AF560784

AT THE CONFLUENCE OF TWO RIVERS

Muslims and Hindus in South India

At the Confluence of Two Rivers

Muslims and Hindus in South India

JACKIE ASSAYAG

MANOHAR
2004

Translated from the French
by Latika Sahgal

First published 2004

ISBN 81-7304-512-7

Published by
Ajay Kumar Jain for
Manohar Publishers & Distributors
4753/23 Ansari Road, Daryaganj
New Delhi 110002

Typeset by
A J Software Publishing Co. Pvt. Ltd.
New Delhi 110005

Printed at
Lordson Publishers Pvt. Ltd.
Delhi 110007

For the two new Easterners,
EVE AND LAURE

Our heritage is not preceded by a testament.
RENÉ CHAR, *Feuillets d'Hypnos* (1944)

Contents

Illustrations

Maps

Figures

Tables

Stories and Songs

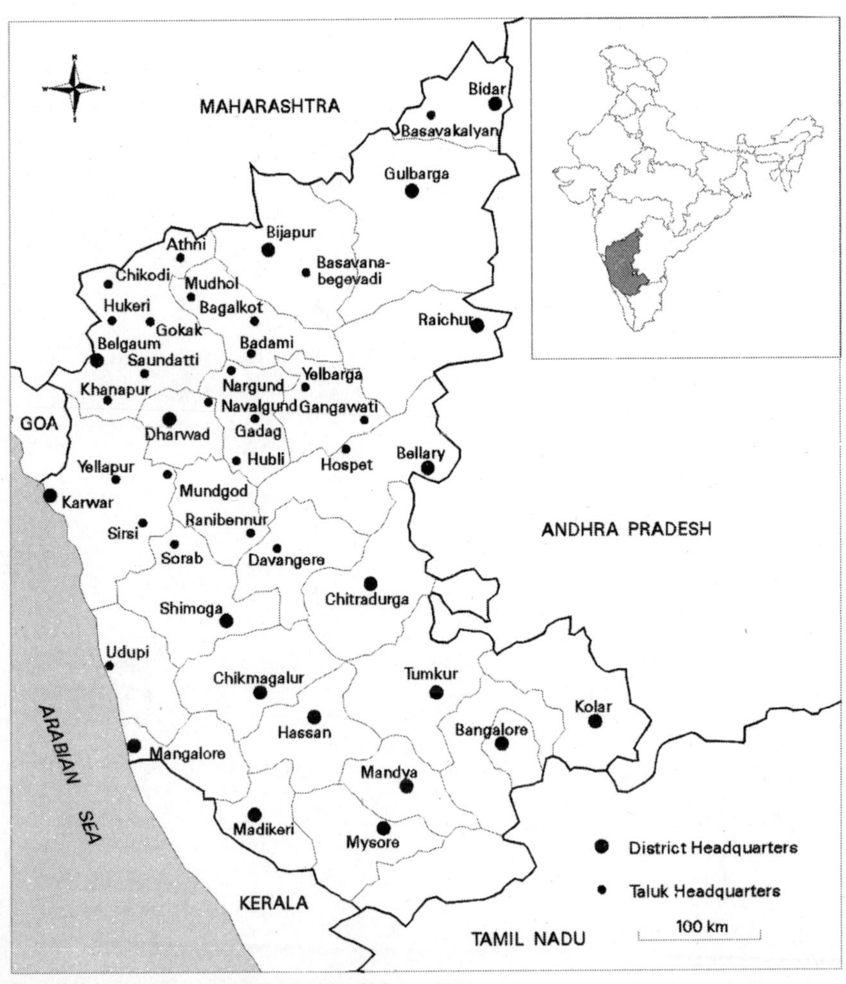

Source: *Census 2001*, Indian Administrative Divisons, 2001.

Map 1: Karnataka state: districts divisons

Preface to the English Edition

Although social sciences aims to achieve clarity—by rendering intelligible the complexity of a local situation at a given moment—history is never a straight line, nor a cumulative process. Nobody is any longer unaware that 'the past is a foreign country'. This book was first published (in French) in 1995. It is based on fieldwork carried out in south India from 1990 to 1994. The picture of the relationships between Hindus and Muslims which emerged at that time makes yet more unbearable the carnage that took place in Gujarat in February-March 2002 and the so-called 'genocidal' violence perpetuated by organized groups backed by the machinery of regional and central states. This pogrom or 'ethnic cleansing' has changed the past into a utopia.

At the Confluence of Two Rivers is a close examination of shared religious sites, spaces, practices and beliefs of members of the two so-called 'communities' living in day-to-day proximity during the 1990s. This picture testifies that the so-called 'war' between the gross categories of Hindus and Muslims is not a rule, but a historical falsification originating in xenophoby and ethnic-nationalism. The scholastic imagination too often assumes that 'Islam' and 'Hinduism' are somehow truly monolithic entities. What I have called 'acculturation' and 'counteracculturation' was not however attempt to observe exclusively sectarian relations or to celebrate supposedly harmonious communal peace of a Golden Age (to which we may return at will). I am definitively not an idealist but a liberal. The empirical evidence of fieldwork shows that coexistence may be a matter of competition—'competitive sharing'—and a model of competitive syncreticism—'antagonistic tolerance'—among Hindus and Muslims. The supposed syncretistic nature of the shrines and spaces, practices, powers and cosmologies, historical resources and cultural values, always reflected contestation by social agents who were variously involved in the local, regional or national political systems. Co-existence between groups was very often a matter both of competition and negotiation; compromise and arrangement were not synonymous of brotherhood; conflict and sharing were not antithetical.

This social and cultural historical landscape was a living testimony to the dynamic exchanges that were then prevailing between agents of so-called 'majority' and 'minority' social groups. The aim of this monograph is twofold: first, to provide a critically-informed view of the plurality of histories and cultures, of practices and narrations, constituting the Indian social fabric; second, to illustrate and understand this plurality and specificity. The locally-grounded study also offers some teachings of a more general nature about 'tradition', 'community', history and events, and the power of interpretative anthropology. Today, the best purpose to which this monograph could be put is to convince ourselves that the costs of intolerance are too high.

'Times they are a-changing'. The last book I published (in French), in 2001, was an attempt to explore the Hindu/Indian desire for the nation in the 'longue durée'. Its aim was to study how the xenophobic relationships between Hindus and Muslims are imagined and experimented in India. 'Times they are a-changing' for sure, but do we have every reason to fear the worst? Following the footsteps of Friedrich Nietzsche rather than the imprint of the svastika, it is maybe re-invigorating to think that time could be a circle. . . .

Paris, 13 November 2002 JACKIE ASSAYAG

Preface to the French Edition

> I believe that the very attempt to explain
> is a failure because one assembles
> correctly only what one already knows, without adding
> anything; and the satisfaction that one seeks to
> obtain through explanation comes automatically.
>
> L. WITTGENSTEIN, *Remarks on the Frazer's Golden Bough* (1931)

The mingling of Hindus and Muslims in South Asia for more than a thousand years can provide lessons for the present, in which we are witnessing the rise of various fundamentalist movements. Relations between Hindus and Muslims deteriorated considerably in some parts of India during the 1980s, drawing to it the legitimate, if somewhat exaggerated, attention of the world. Yet in most parts of India people of the two faiths used to live together without continual antagonism.

Hegel said, 'All gossip must stops when confronted with the seriousness of history.' This ethnographic study is supported by basic facts and common sense. Conducted over a period of four years in a small area in the southern part of the Indian peninsula, it examines the varied, complex and controversial relationship between local Hindus and Muslims.[1] We may discount the notion of different cultures as preconstituted blocs, and religious affiliations as concrete entities, but let us attempt to understand intercommunal microrelations. This casts light on the dynamics of the present adjustment of Muslims to society in northern Karnataka.

This study does not treat Hindus and Muslims as separate 'communities', but aims to explore the numerous ways in which they come together or move apart. The object of this deliberately 'discontinuistic' approach is to diversify the context and temporality within which the interactions between Hindus and Muslims acquire meaning and weight.

Guided by the notion that social relations are expressed in

symbolic forms that give them a structure, I have attempted a cultural analysis of the social milieu in order to identify these forms and determine their impact. There are social divisions and ritual exchanges organized along hierarchical lines, even though this hierarchy is occasionally challenged by the social agents who are forced to live together. This is an opportunity to reflect on the devices that, in the space of a brief history and over the whole social spectrum, allow us to recognize the multiple forms assumed by Islam and Hinduism. Despite constant contact and frequent exchanges, routine cooperation and mutual adjustments, Hindus and Muslims continue to be distinct, even though the lines of separation sometimes shift in an unexpected manner. People interact periodically with one another, absorbing the influence of both cultures and communities, but are guided by certain references that are revised at particular points in time. Attitudes of the present rekindle themes from the distant past. Consequently, communal distinctions emerge in the face of real or imaginary threats conjured by the confrontation of identities in the process of being (re)shaped. Thus it is imperative to examine situations of competition, struggle and open conflict in areas where the ideologization of religion and the politicization of material interests are the determining factors.

But first let me explain the metaphorical title of this book. It has been borrowed from a Persian treatise, the *Majma'al-bahrain*, by Dara Shikoh, son of Shah Jahan, who in the seventeenth century aspired to unite the 'two Oceans' of Hinduism and Islam.[2] This being a regional study, the term 'rivers' was preferred to 'oceans'. What interests me are not religious beliefs but social practices. There has always been greater emphasis on the adaptation of Islam to the Hindu environment rather than the other way around. On Indian soil, the Prophet's religion—or rather the bits of tradition that the Muslims brought with them believing them to be a part of the faith—was forced to undergo changes. It did not lose itself or get completely distorted while it continued to exist in this modified form, although always faithful to the letter of the Islamic law. Undoubtedly, the culture of those who embraced Islam for one reason or another, also underwent change. But this change was partial and did not conform to Muhammad's original teachings. The Muslims adjusted to their new cultural environment; but they managed—both consciously and involuntarily—to maintain their Muslim identity by means of a contrastive adaptation that transformed

Islam at the same time. This adjustment, which testifies to the pragmatic, relativistic and negotiable nature of cultural models in India, is a game of skill thanks to which the Muslim community was able to preserve its essential character despite the contradictions involved. On the one hand, Muslims—defined not so much by normative solidarity as by a web of flexible relations built on a foundation of mutual obligations and loyalties—assimilated with the Hindu population by borrowing some of their traits or by adopting their ethos. The same thing happened to the Hindus who became Muslims—in most cases as a result of a growing number of group conversions.[3] On the other hand, over the long term Muslims preserved their distinctive identity through a series of adjustments in hierarchical orders and customs. Though there are frequent references to the assimilatory or acculturative aspect of Indian Islam (tactlessly called 'syncretistic' at times) any study of the acculturative strength of the Muslims, which forced Hinduism to redefine itself continuously, was usually neglected. Sustained by borrowing and thriving on exchanges, relationships were nevertheless so full of distrust that during a crisis people fell back on a reinforced identity to face the other community. In the study of the creation of such reciprocal identities we must however take the following precautions.

In the first place, we must take care not to depend entirely on oral statements, because they do not always correspond to actual practices. The image the players have of themselves is marred by suspicion, as both Hindus and Muslims have a tendency to believe that they are radically different, although they are not really so. Perceptions of socio-religious differences take the upper hand when they define themselves consciously, reflect on their identity, or answer questions about it. But this identity is not so noticeable when you observe them behaving normally in their day-to-day life.

We must also guard against prevailing notions, ideological, political or economic, of the 'position of Muslims in India', as well as taking as a given just what we are supposed to study. Undoubtedly, Muslims as a community are a relatively independent group whose members have over the years built up networks of solidarity through professional brotherhoods, artisans' and merchants' guilds and neighbourhood groups, in addition to their dynamic religious institutions and reform movements. But in order to understand Indian Islam and assess the features it has acquired as a result of borrowing or internal change, features that have defined it over the years, it must not be separated from the Hindu environment in which it has evolved. Neither should it be isolated from the cultural conditioning to which it has been subjected in different regions. So, if the area covered is too vast and surveyed from atop an observatory, the sociological study tends to overshoot its target. Only a monograph can successfully hit the bull's eye because the author can observe from close quarters the countless interactions between diverse cultural forms whose continual renegotiation conditions sociability.

Third, taking sides cannot undo the injustice a minority suffers: an iniquity that studies concerned with Muslims alone have to face, together with the risk of making a fervent plea in their defence.

Finally, the relations between Hindus and Muslims should not be shown only in the light of communal conflict, because confining oneself to these conflicts is likely to distort the investigator's vision. It is true that they arrest our attention and are also revealing; but they are not very frequent and form only one aspect of the myriad relations between the two communities.[4]

The continual assimilation of Indianness by Hindus and Muslims could very well have served as the subtitle of this book. This subtitle conveys the dimensions of the problem covered in its six chapters.[5] Though essentially ethnographic in nature, there are frequent digressions into history in order to assess its all-pervasive effects. The Introduction describes the encounters of Islam with south Indian society over the centuries.

The relations between Muslims and Hindus have been explored in various contexts: the village (Chapter 1) or the tombs of saintly healers linked with demons (Chapter 2). The third chapter refers to the ceremonies conducted by fakirs, considered important by members of both communities. The fact remains that while establishing mutual relationships and depending on exchanges, living together imposes certain hierarchies and also gives rise to conflicts. We also observe the appearance of differences dividing the two communities, which are accentuated in the following chapters. The existence of hybrid cults bringing together Hindus and Muslims (Chapter 4), possession of certain persons by a goddess or a saint from the nearby temple or mausoleum (Chapter 5) and the socio-historical study of the growth of communalism in an urban environment show how the drawing of boundaries, albeit secular, in areas where they did not exist earlier has fuelled communal exclusivism even in the furthest recesses of collective memory (Chapter 6).

The reader will surely appreciate the methodological and theoretical problems encountered in the course of this study of acculturation. It involved a detailed analysis of the relationship between people of the two faiths, their exchanges and their exclusivist tendencies. A wide field of observation, encompassing diverse points of view, was covered. But, by choice the approach is thematic, not restricted to a simple monographic view through the analysis of relations between two communities in small locality. The intention is to explain the tenuous but dynamic nature of a composite culture, even in its harmless and trivial aspects. The boundaries of this composite culture, which places identities at the centre of phenomena of social change, remain undefined and changeable, particularly since the study depends mainly on oral sources concerning a cultural domain about which there are few conceptual tools.

I have attempted to provide a few concrete examples of encounters that reflect neither harmony nor open conflict, but rather an acculturation that exposes a persistent tension between two ways of looking at the role of Islam in the subcontinent. On the one hand, there is the Indocentric view of the poet musician Amir Khusrau (*d.* 1325), for whom India was a country where 'even the fish are Sunnis'. On the other hand, in the eighteenth century we have Shah Waliullah who said, 'We are Arabs whose fathers feel they are in exile (*ghurba*) in the land of Hindustan, and our Arab genealogy and our Arabic language are our pride' (quoted by Schimmel 1993: 6).

It remains to highlight the complexity of the 'sociogeneses' implied in acculturation and also the changes that place it in a wider context. We shall view the dynamic product of a unique history where local and world perspectives meet. I have dwelt on minute points through the observation of extremely subtle and often evanescent details of social interaction in preference to evidence that appears bulky, but is in reality misleading, and general observations that base social life on a particular concept or values. In brief, one must not say more than one knows. This approach, besides, is capable of throwing light on the complexity and dynamism of cultural forms associated with the dyad alterity/identity.

NOTES

1. The study was conducted in Karnataka from 1990 to 1993. It was funded by the Centre National de la Recherche Scientifique as a part of my research at the Centre d'études de l'Inde et de l'Asie du Sud (EHESS), and by the French Ministry of Research and Technology under the 'Cultural Adaptation of Christianity and Islam in the Hindu Environment' project. The contribution of the team's permanent members—C. Champion (CNRS), C. Clémentin-Ojha (EFEO), M. Gaborieau (CNRS/EHESS) and G. Tarabout (CNRS)—and of some thirty guest researchers helped define the problem. A grant from the Fyssen Foundation made the writing of this book possible.

   But my thanks are due above all to all the Indians, some of whom have become my friends over the years, especially the *fakirs*, mullahs, *mujawars* and others not having any specific Islamic title. They are too numerous to be mentioned by name; but without their active, and sometimes learned, collaboration I could not have undertaken this task, let alone completed it. I must however mention the names of some of my most loyal and informative guides such as Babu Aprajanavar, Shah Wali and his brothers, members of the Imamdar Basheban family, Khanum M. Pathan and V.G. Dixit, as well as Idriss, Ibrahim, Khasim, Pirsab and Alisab.

   I am grateful to C. Clémentin-Ojha (EFEO), M. Gaborieau (CNRS/EHESS), M.L. Reiniche (EPHE V), M. Van Woerkens (EPHE V) and F. Zimmermann (EHESS) for taking the pains to read the manuscript and giving me the benefit of their critical observations. V. Bénéï (CNRS/LSE) provided valuable help for both French and English versions, T. Ganeshan (IFP) helped me to overcome language problems and O. Floret, S. Robert (IFP), Rammohan (IFP) and Sattia Vingdassamy (IFP) provided technical assistance in the field of computer graphics and the preparation of the manuscript, where Christine Selvanadin (IFP) was also very helpful. This work was done during my tenure in the Social Sciences Department of the Institut Français de Pondichéry. Thanks are due to M. Legrand et F. Pirot who kindly carry out all Maps, Figures and tables (CNRS-SIS-UMR 8564, Centre of Thematic Skill 'Modelization, Spatial Analysis, GIS).

2. Dara Shikoh, like his other two brothers, fell victim to his brother Aurangzeb, who seized the throne and got him executed as a heretic in 1659 because he was sympathetic to Hinduism. The title of this treatise written in 1654 was inspired by *Surah* 18/60 of the Koran, where Moses tells his young servant, 'I will not stop until I have reached the confluence of the two seas, even if I have to walk for years.' According to Dara Shikoh's interpretation, this confluence stands for Hindu-Muslim unity in India.

3. The notion of conversion calls to mind a sudden change like the adoption of a new religion by an individual, who is transformed by this action. In India, however, it should be considered more a process of the slow impregnation of a people over several generations; see Hardy (1979), Frykenberg (1981), Lawrence (1984) and Eaton (1994).
4. Readers can find themselves submerged in a multitude of books on communalism. Apart from the book by Chandra (1987), which discusses the possible definitions of the term, it would be advisable to read the analysis of specific cases: Engineer (1984), Saksena (1990), Kumar (1992), and Das (1992) and, finally, to keep in mind the 'deconstructionist' approach adopted by Freitag (1989) and Pandey (1990).
5. Four of these were originally published elsewhere rewritten for this publication. The first chapter appeared in *L'Homme*, 31 (1994), pp. 29-55 under the title 'Pouvoir contre "puissances". Bref essai de démonologie hindoue-musulmane'. The third was published in *Revue de l'histoire des religions*, CCIX (3) (1992), pp. 259-94 under the title 'Invulnérable au fer et au feu. Soufisme et fakirisme dans le Sud de l'Inde (Karnataka)'. The fifth appeared under the title 'La déesse et le saint. Acculturation et "communalisme" hindou-musulman dans un lieu de culte du Sud de l'Inde (Karnataka)' and the sixth as 'Violence de l'histoire, histoires de violences. Frontière, "communalisme" et mémoire en Inde du Sud', in *Annales*, the former in 4/5 (1992), pp. 789-813 and the latter in 6 (1994), pp. 1281-1313.
6. Although neglected in studies covering South Asia—except for M.I. Khan's book (1994)—the notions of 'acculturation', 'syncretism', 'sociogeneses' and 'cultural dynamics' enabled me to define the area and method of research. Their heuristic value is obvious from the point of view of general anthropology in the work of R. Bastide and G. Devereux. But the most penetrating observations in this field have been made by S. Alberro, C. Bernand, S. Gruzinski and N. Wachtel. Their approach to acculturation is essentially monographic and punctuated by quantitative data, divided into periods and along different scales, placing it in a wider sociological and historical context.

Introduction

Muslims in South India

> It should not be forgotten that India is as much a part of the Middle East as Arabia, Persia and Asiatic Turkey.
>
> H. MICHAUX, *Un barbare en Asie* (1933)

India has one of the largest Muslim populations in the world. There are about a billion Muslims in the world today and, according to present estimates, between 80 to 120 million of them, or about 10 per cent of the world community of believers (*umma*), live in India (Table 1). Two figures will suffice to bring out the unique situation of India's Muslim population.[1] Although Indian Muslims constitute a minority amounting to just 12.12 per cent of the total population of India according to the 1991 census, they nevertheless make up the world's third largest Muslim community after those of Indonesia and Bangladesh.[2]

More than half of India's Muslim population lives in Uttar Pradesh, Bihar and West Bengal. The disparity between the northern and southern states—explained by the history of the spread of Islam in India—makes us forget that the proportion of Muslims is higher

TABLE 1: INCREASES IN HINDU AND MUSLIM POPULATIONS FROM 1961 TO 1991

		1961		1971		1981		1991	
	Religion	Pop (M)	%	Pop (M)	%	Pop (M)	%	Pop (M)	%
India	Hindus	366,257	83.4	453,350	82.7	548,77	82.6	672,599	82.41
	Muslims	46,941	10.7	61,418	11.2	75,512	11.3	95,223	11.67
Karnataka	Hindus	20,583	87.3	25,382	86.5	31,907	85.9	38,432	85.45
	Muslims	3,328	9.9	3,113	10.6	4,105	11.0	5,234	11.64

Sources: Census of India 1981 and 1991.

in Kerala (23.33 per cent) than in Uttar Pradesh (17.33 per cent) or Bihar (14.81 per cent). Muslims constitute 64.16 per cent of the population of Jammu & Kashmir (1981), but only 1.18 per cent of the population of Punjab and 1.83 per cent of the population of Orissa. An even more striking difference is the presence of 94.31 per cent Muslims in Lakshadweep as against 1.38 per cent in Arunachal Pradesh and 0.66 per cent in Mizoram. But despite these variations, numerical data do not convey the complexity or the marked socio-economic, cultural and linguistic differences within the Muslim population any more than they reflect regional disparities or reveal the extent to which Muslims are assimilated with the local population (Map 2).

If we take into account the four southern states and the percentage of Muslims in each of them—Kerala 23.33 per cent, Karnataka 11.64 per cent, Andhra Pradesh 8.91 per cent and Tamil Nadu 5.47 per cent—and if we divide their total percentage by the number of states, we find that approximately 12.34 per cent of the population in peninsular India is Muslim: higher by 0.12 per cent than the national average (1991 census). In spite of their heavy concentration in the Indo-Gangetic plain, in statistical terms Muslims appear to be more numerous in south India than they are in the north. This suffices to demolish the widely held stereotype of an Indian Islam that belongs essentially to the north (Map 3).

Let us now concentrate on Karnataka. This southern state provides the geographical and cultural framework for our study.[3] This was carried out in both urban and rural areas, even though this distinction is often a tenuous one in India because of the frequent movements of large portions of the population between rural and urban areas.

In 1991, Karnataka's Muslim population, which constitutes 5.5 per cent of India's total Muslim population, was 5,234,023 or 11.64 per cent of the state's total population of 44,977,201. It is therefore quite close to the national average which, we may recall, is 12.12 per cent. Of course, the density of the Muslim population decreases as you move southwards, so that while the northern districts like Bidar (No. 4) and Gulbarga (No. 10) have 18.99 per cent and 17.30 per cent Muslims, their number is no more than 6.88 per cent and 5.62 per cent in the southern districts of Mysore (No. 15) and Hassan (No. 11) (Map 4).[4]

Far from being exceptional, these variable degrees of concentration are the rule for the whole of the subcontinent. But in Karnataka, the

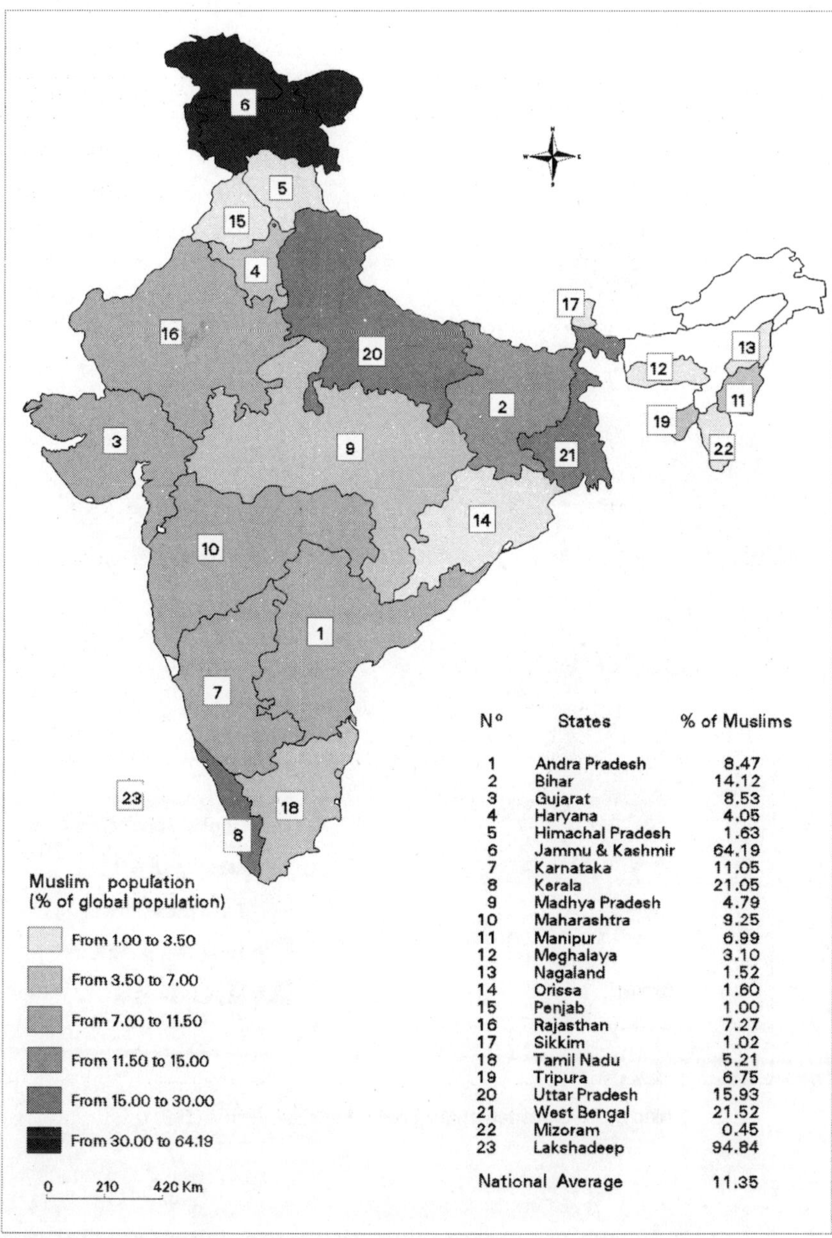

N°	States	% of Muslims
1	Andra Pradesh	8.47
2	Bihar	14.12
3	Gujarat	8.53
4	Haryana	4.05
5	Himachal Pradesh	1.63
6	Jammu & Kashmir	64.19
7	Karnataka	11.05
8	Kerala	21.05
9	Madhya Pradesh	4.79
10	Maharashtra	9.25
11	Manipur	6.99
12	Meghalaya	3.10
13	Nagaland	1.52
14	Orissa	1.60
15	Penjab	1.00
16	Rajasthan	7.27
17	Sikkim	1.02
18	Tamil Nadu	5.21
19	Tripura	6.75
20	Uttar Pradesh	15.93
21	West Bengal	21.52
22	Mizoram	0.45
23	Lakshadeep	94.84
	National Average	11.35

Source: Census of India 1981.

Map 2: Percentages of Muslims in various Indian states (1981)

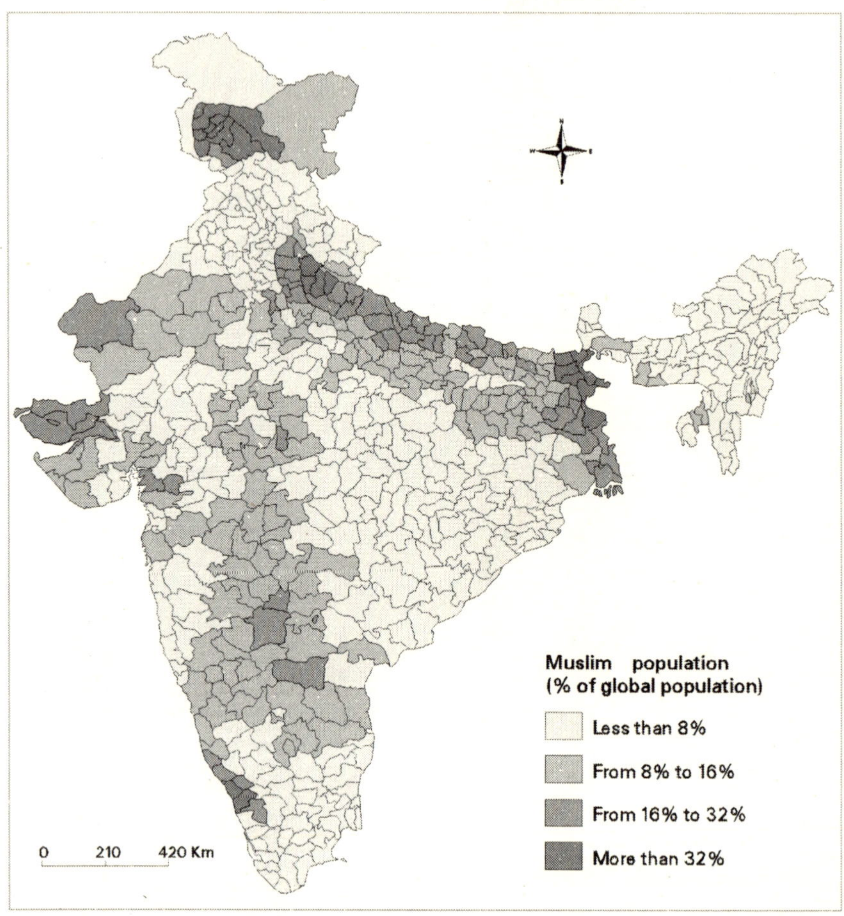

Source: *Census of India 1981*.

Map 3: Percentages of Muslims in India, by district (1981)

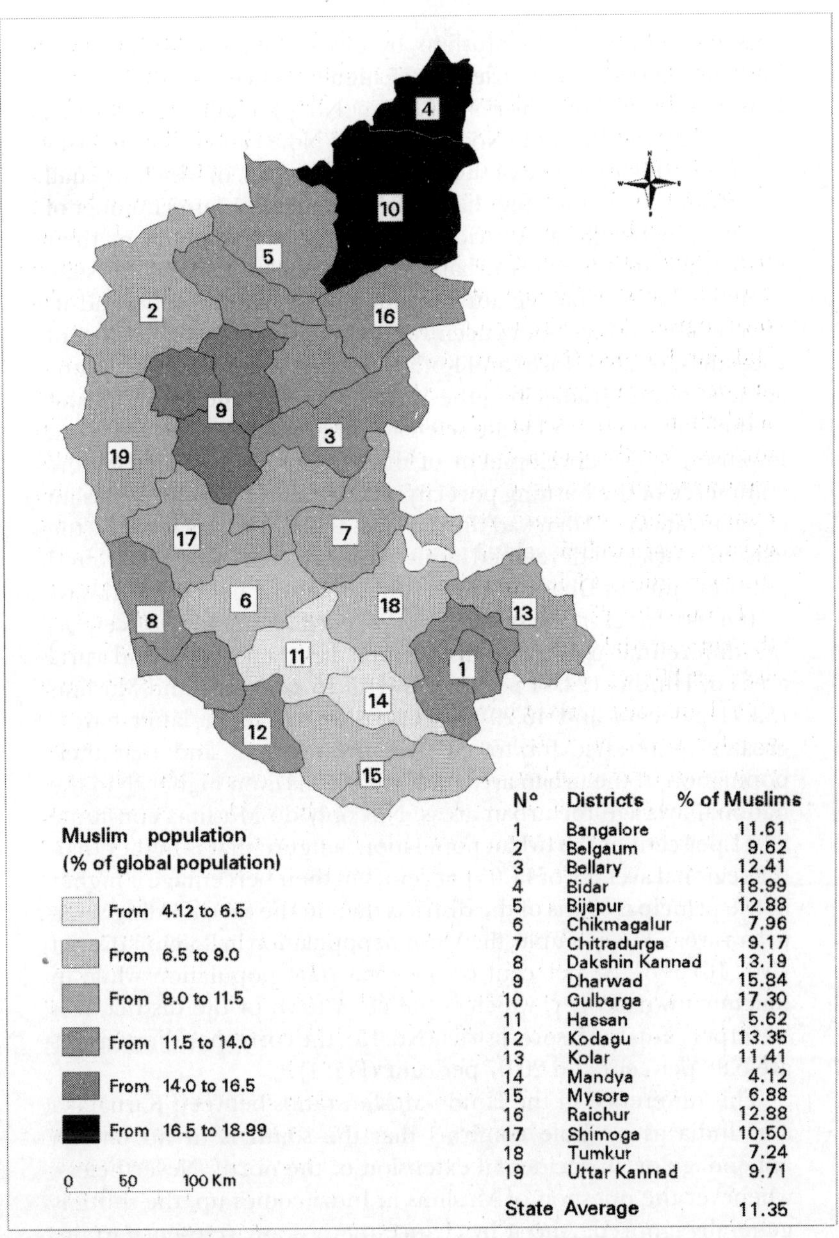

N°	Districts	% of Muslims
1	Bangalore	11.61
2	Belgaum	9.62
3	Bellary	12.41
4	Bidar	18.99
5	Bijapur	12.88
6	Chikmagalur	7.96
7	Chitradurga	9.17
8	Dakshin Kannad	13.19
9	Dharwad	15.84
10	Gulbarga	17.30
11	Hassan	5.62
12	Kodagu	13.35
13	Kolar	11.41
14	Mandya	4.12
15	Mysore	6.88
16	Raichur	12.88
17	Shimoga	10.50
18	Tumkur	7.24
19	Uttar Kannad	9.71
State Average		11.35

Source: Census of India 1981.

Map 4: Percentages of Muslims in the various districts of Karnataka (1981)

present distribution of Muslims by district is a consequence of historical developments. Clearly, the highest concentrations of Muslims, in the northern districts of Bidar (No. 4), Gulbarga (No. 10), Bijapur (No. 5), Raichur (No. 16), Bellary (No. 3) and Dharwad, bear witness to the influence of the Deccan Sultanates, of which we shall shortly speak. On the other hand, the presence of a large number of Muslims in Bangalore district (No. 1) can be explained by their traditional attraction to urban areas, Bangalore being the state capital, whose influence attracts immigrants from well beyond its own region. As for their concentration in the two coastal districts of Dakshin Kannad (No. 8) and Kodagu (No. 12), this bears testimony at once to Arab trade along the Malabar coast in ancient times and to their tendency to be attracted to urban areas, since the main impulse for the development of this region was provided by the commerce of the bustling port-city of Mangalore. Similarly, Muslim concentration in Dharwad district (No. 9) can be explained by the existence of a well-developed industrial and commercial belt around the twin cities of Dharwad-Hubli situated on the national highway.

It must therefore be stressed that, according to the 1981 census, the differential numerical distribution between urban and rural areas of Hindus (24.84 per cent and 75.16 per cent) and Muslims (53.71 per cent and 46.29 per cent) shows that the latter have a greater preference for towns than the former,[5] and that their population in the urban areas of Karnataka is even higher than the national average for urban areas. Not only do Muslims constitute 22.11 per cent of the urban population, a figure that is higher than the regional average of 11.05 per cent, but their percentage is higher in the principal towns of the districts than in the surrounding semi-urban areas. For example, the Muslims population in Raichur district (No. 16) is 12.88 per cent of the total state population while in Raichur town proper, which is the chief town of the district, it is 34.60 per cent. In Mysore district (No. 15), the corresponding figures are 6.88 per cent and 20.07 per cent (Fig. 1).[6]

This difference in the Hindu-Muslim ratios between Karnataka and India as a whole confirms that the south is in no way an appendage or an accidental extension of the north. Nevertheless, whenever the question of Muslims in India comes up, the south is generally ignored. And if by chance there is any reference to the south, it is usually viewed from the perspective of New Delhi or Lucknow. It is therefore necessary to reverse this perspective, and

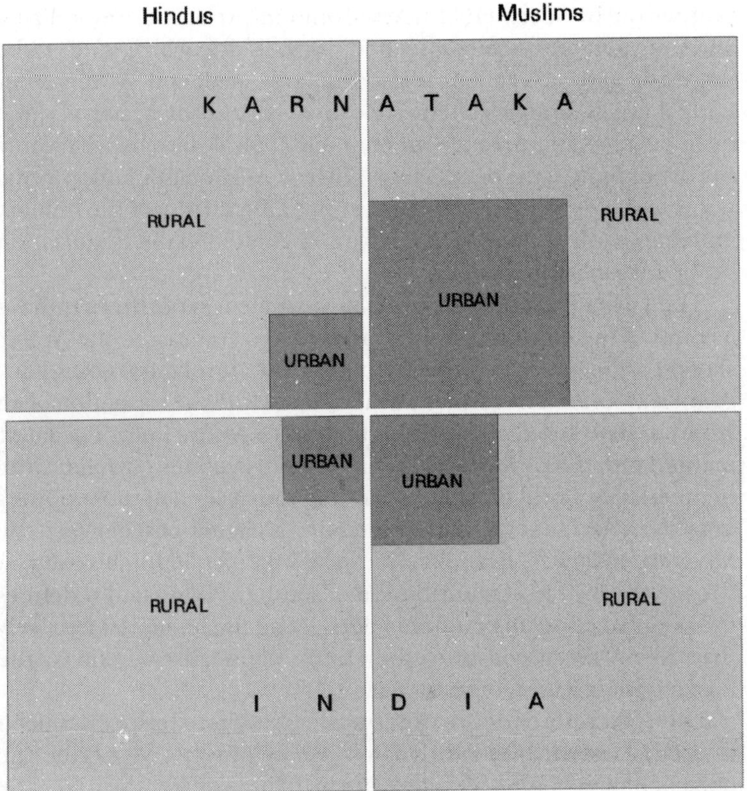

Figure 1: Distribution of Muslims and Hindus in rural and urban areas

this is exactly what this book aims to do. Regional though it is, this Islam of the south deserves all the more attention in that it reveals an independent structure that is all its own. In brief, the study of Islam in Karnataka enriches our view of Islam in general.

A Historical Overview

To come back to India as a whole, it is interesting to see how a journey through this land situated at the so-called periphery of the Islamic world saves us the long journey from Morocco to Indonesia. As a matter of fact, India, situated halfway between these two countries, has tested on its soil the two extreme tendencies of the Islamic faith pointed out by Geertz (1968). At the one end, we have the moralizing and individualistic activism seen in north Africa, which tends to be dogmatic and warlike, but is also humanly mediated. At the other end, there is Indonesia's level-headed syncretism which is quite distinctive and surprisingly phenomenological, because it favours the dissolution of the personality. This essentially cultic and spiritual polarity corresponds in some measure to the duality of the military and mercantile traditions that have contributed to the Islamization of the Indian subcontinent.

The Turko-Persian version of Islam prevalent in northern India as a result of the Ghorid conquest presented a contrast to the Arabic version of the south, a product of maritime trade relations going back to ancient times. The former was associated with the formation of an agrarian state based on taxation on western Asiatic lines. The latter merged with the Indonesian archipelago to become a dynamic hub of the Islamic world economy following the decline of those powers in western Asia that had earlier served as a staging-post between the Mediterranean and the Indian Ocean (Wink 1990: 360). This contrast stresses the historical contribution of southern Islam and redefines the peninsula's socio-cultural image, giving the lie more effectively than its northern cousin to the Hindu nationalist version of the forcible Islamization of south Asia.

Let us therefore restore order to an area whose history has been to a large extent falsified. It is not really possible to ascribe the entrenchment of Islamic culture in north India only to the raids (the historian Wink uses the expression 'goldrush' to describe them) of that great champion of Sunni Islam and even greater looter, Mahmud of Ghazni (AD 999-1030) (Gaborieau 1975). While harping on the Ghaznawid and Ghorid raids, we tend to forget that Delhi became a 'second Baghdad' once the native Muslim nobility, supported by Hindu allies, replaced their 'foreign' coreligionists. This process of civilization formed the basis of a new reciprocal alliance between Hindus and Muslims, the ground for which had been prepared by the Sufi missionaries of the Chishti and Suhrawardi orders. This Hindu-Muslim alliance was all the more singular as the loyalist compromise led to the consolidation of Muslim power with the support of local Hindu nobles in exchange of the payment of a discriminatory poll-tax (*jiziya*) or feudal dues (*iqta*'). This set-up was quite different from the asymmetrical relationship between dependence (*dhimmi*)—where the 'people of the Book' (*ahl al-kitab*) were treated as 'protected subjects' (*ahl adh-dhimma*)—and slavery—the condition of the others—that characterized its hegemony in countries other than India.[7]

There is no doubt about the violent and bloody nature of the early years of the Turkish conquest leading to the establishment of the Delhi Sultanate two years later. But in south India Islam took root in very different circumstances, wiping out the notion of conquest by a 'holy war'—the cliché bandied about today by militant 'revisionists' to fuel their vengeful chauvinism.

Though its origins may be obscure, it is a fact that Islam established itself in southern India through peaceful means long before the events described above—as far back as the first two centuries of the Hegira. It was brought by Arab and Persian merchants known under the generic name of *maraikkayar* (boatmen) such as the Navayats of Karnataka (D'Souza 1955) or the Mappilas (or Moplahs) of Kerala (Dale 1980). They were all Sunnis belonging to the Shafi school (*madhab*). They settled down in the coastal areas and took Indian wives according to the Muslim marriage law called *mut'a*, which allowed sailors to set-up a family in every port they visited. They developed overseas trade with some success, thanks to their links with Egyptian merchants' guilds, the Karimis, who succeeded in the twelfth century in setting up their agents in all the Indian Ocean ports and coordinating the overseas trade. There was also the support of foreign traders (*pardesi*) who gave generous donations to mosques and Koranic schools on the west coast. Around 1330, the learned Moroccan traveller from Tangiers, Ibn Batuta, was surprised to see so many religious institutions, including schools for girls, spread down the Konkan and Malabar (Schimmel 1980: 63).

Only a small proportion of these merchants could penetrate the Deccan peninsula. Although the expansion of the Rastrakuta empire (AD 743-974) depended a great deal on overseas trade with the Islamic world (Wink 1990: 305ff.). In any case, the relative importance of commercial activities in peninsular India, especially those related to long-distance trade, is a matter of dispute (Subrahmanyam 1994: 12ff.). It was probably the descendants of these early settlers who penetrated the interior, making the most of the policy changes under the Cholas who sought to control the intersections of the trade routes between Karnataka and Tamil Nadu (ibid.: 323). This infiltration occurred, with interruptions, over a long period and very unevenly from place to place. It was very gradually that foreign traders assimilated with the native population (whom we shall call 'Hindus' for the sake of convenience). Owing to the paucity of documentation, we are ignorant about the original cultures of the groups with whom came into contact. But we must note that if the Muslims either followed or initiated the progress of monetarization and urbanization in those early years, they continue to do so today. The prototype of the Indian Muslims is the town-dwelling merchant. This characteristic inevitably contributed to the transformation of the social and cultural landscape in an 'exotic' land whose economic *realia* remained linked to its *mirabilia* (Le Goff 1977).

This progressive assimilation was followed by the arrival of large numbers of Turko-Persian Muslims from the north, especially after Timur turned Delhi into a 'graveyard' (Schimmel 1980: 36). (The term was an exaggeration, because the city continued to share the status of a capital with Daulatabad [Ernst 1992: 112].) Among the northern Muslims, there were a number of Sufi Shaikhs. Though some of them were warriors and reformers, others, or sometimes even the same persons, later became aristocratic landowners or respected local chieftains. Some of them became famous as learned mystics or men 'dazed' by God (Eaton 1978). It was only by adapting their message to the local culture, i.e. by spreading the cult of Allah's saints instead of resorting to violent conversions, that they attracted a fairly large section of the population, such as the Labbais of the Coromandel Coast, who became Hanafis.

This is how Arabic and Central Asian Islam, including its Shiah version, met in the heart of the Deccan peninsula, though not entirely without friction, as ethnic and sectarian divisions continued to exist. But although their synthesis was volatile, it allowed the establishment, for whatever it was worth, of a series of dynasties of Islamic faith and Persian culture over a period of more than three hundred years. It was Muhammad ibn Tughluq who was responsible for the foundation of the first independent Muslim kingdom in the Deccan: namely, the Bahmanis (1347-1527). He managed to transfer a significant part of the intelligentsia, consisting of Sufis, writers and courtiers, from Delhi to the town of Deogiri (the present-day Daulatabad), which had been conquered by Ala'uddin Khalji a little before AD 1300. This kingdom was founded by an Afghan nobleman with the help of a Brahmin named Ganju, and he brought to his capital in Gulbarga learned men from Iran and Arabia and also defectors from Gujarat like the famous Chishti saint, Hazrat

Bandanamaz Gesudaraz, whose tomb is still worshipped as the Mecca of the Deccan.

The weakening of this empire after 1428 saw the rise of five other independent kingdoms in the Deccan—Bidar, Golkonda, Ahmadnagar, Bijapur and Khandesh. Born out of a war of conquest, these Sultanates were controlled by a military oligarchy of foreign descent that ruled over a largely native population consisting mainly of Hindus. To convert this population to Islam, they continued to wage war. Khuldabad district, adjacent to Deogiri, epitomizes this phase of regional history (Ernst 1992: Chapter 6). Among the hundreds of tombs in its graveyard, you can see the tomb of the polymath Azad Bilgrami, a member of the family of the Nizam of Hyderabad. This is also the burial place of Aurangzeb, who put an end to the supremacy of the Deccan Sultanates by capturing Bijapur and Golkonda in 1686-7. Aurangzeb spent almost thirty years of his life in this region.

So even though the Muslims conquered the Deccan, they in their turn were conquered by it. While laying too much stress on the assimilative nature of Hinduism, we tend to overlook the absorption of Hindus and their customs in Muslim society. While the Muslim religion adopted attitudes peculiar to Hinduism and its architecture borrowed Hindu motifs and techniques, Hindu kingdoms—even prominent ones like the Rastrakutas and Vijayanagar (Ghauri 1975: 152)—employed several Muslims (Arabs and Abyssinians in the case of the former and Navayats, Mappilas and Ilapats in the case of the latter) in their service, because they were aware of their economic value, especially as horse-traders. They introduced Islamic practices in their royal courts and adopted military techniques brought by the 'people of Allah'.[8] In addition to this acculturation 'from above' there was also an acculturation at the 'popular' level[9] as a result of which Islam spread in the lower and religiously heterogeneous strata of Indian society. Among the latter there were many who came in search of refuge and comfort to the 'friends' (*wali*) of Allah or the miracle-making *pirs* patronized both by Hindu princes and Muslim feudal chiefs. It is true that this tolerance was not so much a sign of religious affiliation as a show of piety meant to increase their power, because acquiring a legitimizing control over sacred space was more important than recognizing its denomination. Thus, while Tipu Sultan donated generously to the Sringeri *matha* and mediated in disputes between various Hindu sects in the Melukote temple (Bayly

1986: 45), to which he donated elephants and silver urns, the Wodeyar Rajahs of Mysore, who went on an annual pilgrimage to Melukote, also presented sumptuous donations to Sufi *dargahs* (Bayly 1989: 181-2; Brittelbank 1993: 51).

Although there was a strong interaction between Islam and Hinduism in other regions as well—especially Gujarat and Bengal—nowhere outside this region governed by the Deccan Sultanates was the interpenetration of cultures so continuous and so significant. But this was an unstable combination between a politically dominant Islam unable to subjugate the entire Hindu population and a socially dominant Hinduism that governed the thoughts and actions of the ordinary people. It is true that the present-day Muslims are heir to the political power exerted for centuries by Turks and Afghans whose culture was essentially Persian. There were few who shared the social customs and manners observed in the royal courts, the majority having absorbed the dominant Hindu culture. As a matter of fact, the region never accepted Islam as a universal and superior force, as in other parts of the world (for example, Java). But this did not prevent Islam from playing a determinant role—firstly, cultural by spreading its message and its teachings in a sizeable minority of the fringe population and secondly, in the political field, by provoking a confrontation some time later with the powerful Hindu kingdom of Hampi (Vijayanagar). It was only after the Islamization of several aspects of the social, administrative and military organization of Vijayanagar that the three remaining Sultanates were able to form a temporary alliance to vanquish the Hindu kingdom (which was not actually hindou in today's sense). In the meanwhile, each of the five Sultanates had, by turns, allied itself with the latter against one or another of its Muslim rivals (Wink 1993: 225).

Thus the balance was maintained for more than two centuries. Even when Vijayanagar's influence was weakened after the battle of Talikota in 1565, the two main Muslim kingdoms of Bijapur and Golkonda resisted the imperial might of the Mughals for the next hundred years. But their final defeat at the hands of the Mughals was inevitable, largely because of the incessant internecine wars conducted by the Sultans of the Deccan, perpetually undermined by the conflict between Sunni Muslims—the first Dakhni colonizers escorted by their Abyssinian (Habshi) soldiers—and the 'foreign' Muslims called Afaqi most of them Shiahs, who came from Iran and Central Asia.

In the interval, the Sultanates played a key role in the region's history, as did Haidar Ali (1717-82) during the second half of the eighteenth century. This military officer founded a much-feared empire through his conquests and his concomitant proselytism, bolstered by an efficient political machinery that, according to historians, was quite remarkable. His son Tipu Sultan (1750-99), the 'Tiger of Mysore', followed in his father's footsteps, aided by his military genius and his hatred of the English. For the local Muslims, Tipu Sultan continues to be a legendary figure to this day.

Sociogeneses and Dynamic Acculturation

Apart from the presence of Islam in India for more than a thousand years, we must also take into account a very wide variety of people who may be roughly labelled as Muslims. As we have already mentioned, the religion of Muhammad insinuated itself very gradually in a Hindu environment already segmented by numerous castes, sects and local traditions. This mixture of disparate elements gave rise to many subtle and complex forms of acculturation, caused by alteration, addition, superimposition and innovation, which vary from region to region. So by absorbing elements that were no longer either strictly Hindu or Muslim, but may have been the result of an earlier assimilation, these cultural forms allowed movement between systems of action and representation that seemed to be mutually exclusive but were capable of changing over several generations.

However, this was not an arithmetical process nor a simply cumulative one. It was always possible to reverse it—sometimes under pressure from a traditional guru bent on reviving an ancient belief reinterpreted by him, and sometimes through the intervention of a reformist spurred by intemperate neo-traditionalism or fundamentalism. In the absence of a centralized state players held together by a village, region, family, lineage, caste or guild or under the leadership of some charismatic figure propelled by missionary zeal, are dynamic units that can change ancient traditions. This happened in such a way that all of these, though some more than others, helped to perpetuate or eradicate some of the sensibilities entrenched in environments that had forged a system of values associated with a certain type of social behaviour. As a result, individuals and groups could, if they wished, join political or cultural bodies modified in this manner. These bodies in their turn broke up into smaller groups or joined larger organizations. At the same time, there emerged other bodies made up of smaller groups with which the former could come into contact.

In view of a social system marked by so much turmoil, it is impossible to consider Islam as an entity introduced into an alien Hindu universe. Such a theory would be acceptable only to those who confuse history with the search for roots and exaggerate the differences between Hinduism and the religion (or one of the religions) of the Book. The ignorance of the different levels allowing routine or original movements from one to the other leads to a misunderstanding of the geneses of socio-religious phenomena and the underestimation of the dynamic nature of cultural contacts. It is quite true that Islam established itself over a long period of time in a varied manner in a segmented Hindu society. But it is also true that Hinduism, with its innate pluralism, is nothing but a semantic and 'syndical' creation of the nineteenth century (Thapar 1985; Frykenberg 1991). As a matter of fact, this term includes a gamut of 'orthopraxes' and thought systems that are sometimes radically opposed to each other (Sontheimer and Kulke 1991), some of which underwent a transformation on coming into contact with an Islam that periodically (re)defined rival doctrines always ready to censure one another. Despite the complexity of these changing cultural forms, it is possible to pinpoint some normative constants. Let us take, for example, the problem of conversions. Because of the paucity of archival material, it is difficult to distinguish between the descendants of Arab-Persian invaders and Hindu converts. However, it is evident that many of the titles currently borne by Muslims are not genuine, owing to the phenomenon of 'Ashrafization' among Muslims similar to the 'Sanskritization' prevalent among Hindus. This may be attributed to two or three reasons. Firstly, contemporary Muslims always seek to establish their nobility (*sharafat*) by claiming that they have been named God, who caused them to be born in the Prophet's family or as descendants of saints who came from Arabia—multiple claims were not forbidden. Undoubtedly, the argument regarding the 'purity' of the group to which a person belongs is in accordance (albeit relatively) with the Islamic canon, at least in the Hanafi and Shafi schools of law. But in the Indian context, it also refers to the (Hindu) notion of superiority of status, still regulated by the distinction between the pure and the impure, which the Muslims refuse to accept, at least theoretically. Consequently, it is not always easy to distinguish between the two types of hierarchies, both based on the 'purity of lineage'. The fourfold divisions of the ashrafs into Sayyids, believed to be direct descendants of the Prophet's family; Shaikhs, descending from the Prophet's tribe; and Mughals and Pathans, who were respectively descendants of warriors hailing from Turkestan and Afghanistan, may be considered as the functional equivalent of the 'twice-born' (*dvija*) class in the Hindu *varna dharma.* This is so even though engaging in commerce is not looked down upon by the Muslims. Although there have been references recently to the ambiguous character of the merchant, alternately applauded and stigmatized in Islamic literature (Subrahmanyam 1994: 21-2), a person's prosperity, which is essentially a secular factor, generally determines his status and increases his prestige (Ahmad 1973: 12). This is illustrated by the following proverb, of Persian origin: '*The first year I was a Shaikh, the second year a Khan; this year, if the price of grain is low, I'll become a Saiyid*' (quoted in *Census of India 1931* [1933: 422]).

The per capita income of Muslims in Karnataka, according to the periodical *Muslim India* (August 1985), is higher than that of their 'brothers' in the north, undoubtedly because these immigrants prospered in the south as traders instead of strutting about as conquerors. They always laid more stress on developing their businesses than on proselytism. It is thus easy to understand why they had to adopt the language and culture of the natives to the extent of creating a vernacular literature in the form of Sufi devotional poetry, where their saints—and even the Prophet—merge with Hindu deities.

Commercial activity—and later banking—reinforced the communal identity, in the south, where cooperative and credit societies such as the Bait-ul-Mals and Akat Funds helped to finance the activities of private entrepreneurs. Though these activities spread through guilds linked to one another by a traders' network, the latter could be superimposed upon an equally close-knit grid of religious brotherhoods held together by more emotional ties. Even today, there are associations of retail traders, fruit and vegetable merchants and transporters in Belgaum and Dharwar-Hubli whose leaders organize and finance every year large festive gatherings that are essentially Muslim. This is also true of the Labbais, settled on the Coromondel coast and mainly concentrated in Kanyakumari, Tirunelveli and Ramanathapuram districts, who are today one of the richest groups in Tamil Nadu. They control a variety of businesses, including hotel chains, the leather industry and also a large part of the black-market trade with South-East Asia. Similarly, on the Konkan and Kerala coasts, the Navayats are a prosperous trading community.

However, in spite of considerable regional variations, the economic condition of the majority of Indian Muslims is precarious. While 70 per cent of them are small farmers and artisans, those living in cities are concentrated in congested areas where they are self-employed in traditional professions, usually as tailors or mechanics. The number of Muslims employed in organized industry, administrative services, banking, transport and police varies from 2 to 6 per cent. And very few work in modern factories or high-tech industries, in research and development, or in the field of education (cf. Appendix 1).

To come back to the socio-religious aspect, it is in their tireless building of mausoleums in honour figures of regional importance, like those in Gulbarga and Nagore, as also innumerable minor local saints linked with votive cults, that the vitality of south Indian Muslims is as evident as that of north Indian Muslims. Though it is far from the Arabic religious axis, from the crossroads of Transoxiana and the radiant focus of Sind, peninsular India welcomes with an equal fervour all those itinerants exposed to influence from the outside: the Sufis, the fakirs and the mystics, be they miracle-workers or mendicant whirling dervishes. These agents and objects of acculturation, or 'cultural mediators' as Roy (1983) calls them, encourage different types of combinations and amalgams in the Indian melting-pot. By mixing with the local population, they promote an ideological eclecticism that leads to unprecedented and continual sociogeneses.

Under the influence of this Indian Islam, not very particular about the pillars of the faith and often mixed with elements of Hinduism verging on 'paganism', the saints were worshipped in such a manner that they could hardly be distinguished from deities. This observation is based on the functional and pragmatic practices that characterize the relations of the Indian peoples with the divine. While sectarian Hinduism turned from polytheism to monotheism or rather henotheism, monotheism among the Muslims was frequently tinged with polytheism. Even though 'associationism' (*shirk*) is considered to be an insult (to God) deserving of death according to the orthodox, orthodoxy was advocated in the subcontinent (as elsewhere) only by a few isolated scholars on the basis of a corpus of texts of which the majority were ignorant. Consequently, it had little effect on the habitual practices of the common people. Largely indifferent to orthodoxy, apart from a few exceptions, South Asian Islam was for the majority of Muslims an Indian religion. We must not, therefore, look for the causes of the growing discord between Hindus and Muslims in their religious practices but in the economic, ideological and political changes that took place before the colonial era.

SEPARATISM, REVIVALISM AND NATIONALISM

C.A. Bayly (1983) explains how precolonial ideologies and institutions determined the structuring of the Raj. He writes that the commercialization of royal power during the seventeenth and eighteenth centuries was accompanied by the growth of a Muslim service aristocracy and also a Hindu merchant class in the process of uniting itself. These two social structures expressed themselves in different cultural idioms and in distinct economic contexts. If the rural *qasbah* brought together the Muslims gentry whose income came mainly from land and public service, the urban market or *ganj* was the realm of an essentially Hindu merchant class. While the former were inclined to uphold more and more firmly a strictly Islamic culture, and their offspring became the ideologues and leaders of Muslim separatism, the latter defended and promoted a purified version of Hindu culture that became a platform for changing Hindu revivalism into political nationalism (ibid.: 449-57).

Following the decline of the Mughals and the expansion of British rule in India, the Muslim elite felt that their culture and faith were under threat, and they tended to revive the Prophet's message of Revelation by retreating into an arrogant and defensive version of Islam. Conscious that they were progressively losing their control over political power, they looked for means to organize themselves in the public domain of civil society to ensure the unity and distinctiveness of their community. Also, from the nineteenth century onward, they promoted the development of academic and religious institutions and movements such as Deobandi, Barelvi, Ahl-i Hadith, Ahl-i Qu'ran, Nechari, Ahmadi, Tablighi Jama'at and Jama'at-i Islami, all of which, in spite of rivalries, tried to redefine the concept of a (good) Muslim (Robinson 1974: XX). The emphasis on the notion that the community of believers was the only one capable of giving Indian Muslims representation was likely to lead to what Hardy calls 'jurisprudential apartheid'. At a time when 'modern' systems of eligibility, representation and association based on the liberal concept of the individual were taking shape, Muslim leaders were struggling with the question of nationalism and trying to restructure their community by reviving an Islamic tradition to define the traits that would distinguish its members as Muslims. Their aim was to reconcile the supremacy of God and the power of the state and prepare for the establishment of an Islamic society on earth. But for the thirty-five million-odd Muslims who chose to stay back in 'secular'[10] post-Partition India (1947), including the south Indian Muslims who faced very few or localized communal problems,[11] the continuance of the Islamic law in the Indian Constitution in matters of marriage, adoption, succession, divorce and other legal cases before the courts was going to create recurring difficulties. The 'Shah Bano case' (1986) in which a Muslim woman repudiated by her husband claimed alimony from him,[12] is the most recent example of a problem that gave rise to a national debate on concessions for ethnic and linguistic minorities in a democratic political regime.

It goes without saying that Muslim separatism is not the doing of Muslims alone. From the middle of the nineteenth century until the 1930s, there was a proliferation of radical and revivalist Hindu sects fired by a zeal to promote the 'true' religion (*sanatana dharma*). The most prominent among them were the Brahmo Samaj, Vibhuti Sangam, Arya Samaj, Nagari Pracharini Sabha, Hindu Mahasabha, Rashtriya Swayamsevak Sangh and Jana Sangh (Jones 1976). But it was mainly under the leadership of the Hindu Mahasabha (Thursby 1975) that they assumed an explicitly communal tone and evolved a specifically anti-Muslim content. At the turn of the century, the Indian National Congress joined the movement in Bengal and Maharashtra, and we know the response evoked by campaigns for a ban on the slaughter of cows, for the general use of Hindi and for the imposition of the *nagari* script, the control of music in front of religious shrines and, finally, the reconversion of Christians and Muslims to Hinduism. This agitation was launched in the name of reviving the glory of the Aryan Hindu religion (*arya dharma*), the religion of the Vedas, which declined after the battle of Kurukshetra according to Swami Dayananda Sarasvati, founder of the Arya Samaj.[13] But it was with V.D. Savarkar, president of the Hindu Mahasabha,[14] and later K.B. Hedgewar, founder of the RSS,[15] and especially his successor, the chauvinistic ideologue M.S. Golwalkar, that totalitarian Hindu nationalism, with its (anti)semitic agenda, was codified (Jaffrelot 1993a: 63-71).

At the same time, the British colonial government encouraged

Muslim separatism in accordance with the ancient maxim of 'divide and rule'. Robinson (1974) shows how this policy was put into practice in the field of education by setting up the Mohammedan Anglo-Oriental College in Aligarh, and, in politics, by creating the Muslim League in 1906. According to this historian, the British did not purposely try to divide the Hindus and Muslims. Actually, they were afraid of the latter, as they felt they threatened the entire British Empire. It was with the idea of reconciling them to British rule that they supported their political expression as Muslims (ibid.: 131): thus, for example, the Morley-Minto Reforms of 1909 accorded them a special status by recognizing their right to separate electoral representation. It is true that the British decision in 1849 not to interfere in religious matters had even before this given a legal significance to 'religious rights' and already shaped religion along political lines.

In the event, these concessions, intended to foster collaboration, led to the strengthening of religious stereotypes, the intensification of competition and the growth of exclusivism between Hindus and Muslims. So much so, that as an answer to the Indian nationalists' dream of a future built on the foundation of 'India's basic unity' the colonial administration invented the (un)historical notion of an India divided into separate communities periodically shaken by religious conflicts (Pandey 1990).

Although the partition of the country brought much violence and bloodshed in its wake, India's independence and the creation of the separate State of Pakistan in 1947—the latter to a lesser degree because the idea of a separate Muslim state remained quite nebulous until the 1940s—were the culmination of a long historical process. The institutionalization of these new hostile geopolitical entities—the former non-denominational and 'secular' and the latter defined by its Islamic religion—brought about a deep division between communal militants and those who supported a composite and secular society in each of these two countries (Hasan 1988: 818). On the one hand, the idea of a secular state was alien to the long tradition of political separatism that had nurtured the majority of Muslims since the nineteenth century and opposed the basic tenets of Islam, according to which 'secularism' only means *ghair mazhabi* or *dini* or, in other words, 'irreligiousness'. On the other hand, it fulfilled the dream of a minority educated along Western lines that wanted to create and actively and consciously religious majority in its own image (Madan 1987: 748). Islam remains the very basis of the legitimacy of the state of Pakistan. As for the secularist consensus in democratic India, it lasted only as long as Nehru was in control. In fact, even before his death in 1964, and just after the Sino-Indian war of 1962, the Rashtriya Swayamsevak Sangh and its political arm, the Jana Sangh (the present Bharatiya Janata Party), denounced the Congress's secularism and suggested that it should be replaced by the principle of a Hindu nation and an exclusively Indian culture based on the slogan: *Hindi, Hindu, Hindustan*! which could be roughly translated as 'one language, one people, one country'. Muhammad Ali Jinnah had rightly foreseen the future when he had declared that Islam and Hinduism were not religions. but two distinct social orders, two nations.

There is no doubt that there were communal conflicts before the colonial era (Bayly 1983: 335-8). But the partition of South Asia upset the communal adjustment that had prevailed until then. In India, it created political borders for hatred, and hatred has continued to demarcate new borders ever since then. As for Pakistan, the 'Land of the Pure', it provided, according to a majority of Hindus, a legitimate nation for all Muslims who actually belonged to Hindustan. It was a foreign but virtual nationality for the Indian Muslims, who sought to strengthen its cultural and religious non-Hindu or Arab-Persian tropism. Since then, South Asian Islam has ceased to be an 'association of truth' and a 'community of the faithful' of continental dimensions. And the Islamic brotherhood experienced once more the disruptive consequences of communalism and nationalism through the rise of militant movements. There are in India religious groups claiming orthodoxy by seeking to purify current practices and beliefs, such as the Tablighi Jama'at, the Muslim Youth Movement, the Students' Islamic Movement and Jama'at-i Islami. In addition, there are parties and organizations like the Muslim League, Muslim Union League, Itehad-ul-Muslimeen, Majlis-i-Mashawat, Muslim Majlis, Ta'amir-i Millat and Islamic Council of India fighting for a better social integration of Muslims. The Jama'at-i Islami evolved in both the countries. While the Pakistani Jama'at does not accept any separation between the religious and public domains, because the Pakistani state is based on the supremacy of God, the Indian Jama'at gave up the idea of an Islamic state and defends 'secularism' as a 'guarantee for a safe future for Islam' (Ahmad 1988: 104).

The fact remains that the splits that brought about the birth of two

Muslim majority countries, Pakistan and Bangladesh deprived the Indian Muslim community of its business, industrial and professional elite. Indian Muslims, more numerous than the total population of Pakistan, found themselves socially fragmented and economically forsaken. At the same time, some Hindus turned them into an internal enemy suspected of owing allegiance to Pakistan. The bulk of the Muslim peasants, being too poor, ignorant or indifferent, had not even dreamt of moving to Pakistan. There were, therefore, many South Asian Muslims who felt that they had become political orphans. Had they not shared the same politico-religious experiences and participated together in socio-religious and cultural movements before the territorial division and the India-Pakistan war (of 1971)?

The ordeal was painful, and its consequences were long-lasting, as evidenced by the subsequent Hindu-Muslim clashes, which have become more frequent, violent and prolonged since the explosion in Ahmedabad in 1969. There were mass killings in Aligarh, Baroda, Moradabad, Meerut, Varanasi, Biharsharif, Pune, Sholapur, Bhagalpur and Aurangabad, and more recently in Surat and Bombay. Alas, the list is incomplete, and there will undoubtedly be further additions.[16]

Consider the furore caused by the conversion to Islam of 1500 (untouchable) Hindus in Meenakshipuram village in Tamil Nadu in 1981.[17] For the Muslims, it was a proof that the most destitute among them would never be able to improve their lot in a casteist society; but the Hindus saw in this action the interference of a foreign agency, namely Pakistani agitators funded by Gulf money! The event was insignificant in itself; but it was cleverly politicized by Hindu nationalist leaders. Their offensive and vindictive statements were publicized by the media and served to catalyse the anti-Islamic sentiments of the 'saffron community' which claimed that it was being besieged on its 'own' soil and its 'own' country.

This 'minority complex suffered by a majority' reached its apotheosis on 6 December 1992 with the destruction of the Babri Masjid in Ayodhya. The bloody clashes between Hindus and Muslims after this incident, unprecedented since 1947, create the impression that each of the two communities wants to go its own way. In fact, Indians readily compare the present situation to the one that led to India's vivisection and the birth of Pakistan.

Since the middle of the nineteenth century there has been a growing tendency towards ideological incompatibility between the two communities, but never have these been so virulent as they are today, especially in terms of the human, ideological and technical means employed to further them. However, despite the unprecedented popularity of the two-nation theory, especially in urban areas, the phenomenon of communal polarization has not yet touched all sections of society. In spite of religious differences and social contradictions, periodic ideological clashes and political opposition, followers of the two religions continue to live together, sometimes in a healthy mixed neighbourhood. It is true that, owing to the dispersal of Muslims over the entire country and the overlapping of populations of different religions, there cannot be a geopolitical solution to the communal problem of the kind that led to the creation of Pakistan. There is no denying that there have been changes, slip-ups and threats, but the members of the two communities will be forced to engage in mutual exchanges at least for some time to come. To observe this phenomenon, one has to delve into the heart of India by means of thorough fieldwork. This enables one to document a situation quite different from that which appears in distorted newspapers and television reports. For example, in the part of north Karnataka where this study was conducted, the two communities have until now shown a tremendous capacity to adapt to each other. The spectacular nature of the communal clashes and the corresponding increase in studies on communalism make us forget that Hindus and Muslims were destined to live not just side by side but together. Unless they want to start a civil war, they have no option but to resort to new compromises everyday. And if they go about it differently today, it is because the recent tragic events have necessitated a restructuring of the acculturation pattern.

Needless to say, studies in political science and conflict studies do not exhaust all aspects of Indian society. Anthropology too has a role to play: by questioning the relationship between religion and politics, it defines the role of secularism in Indian society. It reminds us that history is not created only by the cultural and political elite, and it tells us that we must go to the villages (or the small towns) really to understand the relations between Hindus and Muslims. Not because it is necessary to compare rural Islam or Hinduism with their urban counterparts—because they overlap to a large extent—but simply because more than 70 per cent of India's population lives in the villages.[18]

NOTES

1. Publications on Islam in India, already plentiful as evidenced, *inter alia,* by the thematic bibliographies compiled by Hardy (1972), Schimmel (1980) and (in French) by Gaborieau (1986), or those of a more general nature by Ahmad and Sarwar (1981), Satyaprakash (1985), Harroon (1991), Dallapiccola and Zingel-Avé Lallemand (1993: vol. II, pp. 37-75) and the Osmania University, Hyderabad (*Select Bibliography on Indian Muslims* [1984]), have lately assumed the proportions of a flood. It is neither possible nor necessary to mention all the works forming the base of this study.
2. *Census of India 1991, Religion, Series I: India, Paper I of 1995.* India, Pakistan and Bangladesh contain between them 300 million Muslims, amounting to 32 per cent of the world's total Muslim population and also its second largest Shia population.
3. This study was carried out mainly in the northern part of the state, in villages and religious centres around the medium-sized twin cities of Dharwad and Hubli, where Hindus accounted for 70.10 per cent of the population and Muslims 24.01 per cent in 1981, and in Belgaum city, where the former were 76.60 per cent and the latter 16.11 per cent.
4. *Census of India 1981, Portrait of Population of Karnataka,* B.S. Narasimha Murty (assisted by K.R. Narayana, 1989).

DISTRICTWISE PERCENTAGES OF HINDUS AND MUSLIMS (1981)

No.	Districts	Total	Hindus	Muslims
1.	Bangalore	100.00	83.16	11.61
2.	Belgaum	100.00	85.46	9.62
3.	Bellary	100.00	86.45	12.41
4.	Bidar	100.00	74.98	18.99
5.	Bijapur	100.00	86.00	12.88
6.	Chikamagalur	100.00	88.67	7.96
7.	Chitradurga	100.00	90.22	9.17
8.	Dakshin Kannad	100.00	77.24	13.19
9.	Dharwad	100.00	82.08	15.84
10.	Gulbarga	100.00	81.72	17.30
11.	Hassan	100.00	92.89	5.62
12.	Kodagu	100.00	82.98	13.35
13.	Kolar	100.00	86.61	11.41
14.	Mandya	100.00	95.24	4.12
15.	Mysore	100.00	90.72	6.88
16.	Raichur	100.00	85.86	12.88
17.	Shimoga	100.00	87.81	10.50
18.	Tumkur	100.00	92.26	7.24
19.	Uttar Kannad	100.00	85.47	9.71

5. PERCENTAGES OF HINDUS AND MUSLIMS IN THE VARIOUS TOWNS OF KARNATAKA (1981)

No.	Town	No. of Hindus	%	No. of Muslims	%
1.	Bangalore*	2266290	77.57	422841	14.47
2.	Belgaum*	230079	76.60	48388	16.11
3.	Bellary	137305	68.11	57042	28.30
4.	Hospet*	84869	74.57	26646	23.10
5.	Bijapur	96078	65.22	48130	32.67
6.	Davangere	145525	74.01	46190	23.49
7.	Mangalore*	206744	67.55	46746	15.27
8.	Hubli-Dharwad	369746	70.15	92655	24.01
9.	Gadag-Betgeri	88190	75.14	24616	20.97
10.	Gulbarga	141477	63.92	75908	34.30
11.	Kolar Gold Field*	101540	70.33	13817	09.57
12.	Mandya	79098	78.87	17142	17.09
13.	Mysore*	361628	75.48	96149	20.07
14.	Raichur	78255	62.72	43165	34.60
15.	Bhadrawati*	104747	80.20	17247	13.21
16.	Shimoga	112103	73.86	34101	22.47
17.	Tumkur	75442	69.42	28526	26.25

Note: *City.
Source: *Census 1981.*

6. RELATIVE PERCENTAGES OF MUSLIMS IN THE VARIOUS DISTRICTS AND TOWNS OF KARNATAKA (1981)

Districts	% of Muslims	Towns	% of Muslims
Bangalore	11.61	Bangalore*	14.47
Belgaum	9.62	Belgaum*	16.11
Bellary	12.41	Bellary	28.30
		Hospet*	23.10
Bidar	18.99		
Bijapur	12.88	Bijapur	32.67
Chikamagalur	7.96		
Chitradurga	9.17	Davangere	23.49
Dakshin Kannad	13.19	Mangalore*	15.27
Dharwad	15.84	Hubli-Dharwad	24.01
		Gadag-Betgeri	20.97
Gulbarga	17.30	Gulbarga	34.30
Hassan	5.62		
Kodagu	13.35		
Kolar	11.41	Kolar Gold Field*	09.57
Mandya	4.12	Mandya	17.09

Mysore	6.88	Mysore*	20.07
Raichur	12.88	Raichur	34.60
Shimoga	10.50	Shimoga	22.47
		Bhadravathi*	13.21
Tumkur	7.24	Tumkur	26.25
Uttar Kannad	9.71		

Note. *City.
Source: Census 1981.

7. On these matters, we shall refer to Wink's introduction (1986) and take into account Alam's balanced conclusion, which defines the medieval Islamic compromise in the following words: 'under the existing conditions [it] was to live in peace to the maximum possible extent with little interference in the cultural and religious lives of others and to work together for secular purpose with an ever active sense of separate identities' (1989: 55). Zia'uddin Barani (1285-1360) coined the term *jahandari* to conceptualize a situation where the state permits practices contrary to the *shari'a,* such as religious freedom and respect for non-Muslims.
8. Michell (1986) has assembled the material on the Islamic heritage of the Deccan.
9. In this volume, the term 'popular' is synonymous with 'local Islam'. Strictly, it refers to cultural traits peculiar to the people of a particular place, be they educated or illiterate, theologians or peasants. That is to say, the notion of aberration or betrayal *vis-à-vis* some postulate of 'true' Islam is implicitly rejected. What we have therefore is not Islam as such but cultural expression of an Islam that implanted itself in India owing to its acculturation among the Hindus. For a discussion on the notion of 'popular Islam' in India, see the special issue of *Contributions to Asian Studies,* 18, and the controversy launched by Das (1984) on the basis of his reading of the works of I. Ahmad (1981) and Robinson (1983).
10. In the Indian context 'secularism' means that no religion will get special treatment from the state and that all religions will have the same status and will be entitled to the same respect. It does not imply indifference or hostility, only neutrality. This concept is obviously based on the metaphysics inspired by reformers like Rammohun Roy (1772-1833) and Vivekananda (1862-1902), which holds that all religions are true and that the diversity of religious experiences is but an expression of the multiplicity of paths leading to the same truth.
11. We refer in particular to the Mappilas in Kerala, descendants of Arabs who settled on the west coast during the seventh and eighth centuries, whose revolt in 1921 was an important turning-point in the history of south Indian Muslims.
12. The broad outlines of this case, which started in 1978 are as follows:

Ahmad Khan of Indore divorced his wife Shah Bano, to whom he had been married for 43 years. In accordance with the Islamic law, he returned the *mehr*, i.e. the amount (Rs. 3,000) received at the time of marriage. But, instigated by her sons, the divorced woman applied to the court for alimony. When the case came up before the Supreme Court, the husband argued that as a good Muslim respectful of the *shari'a* he was only obliged to pay *iddat*, i.e. provide for her maintenance for three months. But under Section 125 of the Indian Penal Code, the judge decreed that a husband should provide for his wife as long as she has no resources, adding that this rule was more in tune with spirit of the Koran than the traditional interpretation of the *sharī'a* by Muslims! He also referred in passing to the necessity of a common civil code for all Indians irrespective of their religion.

13. The Arya Samaj founded in 1875 was a Hindu reformist sect advocating a return to ancient Vedic practices based on *Shruti* as revealed by the gods to the *rishis*. It does not accept the caste system but only the principle of merit, it is opposed to untouchability and Brahmanism and refuses to recognize both Christianity and Islam. It had a large following among the educated classes, with more than a million followers around 1930.
14. The Hindu Mahasabha or 'Grand Hindu Assembly', originally founded in Punjab in 1907, was launched on a nationwide scale in 1911 and became an extremist right-wing nationalist party.
15. The Rashtriya Swayamsevak Sangh or 'National Volunteer Organization' was established in 1925 to oppose the British with force. But this organized political group, to which Gandhi's assassin belonged, is now fighting for strengthening Hindu patriotism (cf. Anderson and Damle 1987).
16. For statistical data refer to Map 11, Tables 16 and 17 and Figures 1 and 2.
17. For a detailed description of these events, see Mathew (1982).
18. As opposed to the stereotype of an exclusively urban Islam, an essentially city-based religion practised by shopkeepers and craftsmen gathered around the bazaar or consisting of administrators and scholars centred around the Koranic school, the mosque and the court of justice, it is necessary to remember the importance of the agrarian base in the ethnogeneses of Indian Islam (as pointed out by Eaton 1994: 313).

1

Society: Hindus and Muslims in the Village

> *Compromise,* n. An adjustment of divergent interests that allows each adversary the satisfaction of believing that he has received more than his share and that he has not been deprived of what was rally due to him.
>
> A. BIERCE, *The Devil's Dictionary* (1911)

When studying the relationship between Hindus and Muslims in a rural area, it is necessary to choose a village that is representative of this relationship. But this implies that the pattern of communal relations is immutable and that the rural character of the village taken as a typical example is a legacy of relationships surviving from the past that the ethnologist must explore. When the notion of continuity is understood in its 'popular' sense of tradition, it is wrongly assumed to possess the qualities of stability and durability. But just as the basic expressions of Hindu-Muslim coexistence were neither continuous in history nor the same everywhere, no village organization was ever either perfectly harmonious or totally based on mutual hostility. Affirming the permanence of the conflict or believing in the continuity of 'syncretistic' practices are both illusions. It must be kept in mind that any situation involving several communities is the result of the history of a regional structure. At the same time, it is possible that the cultural similarity that is now evident may disappear after some time, while the differences and social divisions that had disappeared long ago may reappear unexpectedly.

In view of the dispersal of Muslims all over India, their number is so small in most villages of Karnataka, where at least 90 per cent of the population is Hindu, that they usually play an insignificant role, and their visibility is very low at this level of organization.

Living together means that Muslims have to interact with their Hindu neighbours. But these relations are often minimal, because the Muslims are few in number, isolated and sometimes even rejected by the village community whose lot they have to share in spite of everything. But the situation varies from village to village and from caste to caste, because a village is segmented. Muslims are usually closer to the lower castes and the 'untouchables', whose social position may even be higher than theirs. It must be kept in mind that there are both *ashraf* (nobility) and *ajhlaf* (humble classes) among the Muslims. Even so, Muslims have generally been able to develop patterns of horizontal solidarity. Even when they are a part of supra-local, family, religious, commercial or political networks, they belong simultaneously to different types of organizations.

If exchanges within the village are few and of a superficial nature, this is due not so much to religious differences—up to the present the average Indian Muslim has not been very Islamic, and Hindu traits have been more dominant—as to the segregation imposed by high-caste Hindus. The latter consider themselves the purest of the pure, because they have the means to command respect while the growing consciousness of religious identity tends to conform the Muslims' lower social status. But at the same time, when faced with the danger of communal strife, Hindus and Muslims deliberately strengthen their common bonds. Thus after the bloodshed in Bombay in March 1993, the media reported cases where some villagers defended, in their small way, the nation's secular ideals. Far from being mired in tradition, villages present at times a more progressive model of communal integration than cities with their emerging ghettos. This does not, however, mean that communal riots are a strictly urban phenomenon: 46 per cent of the riots in 1985 occurred in rural areas (Rajgopal 1987: 20) (Table 2).

The limited framework of the village—chosen in this case because it yields a volume of data well within the absorption capacity of a single researcher—is only an operational boundary for an empirical study. Unless one accepts the preconceived notion that the village is a 'small republic', or endorses the outdated ontological controversy regarding its social or sociological reality, it does not correspond to an objective delimitation of static or autonomous community. By shutting oneself in the village, one misses out an a gamut of close-fitting adjuncts whose affirmation and extension depends on the individual's status, the place and the time. Not only have modern

TABLE 2: NUMBER OF HINDU-MUSLIM RIOTS IN INDIAN CITIES AND VILLAGES FROM 1961 TO 1970

Year	Towns	Villages
1961	286	153
1962	110	101
1963	68	70
1964	1243	872
1965	346	141
1966	498	75
1967	1076	395
1968	353	122
1969	873	253
1970	526	403

Source: Muslim India, Nos. 81, 103 and 108.

communication facilities had a decisive effect on the remotest of villages, but the complex socio-economic network of which they are a part is supercharged and partly controlled by networks of opinions and positions of the regional and national levels.

In keeping with the 'entomological' approach which means observing phenomena at the lowest level and giving preferential treatment to an examination 'from the bottom', I selected a village where the Muslim community is more numerous and socially more dominant. Within this 'normal exception', to borrow a term from Italian micro-history, communal interactions are numerous and diverse. The predominance of the Muslims makes the representatives of both communities bend over backwards to make minute adjustments—the Hindus in order to adjust to the local balance of power, and the Muslims because of their marginal position on the regional plane. Thus one can observe different types of relations on an expanding scale that affect the interaction and the membership of a medley of social, family, religious and professional and other wider groups. Let us call them 'types' because it is not a question of an exhaustive study, but just of concentrating on a few cases of meaningful interactions. In which context or contexts of collective interaction and with what intensity do Hindus and Muslims collaborate, clash or just ignore each other? It is these questions that were answered by many residents of the Muslim majority village of Shahabandar.[1]

SHAHABANDAR VILLAGE

Situated at a height and surrounded by valleys, the village of Shahabandar is 26 km from Belgaum city.[2] It is linked to the Bombay-Pune-Belgaum Highway by a 3-km district road. At the edge of the village, this road is crossed by another that goes north towards Islampur village (pop. 1,828) and south towards the tiny hamlet of Chikaldinni, before it continues in a north-west direction towards the town of Pachhapur (pop. 6,659). There are regular bus services connecting Shahabandar to the neighbouring towns of Belgaum (pop. 350,000), Hukeri (pop. 15,545), Sankeshwar (pop. 24,018) and Gokak (pop. 42,496) (Map 5).

To give an idea of its size, it may be pointed out that according to the 1991 census, this village with a population of 2,109 has an administrative area of 1,735.9 hectares, including the surrounding fields. There are about 1,500 hectares of cultivated land; the rest is untilled and serves as pasture.

Although Muslims are in a minority in the Hukeri taluk (canton) in which Shahabandar is situated and also in Belgaum district (9.62 per cent of the population in 1981) they are in a majority in Shahabandar. They are also, as we shall see, the more dominant community.

Most of the inhabitants of Shahabandar practise farming, and village activity is largely dependent on the monsoon. The *kharif* crop is cultivated from June to October in fields flooded by rain-water, while the *rabi* crop is planted in autumn and harvested in spring. The principal crops are *jowar* (*Sorghum vulgare*) and *ragi* (*Eleusine coracana*), two varieties of millet that grow well in 'black soil' (*karna-taka*) and constitute the staple food of the rural population. The villagers also grow by rotation other crops like lentils (*Cajanus cajan*), groundnuts (*Arachis hypogaea*), oats (*Dolichos biflorus*) and sugar cane (*Sacharun officinarum*), whose surplus is sold in the Belgaum market. The majority of landlord-farmers have at least one pair of oxen and possibly a few milch buffaloes.

Table 3, bringing together data on changes in the village population, shows a significant demographic decline over a ten-year period. More than 1,500 people of Scheduled Tribes left the village and more than a hundred houses were deserted. However, the village population went down by only 700.

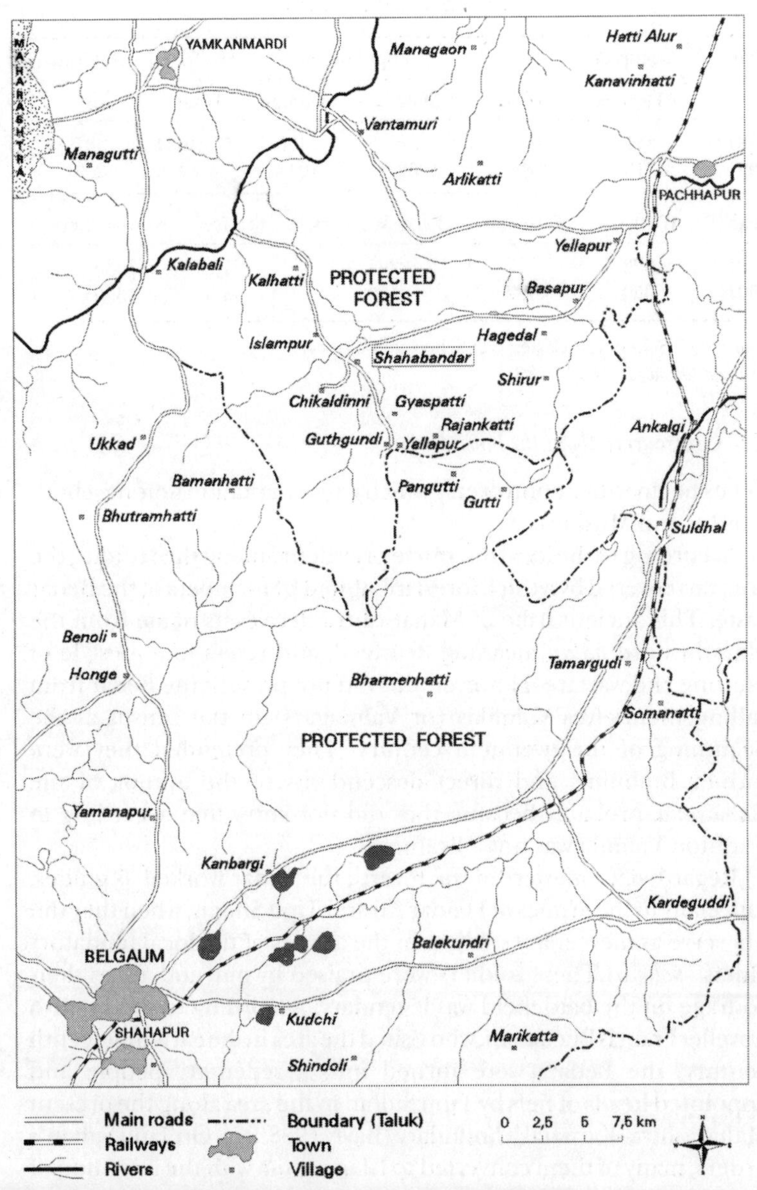

Map 5: Shahabandar and surrounding area

TABLE 3: POPULATION CHANGES IN SHAHABANDAR BETWEEN 1981 AND 1991

Year	Occupied Houses	Population Total	Male	Female	SC/ST* Total	Literate
1981	451	2838	1438	1400	51/1654	307
1991	318	2109	1062	1047	84/0	209

Year	Workers	Farmers	Farm Workers	Service	Non-workers
1981	1002	717	201	94	1636
1991	659	492	129	38	1350

Notes: *SC: Scheduled Castes; ST: Scheduled Tribes.
Sources: *Census 1981 and 1991.*

The Controversy about the Foundation

Let us begin with a controversy which causes agitation amongst both Hindus and Muslims.

According to the local discourse prevalent among the Hindus, the area was covered by a thick forest inhabited by members of the Bedar caste. This ancient tribe of Maharashtra derives its name from the Marathi word *bedar*, meaning 'fearless', and refers to a lifestyle of hunting and warfare. However, this did not prevent the Bedar from calling themselves Valmikis (or Valmagars) in the census at the beginning of the twentieth century. They pretended they were former Brahmins and direct descendants of the author of the *Ramayana*, probably because they did not know that according to tradition Valmiki was not a Brahmin!

Regarded as 'masters of the forest', the Bedar worked as guides, especially in the armies of Haidar Ali and Tipu Sultan, when they did not serve as mercenary soldiers in the armies of the local feudatory chiefs (*poligar*).These soldiers were praised by one and all, as their courage on the battlefield was legendary. According to the English traveller Francis Buchanan, who visited the area in the early nineteenth century, the Bedars were turned into a sedentary people and appointed heads of fiefs by Tipu Sultan in the area along the present Maharashtra–Karnataka boundary (Bayly 1988: 97). On Tipu Sultan's orders, many of them converted to Islam, some with the intention of entering state service. However, their origin is uncertain, as some of them claim descent from Pindari brigands, whose raids were much feared by the peasants, while others claim they belong to various Maratha castes or from Gond tribes.

Local narrative indicates that:

The Bedars took advantage of the thick vegetation to wander about the forest, attack villagers and steal from them. The latter took care to go out of their villages only by daylight and in groups. The only exception was that the Bedars did not attack houses where they had 'eaten salt'. One of them, called Guddappa, who bore the title of *naik* (or *nayaka*) meaning 'one who shows the way', was the leader of the troop and in charge of disposing of the spoils of plunder.

All though the eighteenth century the Bedars are supposed to have taken advantage of the weakness of the local administration. Also, because their exploits disturbed the peace at the beginning of the nineteenth century, the British administration classified these groups of 'armed delinquents' as 'criminal tribes' under the infamous and exceptionally repressive Criminal Tribes Act of 1871 (Pouchepadass 1979: 124).

The Bedars claimed that they made their demands in the name of the goddess Kamalavva. They plundered with the sole aim of offering wealth to her. They deposited it in her little shrine, which exists to this day [although people talk more willingly of the shrine in Chikaldinni village near Shahabandar, where the officiating priests are Bedars].

The latter temple is actually more important, and is believed to have contained in earlier times a golden idol of Kamalavva. This treasure has disappeared, as also the practice of dedicating young girls of the caste to the goddess. They were known as *basavis* and were made to dance before the goddess's statue (Assayag 1992).

Though this story appears historically true, it establishes the Hindu origin of the village on the basis of its divine place-name 'Kamala' by romanticizing the ambiguous relationship that has always existed between the goddess and forest brigands. In spite of their early nomadic history, the Bedars consider themselves to be the founders of the village, and claim the title of Uru Bedar or original inhabitants of the place. As for the story of a caste living on plunder due to devotion to a goddess, it is reminiscent of the Thugs, who committed ritual murder by strangulation in the name of Kali.[3]

Another story, narrated by an old peasant Bedar, confirms this analogy. The British waged a war against his 'criminal' ancestors in the nineteenth century, though no local inhabitant could confirm whether this was the campaign launched by Lord Hastings in 1817 against the Pindaris. On the contrary, they all relished the irony of the story which portrays the British as thieves:

After the British had issued a ban on human sacrifice they came to know that a man had just been burnt in Shahabandar village. They dispatched troops to the village, but in spite of great effort could not lay their hands on the body of the sacrificed man. Instead, they found a bamboo basket in its place. To their great surprise, they discovered inside it a sacrificed ram wrapped in the black blanket (*kambali*) that normally protects nomadic castes during the rains and is also used in some rituals.

The British were so incensed at the discovery that they carried away the golden idol of the goddess, to which devotees would offer jewels when their wishes were fulfilled. The statue was placed in a metal trunk with a solid lock. But all night long, they heard the door of the temple's treasure-room banging loudly against its frame. Nobody could stop the noise. Terrified by the incident, the British resigned themselves to the idea of reinstalling the idol in its shrine in Chikaldinni.

The Muslims agree that the place was thickly forested in the old days. But they refuse to believe that a Hindu bandit and his band of thieves founded the village. They set greater store by what they call history. But their version too is based on oral transmission, and the dividing line between the two versions is very hazy. One of the Muslims, Alisab, narrated a story about Aurangzeb's conquest in 1686 of the Sultanate of Bijapur, ruled by the Adil Shahi dynasty.

One day, an old lady came to the court with a child and beseeched the Emperor to take it under his protection. Since she took care to tell him that the child's name was Muhammad Jamal Shah (Maulana), a name that indicated that he was the son of a renowned mullah of a Koranic school, the Emperor, known for his religious fervour, immediately agreed to provide for the child's education.

The years went by, and the child grew into a wise jurist. Because of his abilities, he had made himself indispensable to the Emperor, who took him along on his frequent journeys. On one such journey, Aurangzeb camped in the village of Padshapur—the present Pachhapur—and asked Jamal Shah to stay on and set up a *madrasa*. It is not known why, but the saintly man refused to do so. Instead he asked the Emperor to grant him permission to set up the school in a nearby spot surrounded by hills that the troops had passed through earlier. The Emperor agreed and granted the land to him as a *jagir* so that he could make a living while continuing to teach.

Year after year, the knowledge and power of Muhammad Jamal Shah grew until they reached such 'perfection' (*kamal*) that he could perform miracles (*kamal dikhana*). As a result, he came to be known as Shahabandar Kamal, which can be literally translated as the 'king of the miraculous village; or the 'miraculous king of the village'. The name was later shortened to Shahabandar.

In spite of repeated questions, I could not find out whether he was referring to Shah Kamal or Shah Kamaluddin (*d.* 1809-10), the Sufi master belonging to the Chishti order, who lived in Belgaum and also spent some time in Chittoor district, and whose *chakki-nama*, or devotional songs composed at his wife's behest (Eaton 1974: 121), have come down to us. But whoever he was, his descendants call themselves mullahs and continue to live in Shahabandar to this day. They enjoy a high status within a complex hierarchy that shows how various social groups are distributed in different residential areas.

The Village Layout

The inhabitants customarily divide the village into two zones: the 'upper district' called *Uppar-keri* where 80 per cent of the Muslim population lives and the 'lower district' or *Nicha-keri.* Each of these is divided into smaller units named after the various castes. Thus, we have not only *Mullah-keri, Lingāyat-keri, Hanabar-keri* and *Bedar-keri,* but also *Badigar-keri* (named after carpenters) and *Lohar-keri* (named after blacksmiths), though there are few of them currently living there.

This simplified plan showing the division of the village into residential areas indicates whether spatial contiguity between the different castes living in the village is possible or impossible, especially when they are presented in the shape of a triangle with two entry points (Figure 2).

Of the hundred-odd Muslim families living in the village, representing a total of 700 persons mainly engaged in agriculture, two called Kasai—butchers by profession—have a very low status. In fact, marriages between Kasais and Mullahs are not allowed, and the latter take the utmost care to avoid contact with the former. This explains why the Kasais have been relegated to the village periphery. None of them own any land and their houses are poor.

The seventy Hanabar families, also called Krishna-Golis, are fewer than the Muslims. Though Hindus, they are not strict vegetarians and most of them are farmers. But three families earn a meagre income by running small groceries. Only twenty-odd of the thirty

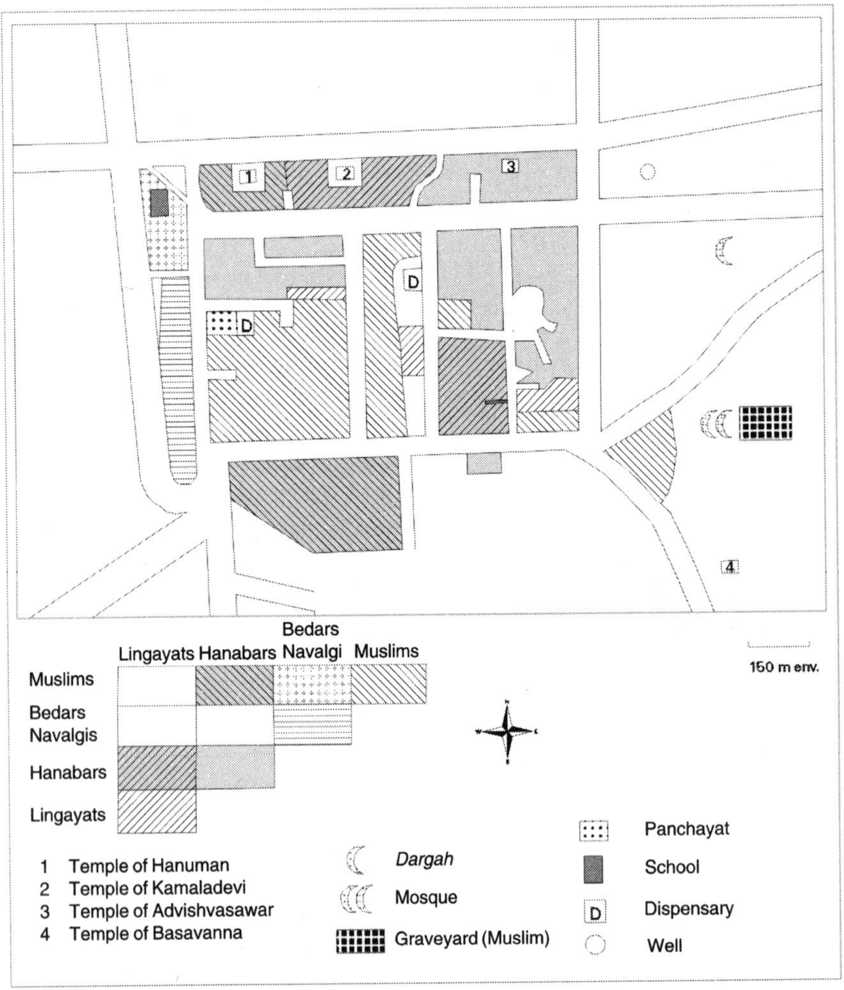

Figure 2: Spatial distribution of castes in Shahabandar

Bedar families figuring in the census records own land, but their holdings are not large enough to satisfy their needs. Many therefore work, for daily wages, for farmers of other castes. One family scrapes a living by running a teashop patronized only by members of the Bedar caste. Another family owns a grocery, where even non-Bedars buy provisions. As for Lingayats—including the fifty-odd *Jangama* (community 'priests') families and the thirty-odd *Panchamsali* (accomplished) families, who are of a slightly lower status[4]—they live on income from their land. The same is true of the Navalgars, who are of a lower status than the Lingayats. Some Navalgars offer their services as barbers in exchange for an annual payment in kind. That leaves the two Brahmin families. One of them lives in the village only on a temporary basis, while the head of the second family is a government employee working as a forest guard.

Eating, Drinking and Marriage Customs

The Lingayats—placed at the top of the caste leader—do not accept cooked food from others, while the Bedars—placed at the bottom—accept food from all castes. Evidently, Brahmins refuse food from non-Brahmins, but, like the Lingayats, accept uncooked food within certain limits. The Lingayats never join in the marriage celebrations of other castes, except Brahmins. But this does not prevent them from giving uncooked food in the form of cereals to other families on various occasions. The Muslims and Hanabars exchange food and eat together in one another's houses. But neither of them have any relations with the Bedars, according to the prevailing rules. The non-Bedars refuse to accept food from the Bedars who, on the contrary, can eat in the house of any other caste, though this does not happen in actual practice. The Navalgars accept food from the Lingayats, but the opposite is not possible. However, they refuse to eat in Muslims or Hanabar houses, though they accept food from them (Table 4).

Entry into the kitchen (*adagimane*) is usually controlled, both to protect the purity of the food and because the domestic altar (*devarakatte*) is usually found there. It is isolated from the rest of the kitchen by a low wall.

Though the Lingayats do not allow non-Lingayats to enter their kitchens, Navalgars allow Lingayats to enter theirs, but refuse this privilege to Muslims, Hanabars and all others. The Hanabars and Muslims allow one another party to their respective kitchens.

TABLE 4: COMMENSAL PRACTICES IN SHAHABANDAR

	Givers / Receivers	Brahmins	Lingayats	Navalgars	Hanabars	Bedars	Muslims
	Muslims	?	○ □	○ □	○ □	⌀ □	
	Bedars	○ □	○ □	○ □	○ □		○ □
	Hanabars	○ □	○ □	○ □		⌀ ?	○ □
VEGETARIANS	Navalgars	○ □	○ □		⌀ ?	⌀ □	⌀ □
VEGETARIANS	Lingayats	⌀ □		⌀ □	⌀ □	⌀ ⧄	⌀ □
VEGETARIANS	Brahmins		⌀ □	⌀ □	⌀ ?	⌀ ⧄	⌀ ⧄

	accepted	non-accepted
Raw food	□	⧄
Cooked food	○	⌀
Missing or dubious information		?

Obviously, no other castes allow the Bedars to enter their kitchens; but in actual practice the problem does not arise as Bedars never enter their houses. It is important to note that the Muslims do not have a special relationship with the Bedars, even though many of the latter are supposed to have converted to Islam during Tipu Sultan's reign.

On the basis of these partial indications, we may conclude that the area where food is prepared is accessible only to members of those castes with whom cooked food is exchanged, irrespective of religion.

Muslims do not eat pork, or animals not killed in the Muslim way. But sometimes lower-class Muslims do kill the animal with one blow. The cucumber too is forbidden, because it looks too much like a snake! Finally, though it may seem heretical, it is believed that the violation of these rules pertaining to food habits would rouse the anger of the village goddess (*gramadevata*). Similarly, the consumption of oil given as an offering to a saint, using the instruments kept in his mausoleum and using for personal purposes the money offered to him by devotees are also forbidden.

The village has only one well, which, as one would expect, creates some tension, especially because the Lingayats insist on drawing their water first. This prerogative is questioned by both Hanabars and Muslims, who say sarcastically, 'If the Lingayats are so pure, why don't they dig their own well?' It is true that, being in a minority in the village, the Lingayats cannot force the other groups to recognize their so-called superiority. In fact, today the villagers follow the rule of first come, first served. We may note that there is no washerman in the village. Dirty clothes are washed in the river, considered non-polluting, without any discrimination, except for the segregation of men and women.

Marriage ceremonies also testify to the complex relationships between groups. Nobody can refuse an invitation, for fear of being ostracized by the village. (An ostracized person is denied the right to take part in day-to-day cooperative activities and to enjoy the fruits of reciprocal exchanges.) Whether it is the marriage of a Hindu or a Muslim, all the inhabitants of the village are expected to take part. This means, in most cases, that a family member has to bring leafy branches from the forest—symbols of well-being and prosperity—to support the canopy of the marriage *pandal*. The *pandal* is erected the day before the marriage, and the whole village, Hindus and Muslims included, is invited to the ceremony. Betel nuts and betel leaves are sent to each house in the village as a token of the invitation.

Among the Muslims, the marriage—called *shadi* in this area—is a more elaborate affair going beyond the few prayers and the simple civil contract (*nikah* or *akha*) registered by the *qadi* according to the Islamic law. Similarly, divorce (*talaq*) and remarriage bring loss of prestige, and are considered immoral, though they are not condemned by the *shari'a*. And like her Hindu counterpart, the Muslim widow loses the auspicious character (*suhagin*) associated with her fertile married status. Just as among the Hindus, a wedding is a costly affair calling for large quantities of rice, numerous offerings of betel nut and coconuts, application of saffron power, payment of dowry (*hunda*) to the bridegroom, collecting a trousseau (*dehej*), presentations of clothes and jewellery—especially bangles (*bangdi*)—and tying the marriage necklace (*lachcha*). The families of the bride and groom always make an offering, called *padi*, consisting of five measures of wheat, rice, lentils, sugar and oil, to the village deity through a priest (*pujari*), who returns it to the family as 'grace' (*prasada*). These offerings are then mixed with the food that is prepared for the numerous wedding guests.

The Muslim marriage system is based on the notion of patrilineage exogamy which determines the identity of each household. The latter may shelter under one roof several families sharing the same cooking stove (*chullah*). A marriage brings together, under the name of *samdava*, the members of two patrilineages. Apart from the exchange of women, this relationship helps forge economic and political alliances that increase the family's influence in the village or in the surrounding area. Members of a *biraderi* have a common ancestor (*ghar ke bade*), whose name often indicates his place of birth. His descendants, having the same 'blood', form a community and share a family deity (*ghar ke piran*), usually a local saint, and ensure his blessings by periodically sacrificing a sheep in his honour.

Marriages between primary parallel and classificatory cousins, the preferred form of union among north Indian Muslims, are not permitted. But here too, it depends on the status: for example, the Meos of Mewat do not follow this custom (Jamous 1991). Although bilateral cross cousins are likely marriage partners among Muslims, there is no particular term to denote this type of matrimonial alliance that distinguishes them from parallel cousins, marriage between whom is strictly forbidden. Even though the husband's elder sister is addressed by the same term as that used for the mother's younger sister, Muslims do not permit a matrimonial alliance between uncle and niece, unlike the Hindus. At the risk, therefore, of this type of matrimonial alliance creeping in, Muslims follow a pattern of categories of relationship that permits marriage between cross cousins (Figs. 3 and 4).

In short, except for some minor differences, Hindus and Muslims in Shahabandar follow the south Indian pattern of family structure and matrimonial alliances. This has been demonstrated by Conklin (1975) in his study of the Dharwad region and confirmed by Hussain Khan in his study of kinship in a village in Gulbarga district (1994) (Fig. 5).

Before concluding, let us refer to a brief news item found in the annals of Shahabandar. It is about a Muslim schoolteacher who married a Hindu woman after getting her converted to Islam. The majority of villagers, irrespective of their religion, disapproved of this union, which was believed to go against nature. 'This is not proper behaviour!' they said, implying that it went against the *dharma* of caste and religion. But censure did not lead to punitive sanctions. This confirms the ambiguous nature of social restrictions, at least from the observer's viewpoint.

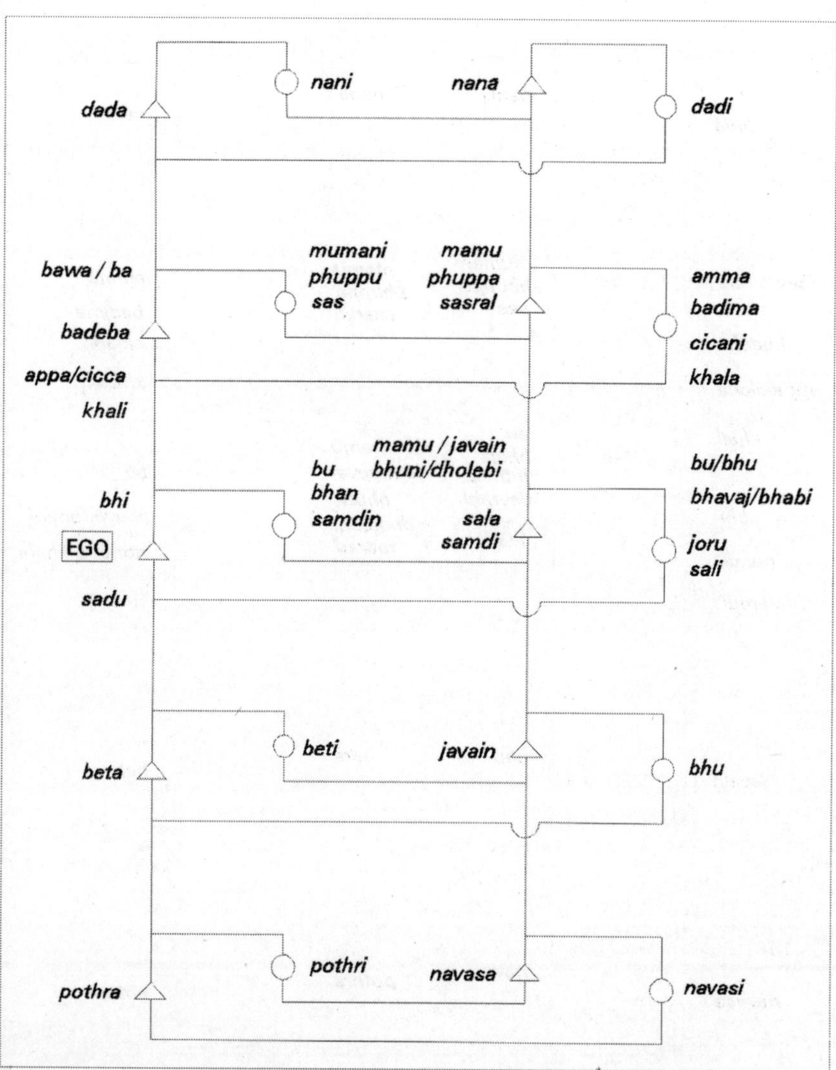

Source: From Hussain Khan (1994: 181).

Figure 3: Terminology of relationships and marriages between bilateral cross cousins among Muslims in North Karnataka (*ego* = man)

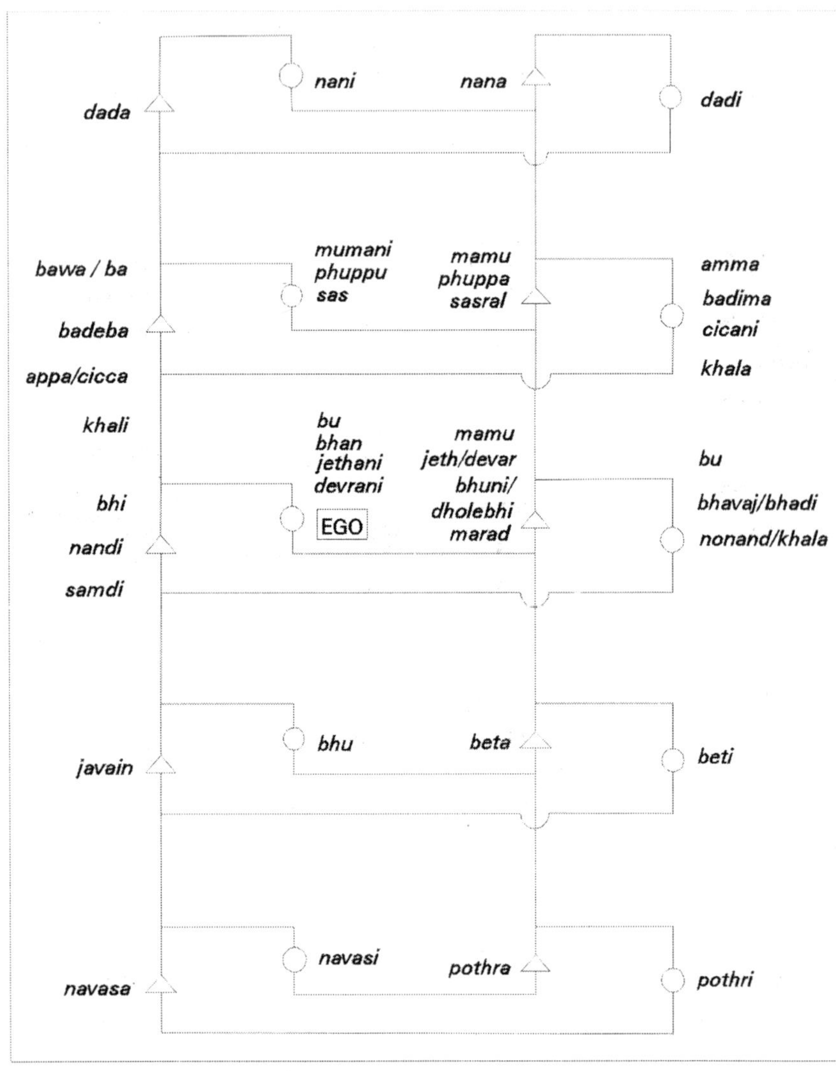

Source: From Hussain Khan (1994: 182).

Figure 4: Terminology of relationships and marriages between bilateral cross cousins among Muslims in North Karnataka (*ego* = woman)

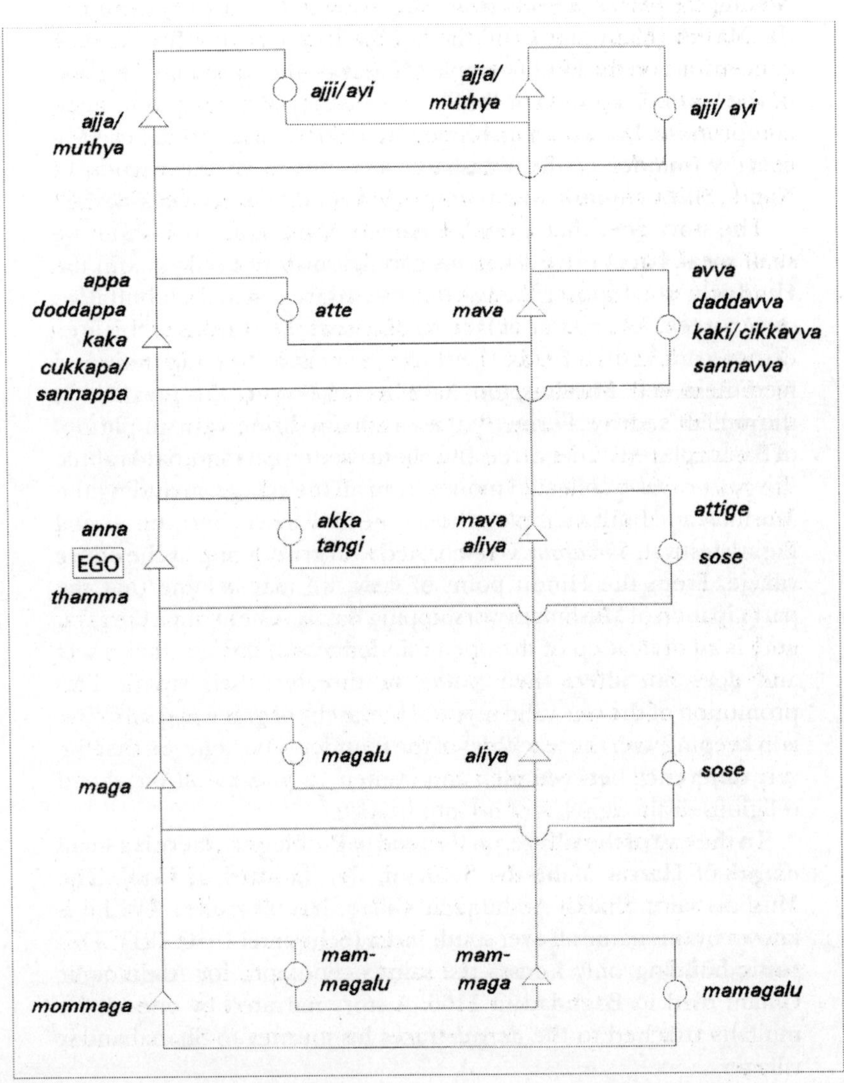

Source: From Hussain Khan (1994: 195).

Figure 5: Terminology of relationships and marriages between bilateral cross cousins among Hindus in North Karnataka (*ego* = man)

Religious Buildings

Among the places of worship are the mosque, the Ankalgi Adveppa, the Maruti (Hanuman) and the Siddheshvar temples. But we shall concentrate on the Hindu temple of Basava—the Kannada distortion of the Sanskrit *vrisabha* or 'bull'—because it indicates a communal compromise. Basava is worshipped here not so much as the twelfth-century founder of the Virashaiva sect, but as an incarnation of Nandi, Shiva's mount, who is supposed to grant his devotees' wishes.

The story goes that a mullah named Abdulqadar (of whom we shall speak later) once asked his coreligionists not only to join the Hindus in worshipping Basava, but also to give rest to their buffaloes once a week. As a matter of fact, on Mondays the Hindus in this area do not work in their fields; they wash their cattle, worship them and feed them well. Muslims, too, have been following this practice on the mullah's advice. Formerly, the Virashaiva shrine was a simple idol of Basava placed under a tree. But about twenty years ago, Sankranna, the *gramasevaka*, collected money from all the village, including the Muslims, and built a temple to house the idol. Since then, the annual Basava festival, *Shivaratri*, is celebrated with great pomp by the entire village. From the Hindu point of view, we may assume that the participation of Muslims in worshipping Basava, essentially a Lingayat god, is an indication of the open-mindedness of the Virashaiva sect and does not affect their power or threaten their status. This promotion of the one valid mystical hierarchy of grace and salvation is in keeping with the teachings of the founder, who believed that the very difference between men and women, as likewise all social and religious distinctions, is of no importance.[5]

To the east of the village, on the road to Pachhapur, there is a small *dargah* of Hazrat Mahbub-i Subhani, the 'beloved of God'. The Muslims saint Shaikh Abdulqadir Gillani has 99 names, but he is known by this name all over south India (Schimmel 1980: 121). This rustic building only houses the saint's cenotaph, for Abdulqadir Gillani died in Baghdad in 1166. A story narrated by one of the mullahs attached to the *dargah* traces his journey to Shahabandar village:

> After a series of epidemics that decimated the population, a mullah named Abdulqadar decided to go around the village, at the head of a procession, holding aloft the sacred green banner of Islam. As he went round the village, he recited *surahs* from the Koran, interrupting his recitation with pleas to

Mahbub-i Subhani to intercede with Allah and rid the village of the calamity. During the night, the mullah saw in his dream a splendid dargah rise magically to the east of the village. When the building was complete, he heard the saint's voice asking the faithful to celebrate his birthday (*ᶜurs*) every year.

When the mullah woke, he called the villagers and told them to join hands to build a mausoleum for the saint; and all of them, irrespective of caste, joined in the effort.

Since then, all the villagers pay homage to the *pir*, and some Hindus, following the example of their Muslims brethren, never fail to invoke his blessings before starting a new venture. As for his anniversary, called his 'mystic marriage with Allah', it is celebrated with even greater zeal on the eleventh day of the fourth month of the Islamic calendar, *Rabi'ath-thani*, because, since the *dargah* was built, there has been no epidemic in the village. Even when the village cattle are affected by an infectious disease, the villagers believe that it can be eradicated by carrying the holy standard in a procession around the village.

According to the mullah who preaches the sermon on Fridays, the mosque, known as *Shahi Masjid*, was built by Sikandar Adil Shah, the last Sultan of Bijapur, who was defeated by Aurangzeb and died in captivity. But some believe that it was the work of supernatural powers (*jann*[6]) who built five similar buildings in the surrounding villages. The Shahabandar mosque is incomplete: a pillar that was to have been placed at the front is still lying on the ground: the djinns were interrupted in their work by the devotional songs sung by women in the early morning while grinding grain. As the dawn broke, they had to leave. As a matter of fact, *chakki-nama* (songs sung while grinding grain) and also *charkhi-nama* (songs sung while spinning yarn) are believed to frighten away demons and evil spirits. They are considered to be even more effective, because the original Hindu songs were retranslated by Sufi saints to sing the praises of Allah, including those translated through the intervention of one of the *pirs* (Eaton 1974).

Some Muslims gather five times a day in this mosque to pray. And every Friday, a mullah reads a sermon before the congregation, which is larger then than on other days. Since there is no *ᶜidgah*—an area on the outskirts of the village bounded by a white wall where Muslims gather before an alcove to say their *ᶜId* prayers—the mosque is also used for prayers on the occasion of *ᶜId ul-Fitr*, celebrated at the end of the *Ramadan* fast, and *ʿId ul-adha*, commemorating Abraham's sacrifice.

Hindus make a sacrifice at *ʿId*, but for practical rather than religious reasons. They thank the saint for having granted their wishes during the year. It is rumoured that a seriously ill child of the Hanabar caste survived by his grace. Since then, his parents give a goat to the Muslims, who sacrifice it for them. A third of the meat is given to them, one-third is distributed among the poor (fakirs) and the rest is taken by the sacrificer. They story may not be very important by itself, but confirms the closeness of the Muslim and Hanabar communities. The latter are clearly Hindus, since they claim to be descended from Krishna; their other name is Krishna Goli or Gauda, *goli* being the name of an edible plant (*Portulaca oleracea*). On the other hand, there are very few Hindus who venerate Khwaja Shamsuddin Mira Saheb, the saint who has a reputation in the region for helping during childbirth and protecting children and adults from demons (*bhuta*). His *dargah*, frequented by Muslims from the village, is located in the nearby town of Miraj. But everybody in Shahabandar knows his story. It is tempting to interpret it as a Muslim metaphor for the relationship between Islam and Hinduism:

Shamsuddin, born in Kashgar in 1333, learnt the Koran and other Muslim scriptures by heart in early childhood before making a pilgrimage to Mecca. But his stay was short, because Allah ordered him to go immediately to Murtajabad, the modern Miraj, to put an end to the extortionist practices of Gangna Dhobi, who tormented men and molested women. Gangna Dhobi was a devotee of a goddess, to whom he made human sacrifices with the help of his wife, a well-known sorceress.

On his arrival in Miraj, Shamsuddin ordered Gangna Dhobi to come and see him. The latter at first refused but then gave in, and finally offered to put himself at his service. Shamsuddin gave him his handkerchief and asked him to clean his dwelling with it. But the magician threw the handkerchief into the Krishna river. To his great surprise, a flame appeared at the spot, from which sprang a cobra that spat venom at him. The magician was instantaneously reduced to ashes.

On hearing the news, his wife came from Bengal to implore Shamsuddin to restore her husband to life. The saint retorted that he had brought about his own death, and if resurrected, would appear in the form of a demon. Only the all-merciful Allah could give him back his original form.

In spite of this answer, the sorceress collected her husband's ashes, and brought him back to life with the help of black magic. Mira Saheb's prophecy came true, and a terrible demon swept down upon her. At the last minute, she managed to escape from his clutches and fled to prostrate herself at the saint's feet. Seized by pity, he threw the demon into a well. From then on, Gangna Dhobi's wife became his devoted servant.

They say that one of the tombs near Khwaja Shamsuddin Mira Saheb's sepulchre, built after his death in 1384 by a Sultan of the Bahmani dynasty—probably Muhammad Shah Bahmani II—is that of the Dhobi's wife.

FESTIVALS

Festivals have always helped people in the past, as they do today, to affirm their identity visibly and publicly by fortifying—even though temporarily and periodically—the community's social cohesiveness.[7] This is largely true of Shahabandar too. First the Muslims form an exclusive group, indifferent to 'others' (and in the last analysis even against them), when they stay awake at night to devote themselves to prayer and take part in nocturnal ceremonies. This happens thrice a year: on the twenty-seventh day of the seventh lunar month of *Rajab*, commemorating Muhammad's ascension to heaven (*shabe-mi'raj*); on the full-moon night of the eighth month of *Sha'bān* called the 'Night of the Decree', which decides the events during the coming year (*shabe barat*); and on the twenty-seventh day of the ninth month of *Ramadan*, the 'Night of Power' (*Lailat ul-qadr*), when the Holy Koran was revealed for the first time. Also, the Muslims refuse to take part in essentially Hindu festivals such as *Naga Panchami*, *Dasara*, *Dipavali* and *Ganesha Chaturthi*.

However, some celebrations—both Hindu and Muslim—seem open to all. A larger number of people take part in them, and their composition is variable.[8] Of course, these festivals also provide the occasions (more at present than in the past?) for violent communal disturbances. But the inhabitants of Shahabandar have a more liberal concept of culture: the staunchly polytheist Hindus do not hesitate to propitiate Muslim saints worshipped by Muslims as though they were deities. In short, in spite of the strong cohesion within each of the two groups, symbolized by their worship of specific divine figures, we do not see in Shahabandar, especially during festivals, two homogeneous and watertight 'popular' cultures—one Hindu and the other Muslim—within which each player has a fixed and unchanging role. Similarly, and in the same context, there are no strictly demarcated and relatively constant group mentalities, at least if one refuses to separate the ability of cultural elements to express themselves from the situations concretely lived through by their enactors. The following descriptions of some of the Islamic and village festivals—the latter of Hindu origin—celebrated in Shahabandar serve to highlight this pluralistic dimension.

Muharram

The word 'muharram' etymologically means 'that which is forbidden'. Though it is essentially a Shia festival, in Shahabandar, as in other parts of India, it is also celebrated by Sunni Muslims. The Hindus join in the celebrations calling it *Imam Jayanti*. During this first month of the Islamic calendar, the Muslims commemorate the martyrdom of Imams Hasan and Husain—sons of the Prophet's daughter, Fatima—who were massacred in 680 by the Caliph Yazid ibn Mu'awiya. But here in Shahabandar, the latter is simply known as Yazid, a person the Muslims readily associate with some evil Hindu king, while the Hindus identify him quite often with a British colonizer!

Although it commemorates a sad occasion, the mourning assumes a carnival-like character. True, the villagers know the broad outlines of the epic saga of the agony suffered by the two martyrs. There are many Kannada songs describing in great detail the episode in which Imam Husain's head was carried away as a trophy to the Kufa castle by Yazid's victorious army. But to judge by the joyous manner, revealing a strong Hindu influence, in which this festival is celebrated, it is entirely free of that tragic and masochistic character to which the austere piety of the Shi'ites is so inclined.[9]

Of all the Muslim festivals, *Muharram*, it seems, is the one in which religious differences are least evident; and the kind of behaviour it occasions blurs even more than one might expect *a priori* the dividing line between the two religions and identities. Unlike the Muslims, the Hindus sacrifice a sheep. The former prepare a special dish called *rotte* which, unlike other dishes prepared on festive occasions, is not exchanged, because it has to be prepared according to strict rules, and even the shadow of a Hindu can pollute it.

The festival consists essentially in the veneration of the (five) *panjahs*, gilded or silvered metal symbols of the seventy-two saints (*pirs*). These relics are normally stored in a locked chest inside the mosque. A *panjah* is shaped like a hand, generally with only three fingers, in keeping with the Sunni creed which recognizes only the first three Caliphs. But this does not prevent them from also considering them as the 'five pure souls' of the Prophet's family, viz., Muhammad, Fatima, Ali, Hasan and Husain. The Hindus, for their part, claim they see in them Pandu's five son, the five valiant warriors of the *Mahabharata*: Yudhishthira, Arjuna, Bhima, Nakula and Sahadeva!

Let us briefly trace the main events of this festival which, like its model, though greatly rearranged,[10] lasts eleven days.

On the first day the craftsmen build the *ta'ziyas* or *tabuts*, small replicas of the saints' tombs. A bamboo frame is covered with shiny pieces of cardboard. Today, these structures tend to look more and more like the Taj Mahal! Money is collected from every house in the village to pay for the materials.

Until the third day, when Husain set up his camp on the battlefield of Karbala, Muslim families visit one another and exchange sweets. They use this occasion to give alms to the poor (*zakat*).

On the fourth day, the community gathers together to hear the story of the hardships faced by the saint and his army and also the details of the useless negotiations with the Omayyads and the growing difficulty they faced in getting drinking water.

The celebration takes a solemn turn on the fifth day. A procession accompanied by a band carries the chest containing the *panjahs* from the mosque. It goes to the house of the village patel, who also happens to be the mullah. They are thus able to honour both religious and temporal authority in his person. The procession then retraces its steps.

In the mosque, the *panjahs*, fitted with long wooden handles, are raised and firmly fixed on a tent erected a short distance from the rear wall. A few men, helped by children, take charge of their decoration, which mainly involves covering them with multicoloured strips of cloth. Once this task is done, villagers and other visitors pay homage to the holy insignia while saying their prayers. The pious devotees continue to pay homage until the seventh day.

On the evening of the fifth day, those who are keen to have their wishes granted—Muslims as well as Hanabars, whose ancestors followed this custom—disguise themselves as tigers. They wear only dark-coloured shorts held up by a belt, and paint the rest of their bodies orange with black stripes to resemble the tiger's coat. To complete the disguise, they sometimes attach long metal claws to their wrists—although many prefer to carry a round shield, an arrow or a spear—and cover their heads with a shiny tiger mask. Today, painted motorcycle helmets with ears have replaced the traditional mask! In addition a votive armlet consisting of a lemon attached to a peacock feather is tied around the upper arm to protect the wearer from misfortune. Because of the playful nature of this ritual, most (male) children participate in it quite willingly.

On the following days, the tigers, accompanied by an oboe-player and two drummers, visit every house in the village and around. After performing a dance punctuated by aggressive gestures and loud roars—whose slow rhythm and swaying movements, with legs placed wide apart, are reminiscent of *yakshagana*—they collect alms, part of which should be surrendered to the mosque. Sometimes, small groups accompanied by fewer musicians enact short plays in which an (undisguised) actor shoots the tiger with an old gun while a cracker goes off to simulate the noise of the gun and the beast makes a big show of collapsing to the ground.

On the ninth day, called *khatal*, the villagers start making preparations for the martyrdom. They begin by digging a big pit in front of the mosque, which serves as the ceremonial hearth. Toward the day's end many people gather around the pit to watch the fire being built, especially the sight of oxen pulling the heavy logs that are piled one on top of the other. It is believed that by performing this sacred task these animals get extra strength to plough the fields. While the Hindus sacrifice a sheep, the Muslims prepare the traditional *khichadi* and large quantities of sweet cakes. The Muslims and Hanabars offer these cakes to the *panjahs* installed in the mosque. At this point, the village head's family withdraws from the jubilant crowd, on the grounds that *Muharram* is essentially an occasion for mourning, as everybody seems to have forgotten.

Then and on the following day, the majority of Muslims observe a strict fast. Votive offerings start piling up before the *pañjahs*, surrounded by dried coconuts. Childless families offer tiny silver cradles, others light oil-lamps to ensure that their wishes are fulfilled, and as a sign of respect to the saints. Some devotees get their heads shave. Others offer clothes, natural produce and mirrors, which are almost always accompanied by small hands (*panjahs*) or tiny silver-plated horses (*duldul*). These gifts are completed by cash offerings. Before leaving the place, each person touches the feet of the officiants with their hands or their foreheads.

It is surprising to see Lingayats and other Hindus performing *puja* in the vicinity of the *panjahs.* There is a family whose wish for a male child was fulfilled in the past. The father gave a drum to the mosque a few years ago—the same one that is now used to announce processions. Since the miracle happened, members of the family visit the mosque with great pomp on the ninth day of the celebrations, announcing their arrival by bursting crackers on the way.

At midnight, the pile of logs is set on fire. The inhabitants of surrounding villages, Hindus included, gather around the fire, and some of them sing and dance. One of the participants explained the reason by narrating the following story:

> When Imam Husain was killed in the battle of Karbala, his enemies kept a watch over his body on the battlefield during the night. To frighten wild beasts and scavengers, they built a big fire around which the Caliph Yazid's soldiers sang and danced to celebrate their victory.

In Shahabandar, people throw salt into the fire to make sure that their wishes are fulfilled. For those suffering from skin ailments, it is advisable to throw flowers, including flowers made of silver. Once the logs are burnt out, some men rake the pit to prepare a bed of glowing embers so that volunteers can walk on them, one after another. Some walk slowly, others run, and still others carry a child in their arms.

A little later, some twenty men huddle together around the pit. With a single movement, they squat on the ground. They are covered with a green cloth while they mumble their prayers. An officiant approaches with a long-handled ladle. He fills it with burning coals which he throws on the cloth stretched by unseen hands. At almost the same time, another officiant removes the coals one by one with a long stick shaped like a pair of tongs. Thus is known as *angar nilana,* or the 'five baths'.

At half past five in the morning, Bibi Fatima's standard and the saints' symbols, including the *panjahs* and *ta'ziyas,* are taken out of the mosque. The devotees light small oil-lamps before them.

On the tenth day before sunrise there is a ritual called *mulaqhat* (meeting). The explanation is that Bibi Fatima had a premonition of the tragic end and called Husain, Hasan and their seventy-two companions for a last meeting before the great battle of Karbala (in 680). This explanation pays scant attention to the received version of history, according to which Fatima died in 633 while her children were still young. Besides, Hasan was not killed on the battlefield, but poisoned by his own wife Ja'dah quite a bit earlier, in 669.

At 4 o'clock in the afternoon, a procession leaves the mosque. It is preceded by a band and followed by a small white horse carrying Husain's turban on its dramatically empty saddle.

It is followed by the 'tigers' who have been dancing for a long time, and by other grotesque figures, including men wearing bear-masks, a giant sticking out his enormous tongue, and clowns wearing jute costumes and pointed hats. The masked men move on, some engaging in antics, teasing more or less willing victims. Hindus of the Talawar caste from neighbouring villages dance, moving in circles, armed with daggers and swords. The more devout lie on the ground, allowing the *panjah* carriers to walk over them.

As the procession winds its way, the *panjahs* and *ta'ziyas* can be seen against the sky, rising above the heads of the crowd. At regular intervals, the *panjah* bearers become possessed, while the *ta'ziya* bearers whirl their *ta'ziyas* over their heads before pushing them towards one another or towards the crowd, finally coming to a halt before colliding with the obstacle.

The spectators, crowded on both sides of the road, throw dried dates on the procession. The procession splits into two as it moves towards a small stream—the local version of the Euphrates, called 'Karbala'! The *panjah* and *ta'ziya* bearers move apart and go into the water slowly until it reaches their thighs. They plunge their *panjahs* into it and sprinkle water on the *ta'ziyas.* As the crowd watches the scene intently, some people break coconuts, and you see some faces covered with tears, as though they were attending the funeral of a family member. This long sequence, called *pir(a) nadijana* or 'the saints' funeral rites' testifies to the emotional ambivalence of the celebration. Then, it is said, all knots are unravelled and all problems solved.

Finally, the frames of the *ta'ziyas* and *panjahs* are removed from the water, wiped dry and put back into the wooden chest. After chanting a farewell the procession silently winds its way back to the village, in stark contrast to the carnival-like atmosphere that marked its beginning. The chest is put back in its place in the mosque and the *alawa* pit is filled up, after the throwing in of some incense sticks and leaves.

The closing ceremony called *ziyarat,* takes place on the thirteenth day. The root of the word *ziyarat* means 'visiting (the saint)'—according to the local custom—on the third day after the funeral.

This ceremony coincides with the solemn return of the chest to the mosque.

Islamist militants from Belgaum have made several attempts to change the nature of these celebrations. In their eyes, these cheerful or violent outbursts, which follow the consumption of alcohol, lead to fights, and this disturbs the atmosphere of reverence normally associated with a period of mourning. It appears that their original (anti-Shia) intention was to put an end to this practice. They have failed so far because the majority of villagers, for whom it is a local Islamic custom, believe that by stopping it they would incur their ancestors' wrath. Obviously, nobody wants the village to be struck by disease and death.

The Saint's Death Anniversary

The death anniversary of Mahbub-i Subhani, who lent his shoulders to the Prophet so that the latter could reach the divine presence, is observed on the tenth and eleventh days of the fourth lunar month of *Rabi'ath-thani*. Venerated as the guardian saint of the village, guaranteeing its welfare and prosperity, and 'beloved of praise', as his name signifies, he protects people and cattle from disease. For the Hindus, this role is played by the (*gramadevata*). However, if some catastrophe does occur, carrying the saint's standard in a procession round the village is an effective remedy. The saint also has the power of granting wishes, curing sickness, and ensuring the continuity of the family line, even for Hindus, who look on him as a protective deity and call him *devaru*.

On the morning of the tenth day, each family prepares food to be offered to the saint. The food is put on large metal trays together with votive silver horses (*duldul*), symbolizing the mount used by Muhammad to climb from sky to sky until he reached Paradise. In the evening, there is a large procession made up of Muslims and Hanabars. After the small band and *qawwali* singers come the village dignitaries and fakirs, led by a man carrying a green flag. The men in the first two rows behind them carry big baskets on their heads. In one basket there are a large number of votive horses; in another there is a pile of silk brocades; in yet another there are bundles of incense sticks and flower garlands. One man carries a vessel containing sandal paste covered with a cloth, while two others carry vessels containing ashes and jaggery. The procession moves slowly, stopping before every house, where a lady comes out and pours water on the base of the flag-post and on the dignitaries' feet. A small white horse, with a man carrying the royal umbrella walking beside it, forms the tail-end of the procession.

Once it has passed through all the village streets, including those in the Hindu quarters, the procession comes to a stop in front of the *dargah.* The nocturnal sandal ceremony takes place within the walls of the *dargah.* Hindus, too, attend this ceremony, but with their heads covered in Muslim fashion. After a long recitation of prayers two officiants apply sandal paste to the tombstone. Both Hindus and Muslims use sandal paste, which is called *gandha* in Kannada: the former apply it to their idols and the latter to the tombs of their saints. But it is not the same kind of sandal. In addition to the real sandalwood, which is white (*Santalum album*), there is another type called *Pterocarpus,* consisting of two varieties, *indicus* and *santalinus,* containing santalin pigments which give them a red colour. The former, *Pterocarpus indicus,* is called 'Andaman redwood' while the latter, *Pterocarpus santalinus,* is called 'red sandalwood'. I found that the Hindus use white sandalwood and the Muslims use red sandalwood. It may be assumed that, for the Hindus, the ritual unction helps to cool the all-powerful *baraka* emanating from the saint,[11] while for the Muslims, it has a vivifying effect, since the scented paste is red in colour.[12] The tomb is then covered with new brocade cloth, on which the devotees pile garlands of fresh flowers, thus marking the end of the ceremony.[13] As soon as the dignitaries leave, a host of devotees crowd into the little shrine to press their palms on the holy sepulchre so that they absorb the precious paste. The luckier among them manage to touch their foreheads on the tomb. Each person is given a handful of sweets before leaving the shrine. During this time the officiants place their sandal-paste-covered palms against the outer walls of the *dargah* to drive away the demons. There will be new imprints the following year.

The *ʿurs* itself, which the villagers interpret as the saint's ascension to heaven, is celebrated the next day. Muslim devotees sacrifice a sheep and light exactly eleven *ghee* lamps, because the saint died on the eleventh day of the month. The day's main event, apart from the recitation of prayers, is a community feast of mutton curry. And as night falls, the feast gradually turns into a fair.

Two anecdotes show how the compulsory feasting sometimes

causes unexpected accidents. Following custom, on the day of the *ʿurs* the Hindus invite a drama company from Belgaum to perform a play in front of the Adveppa temple. The goddess Kamaladevi and the god Basaveshvara are carried in palanquins to the vēnue to be entertained. But one year, it was not possible to satisfy them. The priests from the neighbouring Chikaldinni village, who carry the palanquins, had fallen out with the people of Shahabandar, and therefore would not come to the hostile village. Many people were afraid that the goddess would be angry. As a matter of fact, she did let them know the next day, through the mouth of a possessed priest, that she was very angry with the villagers because she could not enjoy the play. Another year, the *ʿurs* celebration coincided with the festival of Kamaladevi, the village goddess propitiated with goat sacrifices by the Hanabars—who also worship the saint. But the meat from animals so sacrificed is considered taboo (*haram*) by the Muslims, because the goats are not sacrificed according to the Islamic rite, and even more so if the sacrifice is performed on the saint's feast day. So there was no question of celebrating the two festivals on the same day. It was also impossible to change the dates, as they are decided according to astrological calculations in the almanac. Yet no one could ever consider the idea of cancelling the festivals. After a long discussion, it was finally decided that the day would be split into two halves. In the morning, each Hanabar family would worship Kamaladevi in its own field and would come home after a bath to participate in the *ʿurs* celebrations.

Saints are worshipped in recognized and effective ways, but not according to canonical rules. This is so because over the centuries these saints have come to play the role of 'pivots' (*qutb*) in popular Islam, and because this cultural behaviour has borrowed heavily from native Hindu forms of worship and piety. This is seen particularly in the villages, where religion is not an academic or theological question, but guided by the motives and purposes of all members. Also, despite the influence of saints on the development of Muslim identity, their worship continues to be a melting-pot where communities, who jealously guard their individuality, absorb the culture of other communities.

Right up to the present day, it cannot be imagined that the majority of Muslims would be willing to detach their lives from those of their saints, whom they worship with greater zeal than they show in their strictly Islamic duties. These saints live on within their tombs for ever, and their mission is to bring the heavens closer to earth by listening to the pleas and petitions of their devotees before interceding with God. They act as intermediaries, even though they would be capable of granting their devotees' wishes on their own. The villagers believe that the effectiveness of their prayers to Allah depends on the size of their offerings and sacrifices to the saints, and on the familiarity they have been able to establish with one of Allah's intermediaries.

Adjustment, Reformism and Modernization

However, there are some orthodox Muslims, even in the villages, who do not appreciate the way in which their coreligionists conceive and worship God. This is the case in Shahabandar with the village head who, as we have mentioned earlier, also functions as the mullah. Anxious to discipline their beliefs and eradicate superstition, he periodically upbraids all those who corrupt the 'purity' of Islam by following practices inspired by Hindu polytheism. He would gladly forbid all religious beliefs and practices that attribute to God's creatures powers that belong solely to Him.

He openly admits his close links with those supporters of Islamic reformism based in Belgaum, who condemn the participation of Muslims in Hindu rituals and try to put an end to the worship of saints.

Thus once, on the occasion of the *ʿurs* of Mahbub-i Subhani, he invited Muslim militants of the Jama'at-i Islami party to Shahabandar. The visitors, mostly young men, came to remind the villagers that they must believe only in one God and accept only Muhammad as his Prophet and sole messenger. They illustrated their reproaches with stories seasoned with eschatology, where history took the upper hand over miraculous powers, and painted a vivid picture of how infidels would be condemned, punished and tortured by angels on the Day of Judgement.

The educated young Muslim from the village who narrated this incident to me, pointed out—not without malice—that such a sermon was liable to be interpreted by the villagers as an invitation to propitiate the hordes of evil djinns roaming on the outskirts of the village defended by the local saint.

The mullah's psychological and social position continues to be uncomfortable, because his puritanical inclinations have to adjust themselves to the local balance of power and the not very Islamic majority of villagers on whom his power depends. He may see to it that Islamic prayers are said five times a day in the mosque, but cannot prevent some of the ceremonies associated with the *Muharram* celebrations bearing no trace of piety, since the emphasis is on pomp and rejoicing. He has tried to convince Muslims many times to perform them outside the holy precincts of the mosque, which, according to him, is reserved for prayers. He has explained to them that by occupying the mosque during *Muharram*, they force the more pious among them to say their prayers at home. But every time he has come into open confrontation with the assembled Muslim community, the latter has been eagerly supported by the Hanabars, who have never been backward in organizing the forces of opposition.

Owing to the absence of a suitable building and an institutional body to regulate social behaviour at the local level, the occasional dispensation of justice also takes place in the mosque. It is well known that Muslims are reluctant to seek the help of the police and to place their trust in magistrates, most of whom are recruited from among the Hindus. Whenever a Muslim makes a mistake or commits an offence, it is in his interest to get the matter settled within the community and by it. The verdict given by the *qadi*, who belongs to the same faction as the mullah is publicly proclaimed inside the mosque, thereby giving it the sanction of the *shari'a*.

The village head tries time and again to Islamize local beliefs and practices by taking advantage of his title of *hajji*. He is, in fact, one of the very few persons in the area who has been on the *hajj*. Thus he can pester the villagers to uphold the 'five pillars' of Islam and go to the mosque at least on Friday. He takes advantage of celebrations like *Shabe Mir'aj*, *Shabe Barat* and *Shabe Qadr*, when there is a large crowd, to rebuke his coreligionists. However, his pious efforts have not borne much fruit to date.

Many peasants admit that they neglect their religious duties because they are busy in their fields from dawn to dusk. Most of them claim that their poverty does not permit them to bathe and change their clothes before saying their prayers, as they are supposed to. And not content with using the inflexibility of their farming routine as an excuse for not observing their religious rites, they claim they are guilty of very few transgressions, certainly fewer than the rich, because of their extremely frugal existence, which is mostly spent in toil. Some, who are better adjusted to their cultural environment, or more wily, retort that in any case 'work is worship' (*kayakavekailaśha*), borrowing this adage in an alliterative English version from the teachings of the founder of the Virasaiva sect. In fact, this proclamation is often to be found inscribed on the facade of many official buildings in Karnataka. They claim to be good Muslims because they worship the saint. After all, do they not address their prayers to this 'friend of God' (*wali*)? Do they not fast for him during *Ramadan*? Do they not make pilgrimages to him periodically to make offerings? Do they not give alms to the 'poor'? Except for the offerings, all these actions constitute the 'pillars' of Islam.

However, during the last ten years they have been subjected to growing pressure from Islamists. Young proselytizers, mainly students who are members of the Belgaum branch of the Jama'at-i Islami, go to the neighbouring villages to help the local head organize campaigns to 'purify' current rituals. We have already given an example of their efforts in Shahabandar. The following example is no less eloquent, though it produced just the opposite result.

For the funeral procession, the Muslims use a simple stretcher made of bamboo, which is destroyed after the ceremony. Convinced that this custom was too similar to the Hindu funeral practice, some militants decided to get standard-sized wooden caskets (*doli*) made and had them brought to the village. With the consent of the village head, they were kept in the mosque. The villagers unanimously condemned this action, claiming that it was inauspicious to store coffins in the house of God, and would surely lead to many deaths. There was a violent dispute on the subject, which has now been settled. Villagers now place the dead bodies in coffins made in Belgaum.

Attempts to bring local practices into line with what is supposed to be the professionalization of Islamic norms sometimes produce dubious results. This has happened, for example, in the case of the professionalization of worship. During the *ᶜurs* of Mahbub-i Subhani and *Muharram* celebrations, only the members of the mullah's family have the right to officiate. But for private ceremonies, the families in the village often invite one of their own number to recite prayers on their behalf, just like a Hindu priest. At the time of *Bakar-ᶜId*, the sacrifice is performed by the mullah. Of course, the sacrifice is performed in the Muslim manner, but his position *vis-à-vis* those for whom he is performing the sacrifice is similar to that of a Hindu priest performing a sacrifice for low-caste or untouchable devotees.

We may finally mention that the institutionalization of the mullah's role lies beyond the religious realm in the strictly orthodox sense, as he is obliged to distribute amulets against the evil eye or talismans to counter-attack wicked 'spirits'.

The question of Islamic purity came to the fore with the advent of modern technology. A flour mill was set up in the village following its electrification during the 1980s. This gave rise to the problem of the pollution of the ground meal. In fact, the villagers were so fascinated by this novelty, which would give them more leisure, that everybody, irrespective of rank, came to admire the mill. But as *Muharram* approached, they became more and more worried, because until then it had been customary for a few men—suitably purified and sheltered from prying eyes—to prepare the cakes eaten during the festival. After much discussion, it was decided to take certain measures to avoid contamination. It was agreed that the floor would be covered with liquid cow-dung and the flour mill would be cleaned thoroughly. Also, the grain would be ground during the night, and non-Muslims would not be allowed to enter the flour mill during the grinding.

Ugadi

The traditional new year begins for the villagers on *Ugadi*, the festival that marks the beginning of the agricultural season in the month of *Chaitra* (March/April). All social groups worship the tools of their respective trades on this day. This festival has the same significance for Hindus and Muslims, viz., the fertility of their fields and, consequently, the prosperity of the village. But once again, though this statement conveys the notion of religious syncretism in the village, it does not stand up to scrutiny when one explains how the festival is celebrated. Actually, the two communities worship the tools of their trade quite differently. The Hindus hold *pujas* while the Muslims hold more prayers (*fatiha*). In addition, the latter also give offerings to their saints, which, on this occasion, are identical to those given by the Hindus to their goddess on other occasions. After the land is ritually ploughed, the landowner's wife and the mother of his (living) sons spreads manure on the field, a rite that is also followed by the Muslims, though this task usually falls on Lingayat women, who, under the leadership of Adveppa, the god specific to their caste, play a dominant role in the collective life of the village. The festival ends with a communal meal in the *panchayat*. The raw materials for the meal, which must contain jaggery, are provided by the principal castes, including not only the Hanabars and Bedars, but also the Muslims. The ritual food, cooked in Lingayat homes, is served on eleven banana leaves, corresponding to the combined group of the village's Hindu divinities and Muslim saints. It is also the Lingayats who distribute their shares to the Hanabars, Bedars and Muslims; but the Bedars sit apart from the other castes and are served last.

Before the sowing festival (*kalavvana habba*), all the divinities are invoked in the following order: Mahbub-i Subhani, as the protector of the village—*Khade wali*—receives the first offering of fruit; followed by Kamaladevi—the goddess of fertility; then Halavva, Karevva, Basavaranna and Bandavva—this last worshipped as earth-mother; and finally, Hanuman(tha) and buffaloes called Basava.

Except for the Lingayats, who simultaneously give vegetarian offerings to Hanuman, the male members of all the other castes celebrate *Allahnami* (God's name) on the same day. The Muslims, Hanabars and Bedars gather together in front of the mosque, but the Bedars from a separate group, maintaining their distance from the Muslims. When there is a drought in the area, the villagers celebrate the 'rain festival' (*kara habba*). They do not establish a mechanical link between the lack of water and divine wrath, but assume that the natural order has been disturbed by an as yet unknown worldly cause, such as an immoral or criminal act (incest, adultery, sorcery, or drunkenness). Everybody is fully aware that there are climatic phenomena that do not submit to this type of explanation. To counteract this possibility (because there is no smoke without fire), three sheep are sacrificed, one by the Hindus and the other two by the Muslims. The Hanabars sacrifice their own animal by chopping off its head, and cook their food separately. Thus they show the entire village, and not just the Muslims on whom they depend for the major part of their livelihood because they are employed by them, that they are participating in the festival as a distinct group. At the very end, they offer the Muslims a part of the sacrificed animal together with cooked food. As for the Muslims, it is the mullah who performs the sacrifice by slitting the throats of the animals, who are made to lie down and allowed to bleed. He sacrifices the sheep offered by the Hindus and the two sheep offered by his own community. Though food is cooked separately, it is distributed to everybody by the Muslims.

The situation is somewhat different when celebrating the festival of *Bandavva.* The Hanabars play a dominant role here, even though the entire village contributes towards the expenses. Two sheep are sacrificed, but this time in the Hindu manner, which explains why the Muslims and the Lingayats (because the latter are vegetarians) do not participate in the celebrations, although they contribute grain and some money. This time, only the Hanabars and Bedars eat the cooked meat of the sacrificed animals.

The festival held before the harvest (*shige hunnime*) is also in honour of the goddess Bandavva. The devotees burn incense and offer food to the earth-mother while sprinkling water on her. Though this is a Hindu rite, Muslims too participate in it, some of them even touching the ground with their foreheads. The food prepared on this occasion is thrown on the ground to feed the buffaloes, who are buried there to protect the land against evil 'spirits'. It is said, this custom shared by Hindus and Muslims has its origin in the Virashaiva cult, which considers its founder Basava as an incarnation of Shiva's mount. The Muslims, however, do not go all the way and refuse to celebrate the bull's funeral. Also, they never take part in the nocturnal funeral procession, when the body of a dead buffalo is taken round the village in a cart.

The Hindu festival of *Malledevaru* and the Muslim ceremony of *Barsat-ke-pir* have similar rituals. A young boy is made to undress and go from house to house with a metal basin on his head in the name of the Hindu god Malle or the Muslim saint Barsa. At each stop, the house owner pours a small jugful of water into the receptacle on his head. Local exegetes claim that the black basin represents clouds and the water poured into it symbolizes rain. If the rains are delayed in spite of this ritual, a procession made up of a large part of the village population goes to the hilltop to pray and make large offerings of flowers. Inversely, a ceremony performed in honour of Halavva is intended to make the rain stop and generally to avert calamities.

Two Festivals Held Around a Pit

Two rituals held around a pit, one Muslims and the other Hindu, celebrated by the Bedars, are indicative of similar cultural practices rather than detailed communal arrangements. One of them is strictly vegetarian and the other is centred around an animal sacrifice.

Muslims hold a ceremony to protect the faithful against sickness during the coming year. Various Muslim saints are invoked in order of precedence and offered the first fruits and cooked *jowar* grains. The principal saint is Khade Wali, 'friend of the pit' or 'well'. He has no *dargah* in the village, but resides in a hole in front of the mosque, and the offerings of the first fruits are placed in the hole. It is the custom to invoke and propitiate him every Monday and Friday and before starting a new venture.

Kol Karevva, the Bedar goddess, does not have a shrine of her own, either, because she lives in the earth. A pile of stones at the foot of a tree on the hill overlooking the village denotes her presence. Four days before the festival dedicated to the great Kamaladevi, her 'younger sister' (*tangi*) Karevva is propitiated. But the inhabitants of the nearby villages are informed only a day earlier. A few Bedars are sent to the town to fetch what is needed. Nobody must cross their path, otherwise the ceremony is cancelled. Numerous precautions are of course taken to avoid such a catastrophe. On the chosen day, the ceremony takes place at night on top of the hill. A Bedar is deputed to go there and cook various dishes. He then performs a *puja*, in which he is joined by other members of his caste. The remaining food is put in a pit (*dongara*) dug earlier. A live pig is also buried in it. The Bedars then return to the village. Nobody is allowed to go up the hill for the next two days, because it is believed that anybody who hears the pig howling will die immediately.

Basava Jayanti

The birthday of the founder of the Lingayat-Virashaiva sect is celebrated as Basava Jayanti on *Shivaratri* day, as he is believed to be an incarnation of Shiva's mount. Buffaloes are the heroes of the day, even though they are in any case worshipped every Monday. (A man who was very keen to get a photograph of his old ox before it died, managed to persuade me to take a picture. He placed it in a makeshift shrine, where the animal would be worshipped after its death.) Like the Hindus, the Muslims too look on their buffaloes as incarnations of Basavanna and respect them accordingly, even though they refuse, as was pointed out earlier, to conduct a funeral for them.

Although this is mainly a Lingayat festival, Hindus of other castes, as well as Muslims, give cereals as offerings. But only Hindus decorate their buffaloes and take them in procession to the Basaveshvara temple. On reaching the temple, the whole village sits before the idol of the heroic Shaivite. The Muslims, however, remain in the background, while the meal cooked by the Hanabars is first served to the Lingayats.

Infectious Disease or Sorcery?

When there is an epidemic affecting humans or cattle, all the villagers abstain from eating meat for five successive Mondays. And they all take up voluntary work for the common good, such as cleaning the streets and religious buildings. Oil-lamps burn continuously in temples and shrines.

Although this observance, called *wara*, is obviously Hindu, Muslims too follow it. They clean mosque and *dargah* and carry the standard of Mahbub-i Subhani in procession round the village. The Hanabars join the Muslims, who recite their prayers in unison, particularly at the four halts marking the village's four cardinal directions. When the standard is brought back to the *dargah*, a solemn prayer precedes the offering of an impressive mound of jaggery collected from all the houses in the village. Mahbub-i Subhani would thus deserve the title 'intoxicated by sugar' or *Ganj-i Shakkar*, common among Indian saints, though one would have to translate it into Persian as 'storehouse of sugar' to signify the transfer whereby offerings of sugar are converted into an accumulation of *baraka*. On the following Monday, the Muslims make a new offering of jaggery, and every household hangs garlands of fresh flowers on the saint's standard. There is another procession, and everybody asks Mahbub-i Subhani to keep sickness away from the village. A community meal eaten near the dargah marks the end of the ceremony. The Lingayats attend, but do not accept even a cup of tea. Thus the ceremony takes place with minimal transactions between the different participating communities. It is obvious that collective identities are formed on the basis of a host of relationships, but also by the skilful manipulation of the common boundaries that separate them, something that calls for a well thought-out strategy to ensure smooth exchanges between different castes and communities.

When a villager is suspected of practising sorcery, an elderly widow may become the target of suspicion. But first it is necessary to make sure that she is really guilty. Either the mullah or his son then takes the responsibility of carrying the standard as part of an ordeal. If he does not feel the weight of the standard during the walk, that means that there is no 'sorceress' living in the part of the village he has just passed through. If the standard become heavy and suddenly changes its direction in the lower part of the village, for example, it means that the guilty woman has taken possession. Everyone hopes that she will utter the words: 'Don't torture me, I will go away!'. This admission will set the whole village free. Thus the saints in Shahabandar perform all the functions normally performed by Hindu gods.

But in addition to this public management of troubles affecting the village, there are specialized institutions to deal with distress and affliction, as we shall see in the next chapter. In this Muslim majority area, there appears, as if by miracle, an 'old man' or *pir*, or a 'grandfather' (*baba*), who takes the responsibility of protecting the community. From birth to death, he shows signs of his miraculous powers. For example, he masters the Holy Book and performs the pilgrimage to Mecca at a very early age. Allah orders him in a vision to leave his native Arabia and go to Hindustan. He flies across the skies, or travels in stages, meeting well-known masters who initiate him into spiritual truths. He is involved in supernatural fights against a demon, a *yogi* or a fakir belonging to another brotherhood. Finally, he settles down in the village, attracting many followers. He leads an austere life, strictly observing the vow of poverty, punctuated by periods of severe penance. He possesses the gift of healing and cosmic powers and, finally, he rises to heaven with his eyes open. These are proofs of holiness that acquire an institutional character, and thereafter become an integral part of the day-to-day Islamic cult based on touch, participation and immanence that confer on the incorruptible bodies of the saints that most effective of symbolic powers, the ability to crystallize demons.

NOTES

1. The quantitative data have been obtained from the Census Reports of 1981 and 1991 and a considerable amount of information about the village has been provided by Pathan (1979).
2. For a description of the city, refer to Chapter 6.
3. Gordon (1994) explains how the British fabricated the category of 'criminal tribes' on the basis of the equally artificial but by now legendary category of Thugs.

4. For the internal hierarchy of this Shaivite community, torn between its sectarian ideals and its caste organization, see Assayag (1986).
5. This system is similar to the one used by the (Lingayat) Banajiga, who are landowners and also officiate as priests in the temple of a local goddess (Assayag 1994).
6. *Jann* is the plural of *jinn*; but henceforth we will use the Anglicized form 'djinns'.
7. While according to Fruzetti (1981: 109) and Kumar (1989: 158ff.) the celebration of *Muharram* serves to integrate Muslims into the Islamic community (in the face of non-Muslims), according to Saiyed (1981: 136-7) it helps to strengthen the social cohesiveness between Hindus and Muslims.
8. On the basis of official reports, especially those from the nineteenth century, Masselos (1982) shows that all castes of Hindus and Muslims joined in celebrating *Muharram*; but the stresses their rivalry and the changes that came about in the processions in the twentieth century. Hardy points out that, at least since Mughal times, Hindus and Muslims shared the same rites and took part in the same festivals in cities as well as in villages (1972: 19, 27).
9. In July 1991, taking advantage of the presence of a community locally known as Iranis and consisting of some forty families settled around the *Imambara* on the outskirts of Dharwad, I attended the Shia celebration of *Muharram*. To avoid conflict with the Sunnis, because the Shiah festival ends with the immersion of *panjahs* in the same stream as is used by them, the authorities take care to allot different times and routes for the processions organized by the two communities. After the emotion-charged recital of Husain's martyrdom by the *Imam* dressed in black, punctuated by the weeping and moaning of the devotees, the procession heads towards the stream, as the pious flagellate themselves (*matam*). The men slash themselves with razor blades until the blood flows from their bodies. Children too beat their chests violently, loudly calling out Husain's name with each blow.
10. The celebration does not follow in detail the twelve episodes of the martyrdom, locally called *manjali*—quite the contrary, as is revealed in the detailed story of the Karbala saga given by Hollister (1953).
11. S. Bayly interprets the ritual, even for the Muslims, in the following terms: '. . . application of sandalwood paste through which devotees seek to cool, damp down and channel the all powerful *barakat* (or *Shakti*) which emanates from the *pir* and his tomb shrine' (1993: 483).
12. Although this unction refers to the Arabic region during the Prophet's time and even though it is no longer seen there, Goldziher's article on 'the worship of the dead in paganism and Islam' throws some light on the use of this ritual during the veneration of Indian saints. He shows how the worship was transferred from the father, the ancestor buried in

an inviolable tomb, to the saint in general (1967: 216) and how later elegiac poetry (after the third century of the Hegira) asked those passing by a tomb to sacrifice an animal by sprinkling its blood on the tomb (ibid., p. 219) before feasting there (cf. similar indications also given by Chelhod (1955: 119ff.). We may note in passing that *Pterocarpus santalinus* is known for its healing properties: the paste is used for curing inflammations, headaches, skin infections, and used in the form of a decoction for treating chronic dysentery.

13. According to Goody, this amounts to vivification through flowers: 'The wonderful stories about these saints (*malfūzat*) sometimes mention the scent of flowers placed on their tombs; or they relate how the dead body disappeared and all that remained in its place were some flowers' (1994: 393).

2

Demonology
Power *versus* 'Powers'

> Only evil makes you notice and learn, and enables you to analyse mechanisms you would not otherwise understand.
>
> M. PROUST, *Sodome et Gomorrhe* (1922)

Only by observing popular Hinduism and Islam, that is to say functional everyday religion, can one understand the importance and ambiguity of those powers that are usually referred to as 'demons'. It is demons who decide whether a person will be healthy or sick, fortunate or unfortunate, poor or prosperous. Observation also reveals that there is a certain amount of ambivalence in the representation of divinities whose iconography and attributes may change from place to place and from time to time. Often, it is not clear whether they are good or evil; and at times they change their nature quite suddenly.

This observation is further strengthened as one goes lower down the pantheon. These volatile and amorphous 'powers' that haunt open spaces, seem to be independent of the world of gods and generally exempt from the relations that bind human beings to gods. Being neither temple gods (*devgudi*) nor village gods (*uradadevta*), they are not associated with either personal (*ishtadevta*), family (*kutumbadevta*), or household deities (*manedevaru*). It is only after going through an exorcism that the possessed person realizes that he or she had actually been possessed by one of these powers. In short, they do not rule over the village nor do they protect it, although they are sometimes involved in protecting the patriclan. Not having a fixed home nor any protective function—if not the contrary—they do not generally fulfil wishes. And the use of such circumlocutions based on a negative theology to convey their indescribable nature is tantamount to saying that they are dangerous.

Hindus look on demons as *bhut(a)* or *pishac(a)* or as a particular type of deity (*daiva*), a generic term covering the great gods as well. Muslims believe that *jinns* were created by Allah Himself (from fire) at the same time as 'angels' (*farishta*) and 'demons' (*shayatin*). The complementarity in popular Hinduism of the 'Lord of Demons' and the goddess (*devi*), though not necessarily the village goddess,[1] has been pointed out quite frequently; but to the best of my knowledge, nobody has ever pointed out the parallel between the 'saints' (*pir, wali* or *baba*) revered by the Muslims as 'masters' (shaikh, malik) of 'demons', even though they do not belong to the same category.[2] The significance of this parallel goes beyond the local effect of acculturation on the members of the two communities, which in itself is a very complex phenomenon. A comparative ethnography of the way divinity and sainthood are used by the protagonists of the two communities shows that the local conceptions on which they are based are far from opposed to their respective canonical traditions. It is therefore futile to try to reduce 'popular' religion to a form of folklore bogged down in superstition.

According to scholarly Hinduism, 'celestial gods' (*deva*) and the denizens of the Kingdom of Darkness (*asra*), though in constant conflict, are identical (Biardeau 1981b: 294); only their function is different, as day differs from night by chasing it away (O'Flaherty 1976: 58). Also, it is difficult to imagine that one type of god or goddess represents a single function in a polytheistic system (Toffin 1992: 690).

As for scriptural Islam, not only are *jinns* accepted without any reservations, but they also enjoy a legitimate, though somewhat controversial status. We may point out that in the Koran, the world of 'angels' (*farishtagan*) overlaps with that of 'satanic beings' (*shayatin*), incarnated by the ambiguous figure of Iblis who belonged to the tribe of angels (*aj-jinn*) before he was cursed (McDonald and Massé 1961: 549; Fahdh 1971: 176-7).

In support of observation of the worship of saints specializing in the treatment of 'demons'—let us repeat that their mausoleums are usually frequented by members of the lower castes. But this must be understood in a wider sense. It matters little whether they are Hindus, Muslims or Christians. What is important is the effectiveness of the action taken to control these evil powers, which appear and disappear in no time. When it a question of combating disease or affliction, religious affiliation signifies only a superficial variation in a common cognitive universe of evil, its causes and its treatment. And it is the same in the case of divine power. In spite of recent communal tensions, this model is followed by the members of the society of devotees (*bhakta*) and the community of believers (*umma*), occupying a well-defined slot in the Indian caste hierarchy.

It is therefore easy to understand why, in the course of our study on acculturation, we should be conducting investigations into the palace-like *dargahs* where Hindus, Muslims and Christians mingle to express their devotion in an intense, theatrical and sometimes turbulent manner. For this is a new example of the Hinduization of Islam and, to a lesser degree, of the Islamization of Hinduism in the subcontinent.

Demonology in North Karnataka

Demoniac Nature

Anybody carrying out a study on 'minor powers'—whether one calls them *jinns* or *bhut*(*a*)—among low-class Hindus and Muslims in south India, faces two interrelated problems. One of them is the anxiety caused by these creatures, and the other is their essentially changeable and volatile nature. As a matter of fact, people do not like to talk about them, and refuse point blank even to mention them. As for the possessed, their experience is by definition indescribable. Most of them are reluctant to utter the powers' names because any mention is likely to resurrect them. And everybody knows only too well that this transient but stubborn materialization will be tantamount to an evil action. If one of these forces appears to them, they are threatened with misfortune. If it visits them regularly, misfortune will befall them immediately. Following such an encounter, synonymous with certain disaster, they are doomed to suffer.

The fact that they are considered the most impure and predatory of powers belonging to a lower (or the lowest) order, obviously means that these creatures are very powerful and greatly feared. Although they stand at the bottom of the pantheon's hierarchy, they possess the extraordinary power of manifesting themselves to persons belonging even to the middle and upper castes because, as Fuller (1988: 33) points out, the pantheon does not correspond exactly to the structure of the caste-based Indian society. They are feared even more because they live in the vicinity of human beings and occasionally enter their bodies. These powers, with their pragmatic nature are intimately involved in day-to-day human activities and are thus opposed to the great divinities, who are more distant and transcendent (Babb 1975: 239).

The obsessive fear arouse by demons is proportionate to the sudden and sporadic nature of their manifestation: they disappear almost as soon as they appear. This ontological evanescence is expressed in the etymology of the term *bhut(a)* derived from the Sanskrit root *bhu*, which means 'to become'. Similarly, the word *jinn* conveys the sense of 'being hidden or concealed' (*ijtanan*). Not having a lasting identity or a well-defined character, unlike the Ethiopian *zar* (Leiris 1980) or the voodoo spirits of Haiti (Métraux 1959), these 'forces' can by definition resist all efforts to apprehend them. This explains the semantic shift in their names—*bhut(a)*, *jinn*, *pishac(a)*, *pret(a)*, *rakshas(a)*, *asura*, *bala*, *dayam*, *devva*, *gali*, *dhuli*, *yaksi*, *curali*, *caitan*, etc.—and the difficulty of translating them as 'demons', 'spirits', 'genies', 'phantoms', 'ghosts', 'winds', 'evil beings', etc. So many 'powers', difficult to understand and all the more enigmatic because 'their range is vast and their intervention prompt', as a *hadith* puts it (Fahd 1971: 183).

We will try nevertheless to define them.[3] There are male and female demons, but some do not have a fixed gender; or they have two genders simultaneously. And though some of them are married, most of them are not. This is probably a way of saying that they are uncontrollable because of their independence, as opposed to the multiple and reassuring ties that generally bind together the interdependent gods in the pantheon. The confusion is all the greater because the 'powers' referred to here are 'souls' (*pret*[*a*]) or 'phantoms' (*pishac*[*a*]). They do not have a permanent form or cultural set-up, unlike 'spirits', which, being linked with a goddess or goddesses, are given, after they are struck down and transformed into devotees (*bhakta*), the martial function of guarding the locality (*kshetrapala*). This means that they have to be materialized and immobilized in shrines where, once pacified, they become deified demons and join the society of gods. We may cite the example of the demons enshrined in a large number of imposing religious complexes (*bhutasthana*) in the Tulu-speaking region on the west coast of Karnataka, where they are worshipped with pomp and ceremony. They are such an integral part of the divine pantheon that one would hesitate to treat them as real demons. Their well-organized and institutionalized worship, which resembles a form of theatre and serves as entertainment, seems to have subdued them.[4] Till fairly recently, aesthetically presented dance-dramas (*yakshagana*) could be seen in similar shrines in Kannada-speaking areas.

In north Karnataka, evil powers are not pacified by worship in shrines (*bhutasthana*). These and the souls of dead ancestors are given offerings (*pinda*) during the funeral ceremony and belong to the private domain. They only concern a particular family and their exorcism essentially needs the individual expertise of a magician, sorcerer, exorcist or possessor of the evil eye.

Such an institutional function does exist in Karnataka today, but it belongs to a few Muslim saints called *pir* or *baba*, capable of driving out demons (*bhut*[*a*]-*avesa*). They are entrusted with the task of neutralizing volatile and ferocious 'troops of evil demons' (*bhut*[*a*]-*gana*) brought to their tombs, if we may put it so, by the possessed. And similarly to what was observed in northern India by Pfeiderer (1981: 205-6) and Kakar (1982: 64), a small area is set apart in the religious complex for the possessed, and the more violent among them are fixed to the wall with heavy iron chains.

The Demonic Continuum

In the continuum of 'supernatural beings' there are gods and goddesses and deities of a lower order, but also spiritual beings that do not come under any of these categories. These beings of the third type are considered demons, but there are demons and demons. On the one hand, there are those called *bhut*(*a*)-*devaru*; and on the other hand, there are the *bhut*(*a*)-*devva*.

The former, being divinities of a lower order, reside as auxiliaries in the pantheon because their importance, their names and attributes differ from village to village. Most of the time, they are brothers and sisters, and all are related by blood or marriage. Some of them control certain specific domains: Pilichavandi is in charge of agricultural lands, Kodamantappa is in charge of the harvest and Korragamma is in charge of cattle. Still others control diseases and tend to get mixed up with local goddesses like Maryamma, Yellamma, Gangamma and Udutsamma. They can be subjugated by a master who is not one of them, a god having relations with a *devi* (Dumont 1975: 109). Having characteristic forms, they are anthropomorphic and are ultimately related to the terrible 'great divinities' like Bhairav(a)-Kali. At times, they assume an animal form, such as that of a serpent (*sarpa*)—Nagadevate, Nagakanne, Nagabrahma, Nagappa, etc.—and devotees erect stelae to them that receive votive offerings. Sometimes, their idols are installed in a shrine so that they can be propitiated and interrogated publicly.[5]

The latter, on the contrary, constitute of myriad of powers, most of them without a specific name or form. They are also independent, like, for example, the *bhut(a)-bhadhe*, volatile and fairly mysterious phantoms held responsible for unexplained sickness and death. The sickness they cause is called 'wind' (*vata*), because they move freely like air and enter the flesh. Similarly, some of the spirits are called *dhuli* or dust particles.

It seems that nothing can ever tie down these powers. They disappear when any effort is made to give them a form, except the seductive form they assume to entice their victims before they suddenly change themselves into succubi to penetrate their bodies. This is true of the most feared of the lot, the *Brahm(a)-rakshas(a)*, a hairy cannibal, who goes about devouring intestines and drinking blood from open skulls and is believed to take away the lives of those who stray into the night. The untouchables believe that he is the 'soul' of Brahmins who are unable to enter heaven in this age of catastrophe (*kaliyuga*), and torments men to seek vengeance. He has a female counterpart, *Mari*, who is believed to have a fiery look.

Part of day-to-day life, these 'powers' are dangerous when they manifest themselves in the form of light or sound, either as a zigzagging flashes of lightning or the jingling of bells. Just after nightfall, you can see the *Kollidev(va)* flashing like torches or will-o'-the-wisps because of their erratic darting movements, exactly like those of *jinns*. They may be compared to the vengeful spirits of the victims of foul play or consumption of spirits of ancestors not provided with a proper tombstone. However, decent burial does not always guarantee that the departed soul will rest in peace, unlike cremation, which promises a final release. And if a person wants to go hunting or looking for firewood in the forest, he or she must watch out for the *Sambali* or *Sankalidev(va)*, who betray their presence by the tinkling of bells.

These short-lived apparitions—etymologically *yaksa*—are even more worrying because, in actual fact, the distinction between an angry god and an enraged demon is not clear. The demoniac spectrum moves upwards towards the divine, unless the reverse applies, and the dividing-line between the two types of *bhut* remains uncertain. The importance given to some 'powers', whose names are related to well-known divinities like Bhairava, Bhadrakali, Mahakali, Nagabrahma and Maharajanaga indicates that they are considered 'kings' (*bhut*[*a*]-*raj*[*a*]) or 'sovereigns' (*bhut*[*a*]-*isha*) reigning over a cohort of demons (*bhut*[*a*]-*gana*), always on the point of disappearing. Muslims too refer to Shaikhs, Maliks, Sayyids ruling over nameless *jinns* in an invisible world with its own hierarchy.

The proliferation of powers on the outskirts of villages, in forest areas and in burial grounds suggests that this menacing ring also has a protective role. This ambiguity is an indication of their ambivalence. Some *jinns* do not seem to be systematically evil. They act like guardians or protectors, keeping to the letter of the Koran, like those who built the village mosque in Shahabandar, mentioned in the previous chapter, or the one behind the cenotaph of Bar Shah at the approach to the Yellamma temple in Saundatti, of which we shall speak later (Chapter 5).

There is a general belief that *jinns*, who are not manifestly evil, may become so later. This would mean, strictly speaking, that there are no good genies. These evanescent, shadowy 'non-beings' are believed to be capricious, which explains the arbitrary nature of their interventions. But the arbitrariness may be only apparent. Ignorance of the motives that drive them to a particular action does not mean that they do not have their own reasons. But let us keep away from moral connotations. These 'powers' are neither 'good' nor 'evil' because, though they are rid of the weight of their bodies, they too have needs that require satisfaction. This is what makes them appear irrational and also vulnerable. As if human, they are hurt or insulted at the slightest thing. They take revenge by entering the bodies of those who ignore them, provoke them or even assault them unknowingly. They are all the more menacing because one never knows whom they will attack, when, where and how. They are all the more worrying because anyone may be possessed at any time for a lapse or transgression.

It seems that nobody is considered unimportant or uninteresting, and once the attack (*kata*) is diagnosed, there is a plethora of conjectures regarding what could have motivated it. The exorcist (*ghadi*) is obliged to go back in time and reconstruct the sequence of events that led to this misfortune with the help of clues provided by the possessed person, or his/her relations.

If the reason is known, say, the failure to observe a taboo (*haram*) or perform one's duties towards a saint, the same general line of treatment is followed. Sometimes the treatment involves a slow and patient restructuring of past events to awaken the victim's subconscious and find out the dynamics of family relationships. The therapeutic cult practised in the *dargah* could thus be defined as an attempt to reshape the patient's emotional make-up by readapting him/her to his/her social environment, a process conditioned by the renewal of limited exchanges with the divine. However, we must take care not to idealize these traditional methods of treatment where the 'anxiety to cure and to expel come together'; for here too 'people are being locked into the sacred space of the miracle' (Foucault 1972: 21, with reference to the treatment of the insane in the Middle Ages).

The Demon's Name

Some *jinns* or *bhut(a)* are known by specific names, but not others. Namelessness only means that nobody has been able to name them. It is said that every single one of them, without exception, has a name. These names are a part of the demon onomastics, peculiar to the local culture, which anybody can refer to. It is nevertheless difficult to know the name of a demon who acts so fast that the refusal to divulge its identity becomes confused with the nature of its intervention. What better way can there be of avoiding recognition and being named? As a matter of fact, every power bearing a name can be immediately materialized, propitiated and transformed into a divinity. And as Dumont (1957: 405-6) points out, a stone or shrine is then erected in its name to 'subdue its power' (*shakti*).

Considering that the demon's evil powers reside in its name, the effectiveness of its action is proportionate to its ability to remain hidden as long as possible. Exorcism means forcing the demon to reveal itself or, in other words, to communicate its name, an operation that amount to identifying the *bhut(a)* or *jinn* who has taken possession of a person. But it is not enough to name it. It is for the possessed person to name the demon or recognize the name mentioned by the exorcist. Even this may not always work, for the changed speech of the possessed person—when it is not accompanied by a refusal to speak—belongs to another unknown person. Actually, the possessed person does not know who is speaking through him, even if he expects the unknown being to disclose his identity. Pressure is exerted on the demon by the saint's intimidating presence, or, if the need arises, that of his instrument in the form of the exorcist. But no matter how powerful the saint and how clever the exorcist—especially in his master over the onomastic list of demons—the name must be confirmed by an admission by the stranger speaking through the possessed person.[6] Besides, after the name has been extracted, it must be ascertained that it is not a false name. It happens quite often that one name hides another, with the demon giving a borrowed name to maintain its anonymity. Further, once the name is known, it can be kept secret by a few privileged persons who have gained knowledge (*bhut*[*a*]-*vidye*) about the demons' dreadful world, especially those who know the magic formulas (*mantragara*).

Other practical remedies can be used to drive a demon to the wall to force it to reveal its name. For example, reciting *surahs* from the Koran and burning large amounts of incense is a technique used by a 'servant' (*khadim*), an officiant in the shrine (*mujawar*), or an expert in demonology (*bhut*[*a*]-*vidye*) engaged for this purpose. Somebody holds a bundle of burning incense-sticks, containing a psychotropic substance, under the nose of the possessed person until the demon within him is suffocated and forced to utter its name. In villages it is more common to burn red chillies, which produce a thick and stinging smoke. At times, the possessed person is made to chew grains of Malabar pepper. These are all ploys to irritate the demon. I have learnt that a simple musical ceremony (*qawwali*) carried to the point of frenzy can also have the same effect as an exorcism. This kind of music therapy seems to be more common in *dargahs* in north India.

In all these cases, it appears that sound prevails over the other senses, and 'breath' (*shvasa*) is considered to be effective. The *mantravarati* or 'the one who chants the *mantras*' and is endowed with special powers (*siddhi*), whispers the sacred verses into the possessed person's ear. Or else, the exorcist (*ghadi*) blows hard on the spot where the evil spirit resides and on the different parts of the victim's body through a small bamboo pipe (*kolavi*). The demon is tortured and castigated in this manner until it is finally forced to leave.

However, it is also believed that these procedures are effective only because of the *pir's* 'radiant knowledge' (*nuri'ilm*). Associated with the names and attributes of God, this knowledge helps the patient to speak. 'Breath of life, energy and spirit' (*dam*) are supposed to be concentrated in the *dargah*.[7] The shrine is open to divine power, and devotees come here not only to 'hold their breath' (*dam sadhna*), 'recite prayers' (*dam bharna*) or chant 'incantations' (*dam karna*), but also to suffocate (*dam rukna*) and receive the 'breath of water' (*dam pani*). All these techniques owe their efficacy to the energy of speech and the pragmatic power of words, an effective method of action, as Malinowski has so rightly pointed out (1974: 303). It is through the name that the demoniac power is released.

In linguistic terms, the exorcist mobilizes the illocutionary power of speech and exploits the performative value of its utterance. But the illocutionary value of the name depends not so much on its utterance as on the context. The power does not therefore lie magically in the name itself but in the 'essential' extralinguistic condition that influences the 'act of speaking', as Searle puts it. And as Bourdieu insists while commenting on Austin's opinion on performatives, social conditions 'should be satisfied' and 'institutional actions' undertaken 'for the magic of words to have an effect'. The institution, in this case, is the saint's dargah or, to be more precise, his radiant presence.

Saint and Demon

The Space of the Dargah

Such magic works only in the vicinity of the *dargah*, or around the 'tomb' (*mazar*) of the guardian saint, also called 'friend' (*wali*), because 'God has saints (*auliya*) whom he has honoured with his friendship and whom he has chose as governors of his kingdom', according to Ali Hujwiri (quoted by Digby 1986: 62). In the hierarchy of supernatural powers saints occupy the lowest rung of 'substitutes' (*abdal*). They are all incarnations of divine 'friendship' (*walaya* or *wilaya*), and each takes charge of its own realm (*wilayat*) (1986: 63). These areas of spiritual jurisdiction correspond today to the space occupied by the mausoleums in which innumerable Indian saints reign.

Pirs have the power (*baraka*) to perform miracles (*karamat*) and fulfil desires. But even though they have tremendous powers because of their spiritual perfection, only a few are explicitly associated with the treatment of demons or reputed to be particularly effective against them. In this respect, they are doctors, consisting of generalists and specialists! And people use to compare the powers of various *pirs* just as one would grade doctors or hospitals, praising, for example, a particular saint known for curing a certain affliction. This does not however prevent them from simultaneously visiting several *pirs*, though they may eventually show a preference for one of them.

For this reason, exorcism is practised only in a few *dargahs.* This does not mean that the tombs of other saints exude less power, except for cenotaphs (*asthna*), which are known to radiate less power. But this is so because many great learned saints, due to their reserved nature, chose to be discreet about their powers. They refused to use them during their lifetime or to lower themselves by performing miracles, a practice normally associated with rustic *babas* and favoured by 'popular' religion.

But whatever the intensity of the power attributed to saints, it is never so great that they can destroy demons effectively, since it is the *babas* and shaikhs who are locally considered to be the 'masters of demons' (malik *jann*). Sovereignty evidently needs submissive 'servants', for the total destruction of these demons would make them redundant as healers. Mastery is dependent on servitude, as much as on 'powers' belonging to the invisible world, as also on the officials of the shrine and the devotees who bring offerings. It is said that the lack of offerings renders the saint impotent, the demon a pretender, while a continuous flow of power emanating from the tomb deters the demons from threatening the saint's supremacy.

Thus the cult aims to glorify the saint with the help of servants and visitors by maintaining an asymmetrical relationship between the 'master' and his demonic powers so that the latter manifest themselves from time to time, only to be pushed back into submission. As a matter of fact, the demon awakens only when the possessed person comes to the *dargah* and enters the area where the *baba's* tomb is located, makes its presence felt and overpowers the personality of the person it has possessed. It becomes aggressive because of the master's aura, whereas in ordinary circumstances it occupies only a part of the victim's body. Not only does the *baba's* saintliness enable him to rouse demons and force them to appear, it also makes them suffer. It tortures them so that they reveal themselves before running away. However, let me repeat that this disappearance does not mean that they have been destroyed. Once the pressure exerted by the *baba* is relaxed the exhausted demon withdraws into the body of its victim, who then slowly regains consciousness. At least that is how the demon's energy and its abatement are explained by my informants.

Normally, the saint tames the powers by keeping them confined within the space around his tomb, because, even after his death, he continues to give them the same miraculous protection that he had given them during his lifetime. The power that continuously emanates from his sepulchre becomes active at certain times, generally once a week (either Thursday or Sunday), on moonless nights (*amavasya*) and during the *'urs* celebrations. Its intensity changes according to the time of the day, reaching its peak towards seven in the evening with the flickering of the lamp placed before the saint. An *arati* starts after the devotees have had *darshan.*

Yet the saint's vigilance seems to lessen at certain times of the day, as in the middle of the afternoon, at the end of prayers, at nightfall and on moonless nights, when the demons become active. So lamps are lit to dispel darkness, and people who venture out in the night carry salt with them, which can be thrown on the demon if it attacks them suddenly. They talk loudly and answer only when their name is called out for the fourth time, because Odavarra, a female phantom, takes possession of persons after calling them three times. People are extremely scared of crossroads and the confluence of rivers, and they take care to avoid caves, strangely shaped stone piles, trees with high branches known to be dangerous, and places where the placentas of dead infants are buried when they die before being initiated into the community. In short, all places known to be infested by demons, such as old wells, ruined houses and abandoned shrines, are avoided. If, by ill luck, there is a suicide, it is believed that the unfortunate person's soul (*pret*[*a*]) hovers over the area where his/her life ended and attacks the rare living beings who dare to venture there, to feed on them. They are also the favourite food of *yaksis*, 'ghosts' of young girls who seduce young men and devour them, and of *bhavanis,* the spirits of virgins who die at a young age. On the other hand, the *bhuts* become rare in the months of *Chaitra* (March/April), *Pausha* (December/January) and *Ashvina* (September/October), while *jinns* are inactive in the month of *Ramadan* and during important festivals all through the year. It is customary to say that they have been held prisoners by Paighambar, Allah's Messenger.

An indication of the demon's choice of victims can partially reduce the risk. Thus women are advised not to get angry or frightened, as this makes them more vulnerable to attacks, especially during menstruation. Nubile young women and those who are newly married, pregnant or have just had a baby, must be very cautious. After delivery, the umbilical cord is kept for forty days, while the placenta is buried to guard it from evil spirits. In the case of boys, care is taken after the tonsure ceremony (*ᶜaqiqa*) to collect the hair because it attracts misfortune. It is thrown into the river, as far away as possible, to avoid black magic. Recently circumcised boys must also be careful. Dying persons are the preferred targets of spirits, and a lot of precautions are taken to guard them. These examples show that demons are more likely to attack persons on the threshold of a new stage of life, and who are considered impure because of the impending change in their status.

Whatever the nature of the supplicants, the saint patiently listens to their requests in his shrine, but he is more attentive to those whose physical ailment is accompanied by lifelong misfortune. He intercedes with God in their favour so that he can attend to their needs. That is why devotees and not just victims visit his tomb. They come regularly every year and often spend several days or even several months in the *dargah*. By being close to him and through his mediation, they want to imbibe continuously, and for so long as possible, the power emanating from Allah's intercessor. Some devotees rub *vibhuti* on their bodies as a cure for ills; they do it not because they want the holy skin of this living-dead man, but because the ash will frighten away 'evil spirits'. And at night, many of them sleep as close as possible to his tomb because they hope that the dead miracle-worker will appear in their dreams to give them advice and tell them what to do.

The observer cannot but notice the often frantic circumambulations (*tawaf*) of tireless devotees, lasting for hours together, because they hope to pick up his exhalation (Rollier 1983; Assayag 1994).

Self-imposed penance is even more spectacular. A sufferer may place on the tomb the part of his body that hurts most: an arm, a leg, the head; sometimes the sufferer does a headstand. Some remain motionless; others prostrate themselves. Various bodily movements are to be seen.

But it is during the *arati*, announced by the beating of drums and accompanied by the sound of gongs, that the saint's power incites the most extravagant behaviour. There are a larger number of women among the possessed, hyperventilating and quivering. Some of them roll on the ground, while most others brace themselves with both feet and describe large circles with their trunks and especially their heads. They run the risk of banging their heads as with each gyration their long loose hair sweeps the ground. These gestures bear testimony to the punishment inflicted by the *baba's* power, then at its peak, on the 'powers' that torture their victims. This conflict between the saint and the demons, that takes place in the tormented bodies of possessed persons, would cause instantaneous death if its victims were not unconscious. It is said that, come what may, the *baba* protects his followers, and it is the demons who suffer in consequence.

If we look, not just at these wild gesticulations, but also at the collapse caused by depression, the distance that separates the symptoms from the ritual appears insignificant. The expression of existential suffering merges with the act of supplication and veneration. But by putting them in a context where they acquire their complete significance, we come to the opposite conclusion. Within the precincts of the *dargah*, a realm where cures are possible and a stage on which afflictions assume a dramatic aspect, the practices followed are first and foremost religious, and not just a religious codification of anxiety. Except when it succumbs to a crude functionalism, religiosity does not just reflect unease, but indicates transcendence and gives an aura of sacredness to the humdrum life of persons bruised by existence. It is only from the modern and clinical viewpoint of the foreign observer, who starts 'dissecting things anew' according to 'the principle of expression in a language where we are used to recognizing the language of "positive science"' (Foucault 1963: XIV), that the saint, installed for ever in the heart of a community, offers the possibility of symbolizing conflicts and affections to those who come to him for succour. Eschatology plays a key role in finding a medical solution for stress, so prevalent in this type of society. Muslim places of worship—even those specializing in the treatment of *jinns* and *bhuts*—are first and foremost religious shrines where God appears to the living through the intercession of one of his numerous saints.

The Actors and the Exchanges in the Dargah

Since the mausoleum is a living shrine, devotees bring offerings and give donations. Though it is done discreetly, it is a common and effective practice to give offerings for the fulfilment of wishes (*niyyat, mannat*) or to assist healing. Very few devotees come to the *dargah* without buying in advance the things needed for paying tribute to the divinity. They offer coconuts, sugar, rice, oil and lemons, to the saint through a servant (*khadim mujawar*). The bestowal of the respectful title of *pir* on these dargah officials shows that they trace their ancestry to the *baba* himself. Not only is he the 'spiritual head', but also the ancestor of a flourishing line that often functions like a caste. After sanctifying the offerings by keeping them on the tomb for a short while, the *mujawar* returns them to the devotee, who consumes them later. It is believed that the ingestion of food blessed by the saint—called *tabarruk* or 'blessing' and also *prasad(a)*—amounts to absorbing a part of his aura, which now filters through his living *pir*. The worship is marked by the consumption of large quantities of sweets—as we have pointed out, many saints are given the title of 'storehouse of sugar'—in the shape of bright pink saints! Unlike Arabia, where Allah only listens to the Word—prayers, recitations and sermons—Islamic ritual in India has always been partial to the culture of flowers (Goody 1994: 393).

The *mujawar* ends the ceremony by reciting some verses from the Koran while he repeatedly taps the donors' heads, shoulders and backs with the ritual peacock-feather fan. In addition to his 'honorarium (*dakshina*), he is also given horses made of silver or braided cotton symbolizing Ali's army, to support the saint in his fight against demons. Though this practice smacks of Shi'ism, it highlights the martial character of the Hindu deities sitting astride steeds, like Mailar-Khandoba who is very popular in the Deccan for ridding the earth of demons (Assayag 1989c). It may be recalled that 'popular' Indian Islam has a liking for horses. The shrine of the *Ghode pir* in Pune owned by a Hindu and with a Muslim 'priest', is reputed to facilitate the birth of boys. To thank him for fulfilling their wishes, parents dress their children as fakirs during *Muharram* before offering at the shrine a wooden horse with a young colt between its hind legs (Kadan 1988: 283).

Strictly speaking, when you look at these exchanges, you do not see any difference between the ritual worship of a Muslim saint and a Hindu divinity. The only difference is that the Muslim shrine is erected over a tomb, which for the Hindus is an evil and polluted spot. However, this observation does not apply to so-called 'terrible' Shaivism, such as the cults of Shiva-Bhairava and the goddess Angalamman, or some forms of Tantrism practised on cremation grounds. So too Virashaiva rituals are celebrated around the tombs of the founders of monasteries (*matha*) (Assayag 1987). Also, stelae erected in the memory of dead heroes (*vira*), often Jaina and women considered ideal (*sati*) are the objects of ardent worship in this area (Weinberger-Thomas 1989).

However, some practices are peculiar to Muslims, such as placing a garment or an object like a crutch, a photograph or a metal plate on the tomb so that it can absorb the *baraka* that is believed to be capable of protecting or healing. The saint's aura turns into a blessing anything that is obtained from his shrine. There is also the common practice of leaving a copy of the Koran for some time on the brocade covering the tomb, which infuriates orthodox elements, who ask how the holiest of Holy Books can ever become more holy by its contact with the tomb. Another common practice is the distribution against payment of talismans, red-coloured plaited cotton yarn (*lodi*), which the devotees wear round their necks or tie around their wrists. The villagers too protect themselves in a similar fashion; but they hang red chillies on a thread. Further, to increase the prophylactic powers of the threads that are brought home, they make knots in them while reciting a *surah* from the Koran for every knot. Amulets (*ta'widh*) in the form of small copper or metal plaques bearing the saint's name are also worn on a thread round the neck. It is believed that the saint's name will act as a protection against the name or names of demons.

Many devotees write liturgical formulae (*mantra*) or prayers (*fatiha*) together with the saint's name on small bits of paper which are rolled and tied in a black thread and worn round the upper arm, the wrist or the neck. Instead of having to change the piece of paper after three, seven or twenty-one days, it can be slipped into a small metal tube (*tati*) to make it last longer. These examples show that writing is a 'manifestation of language' for the Muslims, as it is also for the Hindus, who tie written notes around their wrists to 'tie up the demons' or wear amulets (*tavisu, yantra*) bearing effective syllables (*bijaksaralu*). This practice complements exorcism, which depends on the spoken word. Though it favours writing, the talisman has the same healing powers. In the case of a grave illness, the 'doctor' writes a verse from the Koran with ash on a plate. Then he pours water over it and makes his patient drink the water. The treatment is more effective if he gives the patient the water used for washing the tomb during the *ᶜurs* celebrations.

It is evident that it is the relationship of nearness and mutual repulsion between the saint and the demons that defines the dargah as simultaneously a place refuge and healing, with its staff looking after both visitors and patients.

Among those who come for help, mentally retarded persons and persons suffering from mental disorders form a separate group. The more violent among these have their feet in chains and their hands tied so that they do not hurt themselves. . . . You can, in fact, see every kind of borderline state among them. There is a belief that these pathological problems are a sign of spiritual experience. But the argument also serves as an excuse to get rid of incurable patients. The latter are always accompanied by one or more family members who organize the patient's stay in the shrine and take part in rituals, adopting a 'systemic approach'—as a modern psychiatrist would put it—towards suffering, conflict and treatment. Considering that good health is correlated with the notion of good behaviour and defined according to *dharma*, which is dependent on each person's *karma*, the affliction (*bene*) involves some or all family members. It does not matter whether the affliction is physical or mental, because it is always seen as a moral crisis, a fault or a 'sin'. That is why all those who are present, whether they are sick or healthy, take part in all the observances and acts of penance to make the medication or treatment effective. Equally involved are the *mujawars*, the representatives of 'sacerdotale medicine' (Marriott 1955: 251, 256), who look after the shrine and keep its saintly powers active by reciting prayers, performing services and giving advice. They are supposed to have a 'magic touch' emanating from the 'initiatory line' (*silsila*) going back to the founder of the order. Finally, various experts in demonology, whom Galen called half or quarter doctors, such as suppliers of medicines, those who administer antidotes against demons, practitioners of traditional medicine (*hakim*) and dispensers of magic formulae are involved in this process. But the most important are the exorcists (*ghadi*), qualified 'doctors of evil spirits' (*bhut*[*a*]-*vaidagara*), whose very title indicates that they are ranked above the others. It is their responsibility to engage the demon in a discussion and subsequently associate various family members in it, to obtain information about the symptoms, and to force the demon to reveal itself by employing spells, cajolery, threats and violence. It is said that they can even make demons visible by pouring a liquid on the possessed person's palm. The recipe for this lotion is a closely guarded secret.

All players strive to mobilize the energy exuded by the tomb in a system(at)ic manner. The *baraka* thus aroused is channelized and redistributed by ritual practice in the hope that it will resolve family disputes, relieve suffering, cure illness and generally put an end to disorder. The *baraka* is a miraculous substance that can be transferred to objects—as illustrated earlier—and to humans according to a set protocol through 'mediums' or, in other words, the saint's 'servants' (*khudam*).

Let us see how headaches are treated. The healer sits close to the tomb. He sways his body back and forth like a pendulum so that at regular intervals his forehead touches the forehead of the patient seated opposite him. Mumbling verses from the Koran interspersed by magic incantations, he transfers God's *baraka* to the saint, then from the saint to the servant and finally from the servant to the patient, a process that guarantees its healing effect. We may mention in passing that sorcery proceeds symmetrically. As a matter of fact, the only way to get rid of the 'evil eye' is to transfer it to others. How is this done? It is necessary to prepare a *lumbu,* a mixture of red chillies activated by a few *mantras* and scatter it at the intersection of three roads; and the first person to walk over it is supposed to take away the spell.

No matter who presides over an operation success is never certain. It is natural for the demon to resist and display its belligerence (especially when it is of the opposite sex) because then it is supposed to have sexual relations with the victim. This shows how difficult it is to get the patient to enter the shrine—sometimes he or she has to be pushed inside—because the demon, who uses him/her as a receptacle or a mount, struggles to avoid a confrontation with the saint.

Possession

In daily life, demons appear furtively, either to punish or to seek vengeance. Their continual presence is seen only in the symptoms and sickness that afflict individuals or, more rarely, in calamities that affect entire communities.

However, within the premises of the *dargah,* the saintly presence forces demons to manifest themselves openly and not insidiously in the form of a disease. It would appear that the saint's *baraka* is a fairly ambiguous force—people often talk of *Shakti*—which, goes beyond fits and afflictions and makes them happen; this perhaps explains the equivocal term *bhut(a) pir* which means 'demon saint' or 'saint of (or against) demons'. Only *baraka* can give life to normally evanescent powers by turning them into beings for a long time, provided that the victim is depersonalized for the benefit of the evil spirit inhabiting him. This calls for a number of special procedures: prior purification of the body, endless chanting and recitation of incantations, inhaling a great deal of smoke, making continuous rotating movements until the patient reaches a trancelike state, a slow or sudden entry into a trance and so on.

Several changes are induced in the victim's conscious—always on an experimental basis with the aim of bringing about a catharsis—in the hope that the demon will submit and the devotee will be freed from its power. By the intrusion of the saint's powers, which are infinitely superior to the power of the demon, the demon is transformed from a power into a being. It gradually acquires a corporeal form and an identity through the changed speech of the possessed person, but struggles to avoid being named. Once its identity is known, the person having *baraka* just has to neutralize or immobilize it. As a matter of fact, the pir 'nails the evil', an expression to be understood literally, because at the end of the séance, the exorcised persons stick three (or five) lemons with long metal spikes into the trunk of a leafless tree growing by the side of the tomb. One would think that the djinn's ability to do evil depends on its mobility, as opposed to the saint's benevolence, which remains permanently in his shrine. But it must be remembered that fixing does not mean killing! Like Allah Himself (Fahd 1971: 155), the saint only pushes the powers that refuse to recognize his power to the periphery of his spiritual domain, which in Allah's case extends to the end of the earth.

If we go beyond the mental restructuring that occurs when the victim affects a strange manner of speech, we find that the saint/demon dyad—transformed by the ritual into the exorcist/possessed couple—is a small-scale model of the macrocosm capable of exerting a religious influence on society, to quote out of context one of Geertz's interpretations (1968: 36). The invasion of a person's body by a power that strikes down its adversary—an agent of impurity and disorder who has taken possession of the victim—is a triumph for the saint and a (new) victory for Islam over chaos and evil. It is even more remarkable because it has its roots, not in a system of beliefs firmly embedded in a theological doctrine, but in a vague arrangement of everyday practice. The power symbolized by the architecture of the dargah, undoubtedly produces a cathartic effect. It is, in fact, due to this double opposition—a horizontal opposition between the saint and the demon and a vertical opposition between the sky and the netherworld—that the victims of schizophrenia are able to dramatize their mental 'schize' (or 'cleave') and display symptoms (Assayag 1994). The abreaction of repressed emotions enables victims to cross the line by setting aside the demands of normal reality, and forms the basis of the therapy (Rollier 1983: Chapter VI). Because of this transition from the latent to the manifest, victims find themselves capable of symbolizing the split and reconstructing, even if momentarily, an identity torn between rejection and acceptance. What we have here is 'two different mental attitudes, contradictory and independent of each other' (Freud 1975: 82), two methods of defence, one focused on reality and the other on mysterious impulses. Only those whose ego is sufficiently permeable are able to attain the symbolic dimension; by contrast, psychotic personalities are permanently foreclosed from reaching the saint Fig. 6.

Once again, we observe that demons and saint seem to belong to diametrically opposite worlds, even though they also both live in the invisible world that borders our own. Further, though their actions and intentions are usually contradictory, their respective identities oscillate between the poles of evil and good. Fortunately for the devotees, the oscillation is not very even. For example, the people of Shahabandar worship a minor saint named Nor Khan. They know that he wanders in the fields to the east of the village and that it is almost impossible to see him except as a fleeting shadow. Even Hindus, Lingayats included, have got into the habit of offering him—under the name of Nanda Rishi—uncooked vegetarian food. They do it through their Muslim neighbours, who add cooked meat

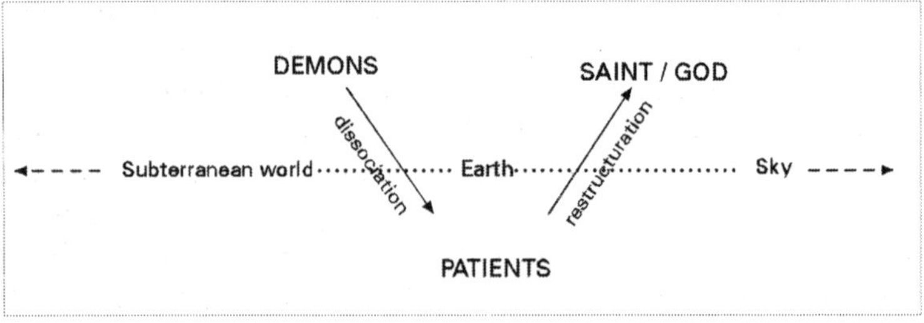

Figure 6: Topical and Therapeutic Organization of Worship in the *Dargah*

to these offerings and place the resultant combination in their fields. The remains of these offerings, regarded as sacred, are shared the next day by the givers. The saint eats only at night, and there is bound to be trouble if he does not find anything! Quick to cast spells, he curses the village with a bad harvest or spreads sickness. The transformation of the guardian saint into a demon occurs mechanically when the offerings are insufficient or missing.

Though it may appear odd, this (extreme) case of metamorphosis illustrates the close link between a saint and demons. Of what use would a saint be if he had no enemies to combat? This idea is stressed in the hagiographies of most *pirs*, with the inevitable anecdotes where he exterminates entire regiments of evil spirits. Demons that were unfailingly victorious would pose a constant threat to our world, thus irretrievably condemned to chaos. So they are accepted with resignation as an essential, but unavoidable, element of human life. But this acceptance does not amount to hospitality. 'Come tomorrow!' the villagers write on their doors, and draw on their thresholds a figure (*disti bomma*) to deceive the evil eye, because two precautions are better than one. However, they do not delude themselves, knowing full well that demons are as necessary as the saint to maintain the equilibrium, precarious though it may be, of the universe.

As a matter of fact, what the *dargah* exemplifies wonderfully well is observed in their day-to-day life: *jinns* and *bhuts* interact constantly with humans, accompanying them at times and surprising them at others, in a wide variety of situations. That is why they are respected, respect being the reverse of fear, since it makes them take adequate precautions. They must be kept at a distance because they are likely to bring turmoil into people's lives. And when such precautions fail, people can always have recourse to the saint, as illustrated by the procession of Mahbub-i Subhani's standard.

Where there is 'popular' Islam, that is to say where its followers have not been recently Islamized by urbanized mullahs, there is no worship of saints without a host of evil spirits around them. Even 'orthodox scholars' who visit villages regularly to spread the concept of a strictly monotheistic Islam (based on the 'five pillars') and to make them understand that Muhammad is the only Messenger of God, describe for propaganda purposes how 'idolators' (*mushrik*) will be tortured by avenging angels on the Day of Resurrection. But we must remember that, in Shahabandar, the villagers do not consider these scholars any different from demons!

During exorcism the *ghadi* draws a circle around the possessed person. This ring of protection prevents other demons from coming in to give a helping hand to the one under attack. Some eminent practitioners even succeed in imprisoning them in pots once the exorcism is over. Another way of treating the possessed is to wave around the person, from tip to toe, a mixture of red chillies and salt previously consecrated by the saint. After the ceremony is over, this is thrown away at the outskirts of the village.

Attack and Exorcism

Not all afflictions can be attributed to demons. There are other naturalistic explanations based on the humours (*dosa*) and related to the theory of the four elements. There are, in addition, ecological, dietetic and sexual explanations, as well as those generally associated with *karma* determined by an earlier existence, the influence of the stars, and present behaviour. Together, they give rise to a local medicinal practice that is in tune with traditional medicine.[8] In fact, demon possession may occur independently of any dysfunction of the humoral system, even if it happens to add to the various factors listed above.

Serious illness caused by a demon attack, can be diagnosed concerning the mode of intervention adopted by *jinns* and *bhuts*, on the basis of the symptoms or scattered morbid manifestations. These are explained by interpreting the signs rather than by 'scientific' study. The psycho-social context is so significant that identical symptoms are interpreted differently according to the subject's environment and life-course.

A clear distinction is made between ailments caused by an internal problem (*olaginaroga*) and those having an external cause (*horaginaroga*). The former may be caused by a poor bodily equilibrium, faulty diet, or thermal imbalance. When it is a question of attacks by demons (*bhut*[*a*]-*kata*), a distinction is made between three types of ailment—superficial, serious and possession.

In the first case, the 'spirit' appears to make a demand and if the demand is satisfied, it disappears and the affliction is short-lived (*galimaiyage-baruvuduga*). In the second case, the body is attacked suddenly and the demon goes away equally suddenly, but only after 'harming' it (*kaikalu-hariyuvudu*) as in cases of madness, mental confusion, epilepsy, paralysis, blindness, delirium and fainting. In the case of possession, the demon lodges itself in the person and settles in. It manifests itself off and on during attacks, and tortures the victims by making demands on him/her. Apart from the fact that their causes are different, in the last case the term *bene* is used to describe the affliction, while the others are called *roga.* In each of the three cases, the intervention of the evil spirit is the result of mistakes or 'transgressions' (*pap*[*a*]), committed by the person who is now its victim. The cause is always attributed to the violation of rules (*tappu*), which causes offence (*neram*) to a deity, perhaps the deity of the clan in which all ancestors are included—the *kula teyyam* mechanism, which has been thoroughly studied in Tamil Nadu.[9]

We must point out, however, that the two types of treatment used for these three types of attacks are not applied indiscriminately. Thus, in the first case, neither of the two treatments is needed, while the second and the third type of attacks have their own specific treatments. The first aims to expel the demon from the body (*hora*) once and for all. This task is all the more difficult because it is a 'major affliction' (*doddaroga*). The attack is sudden and, once the heinous deed is done, the demon disappears. It is therefore impossible to know its name and determine its identity or find the reasons for the attack by engaging it in a dialogue during exorcism. So it is necessary to expel it by using irregular and violent means that match its mode of intervention.

The second treatment consists of taming the demon. It cannot be expelled immediately because it denies its existence. So it is necessary to enter into a relationship that can be called 'symbiotic' (see Crapanzano 1973: 155) because 'the descriptions of possession cults available to us all show that this expulsion can be effected on condition there is a prior pact with the demon' (Rouget 1990: 285). The strategy, therefore, lies in making use of the demon to reach a new equilibrium. This effort at normalization transforms the spirit from a possessor into a protector. But the fact remains that once such a quasi contractual relationship is established, speech becomes an essential instrument of the cure, which is bound to be a long-term process. Since it is impossible to drive away the demon, there is an attempt to remove the symptoms gradually.

So the *khadim* collects information from the victim and his relations to find out where the attack occurred. It is believed that offerings made on this spot, together with the sacrifice of a sheep, are more efficacious than the working through or giving expression to released emotions. Since possession is, by its very nature, chronic, relapse is not ruled out. Even if the demon agrees to leave the patient, very rarely does it go away for good. If it is still present after twelve years—this period is called *patta*, and many spirits are supposed to have a life span of two *pattas*—it is assumed that it wants to kill the person it has possessed. That is why the exorcist begins by making excuses. '*Baba*, what is the matter?' he asks the demon. 'Why are you unhappy? We have never disobeyed you! [Pause.] Pardon us if we have.' Then he starts threatening it. 'Will you go away or not? Otherwise I will beat you! Go away! Go away!' And then you can hear the demon stating its conditions, which include offerings of meat most of the time. It is hoped that when it is tired of battling and satisfied with the offerings, the demon will say, 'Don't hit me, I will go away! But, in future, be sure to feed me.' This result is frequently obtained by resorting to physical violence. The exorcist forces the patient to swallow large quantities of ash until he chokes over it. He suddenly throws water on his face and showers him with blows actually meant for the demon.

Let us take another example. Saints do not actually induce possession (because the demon has to act first)—except in the case of *panjah*-bearers (often Sunni Muslims and sometimes Hindus) who carry the 'hands' symbolizing the seventy-two Shia saints during the Muharram celebrations. But sometimes, a victim starts talking in two voices. There is a reversal of roles in this diphonic dramatization of the struggle between *baba* and demon. '*Baba*', says the demon, 'don't hit me, don't burn me. Let me be. Do you think you are so strong that I can't stand up to you? Are you a *baba* or a *dada* (gang-leader)?' The saint laughs. 'You want to fight with me? Who are you? Why are you laughing? If you are a *baba*, I've seen many like you, just as strong.' The saint bellows with laughter. 'Please stop, don't hurt me! Why are you laughing? If you go on laughing, I won't leave, I will go on harassing her. Okay, I'll leave her, but I will come back soon!'

Power *versus* 'Powers'

If you confine your observations to the lower and scheduled castes in Karnataka, you will be utterly confused by the different types of demons, many of which overlap one another. Hindus refer to them by the generic term *bhut*, while Muslims prefer the term *jann*. Yet when a member of one community refers to an 'evil spirit' from the other community, he often uses the terminology that goes with the religious identity of the place, or translates it into his own idiom. Even so, because the two communities have the same conception of demonology, the difference in the labels does not matter. Here Islam is not overly concerned with sticking to the letter of the Koran, even if it is a reformist Islam, and Hinduism is indifferent to Sanskritized orthodoxy.

This does not, however, mean that there is a strict parallelism. To the best of my knowledge, it is rare for Hindus to use the term *jann* when referring to the numerous little shrines dedicated to *bhuts*. But Muslims do not hesitate to use the word *bhut* when Hindus are present, or even to the ethnologist, to describe the *dargahs* of holy men specializing in the treatment of afflictions, although they prefer using the term *jann* among themselves. In fact, when a Hindu, as happens quite often, visits the tomb of a Muslim saint, it matters little to him what the spirit tormenting him is called. However, one anecdote highlights the importance of a demon's identity. If I were to believe the Hindus I met in the Laxmeshwar *dargah* about 60 km from Belgaum, the most crafty and tenacious demons are Muslims! Such is the voracity of these *bhut-jann*, that it is impossible to pacify them by heaping animal sacrifice on animal sacrifice. This explains why there are so many Hindus in the shrine of Hazrat Sayyed Suleman Badshah Khadar Baghdadi Chishti, commonly known as Dudhpira or Dudhanna, which in Kannada means 'milk grandfather'. This saint is famous for his healing power.

This is a way of placing demonization of the community and the communal conflict in local Muslim space, and deep within the Hindu body—not without ambiguity though, because Hindus come there quite naturally in search of a cure for their ills. This confirms that, despite the difference in names, the same demonic force is at work. The same is true of Muslims who credit some of the 'lower' divinities and several Hindu practitioners, not only with curative powers, but with the power of striking down Muslim demons; and also among the intermediate Hindu castes. In this case, the ambiguity regarding religious identities reflects the ambiguity about the divinity itself. Let us take the example of the power governing 'snake-demons' recognized by both communities. While the Muslims call them Zahir *pir*, the Hindus call them Guga Vir(a), the name of a Rajput prince whose main shrine is in Rajasthan. It is true that this *vira* became a *pir* when he converted to Islam before his death! But both communities agree that he received his initiation from Guru Gorakhnath.

Goddess and Saint

We have frequently pointed out the recurrence in the Hindu sacrificial motif of the subjugation of demons by the goddess, symbolized by the slaying of Mahishasura (Biardeau 1981: 297). But we have dwelt little on the fact that, in northern Karnataka, this amounts more to mythological exploitation than the ritual eradication of demonic powers, so impressive in some Muslim mausoleums. According to legend, temples are set up in honour of Hindu goddesses only after they subjugate the older 'powers' of a lower order inhabiting the place (Tarabout 1990: 223), a victory celebrated periodically during festivals. But the *dargah* continues to be the scene of continuous battle between the saint and the demons. Many stories relate how the latter infested the place before the saint chased them away and settled down there. The battlefield appears all the more tragic because of the psychological conflict within those possessed. For the Hindus, the conflict between gods and demons essentially belongs to the cosmological realm, where it occurred long, long ago (Biardeau 1981b). (It is possible that it has made a comeback recently because of the official ban on animal sacrifice, especially the sacrifice of buffaloes.) Among the Muslims, by contrast, it assumes a very earthy and commonplace aspect as a conflict between saintliness and evil 'powers' supported by an expressly therapeutic cult.

The fact remains that despite the evasive and blurred identities of demons, their modes of existence and action being equally uncertain, each religious group permits the faithful of the other religion to approach them for an explanation of the nature of their affliction, misfortune or calamity. Owing to the absence of a family deity and ancestor worship among the Muslims, the saint is often more concerned with the victim's family, unlike the goddess, who is more concerned with the prosperity of the land. But this refers only to the rites. The hagiographic Sufi literature (*tadhkira, malfuzat*) assigns to the saint (guardian of the locality) the role of the community's cosmic protector. He is the magician who can bring rain to make the crops grow well, the miracle-worker who can eradicate disease and epidemics.[10] However, that many temple goddesses are also family deities whose cult is passed down from generation to generation.

Undeniably, every shrine must have it own appointed demon, but this does not change the basic nature of these powers because Hindus and Muslims living in southern India have the same notions about them. They accept the same cognitive model of a supernatural attack, affliction, treatment and cure and also an identical dynamics of the divine power mobilized to do battle with the subterranean 'powers'. This is undoubtedly because these powers 'control the source of all fertility' on which humans depend. Similarly, the gods themselves are also dependent on these powers, because 'they receive offerings from them' (Biardeau 1981a: 17).

This does not mean that we are denying, in the name of syncretism, the numerous differences between groups of devotees and believers belonging to distinct castes or indeed the individual rituals and the specific socio-religious outlook of each group. Not all these differences are insignificant, not by a long way, even though they may not take into account the opposition between polytheism and monotheism, as one would instinctively expect. But the same logic underlies the thought and action of their members, who are unconcerned about their origin, be it pagan or Koranic, and are not yet affected by the Hindu nationalistic upsurge or by Islamic fundamentalism. This is so because, despite their rustic nature, the practices and perceptions of each community do not really contradict their respective scholarly versions.

Scholarly Hinduism accepts that 'demons'[11] can change into devotees (*bhakta*) or 'guardians' (*kshetrapala*) of the local divinity after their defeat by the latter, if only to justify its 'descent' on earth (*avatara*) as a destroyer of evil. But this is certainly not more orthodox[12] than the miraculous power exercised by one of Allah's intercessors to immobilize demoniac beings and render their scheming ineffective. For every man there is a demon (and an angel), including Muhammad himself, just like the 'sublime swans whose intercession must be sought'. This provoked cultural mediators periodically to draw analogies between the notion of 'Prophet' (*nabi*) and 'incarnation' (*avatara*)—thus changing Muhammad Paighambar into an *avatara* of the 'imperfect age' (*kaliyuga*) and Krishna into the *nabi* of Allah—to make Islamic teachings acceptable to new (or virtual) converts.[13]

One thing is certain though: the troublesome presence of demons around the saint in the Muslim socio-religious world is not a survival from pre-Islamic times (*jahiliya*), just as the interrelation between the goddess and the demons is not an Aryan-Dravidian vestige. In other words, the relationship between divine beings and demons is structural in both cases. This relationship cannot be explained away by the presumed superimposition of the official religion at a later period on the native religion, as affirmed by Rouget (1990: 287). In India, demons exist only as long as they are in conflict with the gods, whose primeval brothers they are in Hinduism (Varenne 1971: 286); and they are likewise a category constituted at the very beginning of Islam (Fahd 1971: 156). Just as the goddess symbolizing sovereign centrality needs her troop of demons, the 'axis' (*qutb*) of saintliness is meaningful only because the world order is permanently threatened and besieged by an army of *jinns*. Hindu divinities need demons since the socio-cosmic order (*dharma*) is accompanied by disorder (*a-dharma*) and is born out of it. As for Islamic 'genies', they have Allah's permission to exist as long as men are unfaithful to him, and they will be destroyed only on the Day of Judgement. It is this anarchic proliferation of auxiliary beings, this mysterious society teeming with demons, that must be constantly appeased, which explains the multiplicity of temples of goddesses and saints' mausoleums that dot the Indian landscape. The former are synonymous with the multiple manifestations of the universal goddess bearing the names of different places, while the latter are respected as the many instances of the intercession of a God who seems very distant because He is the only One.

Certainly, owing to the coexistence of the divine and the demoniac, there is a constant battle between the rival powers to gain sovereignty. The ancient cosmogonic motif called *kurukshetra* in epic and folklore (Shulman 1986; Coccari 1989), is also a recurrent theme—both judico-military and mystical—in Islam, going under the name of *jihad* (Tyan 1961). But can life continue without its shadow, without paying the mortally high price for its much-feared unhealthy other side, into which it is plunged and from which it then withdraws after passing through it?

Finally, it was a fakir from Belgaum who gave me the explanation for this shared gigantomachy, which is both the foundation and the structure of popular belief. Sitting quietly in the Shahabandar *dargah*, he turned the beads of his rosary as he mumbled his prayers. He affirmed that it is enough to recite Koranic formulae to drive away demons and obtain protection against them. He also added that one should spit three times on one's left palm to make sure that they would go far away. On hearing him, I was reminded of the Hindu ritual for removing obstacles: when invoking the Earth Goddess (*Bhu*), the priest strikes the ground three times with his left heel and orders the evil spirits to disappear. Only then can the intended task be performed under favourable auspices. This means that we must now accompany this pious Muslim to Belgaum, where we shall take in impressive séances conducted by the fakirs belonging to his brotherhood.

NOTES

1. Dumont (1975), Biardeau (1981a), Reiniche (1975, 1981) and Beck (1981).
2. Except for S. Bayly (1989), who looks at it historiographically and not an anthropologically.
3. The rich inventory prepared by a team from the *Census of India* led by Padmanabha (1971) reveals the wide variety of figures and *bhut(a)* cults in this area.
4. Apart from the studies conducted by Padmanabha (1971), Clauss (1975) and Upadhyaya (1984) in the Tulu region, we may mention the grand public exorcisms of demons observed by Tarabout (1986) in Kerala, and by Kapferer (1983) and Obeyesekere (1984) in Sri Lanka.
5. The serpent or *sarpa* should not be confused with the divine form *naga*. It is advisable to consult Wadley's (1975, Appendix II) detailed description of a Hindu ritual possession by a royal serpent demon in Uttar Pradesh. It may also be remembered that there is an affinity between *jinns* and reptiles (Fahd 1971: 194).
6. This observation undoubtedly explains the temptation to model exorcism on psychoanalytic procedures. For this, it is advisable to read M. de Certeau's brilliant study (1975a) of the possessed persons of Loudun.
7. This notion of saintliness is also found in Pakistan (Ewing 1984a).
8. The continuity of both the learned and popular systems of traditional medicine in India is confirmed by Zimmermann on the basis of data collected in Kerala. However, it is regrettable that 'passion and possession as such (demonology and psychopathology)' should have been left out of this scholarly study (1989: 195). Nichter's book (1989) is without doubt the richest and the most subtle work on ethnomedical concepts in Karnataka.
9. Dumont's monograph (1957) on the Pramalai Kallars is undoubtedly the first study to provide complex and well-argued material—based on the relationship between religious groups and social and political structures—on temples and 'family cults', called *kula teyyam* in Tamil Nadu. It is also advisable to read Reiniche's exposition (1979) on relations between cult and locality.
10. These characteristics are amply illustrated in Digby's pioneering works on hagiography (1986).
11. The term *rakshas(a)* (cannibalistic demon) is derived from the Sanskrit root *raksh*, which means 'to guard'.

12. Seeing that the worship of saints is not opposed or condemned, as it was among Muslim reformist circles, especially the Wahhabis (Baljon 1989; Gaborieau 1989) or the Deoband school (Metcalf 1982), and not just in India. Gellner, in his work on the Moroccan Atlas (1969), noted the paradox (also applicable to India) of a worship that is not in tune with the teachings of the Koran, although it is an important factor for identification.
13. Roy (1983) gives an inventory of the similarities between Hinduism and Islam in Bengal. For an overview of South Asia see Ahmad (1964). While Akbar encouraged the oecumenical tradition of promoting understanding among different religions, the Sultans of the Deccan did not lag behind. Ibrahim Qutb Shah of Golkonda and Ibrahim Adil Shah of Bijapur both tried to promote exchanges between Hinduism and Islam (Richards 1983: 53). We may finally mention that the well-known orthodox Naqshbandi, Mirza Mazhar Jan-i-janan, proclaimed in the eighteenth century that Krishna and Rama were genuine Prophets (Friedman 1986). Conversely, homology can also incite conflict and vengefulness, as Alam reminds us by quoting the French traveller Bernier, according to whom 'some Hindus' believed that the aim of Vishnu's tenth incarnation would be to free humanity from 'Muhammadan tyranny' (1989: 54).

3

Devotion: Sufism and the Fakirs

> No one possesses the truth, only the one who is himself the truth.
>
> F. KAFKA, *Journal* (1910)

The fakir I met in Shahabandar took me to the Muslim quarter in Belgaum called Khade Bazar. He lives there in a simple but spacious house. The roof of this whitewashed mud house is loaded, rather than covered, with tiles, giving it a rather massive look. It is a shelter for pilgrims and travellers (*khanqah*), also housing his 'wandering' brothers (*qalandar*) apart from its thirty odd semi-permanent residents. On the front wall, just above the narrow door, which is almost always open, there is a green board with the words *Darvesh Arabie Madrasa* or 'College of Arabian Dervishes', written in the Persian script. Then come the words *Hazrat Khanjar Wali Rafai Darvesh Association* in Persian, Devanagari, Kannada, Marathi and Roman scripts in the next five lines, followed by the registration number DR/SOR/33/88-89.

The fakir is a member of the local Rifa'iyya brotherhood, a heterodox order (*be shar'*) that is undoubtedly the most radical of all the Sufi brotherhood. Its founder, Ahmad ibn ʿAli ar-Rifa'i (1106-82), lived in the border area of southern Iraq between Basra and Wasit. It appears that the Rifa'iyya brotherhood made its appearance in India in the fifteenth century. The extravagant behaviour of its dervishes, who bit off the heads of living snakes, rode tigers and ate glass and fire, as described by Ibn Battuta (Trimingham 1971: 38-9), was condemned by reformist movements like the Tablighi Jama'at. Many Muslims do not even recognize them as followers of Islam. However, they are an integral part of the uninterrupted stream of Muslim religiosity, which, despite its showiness, is none the less mystical. These dervishes are 'intoxicated' by their love for God.

Islam and Sufism

Canonists and scholars sought to create an 'official' Islam, that would give men a law, a constitution and a total vision of the world to ensure their happiness—not only on earth, but also in heaven—as expressed in the Koran and supplemented, if need be, by the Sunna containing the practices and teachings of the Prophet. But there developed simultaneously another spiritual discipline based on meditation on the uncreated Divine Word—a 'Muslim mysticism' called *tasawwuf*[1] in Arabic. This experimental path, a systematic way of becoming one with God, was given the name of Sufism. By contrast with what is usually conveyed by the suffix 'ism', it is not a doctrine but an individual experience in the search for perfection, an effort to internalize the Revelation by breaking away from a purely legalistic religion. Centred around different stages or 'stations' (*maqamat*), this 'way' (*tariqa*) began with repentance and glorified poverty and the idea of losing oneself completely in God to gain his love and knowledge—not intellectual knowledge, but the knowledge of the divine truth (*haqiqa*).

Before the twelfth century, which Trimingham calls the 'golden age of mysticism', the spiritual guide (*murshid*) and his disciples (*muridin*) 'travelled together' (*salik al-tariq*) and lived together strictly according to the master's rules in humble shelters (*khanqah*), wherever they found them. Since they lived under the orders of a master of their choice, their behaviour was spontaneous. It was not so much teaching, but a gradual experience in which the harshness of the spiritual battle (*jihad*) was meant to transform and 'extinguish the self' (*fana*) in divine love. This goal was achieved by following certain techniques that lead to ecstasy.

As early as the twelfth century, some mystic communities were formed on more elitist lines by laying down certain doctrinal rules and methods. The imposition of rites and regulations allowed the master to establish a 'chain' (*silsila*). He initiated his 'successors' (*khalifa*), who were chosen from among his own family and not for their merit. Once they were transformed into devotional associations (*ta'ifa*), these brotherhoods began to worship a 'saint' (*wali*). Their members tried to absorb the 'power' emanating from the tomb (*mazar*) where the intercessor was laid to rest. In other words, this was the beginning of institutionalization.

However, regimentation did not stop Sufism from attracting persons in search of a more direct form of piety than the one found in family-based associations or dogmatic circles. Having decided to give up everything, some exalted persons called *darwish* or fakir (poor) or even *majzub* (attracted towards God) were quite willing to live on the fringe of society. These men, who were 'mad about God', travelled constantly, returning time and again to their master's seat for advice or enlightenment.

Among the more zealous fraternities, determination to 'abandon everything after placing confidence in God' (*tawakkul*) was strengthened by listening to 'mystical concerts' (*sama*), through regular exercises (*zikr*), or by repeating mentally or saying (or even singing) aloud sacred formulae or a divine name. In the dervish orders, concerts and litanies were soon combined under generic names like *zikr*, *wird* or *hadra*. These sessions could send some followers into raptures of ecstasy and make them behave extravagantly. The unrestrained atmosphere of the ritual encouraged these men to seek strong sensations. This earned them the displeasure of jurists and austere reformers, who persisted in defining the lawfulness of their own behaviour and corresponding mental states by laying down legal distinctions. They were joined in their censure by those Sufis who followed a more intellectual mysticism, hiding their virtues and powers behind their humility, soberness and conformism.

Nevertheless, the dividing lines were not very clear. This led to confusion. Afraid of fame, and for the good of their souls, other Sufis chose the 'path of blame' (*malama*) and faced censured by deliberately doing what was proscribed and condemned by the *shari'a*. From then on, Sufism attracted men of diverse temperaments who expressed themselves in many different ways. The problem of the relationship between orthodoxy and heterodoxy is as old as Sufism and its history of controversy and deviation bears testimony to its dynamism rather than its decline.[2]

After legendary Sufis like Bistami (800-74), Hallaj (858-922), Gazzali (1058-1111), Suhrawardi (1155-91), Attar (1140-1230), Ibn Arabi (1165-1240), Rumi (1207-73) and many others succeeded in attaining what they had set out to achieve, it was no longer possible to curb the surge of enthusiasm. As Islam spread in conquered lands with different cultures, Sufism became richer and more diverse through these contacts. A network of mystical orders, quite different in nature and often competing with one another, would soon encircle the major part of the Muslim world.[3] And as we shall recount in brief, India was never a land of exile for Sufism, but a fertile breeding ground.

Sufism in North India

India, whose prosperous northern regions came under the influence of Islam in the twelfth century, contributed very actively to the development of Sufism.[4] In 1060, Hujwiri came from Iran and settled down in Lahore. He is still worshipped there as Data Ganj Bakhsh, and the mausoleum of the man who said, 'Today Sufism is a name without reality. In the past, it was a reality without a name' is still thronged by pilgrims. It was said that all Muslims who set foot on Indian soil had to bow before his tomb before proceeding further. And every year, on the anniversary of the saint's death, Maharaja Ranjit Singh (1799-1839) donated to the mausoleum a thousand rupees—a handsome sum for those times.

Through the centuries, as the Muslim rulers advanced further into Indian territory, they brought in their wake Sufi masters who attracted a growing number of followers. Without a doubt, these traditions were imported from Islamic lands; but they underwent considerable change as they spread across India. And it was enough for shaikhs, both big and small, to be considered men of divine essence, and gifted with supernatural powers, for their tombs to become places of worship attracting crowds of devotees. The power to grant wishes and cure afflictions attributed to these saints capable of exercising their power long after their death, the flow of *baraka* through their descendants and the reputation of ecstasy enjoyed by some living masters, made Sufism attractive. This version of Islam, bearing the imprint of supernatural powers and mysticism, peopled by miracle-workers and amulet-givers, satisfied the emotional and spiritual needs of the lowest classes and the poorest of the poor, unlike its legalistic and codified version. This situation persists to this day. Sufism and *bhakti* continue to weave a network of reciprocal influences in India to express the ultimate Islamic experience: the human soul's desire for union with the Beloved. A sublime thought, an esoteric idea, it was, however, experienced in concrete terms through renunciation (*darwish*), militancy (*akhi*), war (*ghazi*) and, sometimes, apparent dementia (*majzub*).

While successive waves of Islamist reformers tried to slow down the deterioration of their faith, the scholar recognizes Sufism as the expression of a truly Indian Islam, because it is related to *bhakti* and the worship of 'holy men'. And though some may disqualify it as a popular and verbose religiosity depending more on emotion than reason and representing a composite culture—Massignon talks of the 'Islamic-Hindu bloc'—this does not mean that it cannot be considered as an honest testimony of faith.

Let us take a brief look at history. In the early thirteenth century, at the beginning of the Delhi Sultanate, there were two great masters in the subcontinent: Mu'inuddin Chishti, who died in 1236 in Ajmer (Rajasthan) and whose tomb is the biggest pilgrimage centre in India, and Baha'uddin Zakariya, who died in 1266 near Multan and received his spiritual initiation at the hands of Shihabuddin Suhrawardi (1234). While the Suhrawardis maintained excellent relations with the political powers of the time, the Chishtis—at least in the early years—refused to have anything to do with the state. They wanted to be away from the 'world', living on alms and devoted to a fervent worship expressed in music. From the time of Qutbuddin, born in 1186 in Isfahan, the musical tradition of the *qawwali* acquired much importance, and it can be heard even today in Delhi, among other places, in the mausoleum of the most famous Chishti saint, Nizamuddin Awliya (1236-1325).

It is interesting that the heterodox groups made their appearance (in the thirteenth century) at the same time as the orthodox brotherhoods (Chishtiyya and Suhrawardiyya), and that in later years they grew side by side with other equally orthodox orders like the Kubrawiyya and the Shattariyya. We must also mention the Madariyya and the Qalandariyya, and especially the Rifa'i, whose members occasionally indulge in violent behaviour, that is often believed to be an indication of their ability to perform miracles. And let us not forget the flamboyant figure of La'l Shahbaz Qalandar (*d.* 1324) called the 'Red Falcon'. This ascetic, who had settled down in an old Shaivite shrine in Sind, took drugs and was adept at performing spectacular dances. The *malang* dervishes, who care ittle for the letter of the Islamic faith, gathered around him. They shaved their heads, dressed in black, and beat the 'drum of Unity' as they ecstatically danced the *dhamal* (Ewing 1984b).

Sufism in the Deccan

With the passage of time, other brotherhoods made their appearance on Indian soil, particularly the Qadiri order, which overshadowed the Rifa'is in the fifteenth century (Trimingham 1971: 40). The latter were present as far back as 1422 in the Bahmani kingdom of Bidar (Eaton 1978: 55; Schimmel 1980: 59). Their saints, who were mostly settled in the north near Ucch, performed miracles—when they were not torturing themselves—like the *chilla ma'kusa,* where the person hangs by his feet from a tree and meditates upside-down continuously for forty days! The founder of this order, Abdulqadir Gilani, is better known as Mahbub-i Subhani in the Bombay-Karnataka region, which Stein (1968: 61) calls 'transitional' for cultural reasons that will be explained in Chapter 6. Islam spread in this area from the fourteenth century onwards with the participation of warlike dervishes in *jihad.*

After the consolidation of the Bahmani kingdoms (1347-1489) and Bijapur (1490-1686), and Golconda further east, there was a spate of Sufi courtiers, scholars, reformists and landowners, as well as dervishes belonging mostly to the Chishtiyya order (Eaton 1978). This order is known for its mystical practices and controversial doctrines. Once it was cut off from its spiritual centre in Delhi, the Chishtiyya order developed independently in the Deccan. Today, the mausoleum of the scholarly mystic, Khwaja Bandanamaz (1321-1422), also called Gesudaraz (long curly locks) is an important pilgrimage centre for the Deccan Muslims.[5] Practically all the local brotherhoods, even those that do not belong to the Chishti order, follow this revered saint.

It would be tedious and futile to draw up a list of all the saints whose mystical ardour gave rise to the original hundred minor orders, ranging from the most orthodox to the most heterodox. Today, there are innumerable holy spots—*dargahs* and *khanqahs*—associated with saints and linked to the different brotherhoods (*tariqa*) spread all over Karnataka which, like other parts of India, is dotted with 'places of prayer' (*ʿidgah, namazgah*) and mausoleums. But after visiting some mausoleums between the towns of Gulbarga and Hubli it is possible to classify them and throw light on different kinds—albeit overlapping kinds—of institutions. There are five types of mausoleums, and we shall follow two criteria, locational and numerical, in presenting them.

In the first type, which can be dubbed orthodox, figures Gulbarga's only religious complex. This majestic edifice, under which Bandanamaz is buried, is surrounded by dozens of other mausoleums of his descendants and disciples. Gesudaraz is the 'pole' (*qutb*) of saintliness, surpassed only by Mu'inuddin Chishti and, that too, only in north India. Here the difference between legalistic Islam and that practised by the brotherhoods is minimal: the same men are both *sufi* and *faqih.* They teach their disciples Islamic jurisprudence as well as mystical practices (*tariqa*), and the impressive complex is linked to a network of Koranic schools (*madrasa*). It is only rarely that you see here the exaggerated or 'rustic' behaviour generally associated with the followers of saints' cults in south India.

The second type, which is not very common, includes the tombs of saints in the vicinity of Hindu pilgrimage centres, like the cenotaph of Bar Shah *wali* situated on the outskirts of the Renuka-Yellama temple complex in Saundatti, of which we shall speak in Chapter 5. The proximity of Hindu and Muslim shrines gives rise to the transfer of myths and encourages complex ritual and sociological interactions between the followers of the two religions.

The third type refers to shrines intended by their officiants to be 'syncretic'. However, I prefer the term 'eclectic'. To my knowledge, there are at least ten such shrines in the region. A typical example of a Hindu-Muslim shrine is the shrine of the fakir-yogi, Rajabag Savar, in Yamanur village. He is shown riding a tiger, holding in his right hand a cobra that serves him as a riding crop, while in his left hand he holds a scorpion which serves as a bit for his mount (Chapter 4).

A more common type of shrine known for its healing powers, has been described in the previous chapter. The saint specializes in the treatment of afflictions believed to be caused by demons. These afflictions may be either physical or mental disorders, or problems of sorcery, sterility or impotence. But such distinctions are of no interest to those who are sick. Usually, entire families come to the shrine, sometimes from faraway places. Their main object is remission, or better still complete cure, as chronic illnesses are legion. For example, near Hukeri, there is the shrine of Pir Hazrat Ranjur, whose name (meaning 'affliction' in Urdu) hardly does justice to his extraordinary healing powers. Then there is Hazrat Malik Rahan, the *pir* of Vishalgad near Kolhapur, known to have cured all kinds of illnesses. The patient just has to go round his *dargah* wearing wooden handcuffs and iron shackles on his feet to be cured of his malady.

As for the last type of shrine, there are any number of them in both urban and rural areas. They are small complexes consisting of a *dargah* that is surrounded by the tombs (*mazar*) of a few of his descendants, a pilgrim shelter with a kitchen opening outward (*khanqah*) and a masjid—seen more and more commonly today. A cult builds up around the local guardian saint, controlled by those *pirzade* who have inherited his powers and gain material benefits from their position. Usually the saint is worshipped only by people in the neighbourhood, who form an association (*jama'at*); but in cities the cult may be linked with a professional guild. However, in both cases, the brotherhood is formed by a 'third order' consisting of lay members who prepare for their eternal salvation in a spirit of solidarity. But at the same time, they are also concerned about material prosperity, because most devotees regularly visit these *pirs* with offerings to express their thanks for the fulfilment of a wish. The *pir*'s *ʿurs* is celebrated with great pomp on the anniversary of his death or triumphal ascent from the earth to heaven. I saw in Dharwad how a *jama'at* was officially created with the aim of reviving the cult of *wali* Hazrat Shah Hadra Qadri Sayyed. This is a remarkable example of Islamization 'from below', so to speak. In the villages, some members of the lower castes among the Hindus take part in Muslim festivals, following certain fixed procedures. The opposite is also quite common, as I noticed in Dharwad and in the villages around Shahabandar (Chapter 1) and in Hirekumbi (Chapter 5).

The Rifa'i or Jalali Fakirs of Belgaum

Having established the historical, continental and regional frame of reference, let us return to our fakirs in Belgaum. I saw them in action for the first time in Dharwad during the *ʿurs* of Hazrat Shah Hadra Qadri. They were invited by the local *jama'at* to take part in a gathering of fakirs after the lover (the saint) and the Beloved (God) had been joined in eternal union.

Never having seen them before, I was carried away by the spectacle. They kept repeating the words *mastan qalandar* (intoxicated wanderers). In answer to my questions, they told me they were Jalalis rather than Rifa'is, to whom they were affiliated. I was able to verify this later, when I read the board on their pilgrim shelter in Belgaum. I did not realize then that the affiliation to a particular order was less important than the activities carried out together, and that the 'path' is built everyday in the service of God. For them this 'divine service' means worshipping God's most terrible attributes, and they do it physically during their collective worship of *Jalal*, one of Allah's epithets. That is why they call themselves *jalaliya*. The word *Jalal* refers to the sombre 'Majesty' and 'Divine Power' as opposed to *Jamal*, 'Beauty' and 'Divine Benevolence'.[6] Jalaluddin Sarpuch, who died in Ucch in 1291[7], is believed to have founded the brotherhood.

It is not surprising that some members of a Suhrawardiyya brotherhood should be simultaneously affiliated to the Chishtis.

Nizami (1974: 272) points out that one of the founders of the order, Makhdum Jahaniyan Sayyid Jalal Bukhari, was himself initiated into the Chishtiyya order. We may even add that this was almost a rule in the fourteenth century. In fact, Dara Shikoh made a distinction between two types of initiation (*hirqa*), *hirqah-i iradat* reserved for affiliation to the main order, and *hirqah-i tabarruk* covering multiple affiliations of secondary importance (Lawrence 1993: 407). As a matter of fact, affiliation to more than one brotherhood is common today, so much so that Gilsenan, on the basis of his observations in Egypt (1973: 61, 90), speaks of 'plural membership'. The advantages of this practice are obvious. By being a member of several orders one can accumulate the *baraka* of many saints. Consequently, their followers do not quite know to which order they belong, and generally they could not careless! The names of various brotherhoods are misleading as they do not always indicate a similarity in the rituals observed. Also, it is not necessary that there should be an organic link between different groups using the name of the same brotherhood.

As mentioned earlier, this small group (often called a *khilafat*) of thirty-odd members headed by a shaikh, lives in Belgaum city. In exchange for their services to the *dargah* 'Abdul Rahman Khanjar Shah Mal(i)khan, the Sufi landlord, a tailor by profession, allows them to stay in the pilgrims' shelter near the tomb. He never tires of repeating that God will be grateful to him for giving his land for the exercise of the Koranic faith.[8]

Apart from keeping the tomb clean and engaging in peripatetic begging, the fakirs' main activity is providing proof of their miraculous powers (*karamat*) after dark. In Karnataka, this is called *mazahir* which means 'showing, exhibiting, displaying' or 'revealing' (Digby 1984: 65). It is simultaneously a show and a ritual, or we might even call it a display of mystical powers.[9] But locally, these meetings are known as *ratib baz(i)*. *Bazi* means 'test or ordeal', 'challenge', 'prayer', even 'game'.[10] This gives the fakirs an opportunity to 'gain' or 'excel', as the verb *bazi lagana* indicates. And it is precisely this aspect of this practice that offends the Tablighi militants.

It was also explained to me that this was a nocturnal *zikr* (recollection), because while *rat* means 'night', *rat* means 'repetition' and *ratna* means 'reiteration' or 'reciting again and again'. The expression can also be translated as 'service (*ratib*) of the drum (*baz[i]*)', because the ritual is performed to the haunting rhythm of the drumbeat. Actually, the expression 'focusing on the drum' gives a better idea of this mystical rite prescribed by the Shaikh for his disciples, who take turns at concentrating on the drum so that they can go into a trance while torturing themselves. This local inversion of 'spiritual listening' (*sama'*) from the root *sm'* (to hear or to listen) is peculiar to the Sufi tradition, and during this rite the Jalalis enter a state of grace or ecstasy.

A '*Night of Ordeals*'[11]

The ceremony can be divided into three main sequences:

- the recitation of the religious service followed by the order's prayers;
- the *zikr* sung to a musical accompaniment, introduced by a special opening prayer (*fatihat az-zikr*), which mainly consists of chanting the names of the saints and God; the prayer called *tahlil* (profession of faith) or *shahada*, literally 'testimony'; '*La illah illa'llah*!' (There is only one God); to which is added *Muhammad rasul Allah* (and Muhammad is Allah's Prophet), the formula that is inseparable from it in Islam;
- and finally, the 'nocturnal game', during which the brotherhood's members perform miraculous feats for several hours at a stretch. Although it was only meant for Muslims in the beginning, the spectacle attracts a large crowd, especially when the musical procession passes through Hindu neighbourhoods before reaching the venue.

The Seating Arrangement

The spectators sit in a circle, leaving an empty space in the middle called *bazi gah*. The heads of some of the local brotherhoods, invited to watch the ceremony, are its 'pivot' (*qutb*). They preside over it and watch it without taking part in it, as is indicated by their impassivity and their position on the outer edge of the circle. Their immobility, a sign of superior rank, is in stark contrast to the restlessness of the participants. By associating themselves with the shaikh-*jalali*, they ask for the intercession of the guardian saint, and get it. At the same time, their presence infuses 'ecstasy' (*hal*) and, to a certain extent, they create movement. If their state is powerful enough to communicate their trance, it should also be able to control the participants. These men, who have attained perfection, experience ecstasy in silence, without moving (in accordance with Ibn Arabi's teachings). That is why they can be called *malamatis*, 'obsessed by the dissimulation of interior states' (During 1988: 100). Though they do not derive any benefit from their charisma, it is because of it that this communion-like performance can take place. But by performing the role of *qutb*, 'axis' or 'pole', they become one with the Ka'aba or a manifestation of God.

All the ritual instruments are spread before them, surrounded by garlands of flowers and coconuts. They bless them at the beginning of the ceremony to propitiate them. Significantly, they do not hesitate to use the term *puja* to describe this 'tribute' ceremony. Before beginning his dance or self-flagellation, each fakir gets his instrument blessed by the spiritual masters.

The Ritual Instruments

The instrument used most often is the *diara*, called *gurz* in Urdu and peculiar to the Rifa'is. It is a pointed iron spike, about 30 cm long, with a cylindrical metal handle to which are attached small chains (*silsila*). It is said that in every séance there must be at least five of them, representing the five pillars of Islam! There are four possible movements and they usually follow one another in a particular order. First, the fakir turns the instrument rapidly on its axis like a prayer wheel, holding it in front of him or over his head. Then he holds the *gurz* in one hand and with a violent movement pokes its tip into his stomach, chest and head again and again. The third movement is similar to the earlier one, but the tip is placed in the corner of the eye so that it bulges out momentarily. In the fourth movement, the tip is placed on a part of the body, either the neck or the chest, and an assistant is asked to hit it with a sledgehammer so as to break the coconut held at the other end of the *gurz*.

An axe (*kulhadi*) is also used, and there are two distinct movements. While turning it around faster and faster, hitting the chest violently each time, the fakir makes one last powerful motion and falls on his knees with the axe planted in his abdomen. Otherwise, the sharp edge of the axe is placed on a coconut on the fakir's head or chest, and the acolyte hits the axe hard with a sledgehammer to break the coconut. The same exercise can also be carried out with a large-toothed curved saw used to cut wood.

Several types of blades are used. The fakir waves the sword (*talwar*) around in wide circular strokes or he holds the hilt in both hands, alternately striking his stomach and his back. The dance ends in the same manner as the one performed with the axe. As for the small daggers called *khanjar* from which the saint gets his name, the fakir makes several cuts on his tongue, switching the dagger from his right hand to his left faster and faster.

Then, there are a series of needles (*tocha*) or spikes, each about 30 cm long and having a crescent or a hand (*pañjah*) at one end. Different parts of the body—the top of the head, the cheeks, the tongue, the skin on the neck or shoulders or the abdomen—are pierced with these spikes. Sometimes, more spikes are added, generally with the help of the shaikh, who also takes the responsibility of removing them very carefully.

A 2 m long whip made of rope is used by the shaikh to flog a disciple repeatedly on the arms and, less frequently, on the calves. Sometimes, the same exercise is performed with two followers standing face to face, holding each other's hands with their arms crossed.

There is a more complicated exercise with beds of nails (*kelum ka talchta*). Not only is a disciple made to lie on one bed, but sometimes two other beds are placed on top. Finally, heavy stone slabs, either square or circular (*duff*), are put right on top. Then, standing at a distance, the shaikh throws coconuts at the stone slabs with all his might so as to break them. Devotees rush to the centre of the arena to gather the sanctified bits of coconut.

Another popular item is one in which the disciple's head is chopped off. The latter is solemnly made to lie on the ground and entirely covered with a long white cloth. While the fakirs move around producing thick clouds of smoke with burning coal, the shaikh crouches beside him and puts a sword blade against his neck. As he starts moving the blade against his neck, the disciple struggles and then stiffens his body. As he is being beheaded, the music becomes faster and faster as the audience goes wild with frenzy. (The intense excitement that reigned during the [simulated] decapitation—a marvel in which the audience has implicit faith—prevented me from finding out exactly how it is done.) Finally, the 'recapitated' man, still quite stunned by the experience, is helped up by his fellow disciples.

It is the shaikh who coordinates the entire operation and ensures its success because of the confidence he inspires among the disciples. As for himself, he does not perform any feats. He is content to help in piercing with the needles or removing them; and almost every time, after the exercise is over, he cauterizes the wound (with hot ash or clarified butter), applies ointment and massages the bruises, which bleed only in rare cases. If the disciple becomes groggy or faints under the effect of shock, he quickly gets the ritual circle cleared by other fakirs.

The séance ends with an ordeal by fire. A red-hot chain, about 1.5 m long, is brought in. With the help of a horizontal stick, two assistants hold it vertically over a large flat vessel filled with petrol. The fakirs come one by one and crouch before the chain. They first dip their hands in the petrol and then move their arms up and down the chain, which catches fire each time.

The Invocations

Apart from the dominant refrain *Wali-auliya Malkhan ta'rif*! which means 'prayer [or respect] to the saint of saints Malkhan!', the Rifa'i fakirs invoke other respected masters from Karnataka, one of whom is buried near Chikamagalur in the south and the other in Gulbarga in the north. The former called Baba Budhan Giri, buried in Attigundi, has given his name to the 2,000 m high hills covered with forests where his shrine is located. These hills were earlier called Chandradrona or 'moon crater'. According to Herklots (1972: 140), this saint, 'intoxicated' by his love for God, brought with him seeds from Moka (Al-Mukha) in Yemen and introduced coffee in Mysore way back in the fourteenth century. But the editor of the *Mysore Gazetteer* (1930: 1137) claims that it was introduced by one Hazrat Shah Jama Allah Magarabi. Whatever the truth, the fact remains that India's first coffee plantations came up on the Baba Budhan Hills around 1840, thanks to the British.

The saint is also known as Hazrat Dada Hayat Mir Qalandar and Baba Qalandar Shah Dattatreya. 'Qalandar' evidently refers to his status as a wandering dervish not too concerned about keeping to the letter of the Koran. However, the inclusion of 'Dattatreya' can be explained by the fact that his shrine is dedicated to this three-headed god (representing Brahma, Vishnu and Shiva) accompanied by four dogs. The cave contains the tomb of Baba Budhan; but some Hindus insist that it is Dattatreya's throne (*pitha*). It is thus an important pilgrimage spot for the followers of both religions. The Hindus claim that Dattatreya's reincarnation, believed by the locals to be Vishnu's last *avatara*, will come out from the 'mouth' of the very cave where Baba Budhan disappeared.

This eclecticism in matters of both mythology and worship, of which we will talk at length in the next chapter, is also seen in the person of the *mahant* who serves as a *pujari* but is a Muslim and carries the title of *baba* or *pir*. It is said that this happened because when the last *mahant*, a Hindu, was about to die, there was nobody at his side—except for a Muslim milkman—to whom he could transmit the mantra for the continuation of the cult. This mantra, an incomprehensible mixture of Sanskrit and Arabic polysyllables, is now mumbled by the Muslim devotees, who outnumber the Hindus. Brahmins too join them to receive *prasada* in return for their offerings of coconuts, milk in a plantain-leaf cone, incense, sugar and bananas (Bharati 1981: 79).

According to another story, Dada Hayat Mir Qalandar appointed Baba Budhan as his successor. A Persian inscription on a wall of the Bhandarkhana *matha* situated near the cave declares that the building was restored by Queen Chennamaji of Ikkeri for one Sayyid Murutuja Shah Qadri Sajjad, whose complete title was Sri Dattatreya Swami Baba Budhan Swami Jagadguru (*Mysore Gazetteer* 1930: 1137). According to the fakir in Belgaum who told me this story, this beautiful Muslim princess (now invisible) is still in the cave for the benefit of all the pilgrims.

A king named Vira-Balla became enamoured of a princess. He asked his men to abduct her in her sleep and place her on a natural platform in a cave hollowed out in the midst of inaccessible mountains. When she was woken up by the fresh mountain air, the princess realized what fate held in store for her. She prayed to God to make her ugly and leave her in the care of the local fakir, Dada Hayat Mir Qalandar. The latter immediately took her under his wing and entrusted her with the feeding of fakirs, but in a way that nobody would see her. So she sat on a platform, hidden from prying eyes, and passed the food through a crevice in the rock. But one day, a fakir, who could not contain himself, caught hold of her hand. Dada Hayat Mir Qalandar was so furious with him that he beheaded him through the sheer power of his curse. Since then, devotees have got into the habit of putting food on the platform because the princess is still there.

The Rifa'i fakirs also pray to Bandanamaz of Gulbarga and some of them tell me that they are regularly invited to his shrine to perform their feats. Digby writes that in 1963 he saw a similar séance there conducted by them (1984: 65, n. 20).

The frequent references to Khwaja Gesudaraz Bandanamaz give rise to four historical comments. First, even if we do not take into account the *hadiths* that condemn the manifestation of ecstasy, we know that his opinion on the *sama'* was highly nuanced. He ruled on its lawfulness by distinguishing between four legal categories borrowed from Burhanuddin (Ernst 1992: 310, n. 25). 'When the listener's thoughts are turned towards God (*haqq*), *sama'* is permissible (*mubah*). When his thoughts are turned mainly towards material things, it is illicit (*haram*). When they are between *haqq* and the world, it is blameable (*makruh*). But when they are turned exclusively towards *haqq* and *haqiqat* (Truth and Reality), then *sama'* is licit (*halal*) (quoted by Hussaini 1970: 178). Ultimately, everything depends on the actors' sincerity, which is very difficult to gauge. True, the natives of Belgaum are ignorant of these subtleties; but these feats seem all the more 'obligatory' (*wajib*) to them because they are performed for all the reasons that Gesudaraz took pride in differentiating.

Secondly, Digby mentions that at the end of the fourteenth century, Gesudaraz condemned the *qalandars* by dismissing their claim that they possessed powers that were superior to those of the great shaikhs (1984: 76-9). The extreme hostility between these two groups is a favourite subject of Sufi hagiographers, who make them meet to defy or combat one another, with the qalandars trying constantly to do away with the shaikhs. The fact remains that (in stories) their repeated attacks with blades and needles have no effect on the shaikhs (1984: 91). It would appear as if the qalandars' behaviour, considered a manifestation of their 'anger' (*jalal*), is systematically subjugated by the superior charisma and benevolent qualities of the shaikhs (1984: 87). It is said that Gesudaraz himself succeeded in bringing about a reconciliation between the qalandars, who seemed too aggressive to him, and the shaikhs. Digby claims (1984: 104, n. 54), that the qalandars now take part in the celebration of the birth anniversary of Mu'inuddin Chishti in Ajmer, where they have a subordinate, but significant, role in the rituals.

Third, though the original traditions of the Chishti order insisted on a certain amount of restraint and self-control (Lawrence 1983; Ernst 1992: 131ff.), it may be observed during the *bund sama'* or private concert on the anniversary of the death of the Saint of Gulbarga (Hussaini 1970: 181, 184) that the writers affiliated to this order clearly defend the principle of excitement and delectation (*hizzat*), both inward and outward, at the different stages of ecstasy (*tawajud, wajd* and *wujud*). 'He who does not experience excitement during the *sama'*, will never experience the pleasure of contemplating the divine face', says Mas'ud Bakk, an Indian Chishti (quoted by During 1988: 111). The benevolence (*jamal*) of the Chishti saints was such that some of them issued *fatwas* favourable to 'spiritual concerts'. Actually, this extrovert notion of *sama'*, an essential element in the popularization of the Sufi doctrine, is exploited by the Rifa'is.

According to Coslovi (1993), Gesudaraz's influence during his lifetime is explained by the political circumstances, particularly the support given to him by Ahmad Han-i-Hanan, brother and successor of Sultan Firuz, who forced him to build his *dargah* outside the city of Gulbarga. But he attributes the continuity of his prestige to the fact that his personality combines traits that are apparently unique in Islam. Thus his theory and practice of *sama'* and his ideas about *wujudi* are in agreement with the ideas of those who value ecstasy in the Sufi experience, as also are his ideas about universal love. They are all in tune with the teachings of the Chishti order, which made him attractive to Indian Muslims, and even Hindus, and he continues to attract them to this day. We must also not forget his mastery of several local languages. On the other hand, his intransigence towards the *shari'a*, his criticism of Ibn Arabi's opinion and his missionary activities in the service of Islamization made him acceptable, and even popular, in more orthodox circles. His popularity among different circles is such that in his *dargah*, 'converted' Muslims (*dakhni*), recent as well as early converts, rubbed shoulders with the 'nobles' (*afaqi*).

Music

Miracles are performed to the music of a drum (*baz*) and tambourines (*daf*). There is no melodic instrument, as there is with the Mevlevi dervishes of Turkey, who use the oblique flute (*nay*) and the Isawiyya of the Maghreb, who show a preference for the oboe (Rouget 1990: 61). The singer (*qawwal*), accompanied by a small chorus (*munshid*), sits to the right of the shaikhs. The drummer, the mainspring of the spiritual concert, sits facing the other musicians. Some of the members present strike their tambourines in unison with the uninterrupted beat of the drum. The chanting is taken up in chorus quite informally by the gathering. Some pretend to meditate, but they are in effect reciting their prayers silently; others are transported by the liveliness of the music. However, no one explained to me that 'the drum is a symbol of the circle of human beings. The skin covering it represents the absolute being; the beats stand for divine visitations. . .' as was claimed by Bawariq (quoted by Molé 1963: 205).

Fakirs listen to music while waiting to go into a trance (Rouget 1990: 448 ff.), but the musicians keep playing without reaching an ecstatic state, quite content with their share of the state of grace. The distinction is clear and no shamanism is involved. The person 'possessed' (by the saint) is hypnotized by the music-makers who are not possessed. The music is played for the fakirs, whose part is to submit to it; and to succeed, they must 'focus on the drum' (*ratib baz*). Although trance is an individual experience, it is also ritualized and socialized, so that the underlying spectacle is a community event. The possessed person is hypnotized by the music because the group demands it of him. But though the trance has to be induced at the outset, it progresses till the person undergoes a change of identity or even a total annihilation, which transforms him completely. At this point, the fakir opens a passage to another world into which he topples (just like a shaman, this time).

Dance

All the expressive gestures follow a measured pattern, with rhythmic leaps, spinning and circular movements, as in dance (*rags*). The footwork, consisting of stamping the ground with the feet, is a movement attributed by the *hadith* to cAli himself. This stamping is not random, but choreographed in perfect time with the drumbeats. The leaps cannot be explained as a simple mobilization of muscular resources, for the dancers give the impression that they are drawing their energy from a supernatural source. Some people say that when they leap about like this, the fakirs, maddened by their love for God, are actually pouncing on demons. The extremely unusual nature of these animated movements, so different from the habitual restraint shown by Sufis, is a divine sign indicating the presence of a supernatural power. And that is the exact meaning of the word *mazahir*, the descent of the supernatural on the dancers as a mark of divine favour that affects not only the mind, but also the body and all the faculties that it harbours. Knowing that the term *majzub* (attracted) is frequently used in the case of fakirs, we may believe with Bawariq that the (dervish's) 'leaps indicate that he is drawn away from the human state towards the state of the One and Only' (see Molé 1963: 206).

Equally important are the whirling movements traditionally called *sama' wa raqs.* These peaceable dance movements precede self-torture. Four fakirs move in a circle, crouching down at regular intervals. They hold a tambourine in one hand, which they move up and down in a very elegant spiral movement.

Generally, the gyratory movements that make them move in a circular orbit are evocative of the nimble movements of the whirling dervishes of the Mevlevi order. But here, because of the unpredictable nature of *hal,* any attempt at formal choreography is completely ruled out, undoubtedly because these dances have a martial air about them.

Offerings

The séance is also an act of grace during which different kinds of offerings are made, thereby enhancing the value of the musical offering. Clothes and money are given, and it is even customary to offer a feast, which is quite sumptuous by local standards. This is an occasion for those who organize and patronize the saint's *jama'at* to affirm their piety and display their importance, and even increase it. The feast, which is both convivial and ritual, necessarily involves distributing large amounts of food believed to have special qualities because it is impregnated by an invisible flow of various virtues (*baraka*). It is clear that like the soul, the body too needs food, music being food for the soul, as mystics often claim. But here, as elsewhere (During 1988: 140), the dervishes dance on an empty stomach; and according to custom, the meal is served only at the end of the séance.

Islamic Piety

A Sufi is not supposed to attach any importance to the sensational and paranormal effects of trance or do anything to encourage them. But the Rifa'is set great store by them. They justify this ostentation, which Massignon treats as pure 'jugglery'! by claiming that it strengthens the faith of the participants and spectators, even helps to attract some irresolute persons to the faith. But the wonderment of the sympathizers apart, this *zikr* 'of the vulgar' (*zikr al'awamm*)—to use Gardet's translation (1952: 650) without accepting it—has been censured by many, including those who watch them, though without earning the disapproval of right-thinking people. The *sama'*, being an instrument of the divine presence, has a profound effect on Muslims as well as Hindus. As Hujwiri proclaimed, 'the true dervish does not bother about the opinion of other men; he is equally indifferent to their censure and their appreciation'.

If the fairs display their 'immunity to the sword and to fire' (Trimingham 1971: 86), it is because God orders them to do so. 'It is an order' (*hukm hai*), they say, from the saint or God to his 'servants'. During the 'service' (*khidma*) when these skilled artistes are called *dhu'l jalal*, meaning 'splendid' or 'glorious', the normal laws of physiology do not seem to work, as if by miracle. And even though an Indian *hadith* claims that 'miracles are menstruation for men' (Schimmel 1975: 212), there is hardly ever any blood because the Jalali are gifted with special 'powers' (*dhu'l iqtidar*). According to one legend, Ahmad Ibn ar-Rifa'i, the founder of the order, had himself castrated very soon after his birth! In any case, the Rifa'is do not seem to suffer from the torture and wounds they inflict on themselves. For instances they use a soothing euphemism to designate the instrument of their torture (*diara* or *gurz*), calling it *gul*, which means 'rose' in Persian! As for the sword, they claim to be immune to it because they identify it with their saint Khanjar. The latter should however be understood in its Sufi and mystical sense as a weapon aimed at the 'carnal soul' (*nafs*) (Ernst 1992: 310, n. 25). As regards fire, those who want to show their devotion to the saint submit to the ordeal frequently, as is seen during the *Muharram* celebrations. It is such a common ordeal that it only produces a condescending smile from those fakirs who do not stoop to it.

By scorning their wounds and burns, the fakirs mobilize the saint's *baraka*. At that point, they are no longer human beings indulging in superhuman feats, but an incarnation of the saint, who literally shows himself to the world through them. Once again it is the epiphanic sense of the term *mazahir* that defines the ceremony. Through this torture leading to an ecstasy that transfigures them, the fakirs to a certain extent embody the saint's power. That is why they are called *dhu*, meaning 'possessor of' or 'gifted with' his charisma. It is only this temporary identification with the saint, while they are in a trance, that gives the Rifa'is the strength to go through the ordeal and prove their invulnerability. Because the saint is within them, because they are possessed by him, the self-inflicted torture does not cause any pain. They become the saint's flesh and are in a position to 'meet' or 'find' (*wajd*) God. Their human qualities disappear, and they can cross the bounds of their human existence through revelatory inspiration. In mystical terms, they reach *fana*, which lies beyond *wajd*. Thus the fakirs' behaviour seems to point to the doctrine of the 'Uniqueness of the Being' (*wahdat al-wujud*) and illustrates Hallaj's prayer: 'Thus You and I are one, no longer separated'. This does not, however, apply to them, because, according to the classical tradition, they do not claim to become one with Him. Of course, their union with the saint by transforming them annihilates their human existence and sublimates it in a divine superexistence. But this does not rise to God. There is nothing scandalous about the fakirs' way of worship because the saint is always the mediator. It is even advantageous to have a saint as an intercessor, because in a religion believing in transcendence, it is possible to get close to the divine presence. By exposing themselves to the dazzling attributes of the divine Majesty (*jalal*) or *mysterium tremendum*, the fakirs become the 'mirrors of God', to paraphrase Massignon's elegant expression.

Annihilation in God (fana)

Apparently sensational, these ceremonies are essentially mystical and Islamic. They are mystical because they involve the practice of *zikr*, a term derived from *dhakara*, which means 'to remember' or 'to recall', called *jali* in this case. It is a type of musical recitation of the divine word that requires '*claire-audience*' according to During's play on words (1988: 52). Remembering Allah and constantly repeating his saint's name in order to reach a state of rapture is Islamic in character and quite different from the *yoga samadhi*. As a matter of fact, according to Filliozat's definition, the latter calls for 'stabilization of thought and latent physical tendencies' in order to suppress representation altogether (1963). Eliade prefers to call this kind of experience '*enstase*' as opposed to '*extase*' (1948: 93). On the contrary, in the case of the Rifa'is, it is an 'ecstasy' (*wajd*) or an 'excitational ecstasy' (*tawajud*) that resorts to overstimulation of the senses through singing, dancing and self-torture. It is a hypersensitive experience that needs to be controlled and, even better, sublimated. In fact, a great deal of 'concentration' (*tawajjuh*)[12] and a lot of 'self-control' are need to undertake the 'journey' (*sayr*) towards extinction.

The second type of control is exercised by the shaikh as he

accompanies the disciple during his efforts to annihilate the self (*fana*). In this way, the *murshid's* spiritual powers are transferred to the *murīd*, and the latter gradually becomes a part of the former. But the process does not stop there. The *pir's* powers have to be conquered, and then those of the Prophet (even those of Allah himself, as is claimed by some). These are the four 'stages' (*maqamat*) of absorption in God, or at least that is how they are interpreted by local scholars. This absorption, resulting from a conjunction between an ascent and a descent, is similar, on the one hand, to a shamanic exercise, and on the other, to possession.

First, there is an ascent towards God divided into a series of *maqamat* or 'abodes', which can be compared to so many steps to be climbed to reach, at each stage, a new level of being. Or else, in the Chishti doctrinal order as interpreted by the Sufis of the Deccan,[13] to attain 'exoteric knowledge' (*ʿilm*), the 'way' (*tariqa*), 'truth' (*haqiqa*) and 'esoteric knowledge' (*ma'rifat*) (Eaton 1978: 146). This normally takes some time; but the Rifa'is skip over some stages and reach their goal quickly by going into a trance. This brings us to the Shattaris—an important order in the Deccan going back to Bayazid Bistami, one of the earliest 'intoxicated' Sufis (*sukr*)—whose name very aptly means 'speed' (Subhan 1970: 306).

Then comes the descent from God into the heart of the 'traveller' (*salik*) because, at the end of the four-stage path (*rah*) leading to it, he reaches this 'abode of proximity' (*maqam-i qurb*), which is transcendent and indescribable. It represents dazzling grace and is gift to the undeserving servant. This 'state' if ecstasy (*hal*), which unorthodox Sufis of the Chishti order recognize as *fana* and interpret as man's union with God (Eaton 1978: 149-50), is by definition short-lived. So the divine descent is an answer to the mystical ascent, and it is the meeting of the two that is the real illumination or *tajalli*, the divine manifestation that summarizes the 'way' (*tariqa*). As Abu'l Qasim Junaid said, 'Sufism means that God makes you die to resuscitate you in Himself'.

Jihad

Usually the word '*mujahada*' is used to denote the torture fakirs inflict on themselves. It is derived from the root *jahad* (to fight against) from which is feigned, that the extraordinary performances are illusions or a conjuror's tricks. There is no doubt that the members of this brotherhood like to show off in public and indulge in histrionics, because the Rifa'is are good showmen. It is also indisputable, as pointed out by Trimingham, that there is (or has been) a 'mechanization (if we may say so) of the mystical experience' (1971: 199), as the Rifa'is sometimes have a kind of commonplace charisma. It cannot however be denied that despite the commercialization and automation of the trance, it continues to be treated as a divine inspiration attributed to the saint rather than to Allah himself.

In fact, the Rifa'is have managed to keep alive a very vibrant tradition of transcending the self as experienced in 'popular' religiosity. This tradition is thus the vehicle of a Sufism that is more devotional than mystical. And because it is so closely linked to the worship of saints, it has done a lot, historically, for the spread and implantation of Islam in Indian society and elsewhere. For example, their gestures correspond to the beating and mutilation of the body practised by Iraqi dervishes during the *zikr.*

And if today, as in the past, canonists and others treat this 'self-mutilating exaltation of the self' either harshly or with condescension, a large segment of the population Hindus included, sees in it the imprint of intense religiosity. In the parallel Hindu tradition of music and song linked with mystical experiences, *kirtans* and *bhajans* perform an identical function. However, among the Hindus the practice of devotion does not normally require the participation of professional singers and musicians. Any one who is willing, whether a professional or an amateur, can join an informal congregation and sing or play an instrument, although the congregation is usually led by a few persons who choose the texts and guide its rhythmic progression. Undoubtedly, impregnating the mind through the ceaseless repetition of music and poetry is common to both religions, as is their aim to induce a feeling of closeness, and even union, with God; and they both seek primarily to transmit emotions. But the Hindus show a preference for a dramatized theophany that transports devotees into the divine world, rather than the violent spectacles presented by the fakirs. Of course, in both cases 'mystical hearing' which, as Rumi said, is the 'food of those in love with God', is treated *jihad,* meaning 'do battle against infidels', is derived. According to Subhan, the two terms are interchangeable when they are used in the sense of 'doing battle against oneself'. According to the Koran (*Surahs* 29, 69), this battle opens the 'way' (*tariqa*) (1970: 6, 89). *Mujahada* generally means penance and austerity; also prolonged fasting and the tireless repetition of divine names, night and day, and giving up the ordinary comforts of life.

It is therefore a 'battle of the heart' (*al-jihad al-qalb*) considered to be 'greater' (*al-jihad al-akbar*) than the military battle called 'small' (*al-jihad al-asghar*). After the battle of Badr in 624, thanks to which is Islam became a universal religion, Muhammad is supposed to have said that the greatest battle is the 'battle against oneself' (*mujahadatu'n-nafs*). Commenting on the Prophet's statement, Maulana Jalaluddin wrote, 'Until now we have waged war against shapes, we battled against enemies having a shape; now we fight against the enemies of thoughts, so that good thoughts destroy bad ones and expel them from the body's realm. The great war and the great battle are this war and this battle' (quoted by Vitray-Meyerovitch 1977: 147). But divine reality manifests itself clearly and indubitably only when the mirror of the heart is not tainted by the impurities of this world. The gradual corruption of the heart by sin is compared to the slow accumulation of rust on metal. This explains why asceticism is compared to polishing, and why it is necessary to launch a *jihad* against the carnal and lustful soul (*nafs*) that obstructs the climb up the ladder leading to God. Also, knowing that the self-torture of lowly souls is worth more than the holy war against infidels, the former suffer more. That is the meaning behind the fakirs' restlessness, exorcism, and bellicose dances.

Thus, as opposed to the Jamalis, who try to channel or suppress the *nafs*, the Jalalis try to excite it and stimulate it to the highest degree by following the 'burning' path in order to exhaust its energy (Kurin 1984: 214, n. 21). These are two different methods of reaching the same goal, which is to preserve spiritual communication between man and God with the saint's intercession.

The Powers of Metaphor

While watching these spectacular demonstrations, one is bound to think (and this applies not only to foreign observers, but also to the natives) that it is a pretented transe and that this extraordinary worship is only an illusion or prestidigitation. There is no doubt that the members of this brotherhood like to show off in public and indulge in histrionics because the Rifa'is are good showmen. It is also indisputable, as pointed out by Trimingham, that there is (or has been) a 'mechanization (if we may say so) of the mystical experience'

(1971: 199) as the Rifa'is sometimes have a kind of commonplace charisma. It cannot however be denied that despite the automation of the trance as a result of its commercialization, it continues to be treated as a divine inspiration attributed to the saint rather than to Allah himself.

In fact, the Rifa'is have managed to keep alive a vibrant tradition of transcending the self as experienced in 'popular' religiosity. This tradition is thus the vehicle of a Sufism that is more devotional than mystical. And because it is so closely linked to the worship of saints, it has done a lot, historically, for the spread and implantation of Islam in Indian society. This is true not only of India but also of many other countries. For example, their gestures correspond to the beating and mutilation of the body practised by Iraqi dervishes during the *zikr*.

And if today, as in the past, canonists and others treat this 'self-mutilating exaltation of the self' either harshly or with condescension, a large segment of the population sees in this display the imprint of intense religiosity. And this includes the Hindus among whom there developed a parallel tradition of music and song linked with mystical experiences where *kirtans* and *bhajans* perform an identical function. It must be pointed out that among the Hindus the practice of devotion does not normally require the performance of professional singers and musicians. Any one who is willing, whether a professional or an amateur, can join an informal congregation and sing or play an instrument, although the congregation is usually led by a few persons who choose the texts and guide its rhythmic progression. Undoubtedly, impregnating the mind through the ceaseless repetition of music and poetry is common to both religions, as is their aim to induce a feeling of closeness, and even union, with God and they both seek primarily to transmit emotions. But the Hindus show a preference for dramatized theophany which transports the devotees into the divine world rather than the violent spectacles presented by the fakirs. Of course, in both cases 'mystical hearing' which, as Rumi said, is the 'food of those in love with God', is treated as a form of worship and a means of spiritual advancement. But the fact remains that, for both Hindus and Muslims, Islam is what the Rifa'is do, because they are Islam, according to the expression used by Gellner regarding the saints of the Atlas (1969: 48). It is the manifestation of a genuine mysticism—though dramatized—and mental and physical states opening out to another world. It is because of the excitement and music, and not despite it, that 'the gates of Paradise creak open', as Rumi puts it. No matter how the word is understood, the fakirs are the wild-eyed fanatics of Islam, its 'army of prayer', to borrow an expression from Emperor Jahangir (Eaton 1978: 242).

This last expression is, of course, only a metaphor. But we know full well that religious discourses abound in metaphors. The heterodox are quite pleased to hear them used in the right way, and they keep to the letter of the Koran, which they magnify through their seemingly deviant behaviour. It is for the anthropologist to interpret this behaviour and show that it actually reflects a set of mystical beliefs, and recognize the nature of the men indulging in such behaviour, who are in truth fundamentalists acting like fanatics. Confusing mysticism with the highly rationalized restraint of the recluse amounts to a strictly one-sided, limited and fairly disillusioned view of mysticism. It means forgetting, as Mauss points out, that 'the body is the prime and the most natural instrument of man' (1960: 372) and that 'at the bottom of our mystical states' there are 'bodily techniques' or, in other words, 'biological means of entering into communication with God' (1960: 385).

Even the conjuring tricks and the beheading of the disciple described earlier have a deep mystical significance. It is an enactment, in the most literal sense, of the indescribable experience of *sama'*. In fact, the saint Qutbuddin Binadal-i Ghawthi, the last *qalandar* to live for more than a hundred years (1373-1518), was known as *Sar-andaz*, 'one who rejects his head'. It is said that he was given this name because so great was his concentration on the divine litany during *zikr* that his head separated from his body (Subhan 1970: 312).

This act of Islamic oblation, the beheading of the fakir in Baba Budhan Giri's cave, the biting off of snakes' heads by the Rifa'is and Husain's decapitation have made such a strong impression on the Muslim imagination that the Urdu word '*gaus*' has become a title for saints whom devotional ardour leads to beheading! This kind of mutilation also appeals to the Hindus. We just have to look at those Hindu heroes (*vira*) who cut off their own heads, to prove the intensity of their devotion to the goddess, or the goddesses shown without heads, or those beheading themselves.[15] True, no analogy is involved, but it is because of similar ways of thinking, in spite of radical differences, that parallels were established between Islam and Hinduism. There are more or less convincing analogies at the bottom of repeated attempts of these two religions to come closer. By devoting the next chapter to cults that aim to promote the so-called 'syncretism' we shall put forth the view that such a makeshift arrangement does not eliminate social conflict or hierarchy.

NOTES

1. Etymologically speaking, the word is usually believed to be derived from *suf* meaning wool, denoting the cloak worn by some Sufis as an outward sign of their poverty, or at least their desire for detachment. But according to another theory, it is derived from the Arabic *safa, safwa* (purity); and according to yet another theory, from the Greek *sophos, sophia* (wisdom). Massignon points out that Abdulqadir Baghdadi, in the eleventh century, and Nicholson, in the twentieth century, were able to collect respectively 1,000 and 78 different definitions of 'Sufism' (1954: 156)!
2. The history of Sufism often creates the illusion that it was perfect when it began. For example, Nizami writes, 'By the middle of the 13th century, mystic thought, both in prose and verse, had reached its finale' (1974: 56). This is just the opposite of Trimingham's thesis that 'this development into orders, and the integral association of the saint cult with them, contributed to the decline of Sufism . . .' (1971: 70). See Arberry (1950: Chapter XI) and a criticism of this scholarly prejudice in Lawrence (1982: 27 ff).
3. Popovich and Veinstein (1986) present an eloquent perspective of the brotherhoods of the Muslim world.
4. The importance of Sufism in the spread of Islam, even in southern India, has been pointed out by Nizami (1974), Eaton (1978) and Siddiqi (1985). See also Subhan (1970), Rizvi (1978, 2 vols.), and Gaborieau (1986).
5. There is very little literature on him except for the rather disappointing book by Sayyid Shah Khusro Hussaini (1983). However, it is worth reading the few pages on him by Rizvi (1978: I, 250-6).
6. Traditionally, a distinction is made between the attributes of power (*ism-i-azam*) and those of glory (*asma'ut-husna*) which are of two different kinds: 'proud' and 'terrible' (*jalali*) and 'airy', 'benevolent' and 'loving' (*jamali*). Thus the *jalal* ('fear', 'terror' and 'anger') of 'terrible' fakirs, who are wanderers and not attached to worldly things, is opposed to the *jamal* ('beauty' and 'benevolence') of the worldly, peace-loving fakirs, who spend their time in prayer. But as Digby points out, the two terms are complementary (1984: 81).
7. For information about this saint and the genealogy of his descendants who contributed to the development of the Jalali brotherhood, Subhan (1970: 236-7), Trimingham (1971: 20-2 and Appendix C), Nizami (1974: 277), and Schimmel (1980: 33 and 36).

8. For a description of the *dargah*, Chapter 6.
9. It may be seen as an Indian version of the *hadarat* such as the *darb al silah* of the Syrian Sa'diyya and the iron and fire ordeals of the Algerian Aissaoua, without mentioning the 'piercing by sword' (*darb shish*) or metal spikes practised by the Rifa'iyyas of Aleppo and Kosovo. Similar practices in Java are described by Lombard (1986).
10. The analogy between 'game' and 'prayer' is the guiding notion of van der Meer's description of the Rifa'is in Surat (Gujarat).
11. A video-film has been made on the 'Mystical Marriage' of this saint and the ceremony performed by fakirs after it (Assayag 1991).
12. In a highly evocative article, Digby shows the link between *tawajjuh* and *jihad*, taking as an example Baba Palangposh, who helped the army of his master Ghazi Al-Din Khan during a battle just by dint of 'concentration' (or 'attention'). 'The Pir', he writes, 'is one who can remove obstacles (*mushkil-kusha*)'.
13. This should be compared with the classical Indian Sufi concept which, as explained by Subhan (1970: Chapters III and IV), makes a distinction between 'repentance' (*tawbat*), 'conversion' (*inabat*), 'reconciliation' (*zuhd*) and 'confidence' (*tawakkul*).
14. For examples of possession among Hindus in the same region, Assayag (1989b).
15. Regarding the theme of decapitation in popular Hinduism and the cult of the goddess, refer to Assayag (1992).

4

Mythology: Let us Pray to Allah in the Name of Vishnu

> Strong belief only proves its strength,
> not the truth of what is believed.
>
> F. NIETZSCHE, *Human, All too Human* (1878)

I owe my knowledge of Hindu-Muslim worship, discussed in this chapter, to the regular companions of the teashop in the little village of Hirekumbi in Saundatti district. It stands right next to the majestic banyan tree that serves as the local bus-stop.

One day, while I was talking to them about the relations between Hinduism and Islam in India, one of them surprised me by quoting Mahatma Gandhi in a mixture of English and Hindi, '*Ram and Rahim ek hai*!'. Translating the above sentence, he immediately added, 'God is One, whether He is Hindu or Muslim!' and gave the example of '*Changadev gudi*, or *Rajabag Savar dargah*'. He explained to me that this was a place of worship in Yamanur village considered indiscriminately as the temple (*gudi*) of a Hindu guru and the *dargah* of a Muslim saint. It is a curious shrine where an *avatara* of Vishnu and an intercessor of Allah are rolled into one in the person of an ascetic who renounced the world, was a tolerably good magician and miracle-worker, and was enrolled simultaneously under the ochre banner of Vaishnavism and the green banner of Islam. The charisma of this saint draws to his tomb followers of both the religions, as is common in popular religious practices.

What is not so common, however, is that Hindu and Muslim servants officiate side by side in this shrine. What is even rarer is the deliberate mixture of symbols associated with both religions, which allows the devotees to express their preference for either monotheism or polytheism as they worship together. Further, as I discovered soon enough, this 'integrated acculturation' (Devereux 1975) has only one distinctive feature as compared to the many other 'cultural hybrids' in this area. So, even though one must beware of generalizations, these examples do suggest that India has witnessed the flowering of numerous types of acculturation between its 'great' traditions through the ages. We tend to presume too readily, on the basis of claims made by their respective partisans, that the main religious schools and sects developed independently. But though these traditions enjoyed a great deal of prestige, they did not influence the development of popular Indian practices as much as the cultural hybrids of which Yamanur is just one example.

When we try to understand this socio-religious phenomenon at the lowest level by studying groups placed lower down in the social hierarchy, we observe that in actual practice Hinduism and Islam are far removed from the conceptions of the 'worshippers of Rama' or the doctors of Islamic law. Keeping this fact in mind, and along with it the rural setting and the relative poverty of the local people, we find that cultural and religious assimilation always gains the upper hand. So they pray to Allah in the name of Vishnu and vice versa.

Purists are scandalized. They condemn these practices, all the more legitimately, so they think, in that this 'low' tradition derives from folklore, a term used to discredit all forms of expression that pay no heed to scholarly sources. But not only did the popular forms encourage peaceful coexistence and creativity; they were also responsible for socio-religious reforms that were mystical in nature and a protest against the established order. That brings to mind the finest flower of Indian 'syncretism'. Kabir (1398-1440),[1] who, according to legend, was the son of a Brahmin widow brought up by a family of poor Muslim weavers. He became a disciple of Ramananda, the *advaita* guru of the Vaishnava sect. If Kabir can be judged by the yardstick of his intentions or his philosophy and poetry, is it right to despise the followers of collective traditions who put his teachings into practice without being aware of it?

There has never been a Kabir in Yamanur, nor is there one today. And to the best of my knowledge, no mystic has ever joined in the common worship of Vishnu and Allah in this little-known shrine, but this centuries-old social experiment is all the more interesting, in its anonymity. It is the actuality of a cross-bred local culture that has flourished for centuries. Owing to mutual hostility the persons involved were obliged to devise suitable rules of modified coexistence. They continue to do so by cobbling together myths, symbols and rites in a manner that is peculiar to those societies so often wrongly described as 'traditional', innovating while constantly referring to the past, but to a past that is always being reconstituted and reinvented.

Rivers, Village and Temple of Yamanur

By a stroke of luck, in the course of a conversation I was invited to join some people going to the temple-tomb of Yamanur, situated between the Karwar hills and the Bijapur plateau. There, between the forest and the plain, I saw the 'confluence of two rivers', Tupurihalla and Benihalla, with their source in Dundashi in Kundgol taluk of Dharwad district. This is the story narrated by the locals about one of these rivers:

(a) Long long ago, an old woman was walking along a stream carrying a big pot of butter on her head. She wanted to sell it in the nearest village. But on the way she slipped on a cowpat, fell into the water and was drowned. That is why this river is called *beni halu*, which can be translated as 'the milk (or butter) of suffering'.

Since then its water has not been fit for drinking. Nor can it be used for irrigation, because it is too alkaline and sulphated. But it is a marvellous antiseptic for wounds, insect bites and burns. It is believed that it can cure skin ailments, boils, alopecia or baldness, itching, eczema, leucoderma, and leprosy, in addition to a host of venereal diseases. It is also supposed to cure all kinds of disease, particularly digestive troubles, since it destroys worms. The liquid is so precious that access to it was formerly guarded by a tiger. And most devotees come to Yamanur mainly to bathe in this river, as this devotional song (traditional from Kannada) says:

All those who suffer come to Yamanur,
They take a bath in the holy river Benihalla,
Their illnesses are driven away,
Their sins are atoned for,
Even though the water is salty
They drink it as if it were butter. . .

The ritual purification is effective only if the devotees go to the temple on foot. It sometimes takes several hours to cover the 2 km long stretch, because the devotees get tired out by prostrating themselves repeatedly on the ground. One Hindu penitent, whom I questioned between two prostrations, justified the ordeal by narrating the following story:

> A family in Yamanur was in the habit of starving its bull of food and water on Thursdays. One day, while the owner was taking the bull to the field, the animal escaped. It went to the river, bathed in it and then wen to the Changadev temple. The same thing happened every Thursday, week after week and month after month. At first, the owner was astonished by the animal's behaviour, but then he started following it to the temple with the other members of his family. Later, he made a vow that he would do it regularly. Finally, his devotion was rewarded, and he became a rich man.

We in our turn followed the animal which led us to Yamanur village, which derives its name from the term *yammiganur* 'the place of buffaloes' because this place was originally occupied by cattle. Known earlier as Yammigahatti, it served as a pasture for the large herd of Lingaraja, the *desai* of Saundatti district, who lived in Sirsangi. Alas! His buffaloes became sterile one day, and blood started flowing from their udders instead of milk. Greatly troubled, the *desai* appealed for help to the local saint, Rajabag Savar. And as though by miracle, his buffaloes became normal and started giving milk.

Without disputing the truth of this story, other local commentators claim that the village gets its name from the god of death, Yama, who was defeated here by Markandeya, 'the enemy of death' (*Yamantaka*) and a faithful follower of Shiva.

But let us take a break from mythology and look at some demographic statistics about Yamanur village. Table 5 will give us an idea of its size and its activities.

TABLE 5: THE POPULATION OF YAMANUR (1981-91)

Year	Occupied Houses	Total	Population		SC/ST*	Literate
			Males	Females		
1981	268	1590	829	761	69/28	780
1991	365	1019	1019	961	98/0	922

Year	Workers	Farmers	Farm labourers	Services	Non-workers
1981	790	331	303	156	800
1991	853	390	314	330	1127

Note: *SC: Scheduled Castes; ST: Scheduled Tribes.
Sources: Census 1981 and 1991.

Once we reached the centre of this poor town, we found the temple of this 'god' or 'saint', whom the Muslims call the *sachcha pir* while the Hindus refer to him as *sad guru* (Fig. 7).

We went past the two 'lamp-pillars' (*dipastambha*) standing at the entrance, now electrified, and entered a 100 m long alley leading to the temple. Several wooden stalls stood on both sides of the path. There were few stall-owners present that day (since it was not a feast day), and they greeted the visitors gloomily. Devotees buy from them the articles needed for worship, such as sugar, salt, oil, camphor and incense sticks, and also small empty glass bottles to carry back the holy water. Oleographs of the hero of Yamanur are sold in some of the stalls.

Before entering the temple precincts, we stop at the porch. On the portal, there is a large multicoloured inscription in Kannada that says, 'Rajabag Savar or Changadev Temple'. Above the arch is a brick-lined room with three large windows surmounted by Islamic-style dual arches. Two anthropomorphic sculptures are placed symmetrically on the roof. One of them is a full-face statue of the Yogi Jnanadeva sitting with his legs hanging down and his hands raised in *varada mudra.* The other is a statue in profile of his disciple Changadev sitting astride a tiger. Between these two figures rises a *gopuram.* I am told that repair and painting work was done between 1982 and 1983 thanks to generous donations given jointly by a Muslim, G. Mehaboob Khan and a Hindu, M. Poojari.

After passing through the temple porch, we discover on the right a statue of Brahmadev(a), to which the Hindus offer salt, oil and Bengal gram, while the Muslims prefer to give jaggery. But I am told that even if the offering does not conform to the devotee's religion, the god is not offended. Brahmadev quietens all crying children, whether they are Hindu or Muslim, no matter how he is propitiated. On the left, there are two tombs in Islamic style, which also receive offerings. The Muslims call them *mazar,* but the Hindus prefer the term *samadhi.* They belong to the first priest of the shrine, Kshetroji Rao Burge, and his wife Narasubai. One of his descendants tell me that Narasubai was fortunate to die before her husband and avoid the curse of widowhood and this auspicious area is called Vrindavana. From Narasubai's tomb, which is smaller than her husband's, there rises a *tulasi* (*Ocymum sanctum*) plant, representing the goddess Tulasi Devi, who, according to Vaishnavites, is none other than Lakshmi. The priest tells us how under the name of Vrinda, the

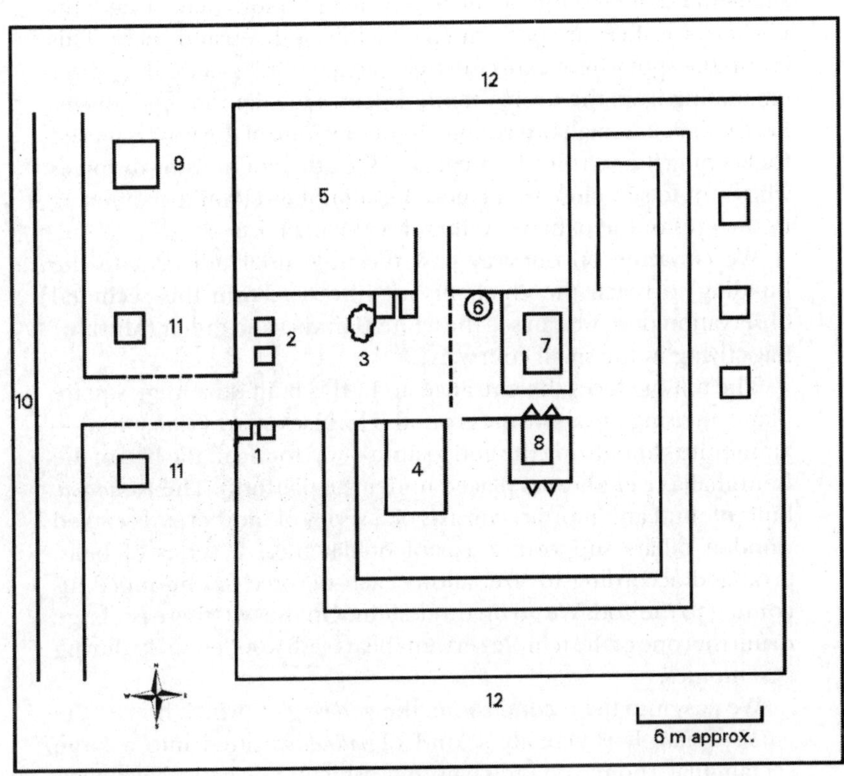

1 Brahmadeva
2 Graves
3 Neem tree
4 Platform
5 Pujari's house
6 Kettledrum
7 Main sanctuary
8 Cradle
9 Trustee meeting room
10 Hubli-Sholapur road
11 Pillar-lamps
12 Surrounding wall

Figure 7: Sketch of the Yamanur shrine

faithful wife changed Vishnu into the *shaligrama* stone for having seduced her, just before throwing herself into the fire like a *sati.* The sacred stone is buried under the temple.

A few metres away is a small stone shrine, which seems even smaller because it stands at the foot of an enormous neem tree. This is where sacrifices are performed—mainly of sheep and cocks. This is also the spot where exorcisms are carried out, because the power emanating from the nearby tombs releases the demons and ghosts. Further left is a small two-roomed building: one of the rooms is used for keeping the sacrificial animals and the other for housing devotees who want to stay close to the god. I shall not dwell on the suffering in the eyes of the patients waiting for the exorcist.

We continue on our way past the little door adjacent to the building to reach the chief servant's house. From this secluded observation post, we can see the white (Hindu) and green (Muslim) flags flying in the small courtyard.

The temple faces the entrance arch. It is built on a huge square platform rising 1 m above the ground. The black stone (*shaligrama*)—ammonite symbolizing the god Vishnu—was found in the bed of the Bennihalla river and was placed under the platform. The *mandapa,* built of mud and mortar, consists of a series of indifferently-carved wooden pillars supporting a roof of flat tiles. A series of bells, arranged according to size, allows each devotee to announce his coming to the god. We go up three steps. On the left, there is a large drum that one of the temple-servants beats with wooden sticks during ceremonies.

We pass into the second room, the *garbha gudi,* which houses the *garbha griha.* It is actually a kind of *mandapa* fitted into a large rectangular room. A gaudy painting, which appears to have been repainted recently, adorns one of the side walls. It has on one side a naïvely portrayed life-sized picture of the 'intellectual' (Gonda 1965: 221) Jnanadeva, dressed all in white and pen in hand, writing the *Jnaneshvari.* On the other side, there is a picture of the 'Great Tantric Yogi' (Vaudeville 1987b: 218) Changadev(a). The name Rajabag Savar is written between brackets in small letters. In keeping with his fierce nature, this *raja* 'rides' (*savara*) a 'tiger' (*bagga*). He uses a snake to whip the tiger, and as a bit he uses a garland of scorpions. His torso is bare, and he wears a white dhoti; he has a beard, and his hair is tied in a bun on the top of his head like and ascetic.

At first sight, this shrine looks like a real junkyard. But on observing closely, you find that the accumulated objects and symbols bear testimony to a well-though-out eclecticism. Gathered together are Muslim and Hindu symbols, both Vaishnavite and Shaivite, placed in a hierarchical order, even though they appear jumbled. Let us make an inventory. Closest to the wall are five big 'hands' (*panjahs*) of silver-plated metal, forming an arch covered by a rich multicoloured cloth, in which red dominates, serving as a canopy for the *mandapa*. These are supposed to have been a gift from Tipu Sultan himself, according to the *Dharwar District Gazetteer* of the Bombay Presidency (1893). In the middle of this installation presides a standing (bronze?) tiger—or perhaps it is a lion, since the Hindus call it Narasimha-Vishnu. A series of silver horses (*duldul*) surround the beast. I counted five big ones, but there were also innumerable small ones surrounding the main idol, though placed at a distance. In front of the tiger-lion are placed the wooden sandals (*khadau/paduka*) of the ascetic Changadev. Small oil-lamps burn on either side, and just behind stand a garlanded *trishula* and a *danda*. I can also see in the dim light copper pots containing water, stone containers holding ashes, and a series of smaller receptacles in wood and metal. Tiny wooden beds are placed lower down, and little parallelipipeds of camphor are burning on trays and incense sticks in holders. The one and only bell-shaped bronze lamp, blackened by soot, is not lit. All this is surrounded by large white and green flags and bamboo sticks covered with cloth, from which emerge peacock feathers. Finally, on the floor there are two fly-whisks used by the priest to bless the devotees. In return, they touch his feet with their hands as a sign of respect, before withdrawing backwards.

Changadev or Rajabag Savar

Several myths explain, or try to explain, this mixed symbolism. One of the stories related by a Muslim pilgrim from Navalgund, says that the divine figure of Yamanur was originally a saint from Gulbarga. The events he talks about took place (according to him) under the reign of Adil Shahi dynasty of Bijapur (1489-1687).

The saint Shah Mirza Abdul Raja Kadiri (of Gulbarga) performed endless miracles. Riding his tiger—which gave him his nickname Rajabag Savar—he decided to visit Khwaja Bandanamaz, who lived in Bijapur. Just as he was about to reach the town, the latter's seven-year-old great-grandson, Nadim Allah, wanting to prove the superiority of his great grandfather's miraculous powers, climbed on top of an old wall and made it move like a horse to welcome the visiting saint astride the tiger.[2]

Disquieted by the power of a small child, which announced the thousand times superior power of his great-grandfather, Kadiri preferred to turn back. But so great was his humiliation that he died of sorrow soon after.

On learning of the cause of the saint's death, Khwaja Bandanamaz cursed the child, who died immediately. After that, the reputation of Rajabag Savar as a master of justice spread far and wide, and he was greatly respected.

Another version relates how Bandanamaz, irritated by his great-grandson's behaviour, cast a glance at the child that made him mortally ill. This story justifies the votive cult that flourishes around the tomb of a child within the confines of Bandanamaz's mausoleum in Gulbarga (Digby 1994: 124).

Other stories from Hindu sources are more explicit and quite detailed, retracing the life history of a Marathi saint linked with the Varakari tradition through his *adi-guru* Jnanadev(a) (1271-93) or Jnaneshwar. A 'series of saints' (*sant*) constituting a specific 'way' (*panth*) attached themselves to this charismatic figure through 'biological descent' (*bindu-parampara* or 'transmission by seed/ semen') rather than spiritual succession (Fig. 8). The Varakaris are an illustrious Vaishnavite tradition (*sampradaya*) of the Deccan, although Vaudeville has drawn attention to their Shaivite background (1987b: 217ff.; 1987c).[3]

These fairly heterodox mystics, Jnanadev, Namadev, Ekanath and Tukaram,[4] lived mainly in Maharashtra and Karnataka between the thirteenth and the fifteenth centuries. They remained faithful to the extremely popular cult of Vithoba in Pandharpur, near Sholapur.[5] The god Vithoba is an incarnation of the divine cowherd Krishna-Gopala, but it is often forgotten that he originated in Karnataka, as is indicated by his earlier name Vitthala (Vaudeville 1987b: 216, 223).

But nothing could have ever brought together one of the incarnations of Vishnu and one of Allah's friends except for the apparent yearning for syncretism of the Maharashtrian priests, willing to tinker with myths to make them accord with the miraculous nature of the shrine. To use such a formula would presuppose that Hinduism and Islam are opposed to each other like two corpora of a hermetically sealed doctrine, whereas at the village level they have constructed themselves through the experience of continuous exchanges down the generations.

Apart from this fusion, these servants claim membership of several traditions, as is seen in the genealogy they invoke (where spiritual

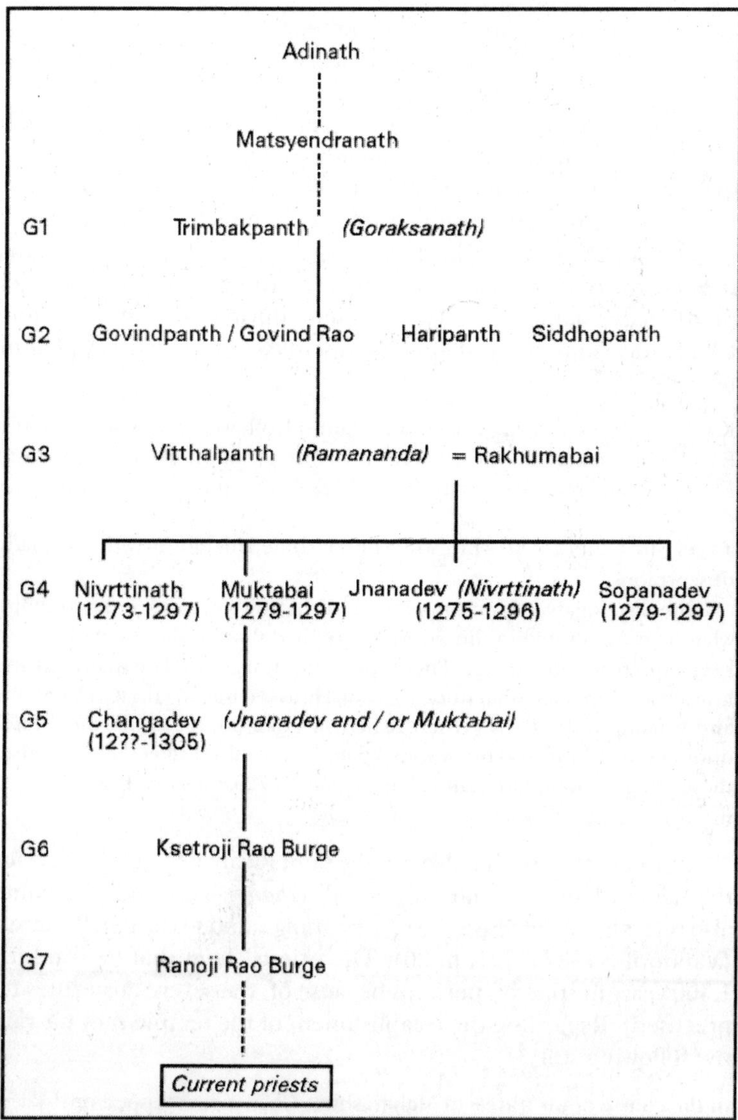

Figure 8: The genealogy of the servants of Yamanur

affiliations are indicated between brackets). Thus the Burge family traces the local cult to the north Indian tantric tradition of the Nath Siddhas, who were followers of Hatha-yoga and *nirguna-bhakti*.[6] At the same time, they link it with medieval Vaishnavism in Maharashtra, according to which the almighty Shiva is the supreme worshipper of the 'spontaneous manifestation' (*svarupa*) of Vithoba/Krishna! It must be noted that there is a genealogical break during the second generation (G2) when the honorific title *pant* is replaced by 'Rao'.

According to the first story, the cult was established by Kshetroji (or Chitroji) Rao Burge, born in Katagaon in the Koregannur taluk of Satara district of Maharashtra. But according to another member of the same family, who was present during our conversation, Changadev himself, and not his disciple, founded the Yamanur temple.

Kshetroji, the head of the village, was a faithful follower of Shah Mirza Abdul Raja Kadiri, hailing from Gulbarga and a disciple of the great Chishti saint Khwaja Gesudaraz Bandanamaz (*d.* 1422). But 'this spiritual king' was popularly known as Rajabag Savar, because he moved about on the back of a tiger with a cobra as his whip, while he controlled his mount with a bit made of scorpions.

One day, Rajabag Savar appeared in Kshetroji's dreams and asked him what he most wanted in the world. He replied that his dearest wish was to keep him by his side for ever. Thereupon, the saint granted his wish by giving him a 'hand' (*panjah*) that stood for him. He asked him to take it to Yamanur and worship it regularly. When Kshetroji woke up, he found the *panjah* under his head and also two wooden batons and a silver tiger. He carried all these things to Yamanur. A little later, around 1720, his son Ranoji financed the construction of a *dargah* in the village.

Although the Hindus also call the saint Rajabag Savar, they prefer the name Changadev, literally 'good' (*chang*) 'god'. But the name also refers to one of Shiva's twelve *jyotirlingas* and to the god Bhairava (Vaudeville 1987a: 221, n. 20). The priests claim that he lived for 1,400 years in spite of, perhaps because of, the severe austerities he practised![7] Regarding the establishment of the temple they narrate the following story:

In the course of his travels in Maharashtra, Changadev stopped one day in the village of Koregaon. There he received hospitality from Kshetroji, who became his disciple. Before leaving south India for the north, where he was to meet his master Jnanadev, Changadev asked Kshetroji to hide an idol of Narasimha in his house and worship it regularly. Kshetroji did so. But it was his son, Ranoji, who migrated to Karnataka in the eighteenth century and built the temple in Yamanur dedicated to Narasimha.

Two other stories, also told by the priests, attribute the establishment of the cult either to Kshetroji or to Changadev himself when passing through Yamanur:

Aware of the progress made by Changadev, Jnanadev ordered him to go and spread his teachings in Karnataka. Accompanied by his favourite disciple, Kshetroji, Changadev arrived in a village surrounded by a thick forest. The village was called Yammahatti. The grass was rich, the land was fertile and thousands of buffaloes grazed on the luscious pastures. Interrupting his meditation, Changadev helped the poorest of the poor, blessed the childless with children, cured the sick and gave advice on how to attain salvation. Even kings asked for his advice. To satisfy his master's wishes, Changadev started travelling again, but he entrusted the task of maintaining the cult in Yamanur to Kshetroji, whose descendants continue the tradition.

The second story highlights the motif of the combat between the *pir* and the *yogi*, which occurs frequently in Sufi hagiography,[8] to justify the gory sacrifices performed in Yamanur.

Changadev got angry when his mother, Muktabai, declared that as compared to his uncle, Jnanadev, his life was vain and empty. He immediately set-off for Alandi, where his uncle lived. It was an impressive sight. He was accompanied by numerous disciples and there was a band at the head of the procession. His devotees cheered him continuously along the way shouting, '*Rajabag Savar, Changadev Maharaj ki jai*!' People could not take their eyes off the saint sitting astride his tiger, which he whipped with a snake and guided with a bit made of scorpions. It is true enough that with his red eyes, the numerous *rudraksha* necklaces around his neck, his unkempt hair, the sandalwood paste gleaming on his forehead, his silver sacred thread and his red-ochre dhoti, Changadev looked like the god of death.

Sitting on an old ruined wall with his brothers and sister, Jnanadev watched Changadev in his frightful trappings. Suddenly, he said, 'By all the power of the all merciful God, I command this wall to move forward.' And the wall started gliding (or flying) towards Changadev! Astounded and full of admiration, Changadev cried, 'I am riding a living creature while he is riding an inanimate object! This man is without question an incarnation of Vishnu.' Changadev got off his mount, which fled into the forest; he threw away the snake and scorpions which, disappeared into an anthill [a Shaivite motif, it should be noted].

With great humility he crouched before Jnanadev, who solemnly said, 'O great Siddha, there is no need to use your power in this manner, Knowledge alone is essential!' Changadev then requested Jnanadev to initiate him. Jnanadev made a sign to indicate that he would accept him, but only on condition he sent away his disciples. But Changadev asked, 'How can I send away these faithful people who have served me for so long?' 'You are mistaken', answered the Master, 'they are not true disciples. Look at them carefully and you will see who is what!' Changadev accepted his conditions, and also promised that he would put his magical powers to proper use in Yamanur, where people were suffering from a thousand troubles. The initiation took place in secret, far away from the village.

The next day, Changadev gathered his disciples together to test their devotion. He asked them to sacrifice their lives for him. He had hardly finished his sentence when he saw them take to their heels. But he cast a spell on them before they disappeared, saying, 'You will be reborn as goats and sheep and you will be sacrificed during my worship in Yamanur!' Only Kshetroji Rao remained, silently prostrated before him.

This wondrous episode, described at length in the brochure printed by the temple (Dixit 1977), was narrated to me by the priests. It illustrates the contradiction between two conceptions of saintliness (and also the source of power, common to both Islam and Hinduism in India). One is peripatetic with an irresistible force, while the other is sedentary, having an immutable power. The former comes to dispute the centrality of the local cult firmly established in the latter's domain (*wilayat*) (Digby 1994: 102). But in this case, it serves mainly to establish the hierarchical relation between the Hindu and Muslim notions of saintliness. To do so, it borrows a number of details from the 'Nectar of Indian Saints' (*Bhaktalilamrit* IV, 137-49), a well-known Marathi work written by Mahipati in 1774 (Abbot 1935: 66-7). But it is known to the masses largely because it was made into a film 'Dnyaneshwar', which has been shown in this region since the 1940s. It is interesting to note that in 1939 the Prabhat Film Company was awarded the Mussolini Cup in the Venice International Film Festival for its film on Tukaram (Edwards 1941: 33ff.).

The Temple Staff

The upkeep of the god/saint needs the services (secondary, no doubt, but necessary) of a number of persons belonging to both religions. There are, for example, musicians from the Bajantri caste who beat the drum during ceremonies. There is also the florist from the Hugar caste, who supplies flowers for the *puja*. They are both

Vaishnavites. As for the sacrificer, he is obviously a Muslim. Also involved are merchants selling sugar (usually Muslims), and salt and empty bottles (to be filled with holy water) (mostly Hindus). They are not really temple servants. They are required to officiate during religious ceremonies only occasionally, unlike the other temple employees, such as musicians, singers, astrologers, exorcists, herbalists and fortune-tellers.

Hindu Servants

The temple, which depends on a Charitable Trust in Belgaum, is the property of the Burge extended family. Its members still earn most of their income by performing religious services. Although they belong to the Maratha caste, they claim to be Suryavamshis.

The five members of the Board of Trustees, which manages both the day-to-day and also the extraordinary affairs of the temple, are selected from among the oldest members of the family. These Trustees also manage the 6 acres of cultivated land donated to the temple (*inam*) and organize the grand annual festival which costs about Rs. 15,000.

Because the family has grown over the years—it has forty members at present—they have adopted a system of rotation of responsibilities, taking into account the total number of members. If, for example, the line of Vishwanath Rao Burge, reduced to a single family today, officiates for only two weeks in a year, the lines of V.B. Burge, consisting of five families, and A.B. Burge, also having five families, serve the temple for three months in the year. In each case, the family performs its weekly duties continuously. It is to be noted that this job, entrusted exclusively to Hindus, always starts on Wednesday at nightfall, which accords with the Islamic division of time.

Actually, fifty-five servants (*pujari*), all aged over eighteen, perform the rites one after another. Though about forty of them have been to school, there is only one university graduate, and nine are illiterate. The fact that five servants are bachelors is quite unusual by Hindu standards, according to which a servant who serves God must be married.

There are two main services in the temple-one at eight in the morning and the other at eight in the evening. Early in the morning, the Hindu priest installs and purifies the feline representation of the god by applying *vibhuti.* Everyday white rice is offered to the divinity, and on Thursdays it is mixed with barley in the form of a paste called *ambli*. During the rituals, the servant gives the devotees water and food in exchange of money (*kanikā*). The older priests wear a *dhoti* while performing rituals, but the younger ones wear trousers or a *pajama*.

Muslim Servants

There are three types of servants among the Muslims, but it is difficult to make an exact count because their number varies a great deal depending on the occasion. Out of a contingent of some hundred *pirs* claiming direct descent from the saint, only ten or so live permanently in the temple. There are also five fakirs and some mullahs living in nearby towns and villages in Dharwad district, such as Hirekumbi, Navalgund, Hubli, Savanur, Lakmeshvar, Hulageri and Anigeri.

The two main 'sons of the saint' (*pirzade*), claiming hereditary rights on the temple, live in the neighbouring town of Navalgund. They come daily to Yamanur to do service. Their duty is to stand at the entrance of the shrine and bless the devotees with the ritual fly-whisk of peacock feathers for a modest return. They also go singing in the nearby towns and villages to collect alms from their followers.

The fakirs, who are sometimes called the 'poor in God' (*fuqara'*), are in the habit of coming to the temple every day—even though they do not enjoy any special rights—to ask for alms. The visitors, however, are obliged to give them something as charity (*zakat*). In fact, the fakirs remind them of their duty, as they bless them by waving the ritual fly-whisk vigorously over their heads. The devotees hope that through this contact they will absorb a part of their saintliness and thus strengthen their link with the saint.

The mullahs living in Yamanur come to the shrine everyday without fail. It is true that while the *pujari* performs the *puja*, one of them recites prayers from the Koran. They are the ones who sacrifice the sheep and the fowl under the huge neem tree growing in front of the temple. Once the sacrifice is over, the devotees cook the meat with rice, which they distribute no only among the *pirzade*, mullahs and fakirs, but also the Hindu *pujaris*. What is even more remarkable is that this is done only after the god himself has received his share of what is called *naivedya*. (Among the Hindus, this term refers exclusively to vegetarian food offered to the deity and then returned to the devotees as a 'favour' [*prasada*].)

During the annual temple festivals, the family members of these three types of officiants take part in the organization and preparations and help the police to maintain order.

On special occasions, the *pujaris*, as well as the Muslim officiants, sit near the entrance covered with black woollen blankets to wait for their regular visitors. They greet them, guide them to the shrine and generally take care of them, and in return for this service they ask for money, which is paid after much discussion.

RITUALS

It is impossible to give a complete list of the reasons that draw devotees to Yamanur. Most people come to get themselves treated for physical, mental and other afflictions. As for families, they generally come to ensure the success of marriage negotiations. This explains the presence of a large number of Helavas, a community of genealogists, who normally act as intermediaries between the families of marriageable young men and women. Newly married couples come to the temple to ask for a (male) child. And finally, the promise of success in their profession or business explains the presence of a large number of unmarried young men, as also the rumour that there are many *jogati* prostitutes around the shrine.[9]

In keeping with the rulers of the Vaishnava cult, Mondays and Thursdays are considered auspicious for Changadev.

After covering the distance between the river and the temple, we hurry towards its entrance. When there is a large crowd of visitors, there is a double line, with women on the right and men on the left, according to the Muslim custom. Otherwise, everybody enters the shrine, and what is very striking is that there is no caste discrimination of any kind. As we wait for the ceremony to start, we listen to one of the many songs that are repeated continuously. There is a slight variation in the words of the refrain depending on whether it is a *bhajan*, sung by a chorus of devotees or the *qawwali*, sung by one man accompanied by a group of instrumentalists:

> Come pray to the pir and sing in the *dargah* [Muslim version]
> Come pray to the *deva* and sing in the *gudi* [Hindu version]
> A saint was born in Sundarapur,
> His name is Changadev/Rajabag,
> He came to Yamanur,
> He is wise, he is famous,
> He is a Siddha,

He practises *yoga,*
He flies in the air,
He controls the wind,
He enters the bodies of those who worship him,
Come pray to the *pir/deva* and sing in the *dargah/gudi* . . .

We join the queue of devotees. It moves slowly, but we can already see the servant in the distance swinging the sacred lamp and bunches of incense sticks. He gives each visitor a pinch of *vibhuti* after having consecrated them. Each person also receives in his cupped palm a spoonful of water from the *tirtha,* which is swallowed immediately in the Hindu manner. A major portion of the sugar offered to the deity is given to the devotees as *prasada,* and the rest is stored and shared with others within the premises of the temple. The priest lightly taps the top of the head and the shoulders of the devotees with a fly-whisk and the ceremony is over. When the ceremony ends, the priest waits for his *dakshina.* Some of the devotees carefully place some lemons on the altar, which they will collect later. It is believed that the lemons will absorb a part of the saint's protective power while they are there.

Finally, we go through the stock of garish prints depicting the deity and buy some printed booklets narrating the life of the saint before leaving the shrine.

Offerings of food, both raw and cooked, are received in the temple; but the main offering is unrefined sugar (jaggery), which seems to be equated with the granting of wishes. It is believed that offering 1 kg of jaggery or, in the case of the more affluent, an amount equal to one's own weight, will bring about favourable changes in one's destiny. Red roses are also added to the offerings, and incense or camphor is burnt. Special sweet dishes (*madali*) made of wheat flour (*huggi* and *kadabu*) are also offered to the deity. Gifts in kind and in silver are not rare, and the little silver horses called *duldul* are offered in large numbers during the *ʿurs* celebrations.

Although the chief servants are Hindu, no coconuts are broken in this shrine. It is said hat a Virashaiva *swamiji* once did so to the great displeasure of the Maratha servants, and roused his ire. From the Muslim point of view, this peculiarity is a proof that the shrine belonged exclusively to their community in the olden days. But on the other hand, the priests perform *homa* by burning wood, camphor and incense before the god. And when a cow or a buffalo calves, the first day's milk is offered to the temple. This offering is called *misalu,* and is usually repeated during the following months. A more characteristic ritual is the 'tying of the thread' (*lodi katuvadu*). The *lodi* is a red-coloured thread of twisted cotton that is knotted round a horizontal metal rod placed at a height of above 5 ft in front of the shrine. The thread is tied when making a wish. Once the wish is fulfilled, the devotee comes back to the temple laden with offerings to untie the *lodi.* Though it is a Muslim practice, it is also followed by Hindus.

A shepherd of Yagaval village in Bijapur district complained that he did not have a son. He came to Yamanur to confide his sorrows to the temple priest. The latter tied a thread (*lodi*) and asked him to become a devotee of Changadev. The same year, the shepherd had a son, whom he named Yamanurappa. To express his gratitude he offered the god sugar equal in weight to his son. After lighting the ceremonial lamp, he also asked him to see to it that his son was properly educated. In fact, some years later, the boy obtained a B.A. degree and became an officer in Belgaum district and later in Bangalore.

Some Hindus prefer to tie a thread similar to the *lodi* around the wrist, and they call it *raja-bandhan.* But the *Muharram* celebration is considered to be such an auspicious time for tying the thread in the sanctuary that Hindus too tie the *lodi.* On the other hand, Muslims tie another *lodi* around the wrist during the eleven days of *Muharram,* and this practice earns them the temporary title of fakir.

The servants also put around their devotees' wrists metal bangles, which are made and sold by them. They are supposed to have not only prophylactic but also curative powers. They are specially recommended for curing skin diseases. If a cure is effected, they are returned to the temple. And listening to the following story about their effectiveness, it is easy to understand why they are so similar to the metal bangles (*kara*) worn by the Sikhs:

After suffering from severe pain in the throat, the ruler of Anegundi, near Hampi, discovered to his great horror that he had leprosy. Doctors rushed to his bedside with various cures. The king cleansed himself ceaselessly in the Tungabhadra river. But nothing seemed to cure him. He noticed one day that his trusted aide Ramsingh wore a silver bangle round his wrist. The latter explained to him that he suffered from diabetes, and he had gone to Yamanur to bathe in its river. He then paid his respects to Changadev and the servants gave him the bracelet and asked him to come back to Yamanur for five Thursdays without a break and keep a fast every time. On hearing this story, the king immediately set-off for Yamanur with his family and followed his aide's example. He was soon cured of his leprosy, and his body was restored to its former healthy state. To express his gratitude to Changadev, he fed all those who were present and donated a piece of land (*inam*) to the temple. Even today, the Burges go to Anegundi every year to collect the income from this land.

All these practices are accompanied by penance, especially in the form of *danda-namaskar* where the devotee prostrates himself at regular intervals during a procession or while performing circumambulations. The *danda* is held in the right hand and he draws an arc with it when he is lying flat on his stomach to drive away to demons. As for *danda-raki*, it involves rolling continuously on the ground around the temple while holding the baton aloft and to the accompaniment of songs.

Come swing the holy lamp before Changadev/Rajabag,
The god/saint born in Sundarapur came to Yamanur,
Riding on a tiger,
With a snake for a whip,
And scorpions for a bit,
He is a miracle-worker,
His life is endless,
He is a god/saint among gods/saints,
For such a man, come swing the lamp before Changadev/Rajabag. . . .

Apart from these rituals, there are animal sacrifices. A place is set aside within the temple premises for slaughtering fowl, sheep and goats, although this is officially forbidden. Of course, non-vegetarian devotees have no compunction about sacrificing animals; but even vegetarians offer an animal to the deity. But before it is slaughtered they feed it a wheat or millet cake. It is the mullah's job to perform the sacrifice while reciting prayers. Oddly enough, he chops off the victim's head in the Hindu manner instead of slitting its throat and allowing it to bleed on the ground. Undoubtedly, this is because the temple *pujaris* are Marathas. In the Hindu caste hierarchy, the ritual practices followed by the Marathas are those that are the closest to Muslim rituals, and Wink believes that this relationship can be compared to the one that obtained between the Mughals and the Rajputs (1993: 22).

Some of the devotees are possessed. In such cases it is possible to watch an exorcism taking place near the neem tree. In most cases, a Muslim expert (*ghādi*) performs the exorcism. He takes charge of the possessed person and talks to him in order to force the demon to reveal its name. The latter grumbles and refuses to obey the exorcist. To overcome the demon's obstinacy, the exorcist strikes the possessed person, more violently each time, with his fly-whisk made of peacock feathers. A few twigs of the neem tree are tied to the ritual instrument to force the demon, ghost or evil spirit to leave its victim. If this method fails, the exorcist forces the possessed person to swallow handfuls of ash or holy water. And if nothing works, he has to resort to physical force to bring the evil spirit under control and neutralize it.

The Annual Festival

The main festival starts on the third day after the full moon of *Phalguna* (February/March). Farmers are free at this time of the year. The celebrations last for three days, and resemble a fair. According to official estimates about fifty to a hundred thousand people visit Yamanur on this occasion.

Once again, the celebrations are preceded by a purificatory bath in the Benihalla river. The first day, which the Muslims call *farz* meaning 'divine order' or 'duty', is spent in preparing special dishes such as *madali, rotte* and *papad* in honour of the god/saint. Although there is no special ceremony on this day, the priests are agreed on its importance, since everybody makes a solemn wish for the coming year.

The second day is generally known as *sandal ratri.* The holy idol is covered with a paste prepared by the priests by mixing perfumed sandalwood powder with holy water. The Hindus call this rite *gandhabhisheka,* or 'consecration with sandal paste'. The Muslims look on this festival as an *ᶜurs,* even though none of the tombs is covered with sandal paste, as is the normal practice in *dargahs.* It is also an occasion for preparing special dishes like *ambli, madali, savagi* and *rotte,* which are offered to the god/saint, shared among the devotees and then distributed to the numerous beggars sitting near the temple.

On the same day, the idol and also Changadev's wooden sandals are carried in a palanquin to the Benihalla river. They are all bathed in the river waters by the Maratha *pujaris* in a ceremony called *devaru holege hoguvadu.* While the Hindus consider the feline figure as Narasimha, the Muslims believe it to be the saint's tiger.

On their way back to the temple, the *pujari* take turns in carrying the idol in their arms. They are followed by two servants, one carrying a white umbrella and the other a fan. Others carry metal receptacles of water from the river for the saint's ablutions at 3 o'clock in the afternoon. Before the procession reaches the temple, the devotees lie down on the ground close to one another over a distance of several hundred metres, so that the garlanded priests have to walk across a carpet of human bodies.

The third day commemorates Changadev's birth. The Hindus call it *rangapanchami* or 'festival of colours' which corresponds to the Spring festival of *Holi.* The Muslims, on the other hand, use the Kannada-Urdu term *Dodda ʿUrs* or 'Grand Marriage', which means that they are celebrating the anniversary of the death of Rajabag Savar. However one looks at it, many fowl and sheep are sacrificed during the day. A Muslim confided that in the old days the *pujaris* of the Burge family were in the habit of pricking a finger to offer five drops of their blood to the saint. But the Burges deny that such a practice ever existed, adding that the blood spilled during the animal sacrifices is more than enough.

As the day advances, the religious ceremony gradually tuns into a commercial fair. In fact, on this day donkeys are worshipped and covered with brightly coloured cloth. The fair therefore looks more like an animal fair. It is true that the animals are of a fine quality. 'After all', say the Kannadigas, 'don't people come from Maharashtra to buy healthy donkeys from Karnataka?'

Some More Rituals

The god's followers try as far as possible to celebrate the rites of passage in the shrine's vicinity. Anybody going through these ceremonies, mostly related to fertility and prosperity, will absorb a part of the power (*baraka*) emanating from this 'king of ascetics' (*rajasamnyasin*), as he is sometimes called.

At the end of the three to thirteen days seclusion, also marked by a ceremony performed at home when a girl menstruates for the first time, she is solemnly accompanied by the women of her family to the Changadev temple. The pubescent girl wears a new green sari, and in keeping with a practice that is becoming common in India, she will come there later to get married. Because they earn some money from such ceremonies, the servants are happy to celebrate them in the temple precincts; but this does not mean, they claim, that they do not hold marriages of poor people in the temple.

For pregnant women, a visit to Yamanur (always with their mothers or mothers-in-law) means that the foetus will grow well and that they will have a normal delivery. When it comes to choosing a name for the baby, usually on the thirteenth or fifteenth day after its birth, it is usually named Yamanaruppa if it is a girl and Yamanappa if it is a boy, so that it will have a good life. Childless couples offer tiny cradles to the god so that he will bless them with a child. There are ceremonies to put young boys under the saint's protection: either the tonsure ceremony in which the grandfather or the maternal uncle cuts the child's hair with a pair of scissors to which betel leaves are tied, or the sacred thread ceremony. The priests are quite happy to perform all these rites as they earn some money in return. Of course, all these ceremonies end with a sumptuous feast at which some of the poor are fed as well as some singers and musicians.

Come swing the sacred lamp in Yamanur,
He is a great god/saint among all gods/saints,
For the well-being of the largest number,
For the good health of the largest number,
For the prosperity of the largest number,
For the wisdom of the largest number,
Come swing the sacred lamp in Yamanur . . .

Eclectic Cults in the Neighbourhood

There are no less than six temples dedicated to Rajabag Savar in North Karnataka and four in Maharashtra, where he is commonly known as Changadev. One source of the diffusion is Vaishnavite having its origin in Sundarapur, but even more in the holy towns of Pandharpur and Alandi. The other is Muslim, within present-day Karnataka, starting from Gulbarga–Bijapur and extending up to Raichur district. And though these two zones taken together constitute a vast religious territory, all these places of worship (except Sundarapur, which lies on the border of Madhya Pradesh) of varying sizes are independent of one another and do not come under the control or supervision of any particular shrine.

Though we are not sure if our list is exhaustive, here are the shrines situated in Karnataka (Map 6). In Ramadurga taluk of Belgaum district there are two temples of Rajabag Savar. The one in Ramadurga belongs to a member of the Burge family, and is said to be regularly visited by the local royal family. Then there is a Yamanurappa temple in Doddamagadi Halli, on the banks of the

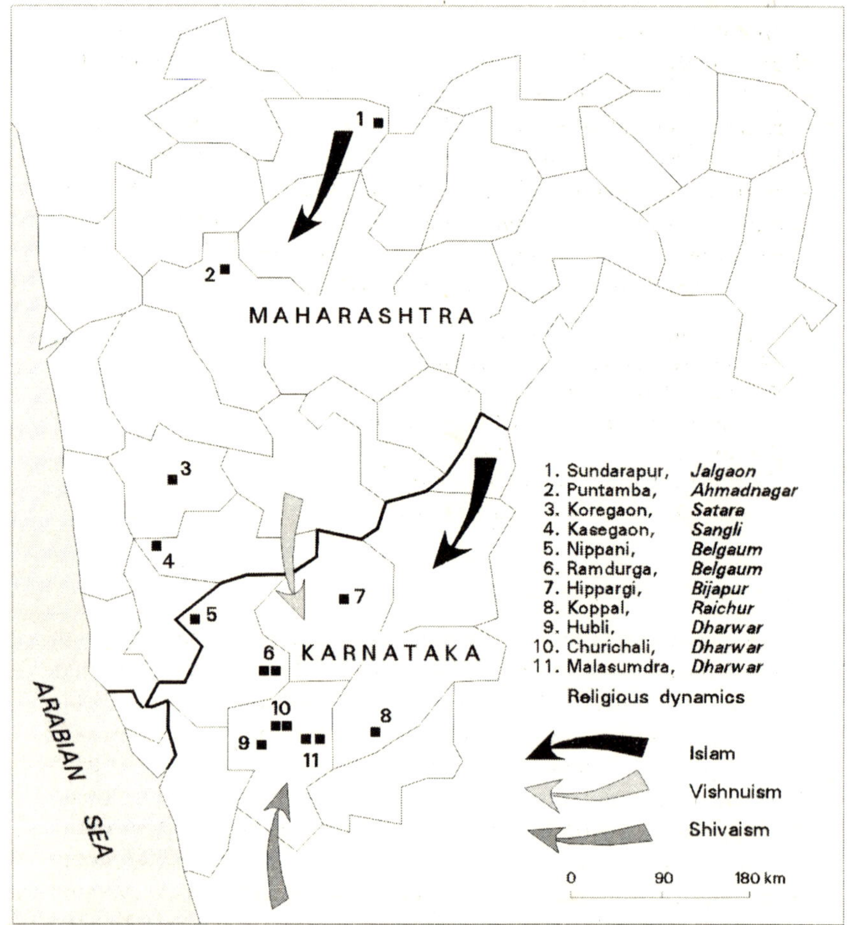

Map 6: Spread of the Changadev/Rajabag Savar cult and relevant local religious dynamics

Malaprabha river. The Maratha priest of the latter temple explains that one of his ancestors was making an offering in the Yamanur temple when a small silver horse suddenly appeared in the little packet of sugar. It was a sign that the god wanted him to build a temple in his birthplace.

The shrines of Chinchali and Malasumdra in Gadag taluk have servants of the Markandar caste. And in Dharwad district, the Navalgund and Hubli temples, especially the latter, mainly frequented by Pattegars and Muslims, were set up by a Maratha disciple of the Yamanur temple. Even more interesting than the Koppal temple in Raichur district and the Nippani temple in he district bearing the same name is the Hipparagi temple in the heart of Bijapur district, built right next to the tomb of Basava (nna), founder of the Lingayat-Virashaiva sect.

As for Maharashtra, we will just give a simple list: Koregaon (Satara district), Katagaon (Sangli district), where Kshetroji was born, Puntamba (Ahmadnagar district) and finally, Sundarapur, situated far to the north in Jalgaon district, where Changadev was born. There is, however, one important observation: Changadev's birthplace in Khandesh is one of the principal hubs of Indian Sufism, centred around the towns of Khuldabad-Burhanpur (Ernst 1993) and the Faruqi dynasty, and constituting a boundary in space and time between the Muslims and the Marathas.

But, it is said, there is also a second reason. As a matter of fact, there are shrines in Karnataka where similar eclectic cults are practised that have nothing to do with either Changadev or Rajabag Savar.[10] In many cases the (relative) integration of Muslims was the work of another sectarian tradition (*sampradaya*), i.e. the Shaivaites. For example, the Virashaiva monastery (*matha*) in Bankapur near Sirsangi town is famous for its two 'exorcists', one of whom, Shivalingappa, was a Lingayat and the other, Fakirappa, was a Muslim renowned for imprisoning a thousand demons; the *Dharwad Gazetteer* (1884) was already describing their use of the techniques they shared in common for driving out demons. There is also the Savalgi shrine near the river Ghataprabha in the Gokak taluk of Belgaum district, about which the following story is told:

At the end of the sixteenth century, when political power was in the hands of the Muslims, the famous saint Khwaja Gesudaraz Bandanamaz kept hearing about the monastic Virashaiva community of Savalageri. Unable to resist any more, he invited its *jagadguru*, Shivalingeshvar, to visit him in Gulbarga. The latter refused. On hearing this, Bandanamaz was angry, and sent soldiers to fetch him. But the Muslim squad was miraculously decimated at the feet of the Virashaiva saint.

Thereupon, Bandanamaz decided to visit Shivalingeshvar, and mounted his tiger. Sensing the saint's intentions from a distance, the Swami sat on the top of a wall that started floating in the air. Terrified by this feat, Bandanamaz decided to become Shivalingeshvar's disciple and, in memory of this episode, Bandanamaz had a huge monastery built in honour of the Hindu saint.[11]

This story, which transposes a theme peculiar to fakirs (Rifa'is?) to the figure of a swami, explains why the two saints are simultaneously worshipped in Savalgi, and why this Shaivaite shrine is partly built in Muslim style. It also justifies the regular change of dress by the 'pontiff' of the monastery, because his followers belong to both communities. It is however interesting to note that most of the time he wears saffron robes, and green only occasionally. And even though the priests and disciples are chosen from among the Virashaiva and Muslim communities, there are more from the former.

What is even more remarkable is that the saint of the Shirakatti monastery, about 19 km from Gadag in Dharwad district, is called fakir Swami. Here too there is a story justifying this practice.

During the rule of the Adil Shahi sultans of Bijapur between the sixteenth and seventeenth centuries, both Hindus and Muslims worshipped the Wali Khalji Aurinuddin because of his miraculous powers. One day a woman of the Virashaiva sect prostrated herself before the saint and placed her dead baby at his feet. Then she left the child and went away, saying she did not have the means to feed her other children who were at home. Thanks to his miraculous powers, the saint brought the baby back to life and made him a fakir. But since the child was born a Virashaiva, he sent him to a monastery of that sect, after assuring its *jagadguru* that the boy was under his protection, and continued to supervise his education from a distance.

After the saint's death, the child saw him appear alive again in a dream. The saint ordered him to go to Shirakatti and use his power to help all those who needed it, irrespective of their religion. The very next day, the child set-off for Shirakatti. When he reached there, he was installed as the *jagadguru*. The miracles he performed were quite spectacular. He was said to be capable of catching snakes, especially cobras, which he wore as garlands around his neck. He could also eat fire and make rain, not to mention his powers as an exorcist. Soon Hindus and Muslims from the surrounding areas came to him for help, and the following and reputation of his monastery grew tremendously.

It is said that Hindus as well as Muslims are eligible to become the 'pontiffs' of this monastery. This is illustrated by the following story, told by a woman dedicated to the goddess Yellamma of Saundatti, a modern version of the temple-dancers of yore locally known as *jogamma*:

The great swami of Shirakatti, who always moved about on an elephant, came across a blind child on the road. The child was of tribal origin; the 'pontiff' sensed immediately that he possessed extraordinary gifts. So he decided then and there to name him his successor as the head of the monastery. As a matter of fact, the child later showed exceptional spiritual qualities.

I have not visited this place, but there are many extraordinary stories about it going around. It is said that the tombs in the monastery are magnificent and the building is made of precious materials. You can always see elephants, camels and horses in the courtyard, and so on. The institution possesses large tracts of fertile land that enable it to spend enormous amounts of money on distributing food everyday. This form of charity is commonly known as *dasoha* in Virashaiva monasteries, while the Muslims call it *langar*. But in both cases, the devotees receive the food as a 'divine favour' (*prasada*). There is a rumour that anybody going there can perform Hindu and/or Muslim rites, and that Muslim priests participate side by side with Virashaiva priests during the installation of the new 'pontiff'. It must however be noted that the office of the swami (of this seemingly utopian monastery), who is supposed to possess miraculous powers, has been held so far only by men of the Lingayat-Virashaiva sect!

Then there is Sharif Saheb or Sharif Yogi, also called the 'Kabir of Karnataka'. He was said to follow the example of the apostle of Hindu-Muslim unity, who sang in his poems the praises of both Vishnu and Allah (in *Kabir sahab ka bijak* [*sabda 10*]) associating Rama (the god) with Nama (the name).

For the Hindus and the Turks, there is only one way
That the master of truth has shown.
Says Kabir, 'Listen O Saints,
What does it matter whether one calls him 'Ram' or 'Khuda' [=Allah]?'[12]

Sharif Saheb lived in the village of Shishuvinal in the Shigganev taluk of Dharwad district. Information about him was given to me by one of his disciples in Belgaum. The saint was born in 1819 in a Muslim family. When he was very young, his father, Imam Saheb, put him under the protection of Hajaresh Khadirlinga of Hulgur, a Muslim saint belonging to a very low caste (the Pinjari or cotton-carders) who received the blessings of the god Muneshwar of Navalgund. The child was also initiated by Sri Sadguru Govind Bhateru, a well-known Brahmin of Kalasa village in Shigganev taluk situated near Shishuvinal, who had set up his seat in Sarosa. An oleograph shows him sporting a beard cut in the Muslim style and draped in a long green shawl.

The influence of the Virashaiva doctrine on him made him an important saint in the region. His followers were Hindus, Muslims, and also Virashaivas, although this last group were the most numerous. He distinguished himself as a leader during the 1857 Mutiny, and was sentenced to death by the British in Belgaum in the following year. This information is of a dubious nature, and seems to combine two historical events of the time. The first was a conspiracy planned in 1857, the year of the Mutiny, by a Wahhabi *munshi*, who was the aide-de-camp of a British officer. He appealed to Indian soldiers to rise against their British masters, and was executed with his companions by a firing squad in Belgaum. The second event relates to a Brahmin chief of Nargund, who also advocated revolt in 1857 after beheading the British Political Agent, Manson. (He displayed the head as a trophy on the gate of the Nargund fort.) A man hunt was ordered, and when he was caught, he was paraded through the streets of Dharwad before being taken to the gallows (*Gazetteer of the Bombay Presidency*, *Belgaum*, 1884: 411-12).

The monastery of Sharif Saheb, whose entrance arch is built in the Muslim style and whose tower is adorned with the statue of a saint meditating in a purely yogic style, is known for its deliberately eclectic cult. The devotees burn bunches of incense sticks in the shrine as they recite verses from the Koran. The religious service consists of giving alms and looking after the poor, particularly by feeding them, and the terms *dasoha* and *langar* are used indiscriminately to describe this practice. The priests, who are Sharif Saheb's descendants, worship in the Hindu manner by braking coconuts, which is forbidden in Yamanur. This shows that when one of the two communities is in control of an institution claiming to be syncretic, it assimilates some of the rituals of the other community without endangering its own identity. As a matter of fact, the Shishuvinal monastery is administered by a Trust Committee with a majority of Hindu members.

Inspired by this mixture of *bhakti* and Sufism, seen quite frequently in India, many inhabitants of Hirekumbi village proudly proclaim that saints like Sharif Saheb of Shishuvinal, Nagalinga Swami of Navalgund, Madiwaleshwar of Gadag and the Swami of Hubli met frequently to discuss religious and philosophical matters. If such an assembly did exist, it is heartening to note that instead of barricading themselves in with their dogmas and looking at each other as 'the other side', Hindus and Muslims in this small area invented a tradition that survives independently of the normative models that orthodox elements on both sides yearn for.

Despite this interpenetration of Hinduism and Islam and their mystic traditions—*bhakti* and Sufism—as also the overlapping of various sects like the Shaivites and Virashaivas and 'paths'—the Natha and Tantra, Kapalika and Kalamukha, and even Sikhism—there is no confusion. Nor can those belonging to these syncretic sects be accused of crass ignorance. It is true that the founders of most of these sects were illiterate. This is also true of many of the Vaishnavite saints in Maharashtra like Gundam Raul, Eknath and Chokha Mela in the days gone by or more recent ones such as Gadge Maharaj (or *Gadge Baba* [1876-1956]) who espoused unorthodox ideas (Zelliot 1987). Lack of learning may be a sign that the person has been specially chosen by God. In the Islamic tradition, some saints, like the Prophet himself, were illiterate men (*ummi*) who learnt directly from God without the screen of human learning. We cannot ignore either the ability of these 'little' masters to create an original world by combining multiple references. This mixture of radicalism and eclecticism often indicates a genuine search for the Absolute, an Absolute conceived as a single God by some marginal mystics, who do not find satisfaction in the 'great' codified religions. And that is exactly the reason why they tried to go beyond these 'great' religions[13] by evolving a new tradition transformed into an anti-hierarchical sectarian movement. Most of the time, this message was expressed metaphorically, promising access to salvation to one and all. This is quite common in India, where there is a proliferation of recognized parallel 'ways'. After all, if the Islamic God has ninety-nine names that do not refer to divinities, the thirty-three million three hundred and thirty-three gods of India may well be the multiple names of a single God.

But what is most remarkable about Yamanur is that it represents not just a convergence between Hinduism and Islam or a special brand of mysticism concocted by an inspired being. It is essentially a regional cult based on this idea. The figure of the Absolute is firmly grafted on to the worship of a god/saint or a guru/fakir by both Hindus and Muslims. It is a dual personality, but ambiguous enough for the followers of both religions to identify with it without any confusion whatsoever. We may wager that it is the indeterminate quality of the motifs, values and practices of popular religion and its pragmatic and segmental approach that is behind this hybrid pattern of worship that ultimately has nothing syncretistic about it.

Power, Conflict and Symbolization

What conclusion can one draw from these mixed cults except that some 'popular' forms of Hinduism and Islam do not in any way resemble our notions of religion and culture, at least on a purely ideological level? Consequently, the anthropologist has to pretend that he does not know what they really are, so that he can observe how they are practised in everyday life. It is only then that he can portray the groups as they present themselves and understand society's ongoing discourse with itself by studying, for example, some of the symbolic patterns that form a coherent system. This is visible in Yamanur in the architecture of the buildings, the layout of the shrines and altars, the exploitation of emblems, the management of recitations and rituals, inter-community exchanges and the mutual collaboration or exclusion of the actors involved. When all these elements are added together, it becomes evident that tradition can never be monolithic or static.

What are the other lessons? What the sociologist calls 'acculturation' is term that raises real problems and actually denotes a graded set of exchanges and interactions that the actors indulge in according to their own conception of Islam and Hinduism. We must understand the different types of practices within the experience that sometimes bring together words and things that are by their very nature incompatible: saint/god, fakir/*yogi*, prayers/rituals, monotheism/polytheism, egalitarianism/hierarchy, etc. Their relationship ultimately depends not only on local systems of communication but also on exchange networks and ties, where one group dominates another, that, taken together, determine the pattern of collaboration and sharing between the two communities.

If one community borrows and assimilates certain cultural traits from the other, or refuses to do so, it is because they are always re-interpreted in relation to a background that gives them a definite meaning. This amounts to saying that adjustments do not always fit in with the intentions declared at the outset, and the attempts of some to impose undisputed norms on everybody always meet with a refusal by the others to comply with them. As a matter of fact, these makeshift collaborations often retain traces of unexpressed rivalry. But it is for this very reason that these accommodations prove to be paradigmatic: first, because the actors interpret the rites and recitation equivocally, associating distinct contents with shared symbols; and second, because they were already renewing the terms of their alliance in its early stages by negotiating compromises. In brief, they devise strategies suited to the balance of power, as they have done through the ages. Have they not learnt for almost a thousand years to live together by symbolizing the relations between them? They have done so by adapting the needs for independence of the individual, the family, the lineage, the caste or the community to the constraints imposed by social cohesion and the need to restructure their traditions in order to face up to changes in their environment.

Unfortunately, it is becoming more and more difficult to live together in this manner. The rise of neo traditionalism and fundamentalism, followed by economic and political pressures from the outside, is increasingly reducing the possibility of living together in the same environment. The more traditionalist or the more politicized actors refuse to continue with the old patterns of collaboration, thereby constricting the definition of identity and, consequently, also that of alterity. This chauvinism is likely, sooner or later, to wreck the understanding between the two communities, which is already quite tenuous everywhere. To come back to Yamanur, the hybrid nature of its divine figure and its composite symbolism are in peril. In other words, all integrated acculturation is fragile.

In fact, some mullahs have ordered their followers to stay away from joint worship. Similarly, Maratha priests, made more aware of their Hindu identity by Hinduist propaganda, are likely to treat their former associates[14] as 'outsiders'. It is also very important to guard oneself against a deceptive retrospective oecumenism, because the divine authority common to the two communities assumes sufficiently equivocal forms not to have ever existed in a socially neutral environment not affected by time.

There is no doubt that the sacredness of a saint, as proclaimed by the servants of both religions, is supposed to transcend religious affiliation and communal identity. However, from the viewpoint of the devotees who crowd the shrine, this is saying either too little or too much. The Hindus look on the divinity as Changadev, an *avatāra* of Vishnu, who is a key figure in their pantheon. For the Muslims, he is the 'friend of God', Rajabag Savar, an Islamic saint who intercedes with God and is the local repository of the *baraka* of the One and Only (Allah) as revealed by his Prophet, Muhammad Paighambar, as he is known here. This is another way of saying that this mixed cult is not syncretistic, nor is it a survival[15] of the good old days. Inquiries in Yamanur support the idea that, despite all the evidences of a so-called 'syncretistic' culture, the unassailable principle (though it is disputed in India) of a hierarchy of values, practices and groups generates fault lines that the two communities embodied in symbols from the very beginning. And they were right to do so, because a lot of money is at stake, in the form of substantial incomes from the shrine and its properties. This explains the Trustees' eagerness to control the shrine and the cult.

In fact, I have not mentioned so far that about 200 m from the main temple in Yamanur there is another one, more recent and also more modest, also dedicated to Narasimha. But the servants in this smaller temple are all Muslims of the Markandar caste, like those in Chinchali in Dharwad district. To justify this monopoly, without however answering why they worship a Hindu god, they relate two vague stories. One of them is about a saint named Tejoddin who was killed by his own disciples, and the other is about Shah Mirza Abdul Raja Kadiri, who came from Gulbarga riding on a tiger. According to them, after the fall of the Adil Shahi dynasty of Bijapur, whose territories were annexed by Aurangzeb in 1686—at the time of the Maratha uprising against the Mughals—the Hindus seized the big temple of Yamanur, which until then had belonged to the Muslims.

It should be noted that these dates correspond to the date of the temple's foundation given by the Hindus, at least if we ignore the historically unfounded Hindu claim that the temple's origin goes back to the thirteenth century, i.e. to Changadev, who was the immediate disciple of Jnanadev, whose historical existence and date are established. According to the Muslims, the usurpation of the shrine by the Hindus in the seventeenth century caused a Muslim revolt that was unsuccessful. This forced them to build a temple of their own in the vicinity of the older temple. The fact that only two descendants of the *pir* now living in Navalgund (their names are mentioned in the list of priests) still retain their hereditary rights in the main shrine lends some plausibility to this interpretation. In any case, though historical documentation is practically non-existent, there are certain indications that the monopoly of services in the Yamanur temple has been the subject of periodic disputes between Hindus and Muslims,[16] which would explain the eclectic nature of the cult. However, it still seems more plausible to recognize in this symbolic cultic pattern an evident acculturation corresponding to the present balance of power between Hindus and Muslims, rather than an accumulation of layer upon layer of culture coming down from the past. Is it surprising after all that some whirlpools should be seen at the confluence of two rivers?

Let us present the little that is known about the Hindu-Muslim rivalry in the past in this region.[17]

In 1784, the Muslims of Mulgund submitted a petition to the court in Saundatti claiming a right to the property of the shrine in Yamanur. The Burges counterattacked, and managed to prove that the temple had been in their hands from the distant past(?). The court decided in favour of the Burges, though the exact reasons for its judgement are not mentioned anywhere.

It may be surmised that this decision was the result of the rapid succession of political authorities in the region at that time. As a matter of fact, in 1778 Haidar Ali handed over the administration of Navalgund district to a 'chief' of the Lingayat caste in exchange for a tribute to be paid as acknowledgement of his supremacy. Between 1795 and 1800, Dhondopant Gokhale, a petty Maratha raja, seized the towns of Navalgund and Gadag. He in turn was dethroned by Ram Rao, a member of the Peshwa family, with the help of British troops commanded by General Munro (*Bombay State Gazetteer*, 1893). It may be remembered that the British were keen on maintaining the *status quo ante* in religious matters, and that is perhaps the reason why the Muslims did not succeed in establishing their claim to the shrine.

In 1826, there was a dispute between Hindus and Muslims about the recognition of the official servants of Yamanur. The two parties approached the *mamuledar* (head of taxes) of Navalgund, the aforementioned Ram Rao. After verification of the recorded decrees by the *patel* named Chanappagowda, and then by the *kulkarni* (chief accountant), named Virappa, who was a native of Yamanur, it was decreed that the temple belonged to the Maratha Burges.

Thirty years ago the Muslims tried once again, this time through their local committee (*jama'at*), to get official recognition of their duties as servants in the Yamanur temple. But once again they met with failure. This did not prevent the less resigned among them from promising themselves that they would try again very soon. But the prospects of success are bleak, as is indicated by a recent judgement in a similar case involving a religious complex dedicated to a popular regional goddess, which we shall deal with in the next chapter.

NOTES

1. In addition to the repeated assertion in his poetry that there is no difference between Rama and Rahman, Kabir freely likens Hari to Hazrat, Krishna to Karim, Kalima to Karama, Muhammad to Mahadeva and Rama to Rahim. The *Allah-Upanishad*, a strange scripture, defies classification, was the result of efforts of Sufis and *advaitavadin* to bring together the two religions. Guru Nanak (1469-1538) merged the *advaita* stream of Brahmanism with Islam. The *Adi-Granth*, the holy book of the Sikhs compiled by Arjun Dev, includes some Hindi poems by Namadeva (1270-1350), the second saint-poet of the Varakari sect (Gonda 1965: 221). And secondly, Akbar (1542-1605) who, in the name of transcendent unity between Islam and India, promulgated in 1582 a syncretic creed called the *Din-i ilahi* (the Divine Religion).
2. Taking note of the frequent association between the saint and the tiger, Eaton (1994: 219, 305) presents a hypothesis (in the case of Bengal) about the connection between Islamization and deforestation. Like the monks in medieval Europe, the pioneer pirs were at the forefront of the movement of clearing forests to make way for the new agricultural civilization. When the frontier was pushed back, the forest peoples also came under the influence of Islam, which had triumphed over their native religion (symbolized by the saint riding the tiger). In a more general manner, van Bruinessen shows the historical depth and the geographical spread of the theme of 'equestrian miracles' in Islam, Hinduism and Buddhism (1991). But the best article on this subject is by Digby, according to whom anecdotes on this theme in Sufi hagiography in India were preceded by those of the Indian Siddhas. He also points to the influence of the Nath Yogis (1994: 103).
3. Though Vaudeville insists that Jnanadev himself is the author of one of the two treatises 'written from a Shaiva point of view, the Atmanubhava and the Changadeva-prasasti' (1987a: 218), Zelliot writes, 'The synthesis

of Shaivism and Vaishnavism is the hallmark of Maharashtrian Hinduism' (1988: xxii). As a matter of curiosity, it is interesting to note that the Portuguese translation of the *Jnaneshvari* was started in 1550. It is one of the oldest translations in a modern language (Halbass 1988: 37).

4. On Maharashtrian Vaishnava saints, Gonda (1965: Chapter VIII) and also the survey by van Skyhawk (1990), although it focuses on the figure of Ekanath whose message was profoundly influenced by Islam, as has been shown by Zelliot (1982) and Wagle (1983; 1991). For the difficulties caused by the use of the terms *sant, panth, parampara* and *sampradaya,* see Gold (1987: 16ff.; 85 ff.).
5. A good description of the pilgrimage to Vithoba's shrine in Pandharpur is to be found in Deleury's monograph (1960), but it is also worth reading Karve's (1962) and Mokashi's (1990) evocative descriptions, if only in the name of 'participant observation'. For a study of the pilgrimage site of Pandharpur refer to Vaudeville (1974a).
6. According to the Marathi tradition, the Nath *parampara* is quite distinct from the Nath Siddhas. But Vaudeville writes, 'The Nath hail from the north, but their propaganda must have reached northern Maharashtra well before the onslaught of the Muslim invaders, and their prestige, at least with the low-caste masses, seems to have been considerable' (1987a: 32). And Alam (1989: 30) recalls that the Nath Yogis proclaimed that Prophet Muhammad was a disciple of Gorakhnath, who taught him *yoga.* Many of the Naths believed that Gorakhnath visited Arabia under the name of Baba Ratan Hajji. But there is no literature in English on the history of the Naths in Maharashtra, even though they occupy such an important place as the 'nine Naths' (*nau-Nath*).
7. The most complete biography, or rather hagiography, of Changadev—written with a short *e* as pronounced in Marathi—the language of the *pujaris*—is to be found in Mahipati's *Bhaktalilamrit* (II-X, 20176). It is possible to learn a lot from Edwards' commentaries (1941: 39ff., 62, 107), but one must be cautious. A song heard in Yamanur recalls some episodes from his life:

   A god/saint born in Pandharpur came to Yamanur,
   He learnt the four Vedas and the six Shastras,
   And all there is to know,
   He went to Kashi to study *yoga,*
   And he came back a *yogi* and *siddha,*
   He was initiated by Jnanadev,
   He wandered in fifty-six countries [of India],
   He offered the *Shaligram* to his disciples,
   He lives in Yamanur.

8. This motif is a favourite topic of Sufi hagiography (Digby 1970; 1994). In addition to the similarities observed frequently between the *bhakti* cult and Sufism, Lawrence assumes that the biographies of Hindu saints borrowed a great deal from the Islamic hagiography tradition (*malfuzat*) (1987: 371). On the contrary, Wagle shows that the two syncretic figures are reminiscent of Shaikh Muhammad and Shah Muni who lived in the eighteenth century and moulded their teachings on Puranic lines (1991: 56-63).
9. For a detailed account of the *jogati* or *jogamma*, devotees of the goddess Yellamma in Saundatti, some of whom engage in prostitution, Assayag 1992.
10. Our inventory does not claim to be exhaustive. For example, in Thinthini village in Gulbarga district, Hindus and Muslims worship a man born in the sixteenth century in Devargonale in Shohrapur taluk. The former call him Monappaiah, and the latter Moneshwarababa. And in the shrine, built in Muslim style, there is a similar mixture of religious emblems (*India Today*, 15 March 1994: 24).
11. Among the tombs in the *dargah* of Khwaja Gesudaraz Bandanamaz in Gulbarga, there is a tomb of a Virashaiva saint named Gurusiddeshwar Swami.
12. Verse quoted by Vaudeville (1987a: 33)
13. Gold (1987) shows that the tradition of *sants* in north India, having its origins in both 'Indic' and 'Islamic' environments, whose teachings glorify a Lord who transcends the orthodoxy of the 'great' religions, emerged when Islamic rule was imposed. As regards the Deccan, van Skyhawk (1993) has shown that the confluence of religious traditions such as Vaishnava-bhakti, Lingayat-bhakti and Sufism is manifested mainly in the figure of Mrityunjaya/Muraja Kadri. But he also refers to Ahmad Shah Wali, the ninth Bahmani Sultan of Bidar (1422-35), a disciple of Nuruddin Muhammad Ni'matullah bin Abdallah Kirmani (1330-1413) and the first shaikh of the Ni'matullahi *silsila*, whose syncretism can be compared to that of Akbar. And if a *jangam* (Lingayat) is associated with the service in the dargah of Ahmad Shah Wali in Bidar, it is because the Lingayats worship him as 'Allama Prabhu' (ibid.: 208).
14. It may be recalled that Muslims entered Maharashtra in 1296, and they ruled the area uninterruptedly from the fourteenth to the end of the eighteenth century. On the way in which Hindus and Muslims of Maharashtra saw themselves in medieval times, refer to the *Hindu-Turka samvad*, or 'The Dialogue between a Hindu and a Turk' by Ekanath, a Varkari from the Mahar caste (1533-99), whose teacher, Janardan Swami, helped him attain spiritual realization by invoking the god Dattatreya, who appeared before him as a fakir (Zelliot 1988: 97). Wagle has translated some extracts from this dialogue that elucidate this

theological controversy by underlining the tensions between the two communities in the sixteenth century (1991). The same historian has earlier presented extracts of a lawsuit between Hindus and Muslims in the eighteenth century (1983); see also van Skyhawk (1993).

15. The concept of 'survival', which has obsessed us for a long time, has turned anthropology into archaeology. It is necessary to go into every historical detail in order to invest it with a meaning, to exhume layers of sediment to reach the origin, which continues to recede further into the past as the work advances. Each observed fact becomes a particular manifestation behind which hides another, more original, one which should really be recognized, however, as the product of a theoretical imagination.
16. It is impossible to know since when Hindus and Muslims have been worshipping jointly in this shrine, albeit as two communities having distinct religious identities. The fact that there are few records prevents us from knowing if there were either 'religious' or 'communal' conflicts in the past. This distinction is important because the latter made an appearance (according to Bayly 1985) only when social and economic groups started looking beyond religious symbols and considering themselves as 'communities' whose interests were defined primarily in political and economic terms.
17. This historical information has been obtained from the *Bombay Gazetteers* of 1884 and 1893 and from Desai (1993).

5

Cult: The Goddess and the Saint

> A society is academic when it judges others,
> a society is barbaric when it is being judged.
>
> BAUDELAIRE, *Exposition universelle* (1855)

During an earlier study of the temple of a goddess in Karnataka, I had questioned a few Muslims who had close links with the servants, officiants, visitors and goddess in that particular shrine. And I found that their answers served to enrich and further complicate my general conception of Hinduism and Islam, or at least the idea I had got by observing Hindus and Muslims as separate groups. Not only did the off-centre viewpoint of this minority group help me discover certain aspects of the working of the temple, intentionally glossed over by the dominant group, it also threw light on the relationship of mutual attraction and repulsion between Hindus and Muslims.[1] Although the Muslims say that they belong to the community of believers, their Hinduization is quite evident, though it expresses itself at a low pitch. There is nothing surprising about this acculturation unless one limits oneself to a refined textual or explicitly reformist model of Islam, one that, furthermore, has become aggressive of late. In fact, such acculturation is quite common in India, where Sufi Islam has generally been assimilative.

Admittedly, in a Hinduized environment like that of the temple, the results of such an investigation are bound to be full of holes. The Muslims, being in a minority, evidently cannot claim to play an important role or contribute to its history in a significant manner, at least in the eyes of those who are legitimately in power. This observation is supported by the evolution of contemporary Indian society. Confrontations between different religious communities are on the increase, and are becoming more serious. With more and more people inclined to flaunt their identity, these communities tend to give up their old alliances, their day-to-day cooperation, their habit of borrowing each other's customs and practices, and their tendency to merge—in short the whole process of acculturation that enabled them to live together until the establishment of the British colonial regime. Then a public space was created that fostered ostentatious and competitive expressions of collective identities, representation, and a growing politicization brought groups into confrontation with each other. From then on, belonging to a particular faith mattered more than affiliation, communal boundaries became more important than solidarity, and symbols of loyalty counted more than the spirit of mutual assistance. And even though it was only for a while, the defence of particularistic interests took precedence over other kinds of sociability. Historians have observed that this phenomenon appeared in the first half of the nineteenth century and became intensified after the 1850s (Freitag 1990; Pandey 1990). Under the leadership of militant organizations whose objects were initially political, these communities endowed with all the virtues of a pristine orthodoxy began to make efforts to eliminate, in the name of a religious purity, these complex forms of acculturation, and as often as not the result was much the same thing: the Hindus fantasized about their Aryanness and the Muslims dreamt about a return to Mughal supremacy or even to the ideal community of Medina in the Prophet's time.

The present case embodies a type of acculturation that is simultaneously 'integrated' and 'dissociative', if we may borrow the categories proposed by Devereux (1975). The Muslims in this shrine recently saw themselves being deprived of the prerogatives they had exercised in the temple not so long ago. So, if the earlier shared worship recalls the labile nature of Hinduism before it became what Romila Thapar (1985) calls 'syndicate *moksha*', it also corroborates the vitality and specifically of Indian Islam (especially in its south Indian version), which may be defined as a process of mutual stimulation of two religions that are opposed theoretically, but whose practices suggest that no predetermined teleology was involved in the creation of their shared traditions.

The Centrality of Hinduism and the Off-Centre Position of Muslims

About 8 km from Saundatti and about 40 km from Belgaum there is a temple of Yellama-Renuka, a Hindu goddess with a large following.[2] Like the temples of other Indian goddesses, the temple of Yellama—called 'Yellama of the seven valleys' (*Elu kollada Yellama*)—

too is located on a hill. The idol is installed in an oblong natural cave, about 8 m long, called 'Yellama's Grotto' (Yellama *dongara*). All the rituals and celebrations related to this 'Universal Mother' (*Ella Amma*) are held in a crater on the mountainside. The story goes that on watching a king dallying with the ladies of his harem, Renuka's sexual feelings were aroused. But her husband, the ascetic Jamadagni, repudiated her and cursed her with leprosy. He sent her away to the forest and asked their son Parashurama to behead her.

On full-moon days and every Tuesday and Friday, days considered auspicious, tens of thousands of devotees, including groups of Muslims, make the pilgrimage to Saundatti. Individuals, couples, families and caste groups come here to get their wishes fulfilled and their sicknesses cured. They often attribute their life's misfortunes to Yellamma's vengeful anger and her 'terrible power' or *shakti*. So their fate depends on the appeasement on her ire. But in Saundatti, a benevolent Yellamma dispenses kindness and represents not evil, but its redress.

This oval-shaped crater, considered to be the world's navel, is a sacred space holding some seventy shrines, some quite large and others tiny. The focus of attraction, of course, is the Yellamma temple. Two shrines, however, lie outside this area: the small temple of her husband Jamadagni and the mausoleum of a Muslim saint named Bar Shah.

The small Jamadagni temple, housing a black stone idol of the god seated in a 'lotus pose', stands alone a few hundred metres to the north-east of the complex. Jamadagni is separated from his wife by a small river, which is dry except in the rainy season. The off-centre position of this temple, standing in solitary splendour atop Kailasha Parvata and overlooking the other shrines in the complex, has a symbolic significance. Naming this hill after the snow-covered Himalayan peak particularly sacred to the Hindus makes Jamadagni an *avatara* of the great Shiva. The remote and elevated position of Yellamma's chaste husband symbolizes the values of renunciation and asceticism embodied by this god. These values may be peripheral in our world, but they constitute, nonetheless, the very basis of the *bhakti* tradition. The devotees point out a significant detail—even though Jamadagni's right ear is turned towards his wife, from the metaphorically Himalayan peak on which he is perched he cannot hear the noise made by the pilgrims below as they perform their rites and rituals. The latter are only interested in satisfying their earthly desires and the acquisition of worldly goods.

The Saint

If you walk about 800 m away from this shrine, you reach the southern end of the rocky ellipse. Exactly opposite Jamadagni's temple, and therefore to the south of the main site, there is a small Muslim shrine of the Sunni, Bar Shah. Situated quite some distance from the Yellama temple, this complex too overlooks the outer edge of the hollow. But there is another reason for its isolation. Since it is Islamic, the building is considered to be relatively impure by Hindus of the upper and middle castes. Obviously, this explanation is not acceptable to the Muslims. They claim that the building stands on this isolated spot because the saint was in the habit of meditating there for forty days. This deliberate solitude, particularly congenial for prayer, is often interpreted as asceticism, synonymous with the 'internal fire' that Muslims here commonly call *tapas*, a word associated with Hindu sages. Thanks to the heat produced by this internal fire, the saint acquires miraculous powers (*karamat*) comparable to those attained by Siddhas through the practice of *yoga*.

The sketch given below will enable the reader to locate the various buildings and important spots within and outside the elliptical crater of Saundatti (Fig. 9).

Although it is often called a *dargah*, the complex is more in the nature of a *khanqah* or shelter for pilgrims, surrounded by houses, prayer and meeting halls, the founders' tomb and a kitchen. It does not really contain the saint's tomb, but only his cenotaph (*asthna*), a whitewashed parallelepiped covered with a green cloth (*galif* or *chadar*). It is only recently that they have started using a green cloth, because earlier it was covered with a brightly coloured brocade. The seven tombs (*mazar*) within the boundary, which the Muslims themselves often call *samadhi*, a term used in the case of Hindu *yogis*, belong to persons of the 'saint's lineage'. The saint, being celibate, did not have any descendants; but he transmitted his spiritual authority or *wilayat* to a disciple, Shah Madar. Thanks to this successor, it was possible to maintain the chain of initiation that links the present officiants to the founder.

Shah Madar, who is also considered as a 'guide' (*murshid*), had

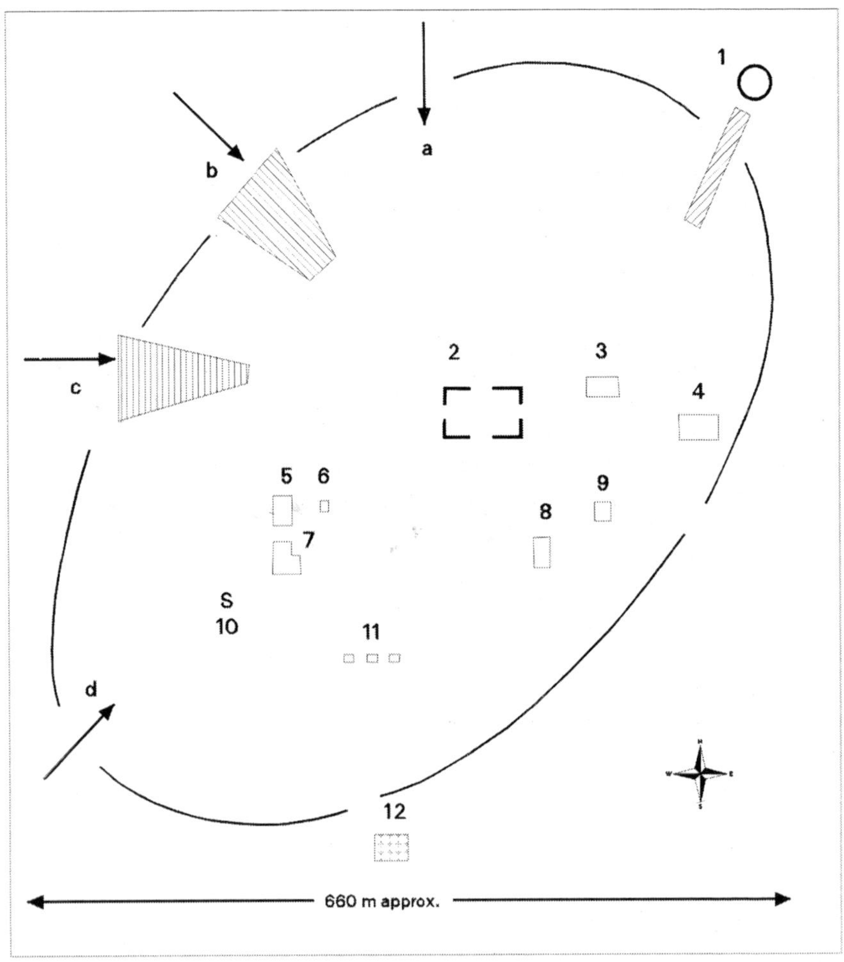

Hindu Sanctuaries: 1 - Jamadagni, 2 - Yellemma, 3 - Kailabhairava,
4 - Matangi, 5 - Parashurama, 6 - Karevva and 'garden', 7 - Revenasiddha,
8 - Ganapati, 9 - Mallikarjuna, 10 - Parashurama.
Ponds, 11 - Yennigonda. a, d: entrance c, d: stairs
Muslim sanctuaries, 12 - *Dargah* of Bar-Shah-Wali.

Figure 9: Sketch showing the location of religious sites in Saundatti

three children, Bavar Shah, Madar Shah[3] and Jangli Shah, who are the ancestors of the present officiants. The religious services in the shrine are now performed by these three families, each in charge for a year following the *palu* system of rotation like the one followed by temple *pujaris*. The officiants attached to the *dargah* are called *pirzade*, sons of the *pir*. However, many Muslims, who visit both the temple and the *dargah* are in the habit of referring to them as *pujaris*, a term normally reserved for Hindu servants. Though the *pirzade* do not perform daily rituals, they burn sandalwood paste before the saint everyday, and some 'disciples' attend the ceremony.

These families, who claim to be of the Sayyid caste, belong to the higher class of *ashraf* (nobles), i.e. real or imaginary descendants of Arab, Turkish of Afghan immigrants. They live in the same village as the officiants, and the servants of the Yellamma temple. The village is situated about 5 km from the temple, because, it is said, nobody can lead a peaceful marital life in its vicinity. Apart from the income provided by the *dargah* through offerings (*nazar*), payment for talismans (*maduli*) and magic threads (*lodi*) given as 'gifts' (*ta'widh*) these Muslims earn their living by selling sweets in the Saundatti complex. They also earn something extra by performing religious services during ceremonies held in people's homes. Their followers never fail to invite them for tonsure, circumcision, marriage and other ceremonies. They are then known as *mujawar*. With five other Muslim 'leaders' from Saundatti town, they take part in the organization and the management of funds belonging to the 'association', presided over by the principal *pirzada*, who assumes for this purpose the title of 'secular administrator of a religious institution' (*mutawali*). These funds pay for the expenditure incurred for festivals, for example payment in cash and kind for the spectacular services performed by the Rifa'i fakirs described in Chapter 3.

Apart from the four buildings for pilgrims, there is a small temple (*gudi*) dedicated to the saint next to his cenotaph. A green flag flutters over the flat-roofed building, open towards the east. Though the architectural style and construction are similar to those of Hindu village temples, there is no idol inside, in accordance with Islamic teachings. However, you can see inside, under a canopy (*chhatri*), the saint's meditation seat (*simhasana*), on which are placed his wooden sandals (*khadau*/*paduka*), the symbol of Hindu royal ascetic (*rajasamnyasin*). It is interesting to note that Sanskrit words are used to denote the objects mentioned above. You can also see 'hands' (*panjah*) with jasmine garlands around them, tiny metal votive horses (*duldul*), the saint's green standard (*jhanda*) and the peacock feather fly-whisk (*morchal*) and a small bench used by the servants. There are in addition ritual utensils, the saint's (magic) staff (*danda*), his rosary with 100(0) beads (*tesbeh*), a receptacle (*chakar*) holding sweets and another full of burning charcoal, whose smoke mingles with that emanating from the incense sticks, a chest for donations (*golakh*) and, last but not least, a copy of the Koran.

At right angles to the shrine, there is a modest covered platform, which some believe is a small masjid where the devotees can pray, although there is no *mihrab*.

The saint's full name is Khwajah Bar Shah Wali, which is usually shortened to Bar Shah. Khwajah, is a title which means 'master' and implies respect, and the honorific Shah, which means 'sultan' or 'king'. The word *wali*, meaning 'one who is close to Allah', is commonly used to designate Muslim saints not only in India but also in other countries. Often the term *pir* meaning 'old man', is used, as is also the title Shaikh meaning 'very old', given to those of Arab lineage.

As regards his actual name, I was given two different explanations.

In Urdu and Persian, the word *bar* means 'greatness' or 'dignity' and by extension 'god'. But it can also be translated as 'giving and audience' when it refers to a 'king in a sitting position presiding over his court', a metaphor with a mystical (Sufi) resonance comparing the throne to a prayer rug. Others said that his name is derived from the Urdu word *bajr*, which means 'heavy' or 'unyielding', but also 'thunder' and 'thunderbolt'. In Kannada, which is spoken by the majority of the population in this area, the saint is often designated by the metonym *bhidu gali* meaning 'staff of tempest', 'thunder' or 'storm' referring to the *danda* in the shrine, which, as we know, is the attribute of the Sufi mendicant. And if some insist on the terrible character conferred on him by this name, with its warlike connotations, others—because of its proximity to the Urdu word *bharan* meaning 'torrential rain'—stress its fearsome aspects, but tone these down somewhat by association with the beneficial qualities generally associated with water in India.

According to the second explanation, in Kannada *bar*(*a*) means 'twelve' or 'twelfth', which is undoubtedly a reference to the Shia figure of the twelfth (hidden) *imam*, Mahdi ᶜAl Muntazar, the 'Awaited'. It may be remembered that the powerful Adil Shahi dynasty, which ruled over the north-western part of the Deccan from its capital Bijapur from 1489 to 1686, belonged to the Shia sect. In his fascinating history of the Bijapur kingdom, Eaton has highlighted the efforts made by this powerful line of nine sultans—patrons of the Muslim saint Hazrat Bandanamaz as well as the Hindu goddess Sarasvati—to bring together court poets, scholars and Sufis in the royal court. The latter preferred to use the local vernacular to spread there message tinged with mysticism in the entire Deccan area (Eaton 1978: Chapters 8 and 9). We must mention in particular that in Hirekumbi, about 15 km from the Saundatti temple, there is another tomb of Bara Imam, the Twelfth Imam. This village is dominated by the Shaikh and Sayyid castes. This is believed to be the oldest tomb, and is part of a Muslim complex dedicated to the saint Makhdum Husaini, which is considered to be more important in this area.

If you go about 300 m to the east, you reach the *dargah* of Bara Imam. It is a curious spot, not because the religious complex is perched on a hill overlooking the village, but because, beside the shrine of Bara Imam, there is an enormous pile of stones representing the tomb of the tiger who served the saint during his lifetime. This huge pile of stones, about 15 m long and 5 m high, heaped around a fruit tree (*gidda bari*) whose leaves are supposed to have medicinal qualities, grows bigger as devotees place more stones (one or five) on it when their wishes are granted. In front of this tomb, there is a trough built into the rocky ground in which the devotees place offerings of sweets and meat for the animal. When the saint meditated in a cave in the hillside just above his present tomb, the tiger stood guard over him, protecting him from external dangers. (This story reminds us of the lion guarding Husain's body after he was buried in Karbala.)

Actually, these references to Shi'ism do not hold significance for the devotees, who are mostly Sunnis. Nevertheless, the fact that Bara Imam was assassinated, and especially the story about a nocturnal message attributed to his glorious neighbour, are quite suggestive.

> One night, in a dream, Makhdum Husaini asked Bara Imam, 'Where have you been buried?' And Bara Imam replied, 'Get up early tomorrow morning and stand with your face towards the sun and throw a lemon in its direction. You will find my body at the spot where the lemon falls. There you will dig my grave.'
>
> 'But what shall I call it?' asked Makhdum Husaini.

'My real name is different, but here you may call me Bara Imam.'

Apart from stressing the saint's need to hide even as he manifests himself by making his sepulchre visible, this short story explains the profound nature of saintliness: the *Pir* is 'living even as he is dead'. We repeat that many hagiographies relate how saints go to Paradise with their eyes open after a long journey involving spiritual attainment and ascetic practice. And they continue to live thus in the place where they are buried, always helping those who worship them, just as they did when they lived on this earth.

Having heard this story, let us now return to Saundatti to meet Bar Shah, who also received a message in a dream:

Bar Shah's father, head of a *madrasa* in Mecca, took charge of his religious instruction. While he was still very young, some miracles and other revealing signs were noticed by the people around him. He was such a precocious child that he mastered in no time the teachings of the Chishtiyyas and Qadiriyyas and already had four disciples (*muridin*), who refused to leave his side. To perfect his knowledge, he went to Baghdad, where he met the saint Mahbub-i Subhani. Then he went to Ajmer in Rajasthan to learn at the feet of the great Indian saint Mu'inuddin Chishti. During a dream, the latter ordered him to go south, first to Gulbarga to saint Bandanamaz and then to Parasgad, the ancient name of Saundatti.

His four disciples, who had faithfully followed him, also became venerated saints and settled down in an area of 35 km on the banks of the Malaprabha. The first, Jangli Bar Shah, settled in Nagudi village in Ramdurga district; the second, Lakdak Diwan Shah, made his home in Toragal in the same district; the third, Dilawar Gori, chose Yakkundi village. As for the fourth, his name is not known and no one knows where he settled! The power of these saints was such that they all 'made disciples' (*piri muridin*).

If one believes this short biography related by the principal *pirzada*, who is without a doubt the only repository of the saint's story, Bar Shah Wali was born in the seventh century of the Hegira and must have reached Saundatti some time in the fourteenth century, which would be just before the installation of Yellama. This claim is justified by the following legend:

While Bar Shah was practising his forty-day meditation (*chilla*) on the site, every morning he found, to his great surprise, that his house had been carefully cleaned and all the household chores done miraculously without his noticing it. Twelve years passed in this manner.

Finally, to express his thanks to the devoted servant whom he had never seen, he threw his staff (*danda*) of 'thunder' about 200 m downhill. At the spot where it fell, there appeared the temple of his servant deified as Yellamma, and it became an important place of pilgrimage.

It matters little that in other versions of the story it is the goddess herself who asks the saint for a place to stay, and the staff is replaced by a lemon. What is important is that this story speaks of Muslim efforts to lower the status of the great goddess to that of a servant. This is done according to a pattern peculiar to Hindu mythology, which merges two divinities in one figure. Here we have Yellamma and her great younger sister or servant Matangi, a goddess who is both secondary and important and whose temple is just behind that of her mistress in Saundatti. Mistress and servant figure in many popular tales. They are distinct but inseparable, and always on different planes. This is the source of iconographic distinctions mainly marked by attributes. It makes it possible for one deity, duplicated in a servant, to be worshipped by followers belonging to different classes. In Saundatti, untouchables of the Madiga caste (tanners and peasants) worship Matangi, who is ignored by the Banajiga-Lingayats (traders and landowners), even though both castes are agreed about the supremacy of Yellamma.

There is nothing similar among the Muslims. Unlike the Hindus, the segregation of sexes is of the utmost importance for them even during ritual but caste discrimination plays no role in the worship of the local guardian saint. Regular visits are made to such shrines, called *ziyarat*, with the sole aim of asking the saint to grant wishes. But this does not prevent the same devotees going to a particular Hindu shrine for the same reason. We have seen in Chapter 4 how devotees of both religions rub shoulders at worship.

Hindus, generally from the lower castes, readily visit Muslim shrines, where they break coconuts, burn incense, offer flowers and clothes and give money. For example, the saris given by these devotees are used to cover the poles of the *panjahs* when they are taken out in procession during *Muharram*. Just as the Muslims 'describe a circle' (*hajj*) around the *dargah*, Hindus too make a *pradakshina* of the shrine. While the former go right inside the *dargah* to touch the saint's tomb, the latter only go there to have a *darshana* at the figure they treat as a god. But whether it is just by looking or by direct touch, the result is the same. They both absorb a part of the extraordinary charisma. All rituals performed in the *dargah*, irrespective of the devotee's identity, are meant to mobilize to the highest degree the 'power' of the one who 'carried the burden of rendering the transcendent Allah relevant and accessible to the needs of everyday life and the common man', as Gellner has written with reference to the Atlas (1969: 8). This is what brings Islamic monotheism closer to Hindu polytheism, even though the divinities worshipped by the latter are conceived of as incarnations of the great gods, while the sacredness of the *wali* is proportional to his nearness to Allah, who has chosen him to bring man closer to him.

As for the servant, he is always present in Muslim stories, especially in the hagiographies of saints, but usually a tiger accompanies the saint everywhere. The animal, which devotes itself entirely to its master's service, performs all the household tasks and protects him from danger when he is absorbed in meditation. The wild beast, changed into a tame animal by the saint's aura, embodies the ideal servant and guardian. So too in the *bhakti* tradition the demon defeated by the divinity after a terrible battle becomes a most devoted servant (Shulman 1984). The heroine of this battle is the terrible goddess, and popular iconography depicts her as riding a tiger or a lion as she strikes down her demon enemies. This vehicle is common to the goddess—the 'Tiger Mother' Huligamma, who represents the terrible aspect of Yellamma-Renuka in the Hospet region—and the Muslim saint—not only Bar Shah but also the Yogi Rajabag Savar of Yamanur.

Here is an episode concerning Bar Shah:

> The saint had left Gulbarga and was walking towards the south. When he reached the banks of the Malaprabha, the river that supplies water to the 'holy oil' pond of the goddess Yellamma, her waters started swelling almost to the point of becoming a flood. A crocodile took advantage of the situation to attack the tiger. As he watched the fight in which the tiger was getting the worst, Bar Shah threw his magic staff at the crocodile, which was forced to flee. Bar Shah then climbed on his tiger's back and continued on his way. He arrived in Saundatti astride his tiger, dressed all in white, his long beard set off by his green turban.

Festivals and Rituals in the Dargah

There are very few visitors to Bar Shah's memorial, as very few rituals are performed in his shrine except on the anniversary of his death on the second Thursday of the Islamic month of *Jamadi'l Awaal.* The celebration last for about forty-eight hours. On the first day (which for Muslims begins after sunset) the devotees pray. It is only on the second day that the main ceremony, called *sandal ratri*, takes place, when the devotees apply sandalwood paste to the saint's tomb before covering it with several sheets of brocaded cloth and a thick layer of flowers. The water used for washing the tomb, sandalwood powder and flowers, especially roses, are later sold to devotees as a 'present from the saint'. The proceeds of the sale go to the *pirzade.* The devotees drink this water to absorb the saint's *baraka*, guaranteed by the constant presence of his spirit and his body in this place.

At the time of *Baratha Hunnime*, one of the major Hindu festivals, celebrated in Saundatti on the full moon day of the Hindu month of *Magha* (January/February), during the Muslim feast of *ʿId ul-adha* and also during the 'new moons' of *Jyestha* (May/June) and *Asvina* (September/October), a large number of rams and cocks are sacrificed. These sacrifices are called *bali* by the low-caste Hindus, and also by the Muslims who join in the celebrations. The Marathas, the Kshatriyas of Maharashtra, whose sacrificial practices are very similar to those of the Muslims, as we have already pointed out, are present in large numbers. They behead the sacrificial beast with one stroke of the knife, without reciting any prayers. That is why they perform their sacrifices at some distance from the *dargah* before offering them to the saint. The head and the skins of the sheep are given to the *pirzada*, who in return distributes to the devotees ashes and sweets specially prepared for the occasion.

This *dargah* is reputed for its [male] 'demon stone' (*bhuta kallu*). About a 100 m behind the shrine, near a small cliff down which flow the waters of the Malaprabha, a natural opening at ground level is considered to be the residence of a 'power' whom the Muslims call either a *jinn* or a *bhut.* A story explains its presence here:

> While the reclusive saint, surrounded by a few disciples, was fasting, praying and meditating for forty days a gigantic phantom or demon kept disturbing him. Seized with anger, the saint took a heavy stone and threw it at the demon. This stone is today called *bhuta kallu.*

Muslims and people of the untouchable Madar caste, crawl into this rocky hole. They have to repeat the gesture three or five times. Unless a person is very slender, he has to be a contortionist to pass through the tunnel, which is barely 30 cm in diameter. Also, he must be careful not to disturb the stone, which is near one of the exits. If he is successful, it means that his wish will be granted. Hindus usually consider the *bhut* to be evil, although we have seen that they are often ambivalent. But the presence of this stone, now symbolizing a defeated demon, near the *dargah* makes it benign.

This change, it may be noted, is similar to the change in Yellamma. To begin with, she is worshipped because people are frightened of her anger, synonymous with afflictions and sickness. But if one visits her in her shrine for a specific purpose, she helps and protects her devotees. Generally, the worship of Muslim saints is meant to satisfy desires and make marriages fertile. But in Saundatti, both Muslims and low-caste Hindus approach Bar Shah not only when they want (male) children but also for curing skin diseases, as in the case of Rajabag Savar. These special powers are usually attributed to Yellamma, whose efficacy in these matters is undisputed. In short, it seems as though all the goddess's power (*shakti*) has by contagion deflected the saint's power (*baraka*) in this direction. One myth depicts the goddess as the saint's servant.

While Yellamma was running away to escape the wrath of her vengeful husband, who had cursed her with leprosy, she came across the saint astride his tiger going for his daily bath. On seeing the beast, she was terrified. Bar Shah reassured her and asked her to tell him her story. Taking pity on her, he gave her his blessings, promising to cure her if she bathed regularly in the holy pond. The very next morning Yellamma regained her beauty.

Out of gratitude, she put herself at his service and served him faithfully for twelve long years. But one day, she asked the saint for permission to leave, and to find her a place where she could settle down. Bar Shah granted her wish, and that is how the Yellamma cult was born in the Saundatti temple.

When we narrated this story to Banajiga-Lingayat devotees, they said that they had never heard it, and told us another story about the founding of the Yellamma cult. This is bound to fuel the 'communal' dispute about who came first, because by turning Bar Shah into a devotee, who is punished and then absolved by the goddess, this story claims that Yellamma was the first to settle at this site.

Bar Shah was in the habit of constantly blaming and cursing the goddess Yellamma. Angered by his curses (which happened to be quite innocuous), she decided to punish him and cast a spell on him and he was struck blind. Then he understood his mistake. He started worshipping her and sang her praises incessantly. By dint of devotion and penance, he regained his sight. To thank Yellamma for her kindness, he became one of her most faithful servants.

Exclusion and Accommodation

It is impossible here to reconstruct the tumultuous history of a temple whose control guarantees at once prestige and a considerable income. This is mainly because the dominant Banajiga-Lingayat caste, from among whom the servants of the Yellamma temple are recruited, does not allow anybody to consult the account books of the temple *panchayat*, which have been maintained from a very long way back by the *devasthanam*. These registers are precious from the ethnologist's viewpoint because they give a list of all the staff and the details of remunerations for the services provided by each member. Fortunately, three of these registers, pertaining to the years 1884, 1924 and 1928 were available for consultation. They indicate that during those years recruitment rules were more liberal and access to ritual functions was open to members of castes that are now excluded.

By using insidious methods and muscle-power and by approaching the law courts periodically, the Banajiga-Lingayats succeeded in the 1930s in ousting the Brahmins from temple service, and lately have even thrust out the Madigas. The most recent case involving Muslims concerns only one family out of the seven living in Ugargol and confirms the current ban on the recruitment of new *sevakari*. I must confess that a member of this family became my principal informant over the years. He allowed me to consult the account books in his possession, though in fairly bizarre conditions. He insisted that the relations between the local Hindus (Banajigas) and Muslims were so strained that it was necessary to peruse these registers in secret.

Traditional Rights and Conflicts

The use of various methods of harassment by some Banajigas led to a violent conflict with the Muslims in the year 1970. In 1974, they succeeded in removing the Muslims from the ritual functions they had hitherto been performing hereditarily and finally, in 1978, they dislodged them completely from the temple administration.

The participation of Muslims in temple duties is not an ideal oecumenical model surviving from the past, nor are they acting spitefully just because they feel they are besieged. It is a historical fact proved by an edict issued in 1774. This edict, bearing the seal of the Peshwa, the Maratha dynasty that ruled over this area in those times, stipulates the hereditary right of Muslims to certain services in the Yellamma temple. This officially-authenticated historical document, written in Urdu and translated for the legal proceedings instituted against the Banajigas by my informant's father, confirms the rights of his family line to clean the temple of the goddess's son Parashurama, to light the lamp in the temple everyday at his own cost, to bring to the *pujari* during the ceremonies held on full-moon and no-moon days the utensils required for the *abhisheka* and to prove oil for lighting the lamp during the *Navaratri* festival at the time of the anniversary of Parashurama's birth. Basing itself explicitly on the local customary rights observed in the past, this solemn proclamation confirming these ritual privileges indicates that before 1774 they were accepted, practised and socially recognized. According to custom, the serving family received as payment the offerings (*padagata*) made by the devotees outside the temple. Also by hereditary right, its members officiated as *sevakari* when the deity's movable idol (*utsava-murti*) was taken out in procession. The men belonged to the association of palanquin-bearers, while the women waved the ritual fly-whisk (*chauri*).

Initially, these rights were challenged verbally on many occasions by the Banajiga, until they were legally withdrawn in 1974 by a law passed by the Karnataka state government. This law, passed under the chief ministership of Devraj Urs, restricts ritual functions in Hindu temples to Hindus.

In the 1970s a violent conflict arose between the Muslims and the Banajigas. An orthodox Lingayat, now dead, acted as the principal instigator, if not as an *agent provocateur*. This man, belonging to the Jangama caste, a high caste whose members function as household priests, was teaching Sanskrit, reading *Virashaiva-Agama* texts and the sect's doctrine [*Shakti Vishistadvaita*] and a *guru* of the *pujaris*. Under his leadership, the Banajigas accused the Muslims of trying to gain possession of the Parashurama temple with the intention of changing it into a mosque. This accusation was implausible, considering the difference in numbers between the two communities. However, since it was made in public in front of the shrine, it gave rise to an altercation. The quarrel became violent, and the police had to be called to restore order in this normally peaceful spot.

Once the Muslims were removed from the duties they had been performing for generations (and from which they were deriving an income), the Banajigas set about destroying the dome of the Parashurama temple. According to them, it was a mistake to allow this edifice, which had now become exclusively Hindu, to display features of Muslim architecture. You can still see old photographs of the dome that disappeared so mysteriously. Today a clumsily placed rickety plank ceiling serves as the temple's roof. However much one might, suspiciously, be inclined to recognize in this version of events a 'communalist', not to say paranoid rationalization, quibbling over an architectural feature that had only suffered the passage of time and the repeated onslaught of the monsoon, it would still be hard to understand why the Banajigas, when question on this subject, deny—despite the photographic evidence—that such a dome ever existed. (Other Hindu informants, less involved in the quarrel, in any case corroborated the information provided by the Muslims.)

Power and Acculturation

As far as the Hindus are concerned, the history of the Saundatti temple shows how society focuses on caste in modern India as a community grows more dominant.[4] While appealing to tradition—forgetful memory[5] always glorifies the merits of days gone by—the community uses, as and when circumstances demand it, dissuasive and brutal methods to establish its legitimacy. Ensuring its superior status in this manner, it consolidates its power, which has by now become hegemonic. In India too, right is actually premised on might, and it comes into being with it, as Kant put it.

Of course, tradition can be compared to the foliated structure of a myth not having a precise source in time. But this means ignoring the fact that the 'foliation' is intentional and fulfils certain needs. If the values that legitimize tradition are combined within the limits of an enforced story-line, this makeshift arrangement is not just a simple logical game. It is a takeover by force, expressing the interests of conflicting social groups, who have a stake in affirming their power (*potestas*) through authority and its symbols (*auctoritas*). For the observer, mythology and symbolism may be a game regulated by variations, inversions and transformations. But however little it may be put in its proper context, this game still refers to the pragmatics of social investments, especially if it appears as a 'machine for suppressing time' (Lévi-Strauss 1964: 24)—'history' rather than 'time'.

In fact, what the Banajigas call 'tradition' in Saundatti really amounts to the continuous management of history for the benefit of those who make it triumphantly. Taking advantage of their monopoly as enunciators, influential persons who legitimize the present with the help of the past readily forget certain facts, inscribe after a fashion history in myth, and reinterpret the past by the yardstick of the present. Thus they invent a time that does not move, that is immobilized and summated in a perpetual duration. This then is their tradition, this present which consists of denying it. Bound to an imaginary existence that consists in denying its own historicity, they build myths and create titles, adapt attitudes and functions, in short, provide themselves with effective means for putting an end to unruliness by imposing orthodoxy/orthopraxis here and now.

That is why it is necessary to stress this truism. The Banajigas use symbolism for pragmatic ends, manipulating stories as necessary, adapting their behaviour to circumstances, modifying norms to cope with untoward occurrences, changes in their interests and the importance of the stakes involved. Methods are often adapted to suit the urgency of the moment. The rules that allow them to adapt themselves to changes in power relationships are re-invented periodically.

It is therefore important to emphasize the complexity of the acculturation process, because affirmation of identity continues, even though certain practices may be borrowed from neighbours and different religious environments. For members of various Hindu and Muslim castes, usually the lower castes, who visit shrines belonging to the other group, acculturation is 'dissociated by differentiation'.[6] Hindus perform a Hindu ritual before the Muslim saint as if he were a Hindu god by adapting their offerings (especially sugar) to respect the servant's ritual practices. And when Muslims visit a temple, they adopt Hindu practices, some of which are also followed in the *dargah*, but without denying their underlying religious culture. In both these cases, allegiance does not imply conversion. Further, the advantages gained from these distinct forms of worship are most of the time cumulative. In this way cultural duality is respected at the cost of following behavioural patterns that are barely differentiated. When they worship the saint, it matters little to Muslims that they do it in the Hindu manner. Because within this autonomous ritual space, the absorption of methods peculiar to the dominant group does not in any way affect their consciousness of being Muslims. Perfectly 'integrated' acculturation shocks those who follow a strictly scriptural Islam, but seems plausible to the foreign ethnologist or indologist. Finally, Islamic identity is strengthened when Muslims are excluded from the solemn worship of a Hindu deity. Muslims understand this attribution of non-Hinduness in religious terms and feel that they are being segregated. Compulsory isolation defines a reactionary identity that, in the long run, is likely to provoke more self-proclaiming differentiation. But Muslims are not passive, and they respond to manipulations and takeovers planned by the Banajigas by borrowing, distorting and inverting stories in their turn, by juxtaposing seemingly contradictory cultural patterns that appeal to them. Forced to do so through means determined by existing power relationships, they adapt to the situation as best as they can. But while doing this, they participate fully in the creation of a social space in which cultural patterns are formed because indigenous models, both complementary and contradictory, exist in the same area. In such a situation, the respective identities of the two communities can be affirmed, perpetuated or denied, but only in proportion to the interaction that allows them to adjust to one another. While Indian society continues to see changes in status and rank, and the definition of identity or the membership of a particular community is still of crucial importance, the margin of free play allowed to individuals and groups by otherwise constructive norms persists.

Tradition and Modernity

In view of current upheavals in the subcontinent, my limited example appears inadequate. Focusing on minute details of rituals and mythology certainly seems meaningless, especially when the changes observed affect only a handful of persons in an extremely localized context. But when all is said and done, does not anthropology depend on the observation of minor details? To dismiss singular features as irrelevant amounts to ignoring significant events and forgetting that they often contain the traces of profound changes. In short, it contains the risk of overlooking the whole. Thus it is better to follow the advice of the historian, Carlo Ginzburg and pinpoint all the 'clues' that make anthropology akin to a police investigation. When the method of indications is used, even micro-events acquire a paradigmatic value.

After presenting a local case, we must build up a wider case on its basis. And the comparative ethnographic study of the worship of a goddess and a saint provides three broad lessons.

In the first place, it shows how, in spite of the disproportion in their populations, Hindus and Muslims have built up a common tradition and still share some of its elements by devising stories to suit their interests, adjusting behaviour and adapting opinions and practices according to varying needs and circumstances. Neither religious symbols nor social behaviour remain static as systems inherited from the past and followed mechanically. In fact, it appears more and more unlikely that India has sveral normative systems of ideas capable of being understood by a sociology of values, and it is becoming more and more evident that ideological and pragmatic patterns are being periodically renegotiated by the protagonists. So we must seriously modify our conception of religion, which serves more and more as an instrument. Protagonists are increasingly tempted by the possibilities of manipulation to invoke and reinterpret the most archaic features of their culture.

Secondly, it suggests that the growing awareness of identity has transformed the actors to such an extent that it would not be surprising if one day they refuse to share the symbols and rites that brought them together in the past. It would be wrong to claim that the situation was idyllic at that time with the two communities living together in total harmony and in a state of complete cultural integration. Acculturation and syncretism certainly do not mean symbiosis! Hinduism has never been a monolithic religion, but a loose and often headless association, a juxtaposition of extremely flexible castes and sects, which were however quick to organize themselves along hierarchical lines in small areas and over short periods. Even if we confine ourselves to the Lingayat-Virashaivas, Desai points out that the acquisition of wealth through trade accompanied by a rise in status gave them the ability to persecute Jain monks and destroy their idols in Karnataka. However, when doing this they did not act as the Lingayat 'community' against the Jain 'community', as only a few segments of the Lingayat sect/castes were involved (1957: 397-402). Similarly in Andhra Pradesh, a group of Virashaivas took control of the great Srisailam temple in the fourteenth century and deliberately destroyed all the existing inscriptions in order to efface the memory of earlier Hindu priests (Parabrahma Sastri 1982: 17). As for the Muslims, examples of 'internal' fights between Sunnis and Shias are legion.[7] However, this did not prevent various kings from patronizing religious institutions of communities other than their own, and of this there are numerous examples (Hasan 1991: 112ff.). It is true that the notion of separate Islamic and Hindu communities has existed in India for a long time. But their connotation changed periodically, and they gained significance in South Asia only after the launching of the independence movement, the forging of a nationalistic Hindu ideology and a fundamentalist Islamic ideology, and the birth of India and Pakistan.

And last this study shows on a limited scale the basic changes that are taking place in India. In fact, everyday the subcontinent comes closer to that picture of strictly compartmentalized society painted by the British administration in the nineteenth century. As Brown says, 'The British tended to break up the Indian population in terms of community and analysed Indian society as a plural one of different peoples who needed special outlets in political life' (1990: 374). Such 'imagined religious communities' believe themselves to be, and are in fact, essentially hostile to each other. Hence they find it difficult to live together and, even more, to share rival religious symbols in a society that officially promotes the secular ideal. Unfortunately, it appears that the day is not far off when Muslims will look on Hindus as *kafir* (unbelievers) and the Hindus in their turn will treat the Muslims as 'foreigners' with whom they cannot mix and who should be kept at a distance.

NOTES

1. This idea has been developed judiciously and appositely by Ahmad (1964: vii).
2. A detailed account of the Yellama cult and the Saundatti temple, only a few aspects of which are dealt with here, can be found in Assayag (1992).
3. This name perhaps reveals a link with the fifteenth-century 'outlawed' (*beeshar*') saint, Badi'al-Zaman Shah Madar, a Jew of Syrian descent, who popularized Sufi practices among converted Muslims by borrowing a great deal from the *yogis*. For more information about this astonishing and colourful personality, cf. Ahmad (1964: 161-2) and Rizvi (1978: 318ff.).
4. This process has been described by Assayag (1986) in a wider political context.
5. As M. Douglas writes, 'Anthropologists have a tendency to invert the question. They are inclined to ask not why one forgets but why one remembers, and they make memory their special subject of study' (1989: 63). So forgetfulness too belongs to tradition (the transmission of

cultural data), which is as much loss as remembrance, a system that plays an integration role in social organization, as we are aware since the time of M. Halbwachs. We will revert to this question in Chapter 6.

6. Devereux calls it 'dissociative acculturation by differentiation: adaptation of the middle segment of the manifest culture, but not of the underlying culture' (1975: 283).
7. Hasan (1990) maintains that the rift was more marked and more violent in north India than that between Hindus and Muslims. Cole (1988) has devoted an entire chapter to the conflict between Sunnis and Shias.

6

Politics: The Border, Communalism and Remembrance

The *other* of truth is not error but violence.

E. WEIL, *Logique de la philosophie* (1974)

In 1992 I returned to Karnataka to pursue a project on urban anthropology I had started a year earlier. I had to conduct my inquiries in Belgaum among the Muslim community living around a mosque and the mausoleums of two saints. This investigation was supposed to supplement, fill out and confirm the information I had obtained earlier. But during this second stay, I found Hindus and Muslims in a mutually hostile mood, as they were almost all over the country after the demolition of the Babri Masjid in Ayodhya (1992).

Because of the riots, the inquiry took an unexpected turn. Besides, the eruption of trouble added a touch of excitement to a situation that I knew, like everybody around me, was quite dangerous. All the more because the religious 'war' and the ensuing storm of violence seemed to have pushed into the background the old border dispute between Maharashtra and Karnataka.

I was kept abreast of the latest developments by the Muslims, because the subject of my study had brought me into their midst. I noticed that some people took advantage of these events to revive the past. Not that they were nostalgic about the good old times; but they wanted to glorify an ancient saga, revitalized by their present concerns. But while weaving the present with the past, their leaders had reinterpreted local history and rebuilt communal memory in the mood of the time. Old memory was replaced by a dynamic and edifying memory that they were anxious to pass on to the foreigner. I noted, not without perplexity, the effect of this projectional recollection of past events on the social definition of their identity. Some of my interlocutors had decided to make use of certain memorial sites, as significant for their Islamic identity. To be more precise, they had chosen the tombs of two local saints, one a scholar and the other a warrior, piously maintained in the past for their antiquity. For this very reason, I had been collecting material about them. But I must admit that there was very little available about the second saint.

Today the venerated past is revived and projected in such a lively manner that it is difficult to disentangle truth from imagination in the absence of written records. This matters little to the anthropologist because fabricated stories are likely to imbue local history with more meaning. Instead of looking at the past in a mundane manner, they dramatize significant fragments of the heritage retrieved from the inertia of a humdrum existence. Breathing a new life into the saint who had given them their identity, people embellished and illustrated his exploits to satisfy their need of community solidarity when under siege.

After that I could judge for myself how religious memory, apparently isolated in a temporal society, obeys 'the same laws as all collective memory. It not only retains the past but reconstructs it, with the help not only of material fragments, rites, texts and traditions that it has given up, but also of recent psychological and social data, that is to say, the present' (Halbwachs [1975: 221]). And in the process, I rediscovered the delicate nature of anthropological investigations, which are prolonged indefinitely in spite of their punctiliousness, and at the same time I realized the fragile quality of the academic work that they produce.

Border Dispute to Communal Conflict

Belgaum district shares its border with Maharashtra in the north-west and Goa in the south-west. Belgaum city, which for long time was called the 'gateway' to Goa, has marked the dividing line between the Marathi and Kannada language zones since the twelfth century. Persian was also spoken there, as well as the local version of Urdu called *dakhni*, which was promptly elevated to the rank of a literary language during the long Muslim rule (1473-1750) preceding Maratha hegemony (1750-1818). There are innumerable examples of association and borrowing between Muslims and Marathas, and the latter were able to expand their political dominion only because of their interaction with the Muslims (Wink 1993: 224).

It was only after repeated attempts that the Bahmanis were able to capture the Belgaum fort. The fortress was a part of the Vijayanagar kingdom, from at least 1375, as is attested by an inscription. An edict issued in 1478 by Khwaja Gawan, a minister of the Bahmani dynasty, proclaims that the land between Junnar and Satara and the forts of Goa and Belgaum would from then on be under the government of Fakr-ul-Mulk. Without going into the details of its tumultuous[3] history, we may indicate that after the death of Bahadur Gilani, who started a rebellion in 1486 to gain control of Goa and Belgaum, the latter was given to Khosru Turk, a Persian officer, as a reward for saving the young king Kamal Khan of the Adil Shahi dynasty. He took the name of Asad Khan and ruled magnanimously over Belgaum for thirty-eight years (1511-49). A number of Muslims say that this hero, who was also a patron of scholars, lived for 150 years, and that his charisma kept cholera away from the city! You can still see his *dargah*. also frequented by Hindus, and his Masjid-i Safa, standing near the old arsenal. The Jamia Masjid inside the fort (1585-6) was built by Muhammad Sher Khan, who succeeded him in 1550. He also built the twin city of Shahapur, originally called Shahpet, where traders and bankers got together. Owing to the present development of Belgaum, Shahapur, once famous for its textiles and jewellery, is now growing rapidly.

Taking advantage of strife in the Bijapur court, Shivaji made a successful raid on Belgaum in 1673. But in spite of the plunder that followed, Belgaum was by 1695 a 'thickly populated and prosperous commercial city' according to the Italian traveller, Gemelli Careri. When the Sultan of Bijapur surrendered Belgaum to Aurangzeb in 1686, it was renamed Azamnagar or Mustafabad. It later fell into the hands of the Nizam-ul-Mulk, who gave it as a *jigir* to the Nawab of Savanur province in 1730. In 1754, a Maratha army returning from Mysore attacked the governor, and the city passed into the Peshwa's hands; after the Treaty of Warna in 1756, it was handed over to the Raja of Kolhapur. The Peshwa Balaji Baji Rao, based in Pune, entrusted the administration of Belgaum to the local *desai*. Though the Peshwas lost Belgaum following Haidar Ali's invasion in 1776, they regained it with British support in 1795. Finally, during the Third Maratha War (1818), General Thomas Munro's troops surrounded Belgaum fort. The siege lasted twenty-eight days when victory or defeat was declared, depending on which side you belonged to.

In 1830, the British made Belgaum a part of Dharwad district, but some years later, in 1838, they created a new district with Belgaum as its headquarters (Rao 1989). After that Belgaum, appreciated by the British colonizers for its 'salubrious climate', became an important military cantonment and the meeting-point of the state governments of Bombay and Mysore. The municipality set up in 1851 was converted into a Municipal Corporation in 1977. The identity of the Municipal Councillors representing the city's 52 electoral wards gives us an idea of the relative importance of its three major communities. In 1994 there were 33 Marathi-speaking Councillors, 12 Kannadigas and 7 Muslims.[4]

The town had 7,650 inhabitants in 1880; 29,000 in 1921; 58,000 in 1941; and 274,000 in 1981.

The city has 79 per cent Hindus and 15 per cent Muslims. Scheduled Castes constitute 43 per cent of its population, and 14 per cent are Marathas, 11.94 per cent Lingayats, 9.78 per cent Brahmins, 3.22 per cent Jains, 0.9 per cent Kurubas, 0.81 per cent Gujjars, 0.49 per cent Nhavi and 0.23 per cent Bedars. It is believed that there are about 2.07 per cent 'upper caste' Muslim. Among the Scheduled Castes there are 35 per cent Chambhars, 22.52 per cent Mahars, 12.33 per cent Dhors, 8.78 per cent Mangs and 8.44 per cent Madars.

The almost continuous rise in population in this region may be attributed to waves of migrants from other regions, attracted by the economic and commercial growth of the city (aluminium, chemicals, engineering, automobiles, cotton, silk textiles and sugar).[5] Situated at the crossroads between Bombay, Goa and Bangalore, Belgaum finds itself at the centre of the regional trade network (Tables 6 and 7).

Conversations with various officials of the Belgaum Municipal Corporation in March 1994, helped us to get a general picture of

TABLE 6: POPULATION OF BELGAUM BETWEEN 1981 AND 1991

Year	No. of Occupied Houses	Total Population	Male Population	Female Population Population	Total SC/ST* Persons	No. of Literate
1981	43,618	300,372	158,573	141,799	25,367	198,390
1991	60,429	393,130	204,438	188,692	37,350	278,226

Year	Employed	Farmers	Farm Workers	Services	Non-working
1981	84,553	5,773	1,536	76,244	215,819
1991	118,624	8,457	3,550	106,627	283,788

Sources: Census of India 1981 and 1991.

TABLE 7: INCREASE IN THE PERCENTAGE OF URBAN POPULATION IN BELGAUM DISTRICT

Years	1901	1911	1921	1931	1941	1951	1961	1971
%	8.406	9.81	9.69	-	12.36	24.18	18.02*	20.54

Note: *Loss of Chandgad taluk.
Source: Compilation of the censuses of the corresponding years.

the situation, impressionistic but significant nevertheless, of the trades and occupations in which the various communities specialize at present (Table 8). The major part of the trade in clothing and sugar is in the hands of Marwaris. Most of the cotton and textile industry is controlled by Jains of the Digambar sect, who have been settled in the Deccan (Kolhapur, Sangli and Belgaum) for a very long time, though the weavers are mainly Muslim. But the Jains have made most of their money in the aluminium industry, as they have links with large factories in Madras and Calcutta. They also have close links with the members of their community in Kolhapur, who wield a great deal of influence in political circles. Jains and Lingayats own road transport companies, although the latter are mainly farmers and also hold a large number of teaching jobs in educational institutions. The Marathas are the dominant caste in the villages, and, apart from engaging in trade, they have many members working in the army and the police. The Muslims control the fruit and vegetable trade; but the majority are petty shop-keepers or tenant-farmers.

The economic situation partly explains why the city and its outskirts became a major stake in the boundary dispute between Maharashtra and the erstwhile Mysore state. Both of them laid claim to this high-growth area, so that they could tap its rich resources. The dispute continues, although in 1956 the Government of India transferred what was called the 'Southern Karnatic region of Bombay', together with its headquarters, Belgaum, to Mysore state during the reorganization of the states of the Indian Union on a linguistic basis (Map 7).

However, it is impossible to attribute the boundary dispute between the two states to purely economic reasons. The controversy was aggravated by long-standing cultural differences. Marathi-speaking people lay claim to the tiny area on the grounds that it was controlled by the Marathas in the seventeenth century and later by the Peshwas (1754) until the advent of the British in 1818. Kannadigas, on the

TABLE 8: INDUSTRIES IN BELGAUM DISTRICT (1994)

Type of Industry	No. of Industries	No. of Employees
Small-scale	12,756	57,581
Large-scale	13	14,731
Medium-scale	9	1,832

(A) Large-scale Industrial Units	
Aluminium	
Indian Aluminium Co. Ltd., Belgaum	1,464
Total 1	1,464
Cotton	
Belgaum Cooperative Cotton Spinning Mill Ltd.	849
Gokak Mills, Gokak	5,469
Malaprabha Coop. Cotton Spinning Mill Ltd., Saundatti	374
Total 3	6,692
Textiles	
Gogte Textiles Ltd., Kakti	1,009
Total 1	1,009
Sugar	
Doodganga Krishna Sahakari Sakkare Karkhane, Chikkodi	846
Ghataprabha Sahakari Sakkare Karkhane Ltd., Gokak	656
Halsiddhanath S.S. Karkhane, Ltd., Sankeshwar	482
Hiranyakeshi S.S. Karkhane, Ltd., Sankeshwar	804
K.G. Gluco Bails Ltd., Gokak	60
Malaprabha S.S. Karkhana, M.K. Hubli	843
Raibag S.S. Karkhana, Raibag	751
Ugar Sugar Works, Ugar	845
Total 8	5,287
(B) Medium-scale Industrial Units	
Mahant Oil Mills Pvt. Ltd.	76
Arun Engineering Works	344
Ashok Iron Works Pvt. Ltd.	497
Bemco Hydraulics Pvt. Ltd.	442
B.T.P. Structural India Pvt. Ltd.	81
Crown Fine Chemicals Pvt. Ltd.	12
Jaihind Engineering, Belgaum	307
Katwa Cement Co., Yadwad	66
Mullar Cylinders Pvt. Ltd. (LPG Cylinders)	7
Total 9	1,832

Source: Regional Science Association of Indian Academy of Regional Science and Humanities, Belgaum, 1994.

Source: Census of India 2001, Indian Administrative Divisions, 2001.

Map 7: Incorporation of North Karnataka in Mysore state in 1956 (named Karnataka in 1974)

contrary, invoke the medieval Kannada dynasties, particularly the Vijayanagar kingdom destroyed by the Muslims in the sixteenth century. While the former claim allegiance to the princely state of Kolhapur (in Maharashtra), whose ruler is said to be a descendant of Shivaji Bhonsle (1627-80) who laid the foundations of the Maratha kingdom, the latter swear faithfulness to Vijayanagar and to the Wodeyars of Mysore. This princely state founded in the fourteenth century was conquered by Haidar Ali in 1765 and ruled by his son Tipu Sultan until it was restored to the Wodeyars by the British in 1799. But their rule was short-lived as the Maharaja was deposed following a Lingayat-Virashaiva rebellion in 1830 (Stein 1985) and in 1834, the Chief Commissioner, Mark Cubbon, took charge of the administration, as had been decided in 1831. The British remained in authority for half a century.

This geopolitical tropism was further strengthened by ethnic antagonism between the two dominant groups who wanted to establish their rights to the reconquered territory. Against the prestigious martial Maratha Vaishnavas, accounting for about 15 per cent of the population in 1951, were ranged the powerful Shaiva Lingayats. The latter group made up of several castes constituted approximately 30 per cent of the population at that time. The sociological picture is however even more complex than this, because the Brahmins, though constituting a minority of 4 per cent and divided by their linguistic loyalties into Marathi-, Konkani- and Kannada-speaking groups, played a significant role due to their 'over-representation' in decision-making administrative posts (Tables 9 and 10).

TABLE 9: DISTRIBUTION OF GOVERNMENT POSTS AMONG DIFFERENT CASTES IN MYSORE STATE (1921-4)

Castes or Other Groups	Number	Percentage
Brahmins	570	54.23
Kshatriyas	13	1.24
Vokkaligas	42	4.00
Lingayats	63	5.99
Mudaliars	18	1.71
Other Hindu Castes	197	18.74
Backward Castes	13	1.24
Muslims	89	8.47
Christians	46	4.38
Total	1,051	100.00

Source: Kaul, R. (1993: 63).

TABLE 10: DISTRIBUTION OF UNIVERSITY STUDENTS ACCORDING TO CASTE IN 1916

Castes	No. of Students	Percentage
Muslims	21	2.90
Brahmins	571	78.87
Kshatriya	25	3.45
Vaishyas	10	1.38
Lingayats	29	4.01
Other Upper Caste Hindus (including Vokalligas)	33	4.56
Total	724	100.00

Source: R. Kaul (1993: 60).

This explains the growth of a strong anti-Brahmin movement during the 1920s joined by both Marathas and Lingayats as a common front. On the one hand, the Maratha agitation was supported by the Maharaja of Kolhapur, who was at the vanguard of a progressive socialist movement that remained outside the mainstream nationalist movement because of its strong anti-Brahminism. So by adopting a pro-British posture under his leadership, the Marathas imperilled their integration in independent India (1947). On the other hand, the Kannadiga leaders (belonging mainly to Lingayat castes) readily joined the Indian National Congress, because they were against the Marathas, and also because they realized that the importance of Brahmins would decline in the future (Table 11).

What is surprising is that the first nationalist demands on a regional level came from the Marathi-speaking people of the north. Under the leadership of A.V. Gokhale, a Chitpavan Brahmin who visited Belgaum in 1906 long before Gandhi (he came only in 1920), the independence movement gained momentum in south India, although the Kannadigas were in a majority in Belgaum district. It

TABLE 11: REPRESENTATION IN PERCENTAGE OF MAJOR CASTES/ COMMUNITIES IN THE STATE GOVERNMENT SERVICE IN 1930

Caste/Community	1918	1930
Brahmins	69.60	54.10
Lingayats	3.60	7.70
Vokkaligas	2.40	4.40
Muslims	7.70	12.20

Source: J. Manor (1978: 64).

must however be pointed out that the agitation against the inclusion of Belgaum district in Bombay Presidency by the British was started by militant Kannadigas.

Before Independence, the territory of Karnataka as it stands today came under five separate administrative and political authorities of unequal importance, viz., the Bombay Presidency, the princely state of Mysore, the territory of Coorg, the princely state of Hyderabad, the coastal area of Mangalore and the tiny state of Sandur, which came under the Madras Presidency (Map 8).

The Lingayat-Virashaivas set up literary and cultural associations, for instance, the All Karnataka Literary Body in Bangalore in 1915, and the Karnataka Sabha in Dharwad in 1916, which supported the demand for a unified Kannada state. But the crusade launched way back in 1890 by Chennabasappa was the mainspring in Dharwad of the first organization of this type, the Karnataka Vidyavardhaka Sangha. The movement sought to separate 'Bombay Karnataka' from the Bombay Presidency and join it to Mysore. The first political conference was held in Dharwad in 1920. The proposal was presented at the annual session of the Congress party in Nagpur in 1920 and taken up again at the Congress session in Belgaum in 1924. The same year a Karnataka Unified Conference was held under the auspices of the recently established Karnataka Ekikarana Mahasamiti. This association was reorganized as the Karnataka Ekikara Sangha by S. Nijalingappa (who later became Chief Minister of Karnataka) during the unification conference in Kasargod in December 1947. On the contrary, the Maharashtra Ekikaran Samiti (MES), an association expressly set up to oppose the long-standing programme of their Kannada-speaking adversaries (Weiner 1967: Part IV; Kohli 1991: 97ff.), made its appearance as late as 1946. And it was only in 1960 that the Sampoorna Maharashtra Samiti was set up in the border areas of Karnataka to agitate for the inclusion of Belgaum and Karwar districts in Maharashtra state (Gupta 1991: 574) (Map 9).

Muslims in the Midst of Hindus

The administrative division of the country into states corresponding to traditional linguistic zones under the States Reorganization Act of 1956 and the Official Languages Act of 1963 and its compromise in 1965 put an end to conflicts of this type almost everywhere in India, except for Punjab, as people were more or less satisfied with the newly demarcated states (Brass 1990: 146ff.). However, things were

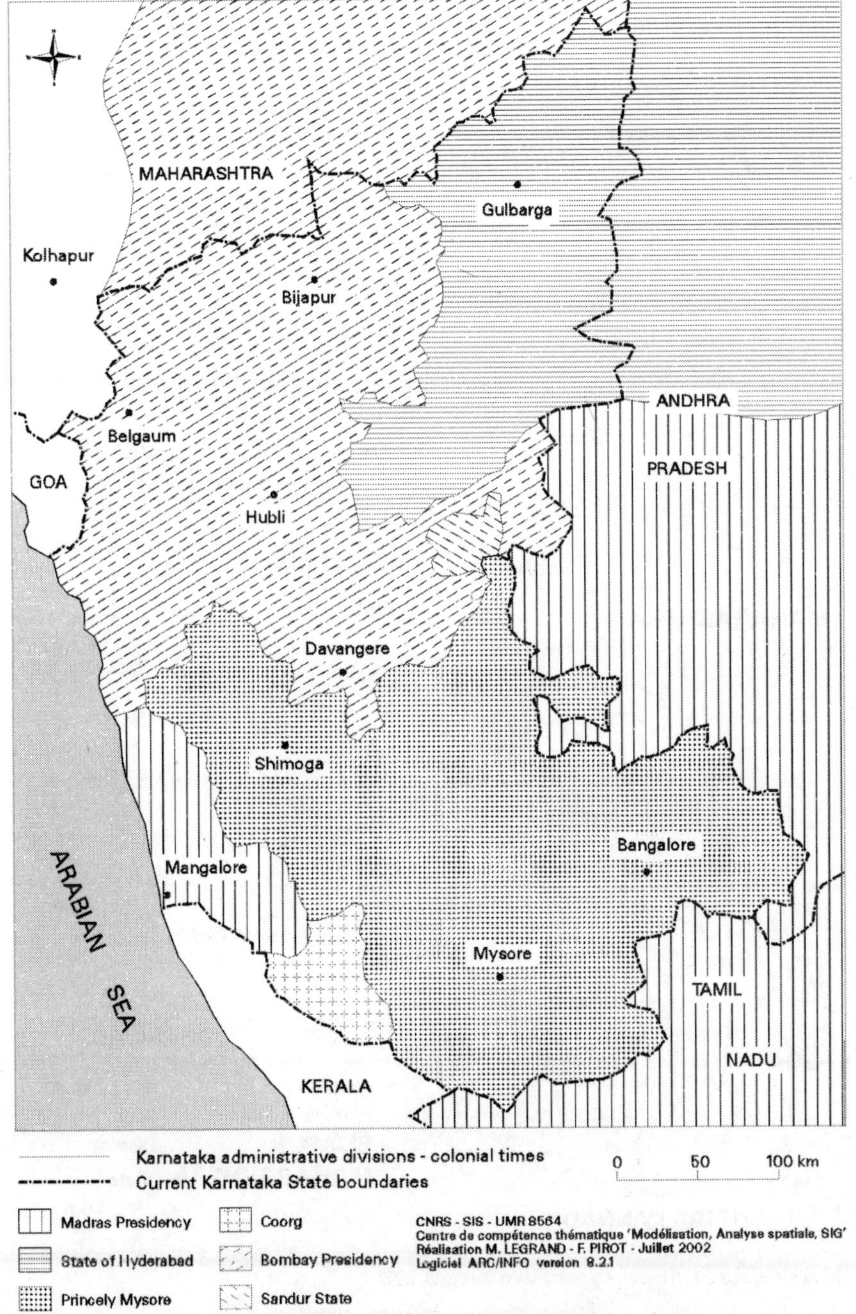

Map 8: The five administrative territories of Karnataka before Independence

Source: *Census 2001*, Indian Administrative Divisions, 2001

Map 9: Cantons of Belgaum district

not the same in 'Bombay Karnataka', especially in Belgaum city where Marathi-speaking people constitute 41 per cent of the population and Kannadigas 53 per cent, with the 11 per cent Muslims included in the latter group.[6]

Following the regionalistic fervour unleashed by the movement for a 'unified Maharashtra' (Samyukta Maharashtra Movement) started in 1949, the Shiv Sena claimed that not only Belgaum city but the entire district should be made a part of Maharashtra, on the grounds that the Marathi-speaking population was in a majority. This contention was naturally opposed by the other half of the population, especially the agitators grouped together under the banner of the Kannada Chaluvalagar.

Maharashtra's claim was further strengthened by the district's geographical proximity and the support of Marathi-speaking middle-class business circles, whose members headed small and medium-sized industries and also cottage industries controlling a large number of small stores. In addition, many of their members held important political positions, where they could influence decisions. At the same time, a substantial portion of the Muslim population had also prospered in small businesses, transport companies and the retail trade in fruit and vegetables, so as to attain the status of a middle class whose opinions counted. This prosperity fuelled their political ambition and their desire to compete with the Maharashtrian, Marwari and Gujarati trading classes.[7] There was need for a different mode of expression: Muslims wanted political representation. Far from displaying 'medieval barbarity', the crystallization of religious identity and communal polarization were thus linked to the self-expression of the mercantile class by the election of members to represent its interests, since this electoral mechanism implanted by the British colonial rulers is now well entrenched in the system of indirect democracy prevalent in India.

On reading the official reports of the Fazal Ali Commission (1953), the States Reorganization Commission (1955) and the Mahajan Commission (1960), we find that the Muslims became a part of the Kannada cultural ethos without much difficulty after Independence. They joined hands with Hindu Kannadigas to oppose the transfer of Belgaum to Maharashtra. It is true that in the 1970s, the Devraj Urs government included Muslims in the category of Backward Classes and Minorities (BCM) (Thimmaiah and Aziz 1983: 823).[8]

Inspired by the Havnoor Commission, this decision was in tune with the Congress party's new political strategy, which sought to put an end to the undue privileges enjoyed by the Lingayats and Vokkaligas and win the support of the Backward Classes by providing quotas in schools and government jobs (Brass 1990: 212-13). In addition to substantial economic assistance, the Muslims finally got an 18 per cent reservation in government jobs and 20 per cent of the places in educational institutions, although they already had a higher representation than other castes in government service in this state (*Muslim India*, 26 December 1985: 551). In 1990, the report of the third Backward Classes Commission confirmed the classification of the Muslims under the second category—besides thirteen other groups including Lingayats, Vokkaligas and Marathas—for whom 28 per cent of government posts are reserved (*Muslim India*, 15 June 1994: 274).

Karnataka was the first state of the Indian Union to appoint a Minorities Commission to encourage their integration in the mainstream and to safeguard their interests (Brass 1990: 111), in sharp contrast to neighbouring Maharashtra, where the Muslim community was treated quite shabbily. In 1985, the Shiv Sena leaders held 76 of the 170 municipal seats in and in 1990 they won 94 seats in the state legislative assembly thanks to a tie-up with the Bharatiya Janata Party (BJP). This same alliance won 138 seats (against 85 polled by the Congress-I) in the 1995 elections, and at the time of writing this book it controlled 30 out of 34 seats in Bombay city and 54 out of 75 seats in the 'sugar belt', i.e. the western part of the state including the districts of Sangli and Kolhapur.

The Shiv Sena, which claims to be the voice of the Marathi-speaking middle-class, was said to have a million members in 1992. The militia movement was originally started for the 'extension of preferences in all job categories, in both the public and private sectors, to those who are Maharashtrian by the definition of mother tongue' (Katzenstein 1979: 26). In other words, this means giving preference to the 'sons of the soil' and those who have been sharing for many generations 'the joys and sorrows of Maharashtrians' as expressed in poetic terms by the local leaders (Katzenstein 1981: 46-7). In 1968 and 1973, the government of Maharashtra agreed to this demand by introducing a system of preferential quotas for the employment of 'native Marathi speakers' (Katzenstein 1979: 133).

The Shiv Sena movement, which was initially directed against the communists and limited to Maharashtra, turned its attention to exposing the ill-treatment of Maharashtrians everywhere, especially in Karnataka (Gupta 1982: 51). At the same time, its defensive stance turned into outbursts of xenophobia, whose scapegoats were, in turn, the Marwari and Gujarati merchant classes regarded as predators upon Bombay's economy and then the Tamils, those 'foreigners' from south India, also accused of the same crime. The militants of the Shiv Sena did not spare the industrious Sikh and Parsi minorities before tackling, more recently, the Muslim 'invasion'.

Having become the Shiv Sena's scapegoats and the fifth caste in electoral terms, Muslims are politically underrepresented in Maharashtra. Except for a prosperous trading class in Bombay, some of whom belong to an urban mafia having ramifications in Pakistan and the Gulf States, Muslims are by and large economically backward and socially unintegrated. This explains why they tend to withdraw into themselves, which adds further to their difficulties. This claim is supported by the fact that there are more Muslim students receiving instruction in Urdu (483,353 or 7.2 per cent of the Muslims) in Maharashtra than in Karnataka (333,009 or 9 per cent) or Uttar Pradesh (3,52,022 or 15 per cent), in an area where there are already 10.5 per cent of Urdu-speakers (Brass 1990: 156-7) (Table 12 and 13).

The Karnataka government has created Chairs for Urdu in the universities of Gulbarga, Bangalore and Mysore, as well as teaching posts in colleges. It has also increased the number of scholarships, provided assistance for publishing books, instituted awards for writers and even assisted the publication of an Urdu-Kannada dictionary. On the contrary, the Maharashtra government has always opposed the promotion of Urdu. As for Belgaum, the linguistic division between its 104 schools (in 1994) correctly reflects its medial position between these two states in cultural terms, as 52 schools have Marathi as the medium of instruction, 36 have Kannada and 16 have Urdu.

The Growing Intensity of the Communal Conflict

The spread of the Shiv Sena's chauvinistic ideology in north Karnataka supported by its recent collusion with the nationalistic 'saffron' wave, has pushed into the background the traditional quarrel between the Maratha and Kannadiga factions among the Hindus. What is worse, they have joined to form a common anti-Islamic front. Forgetting their old grievances about the demarcation of the state border, they

TABLE 12: DISTRICTS OF KARNATAKA WHERE THE URDU-SPEAKERS MAKE UP 15 PER CENT OR MORE OF THE POPULATION

Name of District	Languages
Bangalore District	
Belgaum District	
Belgaum Urban Zone	
Belgaum City (Municipal Limits)	Marathi & Urdu
Bellary District	
Bellary Taluk	
Bellary City (Municipal Limits)	Telugu & Urdu
Bidar District	
Basavakalyan Taluk	
Basavakalyan (Municipal Limits)	Urdu
Bidar Taluk	
Bidar (Municipal Limits)	Urdu
Humnabad Taluk	
Humnabad (Municipal Limits)	Urdu
Chitraguppa (Municipal Limits)	Urdu
Bijapur District	
Bijapur Taluk	
Bijapur City (Municipal Limits)	Urdu
Chikamagalur District	
Chitradurga District	
Davangere City (Municipal Limits)	Urdu
Dharwad District	
Hubli Taluk	Urdu
Hubli-Dharwad Corporation	
Hangal Taluk	
Hangal (T.P.)	Urdu
Gadag-Betegari (Municipal Limits)	Urdu
Savanur Taluk	
Savanur (Municipal Limits)	Urdu
Shiggaon Taluk	
Shiggaon (T.P.)	Urdu
Gulbarga District	
Chincholi Taluk	
Chincholi (Municipal Limits)	Urdu
Chitapur Taluk	
Chitapur (Municipal Limits)	Urdu
Gulbarga Taluk	
Gulbarga City (Municipal Limits)	Urdu
Jevargi Taluk	
Shahpur Taluk	
Shahpur (Municipal Limits)	Urdu
Yadgir (Municipal Limits)	Urdu
Yadgir Taluk	Telugu
Hassan District	

(contd.)

TABLE 12 (contd.)

Name of District	Languages
Kolar District	
Kolar (Municipal Limits)	Urdu
Mandya District	Urdu
Mysore District	
Mysore City (Municipal Limits)	Urdu
Raichur District	
Raichur Taluk	Telugu & Urdu
Raichur (Municipal Limits)	Urdu
Shimoga District	
Shimoga Taluk	Urdu
Shimoga City (Municipal Limits)	Urdu

Source: Muslim India, No. 15, April 1983.

TABLE 13: DISTRICTS OF KARNATAKA AND MAHARASHTRA HAVING A 10 TO 20 PER CENT MUSLIM POPULATION

State	Districts	% of Muslim Population
Karnataka	Bidar	18.0
	Bijapur	12.7
	Dakshin Kannad	13.2
	Dharwad	15.3
	Gulbarga	16.6
	Kolar	11.4
	Raichur	12.3
	Shimoga	10.5
Maharashtra	Greater Bombay	14.8
	Jalgaon	10.8
	Aurangabad	16.0
	Parbani	10.9
	Bid	10.9
	Nanded	11.9
	Osmanabad	11.1
	Buldhana	11.0
	Akola	13.1
	Amaravati	10.9

Source: Muslim India, No. 32, August 1985.

have united against the Muslims. Following the stupendous increase in communal riots, Belgaum has been officially declared a 'sensitive area'.

It has been observed during the last few years that various religious groups tend to divide an area amongst themselves, leading to the phenomenon of ghettoization now visible in most Indian cities. Every town or city now has its own 'Little Pakistan' to borrow a metaphor popularized by 'saffron' propaganda. The situation has become all the more explosive because there is no geopolitical solution to the problem of the growth and poverty of the Muslim minority in peninsular India like the one that led the creation of Pakistan in 1947.

Belgaum: 1984

A communal conflict broke out in Belgaum in 1984 over the naming of a square. This conflict was in fact the violent end of a long-standing controversy over the naming of a square (*chowk*) in the city's market area. The Muslims used to call it Jinnah Chowk but the Hindus wanted to rename it Vir Savarkar Chowk.[9] During one of the meetings called by the Divisional Commissioner, the representatives of the two communities agreed to a compromise—the square would henceforth be called Maulana Azad Chowk. This name was acceptable to the Hindus, because Azad had sided with Pandit Jawaharlal Nehru in the Congress party. But the government rejected the proposal on the ground that only officially constituted 'local bodies' are empowered to decide on the names of roads and squares. This dilatory tactic only served to increase the tension between the two communities.

From 5 October the rumour spread that the Muslims had desecrated a Hindu temple. Whether true or not, this further aggravated the already strained atmosphere, as the local press, Marathi and Kannada, reported the incident in vivid detail, embroidering their comments with invective and anti-Muslim slogans. The result was disastrous. Street-fights broke out everywhere, and shops were plundered and set on fire. The riot lasted for five days in Khade Bazar (Map 10).

It seems that the government's indecisiveness was responsible for the 1984 riots. The government should have acted swiftly, proclaiming an ordinance to put an end to the conflict[10] and the campaign, orchestrated since the 1980s by the periodical *Hindu Ekta Andolan* brought out by a militant Hindu organization supposed to be infiltrated by the Shiv Sena. But neither the government nor the police took any preventive measures against the leaders of this organization, or made an attempt to dismantle the neighbourhood defence committees set up by militant Hindus.

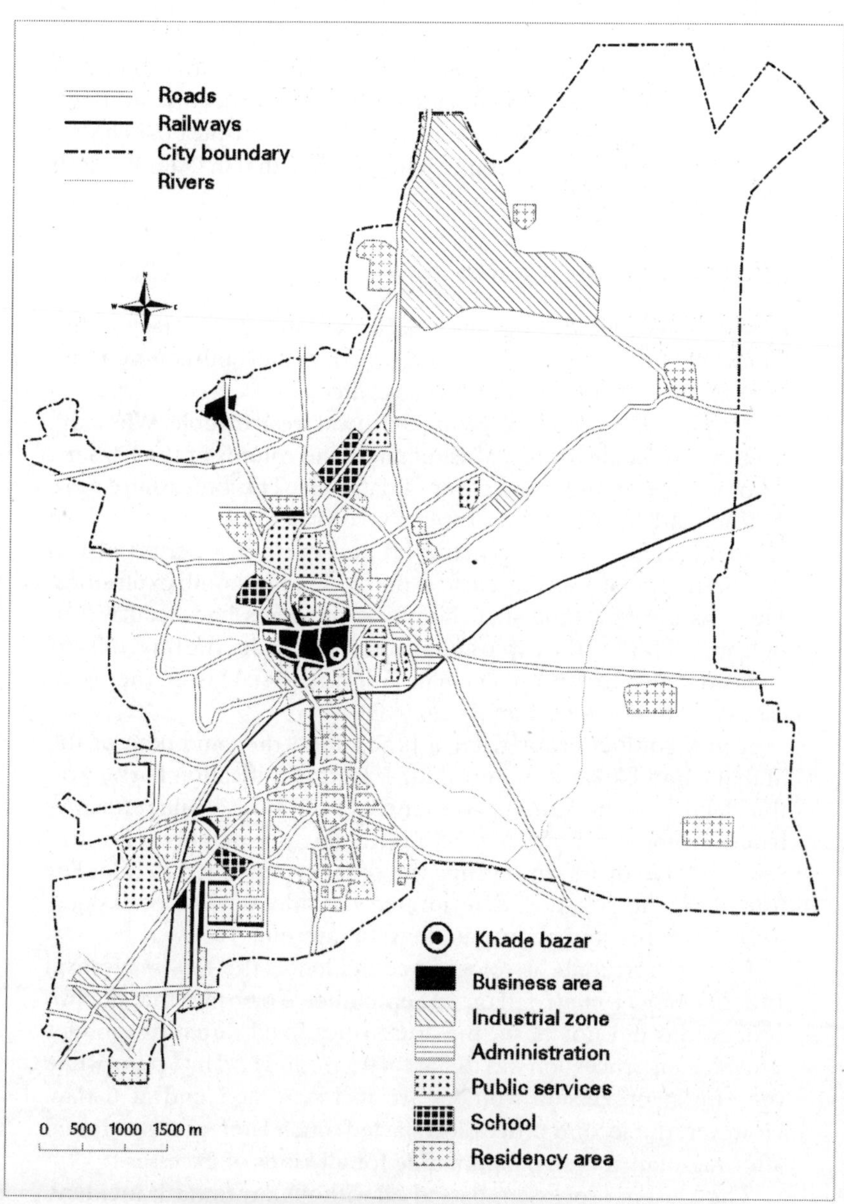

Map 10: Location of Khade Bazar in Belgaum city

After these riots, Karnataka enjoys the dubious distinction of ranking with states that have faced the largest number of communal conflicts. Over a period of three months (October, November and December 1984), there were 37 clashes leading to 15 deaths. Although this number is lower than that recorded by Maharashtra (58 clashes resulting in 280 deaths), it is much higher than that in Uttar Pradesh (32 clashes and 12 deaths).[11]

Belgaum: 1991, 1992 and 1993

In September 1991, during the *Ganesha* procession, there was another Hindu-Muslim riot. Shops belonging to members of both communities were set on fire and one Muslim was killed.

In April 1992, during *Ramadan* there was fresh trouble. When the news about the death of a Muslim made thc rounds of the bazaars, a riot broke out under the cover of darkness. This time, there were 2 dead and 92 wounded (officially recorded by the city's Civil Hospital). The clashes occurred off and on over a period of two weeks. In spite of a six-day curfew, there were two bomb explosions. This was the first time such bombing incidents had occurred in Belgaum. Though the explosions caused six deaths, the final toll was 16 dead, one of them a policeman. As for material losses, they were estimated to be more than Rs. 20,000,000.

A new conflict erupted on 8 June, when the candidate of the Maharashtra Ekikaran Samiti (Maharashtra Unification Party) won the election to the Municipal Council. On 14 June, while returning from a celebratory political meeting, a man—presumably a Hindu—was beaten to death. In revenge the other group killed a child. For four days, the situation deteriorated considerably, autorickshaws were set on fire and many people were injured.

By an unfortunate astrological coincidence, the *Ganesha* festival and *ᶜId-i Milad Unnabi,* fell on 10 September. To ensure that the two processions did not clash, the authorities fixed different timings. The Muslim procession was to start at 9 a.m. and end by 1 p.m., while the Hindu procession would start at 2 p.m. and end at 6 p.m. However, the second procession started much later, and continued after nightfall: a time most suitable for all kinds of excesses.

The Muslim procession passed off without any towards incident. But the other procession was not so peaceful. During the immersion of the *Ganesha* idol, a policeman was attacked and stabbed. An incendiary attack, evidently preplanned according to some, reduced the nearest minaret to ashes. Whatever the truth, according to the official version the fire was caused by an electrical short-circuit. However, a group of young Hindus attacked, plundered and set fire to several Muslim shops the next morning. Three persons were injured in incidents of stone-throwing. The police intervened swiftly, and claimed to have the situation under control. Nevertheless, two days later on autorickshaw driver was beaten to death and his vehicle set on fire. Newspapers claimed that he had been killed because he was a beneficiary of a government scheme reserved for Muslims for training autorickshaw drivers. They also said that vengeance had motivated the subsequent murder of a Hindu from Bombay.

The situation became so tense that the authorities had to take emergency measures and impose Prohibitory Orders under Section 144 of the CPC. The police cordoned off the district and closed the roads leading to the city's main markets (Khade Bazar, Kirloskar Road and Maruti Galli), mostly inhabited by Muslims. All the shops put down their shutters. Banks were closed for two days. However, despite all this, two men were stabbed, one in Kacheri Galli and the other in Kittur Channamma Circle. The situation remained tense throughout October.

During this time, the police recovered a large number of daggers and swords. One hundred and ten persons belonging to both communities were arrested, eleven under the Terrorist and Disruptive Activities Act (TADA) of 1985, which allowed the police to interrogate suspects and keep them in prison for one year without trial. The TADA threat sent the 'gangs' responsible for the riots underground. Among those arrested, the majority age between 18 and 22 years, was a person suspected of murdering the policeman on 10 September. But since he was a Hindu, it was considered to be a case of settling of accounts between the two communities.

The locals cite several possible motives for these clashes, which are never specifically attributed to religion.[12] This is also suggested by the statements published by a journalist in *Indian Express* (19 October 1992).

According to the retired politician Gofar Mujawar, there is nothing communal about these clashes, because *goondas* (miscreants) from both communities create problems to settle scores among themselves. M.G. Takked, former MLA, blames the police and their complicity with the *goondas*, especially the 'godfathers' of the gambling mafia (*matka*), who fight among themselves to gain control of different urban territories. Some people claim that these events were the result of the rivalry between two Superintendents of Police having links with rival gangs, which is vehemently denied. But there is no denying that rampant unemployment encourages the extremely explosive association between jobless youngsters and mischief-makers. On the other hand, an advocate believes that the riots were planned by a group of traders opposed to the construction of a new road (as decided on by the Municipal Council) on the land where their shops stood. These petty shopowners had already gone to court before the work started in March and several shops were demolished. But their case was dismissed. As a matter of fact, the work has now come to a standstill. However, the Mayor brushes this claim aside. He insists that the traders had agreed to the demolition of their shops, which had been declared illegal, and that they were not in the least opposed to this urban development project. As for the President of the Chamber of Commerce, he is more concerned about the enormous material losses amounting to Rs. 1,50,00,000. Another Rs. 20,00,000 were lost as a result of the slowing down of business activities, while the government lost Rs. 50,000 in entertainment tax owing to the closing down of cinema halls. Further, hoteliers, cloth merchants and jewellers suffered irreparable losses, because April and May are the months when they make their maximum profits, because of the marriage season. Owing to the troubles in Belgaum, most people went to the nearby towns of Hubli, Gokak or Kolhapur for their shopping.

Recently, the leaders of the two communities welcomed the idea of imposing punitive taxes on areas where such clashes occur regularly, but this did not prevent the outbreak of riots in the same areas after the demolition of the Babri Masjid in Ayodhya in December 1992!

Communal Clashes in Karnataka

A discussion in 1992 with the state Superintendent of Police in charge of communal clashes, based in Bangalore, gave me a broad idea of such clashes on a regional scale. Although such information is classified as 'confidential', he confided to me that his department had listed 28 violent 'communal incidents' during the first half of 1992, in which 5 Hindus and 6 Muslims were killed and 96 Hindus and 62 Muslims were injured. Further, 620 'minor' cases were registered and 2,600 Hindus and 304 Muslims were arrested. Material losses amounted to Rs. 15,00,00,000. In view of the seriousness of the situation, he confessed to me that the police had received orders to shoot at random at the crowd to dissuade the rioters! He felt that the only way to stop this violence was to check the spread of the wild rumours that were responsible for starting riots.[13] Even though they are nowhere near the spectacular figures recorded in Bombay, where there were 500 dead and more than 1,000 injured up to 13 January 1993, there were nevertheless 50 dead and more than 500 injured in Karnataka (28 and 150 in Bangalore and 9 and 260 in Mysore) (*India Today*, 31 December 1993).

According to the Inspector-General of Police in charge of law and order in 1993, the police now consider Belgaum, Hubli-Dharwad, Davangere, Gulbarga and Shimoga as 'communally sensitive areas', because incidents of violence have gone up tremendously in these cities during the last few years.[14] In Shimoga, in September, stones were thrown at members of the Hindu Mahasabha during a *Ganesh* procession. In Gulbarga, activists destroyed banners during an *ʿId* procession and raised Vishnu's pennant in the Chowk, although the two sides had earlier come to an understanding that there would be no trouble. The police intervened and attacked the troublemakers with *lathis* (batons). In Davangere, there was trouble in October—after a gap of two years, because the earlier clash had taken place in 1990. A farmers' demonstration to protest against certain decisions taken by the local government assumed a communal hue and caused two deaths. The farmers' procession was infiltrated by BJP activists who shouted the slogan '*Raita* (farmers) and *Rama* march hand in hand!'

In Hubli, the dispute relating to the Idgah Maidan has figured regularly in the headlines for the last ten years. The maidan is about an acre of land which BJP activists have been trying to appropriate from time to time. The place is empty except for *ʿId* prayers held twice a year by Muslims and occasional exhibitions. But before it became a political bone of contention, the dispute had legal antecedents.

It all started in August 1921, when the Hubli municipality legally leased this land to the Anjuman-i Islami, which claimed that it had been holding prayers there for the last two hundred years. The land was given to them on condition that they would use it only for religious purposes and not raise buildings on it. A 99-year lease was duly registered in 1930. On 1 February 1961, on the recommendation of the municipal administration, the government revised the conditions of the lease and permitted the Association to put up a commercial building. The decision became official on 8 February 1962. But in 1972, a petition was presented to the municipal judge (*munsif*) regarding the ownership of the site. In his 69-page report, submitted on 7 December 1973, the *munsif* insisted that the land had been leased only for holding prayers, that there was no contract involved but only a licence, and that all orders passed after 1921 were legally null and void. The Anjuman-i Islami and the Waqf Board joined hands and appealed to the Civil Judge, who declared null and void the order passed in 1962. As a result, the building already under construction had to be demolished within forty-five days. An appeal and a petition were submitted to the Karnataka High Court, which rejected the appeal on 18 June 1992, and upheld in its judgement the right of the public to use the land. The plaintiffs then approached the Supreme Court, which ruled on 8 September 1992 that the building had to be destroyed (*Frontline* 9 July 1994).

In the meanwhile, in January 1992 to be exact, the local BJP announced that it would hold a flag-hoisting ceremony on the ground on Republic Day to mark the end of the party's *Ekta Yatra* which would reach Srinagar that day and hoist the national flag in the Kashmir Valley. To honour the potential 'martyrs' to the national flag, BJP members from Hubli and other parts of Karnataka appointed for the purpose a special committee called the Rashtra Dhvaja Gaurava Rakshan Samiti. They started holding periodic meetings shouting, 'We will hoist the flag only here!' They managed to do it for a few minutes in 1992, although the leaders were taken into preventive custody and a curfew was declared. This was the original provocation that led to pitched battles between the militants of the two communities.

But on 15 August 1994, these clashes caught the attention of the nation. Leaders of extremist organizations like the BJP and the RSS—especially Uma Bharati, president of the Bharatiya Yuva aur Mahila Morcha (Movement of Youth and Women) and Member of Parliament—converged on Hubli to give support to the local extremists in the name of Indian patriotism, invoking, we may note in passing, the values of 'secularism'! The 'nationalist Muse' was arrested about 500 m from the disputed ground, before she could make a speech and spark off yet another riot. But there had been clashes and provocations earlier. The police had to open fire three times to disperse the crowd. Then they attacked the 5,000(?)

activists with *lathis.* There were four deaths according to *The Hindu* (16 August 1995), and three according to *Indian Express* (16 August 1995). The number of casualties went up during the next few days. About 40 persons were wounded by bullets and over 300 were arrested. According to BJP leaders, a squad of militants, all candidates for martyrdom, succeeded in hoisting the flag, and singing the national anthem and *Vande Mataram* a little before 7 o'clock. There are photographs to prove that the venture was a success; but the police and local authorities deny it. Though the Prime Minister declared that he did not want another Ayodhya in Karnataka, Hindu-Muslim riots broke out two days later in Bhadravati, 150 km from Hubli, provoking a particularly stormy debate in the Parliament.

On 14 October 1994, during the *Dussehra* festival, violent communal clashes occurred in Davangere. Trouble-makers threw stones at a religious procession. The police opened fire and two persons were killed. They had to shoot again when a crowd of pro-Hindu agitators armed with knives and bottles of acid attacked a Muslim slum. There were two more deaths, and 53 persons were injured, of whom 21 were policemen.

But the most tragic communal clash of the year occurred in Bangalore on 2 October, Mahatma Gandhi's birthday. On that day, the local Doordarshan (national television network) station started telecasting a daily 10-minute news bulletin in Urdu. It should be noted that this was done without any prompting from the leaders of the Muslim community in Karnataka, although, ten years earlier, the Gujral Committee had recommended that Urdu bulletins be broadcast in areas having a Muslim population of more than 10 per cent. The BJP and the Janata Dal claimed that the decision had been taken at the highest level in Delhi, under pressure from the Congress party, then in power. In the pre-electoral period, the Congress was definitely trying to strengthen its Muslim 'vote bank' after the demolition of the Babri Masjid and subsequent riots, and procrastination by Prime Minister Narasimha Rao. But the leaders not only of chauvinistic Kannada organizations like the Mico Kannada Sangha, the Channakeshavapura Kannada Sangha and the SKF Sangha, who mobilized the public, but also of the Kannada Shakti Kendra and the Kannada Sahitya Parishad, claimed that they had launched the movement because they were afraid that the time allotted to the precious television programme in Kannada would be reduced. The Congress party, in power in the state, accused the BJP of 'communalizing' the situation through its student wing, the Akhil

Bharatiya Vidyarthi Parishad (ABVP). Marwari traders in the city, known to support the BJP or the VHP, were accused of funding the trouble-makers. There is no doubt that they are in open competition with Muslim businessmen in the state. The fact remains that riots broke out on 7 October, a Friday, just after the telecast of the Urdu bulletin. Kannadiga processions intentionally marched towards the southern part of the city, where the majority of Muslims live, shouting slogans in front of mosques. 'Uncontrollable' elements attacked Muslim autorickshaw drivers and threw stones at *madrasas*, setting buildings on fire on their way. One week of uninterrupted violence followed, in spite of the announcement by the Chief Minister, Veerappa Moily, that the news bulletin had been stopped. There were no less than 30 dead and 343 wounded, and goods worth several million rupees were destroyed. The market area where the big mosque (in which six thousand persons can say their prayers at a time) is located and Mysore Road presented the sad spectacle of a land ravaged by civil war.

But enough of these dismal figures and accounts of orchestrated violence. Let us see how the apostles of modern ideological dissemination approach the transitional character of this region. On Karnataka's soil several Hindu organizations like the RSS and the Shiv Sena and the Islamic Sevak Sangh (ISS),[15] a paramilitary militant organization created in Kerala on the RSS model, constantly come into contact—often violently. All of them now get financial support from local groups. Though the RSS makes its presence felt in all the districts of Karnataka, for the first time in the state's history four BJP candidates were elected during the 1991 parliamentary elections—two from Shimoga district, one from Bidar and one from South Kanara. In these elections, the BJP polled 28.33 per cent votes in the state, 32.26 per cent in south Karnataka, 36.94 per cent in Kodagu and 31.70 per cent in Malnad. It is also known that, since the beginning of 1992, the ISS has set up bases in Belgaum, Shimoga, Mangalore, Kodagu and the state capital, Bangalore, where no less than 14 antennas can be counted.

Muslim Memorials in the Communal Conflict

It was in the southern part of Belgaum that I met an ISS supporter for the first time. The majority of the city's Muslim population lives in this area. It is a crowded neighbourhood situated right next to the local and regional bus terminus. The Petti Bazar, a labyrinth of narrow streets teeming with vehicles and shops that draw a crowd of shoppers and curious onlookers throughout the day, spreads out haphazardly around the Anjuman mosque (Fig. 10). This faded and run-down building is flanked by a *madrasa* and a library named after Muhammad Iqbal, whose poetry inspired the creation of Pakistan. The students of the *madrasa* are mainly taught Arabic and Urdu, and some thirty mullahs are trained every year.

The mosque was built in 1585-6 at the command of the Sufi, Sher Khan, the local representative of the Shia Sultan Ibrahim II of Bijapur (1580-1626). This scholarly king, was the patron of the historian Muhammad Qazim Firishta (Ahmad 1964: 201-18).

The land on which the mosque stands still belongs to the family that donated it. The present descendant, Abdul Rahim Sher Khan, a tailor by profession, now leads a retired life. A very pious man, he is always willing to talk of his pilgrimage to Ajmer in Rajasthan, twenty years ago. Waqf properties such as this are administered by a committee consisting of ten members, some of them government representatives.

We must point out that in 1978 the Karnataka government pioneered the creation of a Waqf Development Corporation under the Companies Act. If the corporation is endowed with Rs. 1,00,00,000 the Karnataka government keeps 25 per cent of this amount to promote the economic activities of all the Trusts or Waqfs, functioning under the aegis of the Muthavalli Managing Committee. Since then, the majority of these Trusts—there were 19,000 of them in the state at the time of writing this book—are owners or managers of stores, hotels, apartments, industrial and agricultural cooperatives, or educational institutions, whose funding is assured by the capitalization of amounts received as obligatory charity (*zakat*) (Ahmad 1993: 51, 77-8). We may add that the government also constituted a Karnataka State Haj Committee in 1980 to assess the needs of Kannadiga pilgrims going to Mecca and to look after their well-being.

Actually the mosque covers only a part of the land. Behind it rises the mausoleum of Abdul Rahman Khanjar Shah Malikhan, the 'Merciful King-Lord with the dagger'. In the small compound surrounding his unpretentious *mazar* there are six sepulchres belonging to unidentified members of his family. On one side, a small whitewashed mud-brick structure serves as a permanent shelter for Rifa'i fakirs.

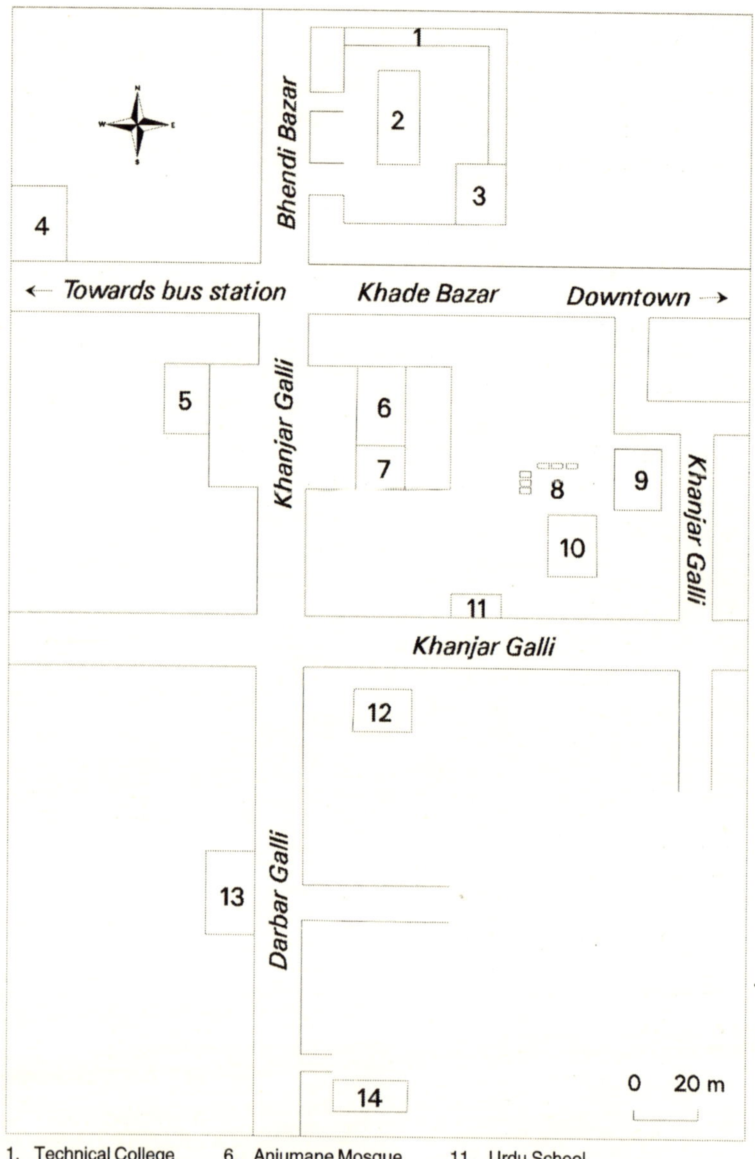

1. Technical College
2. Bashuban Dargah
3. Madrasa
4. Sheetal Hotel
5. Cadi ^{c}Abdul ^{c}Aziz
6. Anjumane Mosque
7. Iqbal Library
8. Graves
9. Fakirs Rifa'i
10. Khanjar Dargah
11. Urdu School
12. Sher Khan's house
13. Darbar Hall
14. Sajjadanashin Shah Pasha

Figure 10: Sketch of the Muslim area in Khade Bazar

Today the saint has no surviving descendant. Local collective memory remembers no more than his name and the date of his death anniversary, celebrated every year during the *ʿurs* after the procession in the neighbourhood. In spite of repeated efforts in 1991, I could not fill in this existential gap except by this short story related to me by Abdul Rahim Sher Khan:

Abdul Rahman was born in Baghdad in the fourteenth century. One night, he dreamt that he was holding a long dagger with a carved hilt inlaid with precious stones. Suddenly the dagger slipped out of his hands and flew away in the direction of Hindustan. It landed, if we may dare to say so, in Belgaum. The saint decided to settle down there after being initiated by many famous teachers on his way from Iraq to India. The place was then a thick forest inhabited by wild animals, tigers and elephants. The saint, who stood out because of his long beard and his impressive white turban, lived alone, leading a life of prayer and meditation. His piety won him many disciples who believed that he possessed miraculous powers . . .

When I returned to Belgaum in 1992 after the communal riots, I was surprised to find myself being offered his biography in private! To be more precise, it consisted of a series of hagiographic elements that all agreed on his sudden and dramatic end, that he died as he fought bravely against Hindu armies. The mullahs declared that he had settled down in Belgaum much later, probably in the seventeenth or eighteenth century, than what Abdul Rahim Sher Khan had given me to understand. The dates mentioned by the mullahs correspond to the building's architectural style. Those professing to know better, traced the events as follows:

After conquering several forts like Raigarh, Chakan and Purandar, and sacking many towns, Shivaji's Maratha troops under the command of Pratap Rao made a second foray into the region. They wanted to conquer the town of Hubli, which was then a prosperous trading centre under the control of the East India Company. But Sultan Ali II (1656-72) of Bijapur opposed this conquest. In the hope of preventing the destruction of Hubli, he sent his troops under the command of Muzaffar Khan, the viceroy of Kanara, who had received as a fief the imposing fort of Belgaum. After a terrible battle, Muzaffar Khan managed to drive out the enemy with the help of 4,000 mounted soldiers, among whom was the Sufi warrior Khanjar, who distinguished himself on the battlefield before laying down his life.

Though these events are historically correct (except for the reference to Khanjar), the story makes no mention of two well-known facts. First, Shivaji welcomed Muslim soldiers in his army (Gordon 1993: 66); and second, although he was a vassal of the Sultan of Bijapur, Muzaffar made a secret pact with the Marathas so that he could become independent (Sarkar 1992: 186).

But most of my informants had not bothered to tell me exactly how Khanjar Shah died. Some claimed that he died while he was a part of the powerful Mughal army raised by Aurangzeb to put an end to the expansion of Shivaji's Maratha empire. Others insisted he was in Tipu Sultan's army, which meant that his death occurred during the war waged by the King of Mysore against the Peshwas, who had formed an opportunistic alliance with the British against Tipu Sultan. But they too omitted one detail, probably because they were unaware of it—that the Nizam of Hyderabad was a part of this alliance formed to vanquish Tipu Sultan! (Desai 1970: 435).

To the best of my knowledge, there is no written proof available either in support of these stories or against them. However oral testimony has taken the place of historical records in the strategy of belief and conviction that turns history into myth.[16] All the stories conspire together to depict the *pir* as a warrior (*ghazi*), the emblematic hero of the Muslim struggle against the Hindus—including the British, enemies clubbed together when convenient, and whose felonious character was always emphasized by my informants. Only one episode recurred constantly. While negotiations were going on between the Sultan of Bijapur (represented by Afzal Khan) and Shivaji, the latter treacherously killed the Muslim general with steel claws hidden on his person. However, official Maratha historiography accuses Afzal Khan of treachery. His attempt to kill Shivaji failed because the wily Maratha chief took the precaution of wearing a coat of mail under his clothes (Sarkar 1992: 51-2). This anecdote has become famous, and is much celebrated in popular ballads (Rao 1969), village fairs, plays and films, apart from scholarly writings. Whatever the truth, the headless Muslim army was easily defeated by Shivaji, although there were many Marathas in the service of the Sultan of Bijapur as the historian Gordon tells us (1993: 68). On the other hand, when the Marathas conquered Delhi during the rule of Shah Alam II (1760-1818) they proclaimed themselves protectors of the Mughal empire (Alam 1989: 54).

Like the various other references to the death of Khanjar Shah Wali, celebrated every year, this last analogy contributed to make the saint a hero of the Islamic faith who gave his life during a holy war against infidels. This process of changing a saint into a martyr is an ancient one, starting before the fourteenth century according to Ernst (1992: 104), the warlike qualities attributed to Khanjar perhaps had a Sufi connotation, since the dagger was directed against the 'carnal soul' (ibid.: 310, n. 25). Some of my interlocutors even dared to compare him with the saint Salar Mas'ud Ghazi called 'Ghazi Miyan' or the 'holy warrior'. This young prince was killed in combat in 1033 at Bahraich in Uttar Pradesh during one of the earliest Muslim expeditions, preceding the conquest of the subcontinent by more than a century (Gaboriaux 1975: 290; Schwerin 1984).

However, the majority portrayed the saint as one who resisted the Hindus, a martyr to the cause of the faith rather than a conqueror. This gives us the feeling that we are dealing with a community that is always on the defensive, since it is quite far from Islamic centres like Gulbarga and Hyderabad in the Deccan, and even further from the large concentrations of Muslim population in north India. This creation of legends is the reaction of a community that feels extremely vulnerable in a hostile, and even threatening, Hindu environment. This also explains why there were so many Sunnis ready to compare Khanjar Shah with Husain, the Prophet's grandson. Thus, while the saint is compared to Husain, Hindus are likened to the soldiers of Caliph Yazid, even though the latter were Sunnis!

The invocation of past events to endow the saint with the attributes of the soldier of God, wearing the martyr's sacrificial garb, is meant to defend that inner frontier within which a community forges its cohesion and its religious identity. The withdrawal of the local community into itself when faced by invaders, whom the mullahs readily identify as 'infidels' revives, at least from the observer's viewpoint, the canonical opposition between non-Islamic lands (*dar ul-harb*) and the Islamic homeland (*dar ul-Islam*), though at a huge distance in both time and space from the original Caliphate. The present pessimistic outlook of the communal situation has changed this brave warrior of the faith[17] into a martyr or even a voluntary suicide for the glory of Allah. After all, a *hadith* by Zainuddin does claim that 'Paradise lies under the shade of swords'.[18]

About 200 m from the mosque stands the mausoleum of the saint Basubhan. The present 'spiritual guide' answers to the name of Shali Pasha Basubhan Imamdar. According to his disciples he is considered saintly because his lineage is linked with the universal genealogy of the *ashraf.* His saintly qualities were further crystallized during his lifetime by the extraordinary *baraka* of the *wali* who represents them.

He tells me that his lineage goes back to Ali and Fatima, although it springs from one Sayyid Abubakar Basubhan, born in Iraq in the eleventh century. But he can actually trace his genealogy to Sayyid Umar Idriss Basubhan, born five centuries later in Yemen. The Muslim system of universal identification, which permits a person to trace his ancestry as far back as possible to Arabic, thereby adding to the family's prestige, effectively maintains and supports the message of local saints. By linking the individual with the universal, believers transform an obscure local saint into an ancestor who is almost a contemporary of the Prophet. And this reference to a chain of initiated saints close to the divine source is meant to attach an 'insignificant' local history to the 'great' Muslim history in order to share its fame and power.

The fact remains that Sayyid Umar Idriss Basubhan was born in the seventeenth century, in Tarim in Yemen. He received the title of *maulana* in Medina after having acquired a deep knowledge of religious science in a *madrasa.* When he was a young man, the Prophet appeared before him in a dream. In his wonderful voice, the Prophet ordered him to preach Islam in Hindustan. Basubhan did as he was told, but broke his journey for long periods to perfect his knowledge. Thus he stopped in Surat, Ahmadabad and Bijapur before settling down in Belgaum, where he died in 1064/1686. During the interval, he gathered around him seven hundred disciples, including five hundred *hakims* (traditional doctors), one hundred *hafiz* (those capable of reciting the Koran by heart) and one hundred *khatib* (preachers). The following episode, known to all the devotees who visit his tomb, explains the origin of his name and also of his saintliness.

While two men were quarreling on a street in Tarim, a four-year-old child happened to pass by. To settle their dispute, the authorities decided that the two opponents should appear before a judge (*qadi*). But before pronouncing the verdict, the judge wanted to call witnesses It so happened that there was only one witness, and the judge was assured that the witness would be produced before him.

The next day, a man brought the child before the judge. The latter declared that it was against the law to record the testimony of a child. On hearing these words, the child got angry and started rubbing his palms against his cheeks. A long white beard grew almost instantaneously. On seeing this miracle, the judge exclaimed, 'He is *abba Subhan*!', or 'a father blessed (by God)'. When the story spread, the town-dwellers started calling the child '*abba Subhan*', contracted later to 'Basubhan'.

This amazing man devoted most of his life to writing a medical treatise or aphorisms (*Nawādir al-tibbiya*), which there is no trace today. His reputation as a healer, mistaken for his wisdom as a 'philosopher', was so great that even today he is known as a doctor (*tabib*).

After his death, his family split into two lines, one from his eldest son, Sayyid Abdul Rahman Basubhan, who had nine children. It is said that a person bearing his name is buried in Khata Bazar in Bombay, while the others are buried in Belgaum. So, what we have here are urban saints who have maintained the prestige attached to pious scholars.

The main representative of the other line, Sayyid Muhammad Basubhan, left Belgaum and settled down in Sulga 8 km away, where the villagers were suffering from the effects of a terrible drought. I learnt the following story from a resident of Sulga.

On his arrival, the saint asked for water for his ablutions. The villagers replied in one voice: 'We don't have water even to drink, so how can we give you water for your ablutions?' the saint raised his stick and violently struck a block of stone, and water started gushing out. On hearing of this miracle, Aurangzeb decided to give him the village as a gift. That is how the saint became a big landlord, an *inamdar* (a name that has now been changed to *imamdar*, and is still used by his descendants). At the end of his life, he went to Mangallela, a village near Kolhapur, where he breathed his last. He is buried there, and his death anniversary is still celebrated on the 27th, 28th and 29th of the month of *Rajab*.

This saint had three sons, and I was told that the descendants of the second son live in Belgaum today.

The memory of these two Muslim saints remains alive, each in its own way. Though in the case of the scholarly saint, Basubhan, its continuity has been maintained because his descendants are heirs to a past that is still alive, this is not so in the case of the warrior saint, Khanjar Shah. There is only a vague memory of his persona. But that does not prevent people from worshipping him, particularly the Rifa'i fakirs, who commemorate his 'mystical marriage with Allah' with great pomp.

It is interesting to see how much the extensive memory of the former is contained within the repetition of a present (combined with the past), whereas the absence of memory in the latter's case allows his devotees to fill in the gaps according to circumstances. In other words, oblivion has helped to bring him back to life. For example, the emotions stirred up by the communal tragedy lend greater depth to his character, making him an ideal instrument for interpreting the present turmoils.

Normally, this availability explains why people run to him for the fulfilment of all kinds of urgent desires, including the birth of a child. His religious image is of a more 'popular' nature because he is venerated as a miracle-worker, unlike the scholarly Basubhan. The latter is the patron of a faith marked by piety, and he benignly watches over the technical college bearing his name in the compound of his mausoleum, where courses are conducted in English.

Each saint inspires a very different kind of worship. Basubhan is visited by the devout because he is an object of peaceful, and sometimes mystical, worship appealing to man's inner nature. Khanjar Shah, on the other hand, presides over ecstatic dances performed to the rhythmic beat of the drum, ostentatious cases of possession by demons and violent demonstrations by fakirs of their mystical powers. While the worship of the latter is made possible by donations from devotees who are recruited without any restrictions, the former owns large Waqf properties, income from which provides for the maintenance of his shrine. These funds are managed by his immediate descendants in close association with patrons mindful of their respectability. For several generations, aristocratic circles of Basubhan's devotees link their identity to his origin, prestigious because it is contemporaneous with the Revelation. They mock at Khanjar Shah's devotees, who are of common stock, and at the rustic practices that are a part of his cult, although 'that way of everyday practices of Muslims changed less than did their way of conceptualizing and lebelling these practices' (Ewing 1988: 16). If aristocratic sainthood were opposed to magico-religious virtuosity, so would the prestige of study be opposed to that of war and the practice of medicine and poetry to that of healing.

We must however take care not to exaggerate this opposition between the two saints, as they are really complementary. In spite of the unvoiced hostility between the warrior-magician and the puritanical doctor,[19] there are links between them, as the devotees of the one readily visit the other's shrine. Though they are generally also normative, feelings of solidarity are partly built around groups that are based on flexible relationships between the cohorts of followers who, because they feel they are surrounded by hostile forces, tend to recognize each other as forming part of a single community occupying the same territory.

Both saints profess the same universal religion; both were exceptional men considered to be mirrors of the Prophet, who himself is a mirror of God, and had the same vocation of bringing Heaven closer to Earth. They represent different types of *baraka*, and embody two different aspects of Indian Islam. Their coexistence, which joins *jihad* to the *shari'a*, empowers them to perform functions that are at once both distinct and cumulative. If the one embodies the militant ideology of holy war and the magical power bearing the seal of his martyrdom, the other exemplifies the respectful behaviour enjoined by the sacred law. These are two ways of demarcating the community's limits—by opposing it to all 'infidels' who, because they do not abide by the etiquette, lie beyond its pale.[20] It is the responsibility of combative violence to protect the habitual non-violence which regulates ordinary sociability—the more so because, since the dissolution of the Caliphate (1924), an event of which the majority of local Muslims are ignorant, the breach between religion and the world does not allow the law to be propagated in India by means of the holy war.[21] These are the two aspects that make up the one (and only) religion, one 'popular' and 'exoteric' and the other more 'canonical' and 'esoteric', which have for a long time permeated all social groups, though in varying measures.[22] They are therefore two types of devotion and two ways of perceiving the spiritual power of Islam, which can also be interpreted as the polarity between the universal and the singular. The former is restricted by boundaries that can always be pushed back further; and the second is confused with the sanctification of a local figure 'firmly entrenched in its place' (Digby 1994: 99).

We must insist that the two religious trends, one characterized by the *ulama* and the other by 'marabouts', coexist even today and influence each other with every swing of the pendulum, however slight, between retention and pretension, between class difference and social solidarity. After all, are not both saints venerated as guardians? Without a doubt, the scholar's centuries-old base serves as a greater obstacle to periodic manipulations, while the warrior's residual image makes him more susceptible to modification in tune with the present. However, this present becomes a refrain for the Muslims, because it merges completely with the tumultuous history of their relationship with the Hindus. Whenever the communal conflict worsens, we can expect a revival of the saint's martyrdom. An attack of amnesia is very useful in this type of projection into the past.

It follows that the memorials can be put to two kinds of use; that there are two types of memory at work in the experience of this regional Islam, which lays greater stress on genealogy than on chronology. The former, based on tradition, is transmitted by the repetition of a story that exalts a learned man who is peace-loving, but is also a protector of his followers, though he is indifferent to current concerns. As for the latter, his military prowess prevails over his ancestry, and he functions through reinventions of history that move from key to key under the cloak of a model that the impact of force renders immediately ready for mobilization.

Memory, History and Violence

When conducting a study in the circumscribed space of a particular 'field' in this manner, it is evident that its limited scope has value not merely as an isolate particular. Not only do its descriptions refer to a great depth of time, but its course opens the way to far distant geographic horizons. When the protagonists narrate what, from the ethnologist's viewpoint, are very minor events and recount their 'little history', it is only because they want to establish their authenticity and make them a part of the 'great history', the history of their country and their religion, which they rewrite as they go along. In the same way, they promote local cults only to relate them better to more universal forms, which they restructure when the need arises. It is therefore worthwhile to decipher the signs and the possible consequences of local events and place them in a context that transcends these events by investing them with a meaning. The collective memory of groups, or of social imagination, is semiotic rather than historical: it freely reinvents the past, changes past events into myths, and subsequently changes these same myths into history. Thanks to this appropriation, made possible as much by lapse of memory as by remembrance, and depending on camouflaged feedback, the past is reflected in the present, and history arranges itself like a metaphor for mythical realities.

We cannot but conclude that memory, this real-life relationship with the world, is a conduit for narration that has an essentially social function, as it is defined by P. Janet.[23] This is amply illustrated by the border dispute between the states of Maharashtra and Karnataka, an echo of the long-standing ethnic, linguistic and political rivalry between the Hindu Marathas and Kannadigas, which takes a backseat when they join hands for a common purpose.[24] When the national communal situation demands it, they form a joint front against the Muslims, or rather 'the Muslim' considered as a stereotype of radical alterity, who remains an alien although he has lived side by side with them for centuries and participated in what is called a 'syncretic' way of living and believing of which there are innumerable examples. In fact, this stereotype of the enemy is all the more frightening because, apart from his nearness, they have to contend with his alien identity, which comes to the fore promptly at the slightest provocation. In fact, the comparative ethnography of the two saints of Indian Islam housed in their respective *dargahs* in Belgaum provides an excellent example of the tendency to build identity on alterity. Though they are both Sufis, their devotees seek their assistance in very different or even contradictory circumstances, and they are brought to life by a hagiographical *topos* that is inseparable from local history (Dakhlia 1990: 195). But when all is said and done, it must be admitted that talking of the dead is a topic that essentially concerns the living, who invoke them in order to conjure away, thwart or reply to repeated attacks by other living beings.

There is certainly a substantial difference in the way the two communities now look at religion. The Hindus are exploiting it to redraw the map of India, which they confuse with the territory of a sacred nation in which the *Ramayana* is continuously replayed, with Rama chasing away demons currently embodied by the Muslims. As for the Muslims, they are using religion to dramatize the fight tirelessly waged by their martyrs to defend the boundaries of the areas occupied by them, which are treated as veritable kingdoms, against the forces of Hindutva.

NOTES

1. On the reshaping of Hinduism on a chauvinistic nationalistic model, see Jaffrelot (1993a), and Gold (1991).
2. An explanation of the trends of Islamic fundamentalism in India is provided by Ahmad (1991).
3. A detailed account of the history of Belgaum can be found in the *Bombay Gazetteer, Belgaum* (1884: Chapter VII).
4. Interview with Abdul Bari Nawab, (Commissioner, Municipal Corporation of the City of Belgaum), on 20 March 1994.

5. For a detailed account of the agricultural development and the establishment of industries in Belgaum district since the nineteenth century, Rao (1989).
6. It is difficult to determine the exact date of the beginning of Islamization of this area. As in other parts of India, it occurred in waves and through a slow impregnation rather than through sudden conversions. According to the *Bombay Gazetteer Belgaum*, 1884, the first to come were Arab traders looking for jobs in the courts of local chieftains of the time. They were followed by Turks and north Indian Muslims, who invaded the Deccan in the thirteenth century. Then came Abyssinians, Arabs and Afghans who settled down here during the rule of the Bahmani Sultans (1347-1490), the Sultans of Bijapur (1489-1686) and the Mughals (1686-1723). The last wave occurred when Haidar Ali and his son Tipu Sultan were at the height of their power (1760-80). During this period and also under Aurangzeb (1686-1707), there were a large number of conversions.
7. This instance corresponds to the socio-economic explanation of entrepreneurial 'micro-level' communalism proposed by Engineer (1991) and Ahmed (1984).
8. Ray and Kumpatla (1987: 1829). This political ploy, as often happens, led to carelessness in classification. The Commission classified the 'Darveshis' as a Backward Tribe, and the 'Kasais' were put in the category of 'Backward Castes and Tribes', though they are both Muslim sub-castes (*Muslim India*, 26 December 1985, p. 552). The following table will give an idea of the political strength of the various groups in the state legislative assembly.

REPRESENTATION OF VARIOUS CASTES IN THE KARNATAKA LEGISLATIVE ASSEMBLY (1952-72)

Castes/ Communities	1952		1957		1962		1967*		1972	
	No.	%	No.	%	No.	%	No.	%	No.	%
Brahmins	14	11.0	9	6.3	8	6.0	8	5.8	11	6.2
Lingayats	45	35.4	47	33.1	45	34.0	49	35.5	43	24.2
Vokkaligas	33	26.0	35	24.7	35	26.5	36	26.1	52	29.2
Other Hindus	12	9.5	22	15.5	20	15.2	17	12.3	37	20.8
SC*	20	15.7	22	15.5	21	15.9	24	17.4	23	12.9
ST*	0	0.0	2	1.4	1	0.8	0	0	2	1.1
Christians	0	0.0	1	0.7	0	0	1	0.7	5	2.8
Jains	2	1.6	3	2.1	1	0.8	1	0.7	1	0.6
Muslims	1	0.8	1	0.7	1	0.8	2	1.5	4	2.2
Total	127	100	142	100	132	100	138	100	178	100

Note: *SC: Scheduled Castes; ST: Scheduled Tribes.
Source: *Karnataka Backward Classes Commission Report*, vol. IV, Bangalore, Government of Karnataka (1975: 822-3).

9. Savarkar, an ideologue and the author of a 'treatise on Hindutva' (Hinduness) that inspired Hedgewar, founder of the RSS, wrote, 'A Hindu means a person who regards this land of Bharatvarsha (India) from the Indus to the Seas, as his Fatherland as well as his Holy land.' This merging of geography (Bharatvarsha), genealogy (Fatherland) and religion (Holy land) enabled him to create an ethnic and political myth—because the Hindu nation (Hindu rashtra) and Hinduness (Hindutva) are congruent—according to which Hindus are descended from the first Aryans who inhabited the subcontinent. He declared, 'All Hindus claim that they carry in their veins the blood of the powerful race descended from the Vedic fathers' (quoted by Jaffrelot 1993b: 226). In 1939, the second RSS leader, Golwalkar, proposed a 'final solution' by moving from Aryanism to pro-Germanism. He says, 'Germany shocked the world by her purging the country of the Semitic races—the Jews. Race pride at its highest has been manifested here. Germany has also shown how well-nigh impossible it is for races and cultures, having differences going to the root, to be assimilated into a whole, a good lesson for us in Hindusthan to learn and profit by' (quoted by Gold 1991: 556).
10. We know that since Independence at least, the proclamation of ordinances is a part of the political strategy employed for 'managing' 'ethnic' and 'communal' conflicts (Das 1992: 11).
11. *Muslim India*, 26 February 1985: 19. These figures do not take into account the communal violence that occurred in November/December 1984 following the assassination of Prime Minister Indira Gandhi by her Sikh bodyguards. The figures here were compiled in official reports on communal riots in India and should be taken with a pinch of salt, as is pointed out by Das (1992: 8). Not so much because official agencies have a tendency to play down the number of casualties (usually more deaths are caused by the police controlling the riots), but because the definition of 'communal clashes' is subject to different interpretations. Thus Freitag's study (1990) points out that, during the 1880s, internal rivalry in a community in Agra was responsible for what was reported to be a 'communal clash'. Pandey reminds us that the narrative structure of communalism was fixed into a stereotype during colonial rule, and says that the historian should be able to distance himself from the dominant viewpoint of nationalistic historiography (1990). Having said this, we present the following table to give an idea of the number of victims from the two communities:

NUMBER OF HINDUS AND MUSLIMS KILLED IN RIOTS BETWEEN 1968 AND 1980

Year	1968	1969	1970	1971	1972	1973	1974	1975	1976	1977	1978	1979	1980
Hindus	24	66	68	38	21	26	26	11	20	12	51	80	87
Muslim	99	558	176	65	45	45	61	22	19	24	56	50	278

Sources: *Muslim India*, Nos. 81, 103 and 108.

12. That is the conclusion of the numerous studies conducted by Asghar Ali Engineer (1984).
13. According to the more optimistic observers, the use of indiscriminate force under the pretext of maintaining order indicates a decline in the authority of the rule of law following the growing criminalization of politics. According to more pessimistic observers, it represents 'state terrorism'. Apart from the large number of deaths, mainly Muslim, caused by the forces of law and order, it may be noticed that the men behind this communal violence are never prosecuted.
14. Riots have become more severe in Karnataka since 1990, when the Vishwa Hindu Parishad (VHP—created by the RSS in 1964 to propagate Hinduism) organized *Ram Jyoti Yatras* (processions carrying Rama's flame). Thus the riot in Channapatna on the Prophet's birthday caused 17 deaths, according to official records, while the riot in Davangere caused more than ten deaths when a procession of 20,000 'devotees' entered the Muslim neighbourhood.
15. The ISS was founded in November 1990 by a violent anti-Hindu agitator named Abdul Nassar Madhani, advocating an Islamic revolution in Kerala in the name of a holy war (*jihad*). The movement has its headquarters in Mynagapalli near Quilon, but it has a very strong base in the district of Mallapuram which has an 85 per cent Muslim population. The movement claims a membership of 90,000 divided into 2,600 branches. The rumour goes that it has set up antennas in mosques and that it has ramifications in the Gulf countries (*Sunday*, 14-20 June 1992).
16. There is an internecine war between history and myth, a kind of family quarrel that determines the position on which M. de Certeau has reflected at length: '(. . .) by struggling against genealogical confabulations, against the myths and legends of collective memory and the deviations in oral transmission, historiography creates a gulf between itself and what is commonly said and believed; and it lodges itself precisely within this difference which supplies it with its accreditation as 'learned' by dint of distinguishing it from ordinary discourse.' (1975b: 66).
17. Bayly mentions the transformation of Sayyid Mustafa of Kalathura into a martyred companion of Tipu Sultan (1989: 187). She quotes several like examples in Tamil Nadu also. Dale and Gangadhara Menon describe the worship of a deified martyred saint in Kerala (1978). Ernst, on the relationship between hagiography and martyrology emphasizes the role played Husain Ibn Mansur al-Hallaj as a model of Islam (1985). Finally, in the realm of political ideology we must mention the Mujahiddin Movement, led by the traditionalist Ahmed Riza Khan (1855-1921), founder of the Barelvi school (which adopted a view that was diametrically opposite to the doctrines of the Father of Indian Wahhabism, Sayyid Ahmad Barelvi (1786-1831).

18. Quoted by Dale (1980: 52). His book on the Mappilas of Kerala explains this militant ideology with reference to the notion of the 'boundaries of Islam' (which he borrows from Witteck's work on the Ottoman empire). He also provides several examples of armed rebellion, spread out over a long period, and some of which were suicidal, against Christians, Hindus and the British. Hardgrave indicates that one of the leaders of these revolts assumed the title of 'Khilafat King' and ruled over two districts (1977: 82). Regarding the notion of 'boundaries of Islam', Richards (1974), Fusfeld (1988) and Assayag (1996), Ernst (1992) and Eaton (1994). The Bir Babas of Benares, guardians of deities, are considered both as 'heroes' (*vīra*) and 'martyrs' (*shahid*) as they died in the battle of the Mahabharata against the armies of Aurangzeb or the British (Coccari 1989).
19. We must refer to Gellner (1981) for the most lucid explanation (in the case of Berbers) of the opposition (and complementarity) between the Islam propagated by scholars and the one propagated by saints.
20. Ewing presents a clear account of the determinants, both ambiguous and contradictory, of the *shari'a* in India.
21. Certainly, when the coalition between Hindus and Muslims (forged against the colonizers) broke up in 1922, the All-India Khilafat Organization dominated by the ulama started working for the restoration of the Caliphate in Ottoman Turkey. But later, 'The passions and energies which had responded to religious appeals and the stimulus of the non-cooperation program had found new outlets, perhaps in the form of communal riots' (Minault 1982: 82). Since them, 'Muslim nationalism' has taken over from 'Islamic nationalism'.
22. 'Two classical religious styles' as Geertz puts it (1968), but within the same society and, what is more important, in the same neighbourhood!
23. This is the main idea behind his book, *L'évolution de la mémoire et la notion du temps,* published in 1928. Ricoeur has expressed the same idea more recently in very eloquent terms: 'Tradition is not the inert transmission of a deposition that is already dead, but the live transmission of a new idea that is likely to be reactivated by a return to poetic action' (1991: 106).
24. This is not entirely true because the *panchayats* of Belgaum and Khanapur taluks, controlled by members of the Maharashtra Ekikaran Samiti (MES), seceded from Karnataka on 15 August 1995, demanding that the Marathi-speaking areas of Belgaum, Nippani and Bidar be included in Maharashtra state.

Conclusion

At the Confluence of Two Oceans

> The desire to associate only with
> those whom we approve on all counts is
> fanciful; it amounts to sheer fanaticism.
>
> ALAIN, *Propos II* (1910)

Some well-known examples in literature and a few cursory sociological studies have led to the belief that Hindus and Muslims either fought incessantly in the past or lived together in perfect harmony in accordance with 'syncretic' principles of thought and action. But present-day field-studies (in the beginning of the 1990s) on problems related to acculturation, remind us that there is a tendency to idealize these references to past events. Without succumbing to either of these views, we may point out that the so-called Hindu and Muslim communities cannot be understood and defined once and for all. Understanding the endless nuances of acculturation in day-to-day life demands that we mistrust conceptual schemes that are manipulated in the rarefied atmosphere of hypothetical reconstructions or abstract ideas. We must therefore be prepared to suspend the ideological debate and concentrate on cultural dynamics and other sociogenetic aspects that have created the communal mosaic peculiar to India and shaped the bilateral relations between Hindus and Muslims.

This study of the modes of thought and action of thousands of people living in a small part of South Asia has led me to conclude that Hindus and Muslims have not been living in separate compartments during the past centuries. On the contrary, they have thrived on constant exchanges that have developed over the years. This is obvious because Hinduism and Islam, as they were practised until very recently, continue to show a great deal of flexibility and a spirit of accommodation in their mutual relations. In fact, they display an understanding that is infinitely richer than the limited sectarian approach adopted by dogmatic and orthodox circles on either sides. When all is said and done, it is possible that the relationship between Hinduism and Islam has been, and still is in some regions, a cultural system, i.e. a codification of the differences between neighbouring groups, a set of changing interrelations within configurations that are constantly adapting themselves to changing circumstances. But what is most remarkable is that the continuous process of acculturation has allowed each tradition to preserve its peculiarities. Better still, in spite of the existence of a network of exchanges and reciprocal actions and the absence of a clear conceptual boundary between them, this process allows these communities to withdraw periodically into themselves whenever the situation (dramatized by the actors) requires them to affirm their social identity *vis-à-vis* the other so-called 'community'. Hindus and Muslims have been able to achieve this not by enunciating basic spiritual truths but through seemingly insignificant though decisive signs, by cobbling together 'little bits of truth', as observed by Freud, during the 'shifting' of traditions (1975: 115). In fact, the aim of this monograph has been to illustrate and understand this plurality and specificity.

It is also possible to draw some systematic lessons of a more general nature from this locally-ground study.

The first lesson is that when we are trying to understand socio-religious practices we should not limit to textual norms or to the viewpoint of the so-called 'great' traditions. It is true that some of these traditions claim to be universal. But it must be remembered that before they were written down and even once they became traditions, those who created them engaged in a multifaceted exchange with other systems of thought and action. This observation also applies just as much to those who continued these traditions after they became what they are today. This is the lesson that we can learn from the composite worship of the hybrid figure of Changadev/ Rajabag Savar (Chapter 4). Moreover, it should be kept in mind that the protagonists are able to create traditions, transmit them or destroy them only under the influence of social interaction. Of course, many traditions are distorted by the very persons who are inspired by them, or even by those opposed to them, or even those usually more numerous—who are either indifferent to them or unaware of them. Ignoring ideas handed down by the history of religions or by civilizations interested only in the study of 'Religion' or 'Civilization' means treating these issues in a contextual and pragmatic manner and avoiding identification with the propagandists of either camp. Different cultural forms are not watertight compartments, but the products of dynamic processes and mutual adjustment. Thus when it comes to notions that oppose the gross categories Hinduism to Islam, polytheism to monotheism, or even egalitarianism to hierarchy, one must be careful not to project them anachronistically in history, or consider them as values on which contradictory conceptions are founded. We may cite as a proof the mutual adjustment between Hindus and Muslims in Shahabandar Chapter 1 or the overlapping of stories about the goddess and the saint of Saundatti (Chapter 5). In this book entitled *At the Confluence of Two Rivers*, I have tried to understand the Hindus and Muslims of south India through the notion of dynamic acculturation.

The second lesson is the thoughtless use of the notion of 'community' and its corollary, the 'holistic' approach to society, because it presumes what is yet to be demonstrated, viz., the supposed organic unity of the whole and the proper demarcation of the groups constituting this whole. The use of the term 'community' implies that each group has always been cohesive and stable, and that all its members are sufficiently alike to share long-term common interests, because they all have the same attitudes. We thus tend to represent so-called communities or socio-religious groups according to an 'ideal-type' that we later pre-import into contemporary reality, even though we may not go so far as to apply it to earlier cultural forms. A case in point is the hostility between the Lingayats and Hanabars—both Hindu castes—or the prohibition on intermarriage between the Kasais and Mullahs, though both groups are Muslims (Chapter 1). Following this procedure amounts to likening the group to a stable object that can be represented very easily and is suited for representation, as it has an identity of its own that is nothing other than its transformation into an object of knowledge. By merging sociological reality, collective representation and social identity in this manner, we forget the series of tactical changes taking place within rival groups in a social set-up that has been created by them jointly. At the same time, we ignore the extreme diversity of practices that are likely to express an identity displayed through more or less institutional channels. Actually, this is what is being practised day after day by the various groups living side by side in Shahabandar (Chapter 1) and in Yamanur (Chapter 4). In fact, the plurality of lifestyles is not determined by stereotyped behaviour or by uniform values, nor is it unified by some vague notion. On the contrary, we may even wager that 'forms of life' are at one and the same time plural, composite and conflicting, and that they have never been, nor are they now, exempt from dynamic contradictions. This brings to mind once more the idea that whirlpools are bound to exist at the confluence of two rivers or, better still, the two oceans represented by Hinduism and Islam.

Finally, an anthropological study (of the present) does not appear to contradict history, and what could be a better testimony to this than the fact that Islam has been deeply rooted in India for at least five hundred years. To support our argument we must not reduce anecdotes (both past and present) to the level of non-events. Fortuitous though they may be, micro-events have their meanings, though those meanings evidently change with the passage of time. Anecdotes, like the symptoms of a crisis in the social order, reveal upheavals and social norms, and although they are experienced on the emotional plane, they are necessitated by history. For example, the incident leading to the exclusion of Muslims from the goddess's service in Saundatti illustrates the heightening of tension between Hindus and Muslims (Chapter 5), while the feigned beheading of the fakir (Chapter 3) has its roots in an ancient theme that is both mythological and mystical. Because history covers a long period of time, it is likely to endorse myths going back in times past. But the existence of several forms of culture today has given rise to another type of historiography in the form of myriads of unwritten micro-histories that are of interest to the ethnographer; hence the 'little stories' about relationships between Hindus and Muslims narrated in some of the chapters, which allow us to conclude with relative certainty that social and cultural identification can be of a temporary nature and are often subject to change. The composition of the devotees visiting the temple of the goddess or the saint's mausoleum is proof enough of this changeableness. It is evident that in the beginning this identification was of a functional nature, even though it tended to persist. In India, of course, this persistence would be used only too readily to be turned into a 'tradition'. But through being associated with a set of criteria that determine the membership of a religion and the ways of making this membership and exclusion manifest, the boundaries sometimes change because they are unstable. At present—as in the past—we see a society subjected to rifts, where norms are many and there are several rival offers. Social structures propose not only a multiplicity of roles but also over-lapping roles, and there is a confusion between various roles. This book has tried to pinpoint the dividing lines according to historically controllable contexts in time and space: over two centuries and in an area that moves between the present states of Maharashtra and Karnataka. It so happens that oceans, like rivers, flow across borders.

The reason for pointing out thus the changing forms of a culture is to prevent them from being reduced to an organic model in which all cultural manifestations have a fixed and unchanging place. It matters little whether they are scholarly or popular, because they belong to different levels of the same realm, as is illustrated by the show put on by the fakirs (Chapter 3) or as testified to by the traditional mullahs mentioned on and off. Apart from the fact that such a conception encourages us to imagine culture as some kind of a lost world of symbolic coherence, it also ignores the fact that stories and values change according to the context and contradict one another in different domains. It is needless to point out that behaviour patterns, because they reflect diverse interests, are first and foremost praxeological forms that do not need to form a perfectly coherent ideological system. Any attempt to conjugate cultural identity in the singular, whether individual or collective, classical or popular, religious or political, fixes and immobilizes in the tracks and ruts of communal rhetoric that ebullition and flow of sociability in which the philosopher Merleau-Ponty recognized a miracle that is repeated day after day. Nobody can afford to ignore the fact that an ideological petrifaction sometimes has tragic political consequences. This is as evident in India (as elsewhere), because organizations like the RSS and BJP recruit the mass of their followers on the basis of such so-called 'eternal traditions' (Introduction and Chapter 6). And if contemporary history has been fond of such ideological fare, there is no guarantee (quite the contrary in fact) that the same fare will still be served in the near future.

Furthermore, tradition should never be considered as heritage, patrimony or ethnicity. It should be considered more as a competition or rivalry between systems, establishing a relationship between social partners who are likely to cooperate but can also come into conflict, and who may consider each other as both identical and different. With this perspective in mind, we selected from the gamut of social interactions those that best convey the interlocking between individuals, groups and sub-groups, whose similarity and diversity are expressed at different levels. At each of these levels, whether it is the village or the town, whether it is rules pertaining to marriage or eating practices, whether it is a mausoleum or a temple, a festival or daily life, trade or worship, therapeutic methods or political claims, there are experiences and rules through which social agents can redefine themselves and create their own identity. Even if cultural receptivity often appears to be intermittent and fragmented, we know too that it can be extremely dynamic. These agents are excellent tacticians, and they know how to combine even those cultural practices that appear to be the most exclusive. The ability to find alternatives and stopgap solutions in social matters, which themselves depend on the intensity of the interactions, bears testimony to the skill of these actors in investing them with meaning. The stake is critically important because it means not only legitimizing a particular way of thought or action, but also discrediting all other ways that are deployed by others in a distinct semantic system. This means recognizing the importance of cases of interaction where it is possible to examine the dialectic of reciprocal sharing, both between individuals and also between groups, which later may be either permanent or temporary in nature. It is also an acknowledgement of the need to give priority to the symbolic arrangements that give rise to these interactions or are produced by them in social life. In other words, it implies that it is possible to study the culture which encircles and embraces them. How does this work today between Hindus and Muslims in north Karnataka? What do they seek to achieve when they come into contact, when they exchange customs and traditions, or even when they share with or exclude others?

Behind the diversity of experiences, it is possible to identify a relatively coherent system. But it is never closed to outside influences. On the contrary, it is always unstable because of its extreme complexity and its acknowledged singularities. Of course, there is a compatibility between subjective culture and dominant cultural values that are considered to be 'objective'. It is nevertheless impossible to look at collective identity as the sum total of individual identities, because the variability of interactions gives scope to inventiveness and in some cases to normative dissension. When explaining this with a limited number of examples, we find that the relationship between different cultural behaviour patterns is often criticized and debated. But, paradoxically, this strengthens the traditions contributed by each of them. In this sense, formulas for identity always seem more flexible, diffuse and problematic—even more so now than in the past, because history offers endless tempatations. The memory-work performed on Belgaum's Hindu-Muslim history (Chapter 6) only reaffirms this.

These observations justify the resort to a style of plural hermeneutics to define the method employed in this book. Of course, such an approach proves to be rather hesitant and uncertain. But it is better suited to the cultural heterogeneity and peculiarities of different types of Indianness, since they offer provisional descriptive grids and develop principles of assemblage suited to the hazardous process of the crystallization of identities undergoing permanent restructuring.

The cult that has developed around demonology and possession (Chapter 2) is not just the actualization of pre-existing elements, but a particular method used to control crucial situations subject to rapid change. Its representation is not the simple affirmation of what is already established, but a creation that, though it generally takes refuge in the sanctuary of tradition, cannot be totally equated with it. Nor is it possible to compare the expression of a cult to the transhistoric identity of the person who performs it, because of the danger of losing the specific character of the idiom through which it is put into action. Especially when intercultural contact is involved—and whatever we may claim, it is doubtful if strictly demarcated cultures have ever existed—the cult functions like a performance given against a backdrop where divergent expectations are integrated and synchronized. Finally, when the cult's agent realizes that two cognitive universes, Hindu and Muslim, are too different to be brought together, he resorts to the mechanisms of borrowing, reinterpretation and accumulation, moving freely from one to the other without necessarily mixing them even when the circumstances appear to demand it.

Therefore there is no static representative relationship between cultural traits, actors and social groups, except for those that are prepared to transfer their ideological representation. In the universe of authentic relationships studied by anthropologists, it is necessary to recognize the articulate expression of cultural sociogeneses that advance in series of non-linear dynamic changes having their own rhythm. Of course, these changes are subject to external constraints. But field studies show that they are shaped in an equal measure by the margin of freedom allowed to the actors or groups. As we are well aware, in order to live, a person has to make compromises and manage to get around contradictions. It is these methods of re-employing the imposed order to one's own ends, just as much as the reciprocity of historical exchanges that cannot be dissociated from power relationships, that have until now bestowed on India what Lévi-Strauss so eloquently called 'the delicate flowers of difference'. These flowers are threatened today by events that are shaking the subcontinent.

India, being as vulnerable as other pluralist democracies the world over, is now in the grip of an ideological and political campaign for religious purification, of a kind it has not experienced since Independence. The Sangh parivar militants have successfully campaigned for a re-evaluation of past events, which, according to them, have been mutilated by the fanatical warriors and missionaries of Islam. Throughout their domination, which lasted several centuries, Muslims are said to have corrupted the integrity of the ancient *Bharat*, the sacred land that many Hindus, and not just activists, emotionally liken to the divine image of the Mother. Not satisfied with redrawing the map of India by incorporating into it a whole network of holy places, temples, shrines, pilgrimage spots, rivers, etc., including some recently invented 'high tech' shrines (like that of Santoshi Ma) and especially those the Muslims are supposed to have usurped, of which there are officially approved lists, Hindus are now planning to take them over by dramatizing the ancient mythology of Hindustan. They invoke Rama, the divine hero of the *Ramayana*, the ideal warrior-king who travelled the length and breadth of the country before ascending his throne. This expert archer, whose mission was to deliver the earth from demons, is now being invoked to free India from the Muslims! Under the influence of popular Hindi cinema, which worships 'Ram (bo)', militants revere his virility and have made him the post-modern muscular defender of the faith—never before has 'Mother' Bharat been so virile! This interpretation is supported by some obliging 'scholars' and historiographers busy collecting 'facts' that have turned the god into a historical character. According to them, Rama was born 9,00,000 years ago in Ayodhya and was reincarnated in 1949 exactly at the spot that is now called Sri Rama Janmabhoomi (Pandey 1994)! Since the second half of the nineteenth century, monotheistic religions have become, by the curious process of 'introjection' of the enemy, models of a new Hinduism in quest of (ecclesiastical) unity to compensate for its hitherto fragmentary nature, which is now despised. Organized on the model of a 'syndicate for deliverance' (Thapar 1985), with an abundance of 'jet-gurus' and other 'godmen' who interpret tradition to suit the needs of their followers, the 'Hinduists' are now fervently appealing for a return to the old notion of royalty based on divine power. In this manner, they hope to take on the modern and secular nation state, which has to date tried its best to protect civic rights and the freedom of expression, though not always very successfully.

We should not let ourselves be deluded by the archaic nature of their inspiration. These zealots invoke tradition *ad nauseam*, but only with the idea of modernizing it. In fact, L.K. Advani travelled over 10,000 km from the extreme south in a Toyota van remodelled to look like Arjuna's chariot in the *Mahabharata* to win over Hindu voters by exploiting religion for purely political purposes. This is because the Hindu nationalist movement has been presenting itself since the 1980s as the only alternative to a Congress party weakened by internal dissension and widespread corruption. Following the latter's failure, the BJP organized a massive procession (*Rath Yatra*). This caravan, with the lotus flower as its politico-religious symbol, set ablaze in its wake a series of communal bonfires fuelled by the feeling of insecurity now shared by all Muslims[1]—quite apart from the socio-economic grievances that have for a long time fed their rancour against the Indian government.[2] Now they consider themselves members of a community under siege in a country that they still perceive as their own, but that is without any doubt becoming less and less so. Maybe the number of those who dream of an ideal society, evidently Islamic, based on the model of the society in Medina in the Prophet's time, is increasing day by day. The more extremist among them believe that it should encompass the entire community of believers (*umma*). This utopic dream goes back to the time when the Muslims first came to India, proclaim the militant Hindus, always ready to diagnose separatist tendencies in the other community to justify their own violence unleashed on the pretext of a 'defensive' nationalism. This is a classic argument for a majority that is prey to a growing inferiority complex.

Even if the history of Indian Islam since the nineteenth century is largely confused with the spread of the separatist ideology now encouraged by activists elements in Pakistan and Bangladesh, it must be admitted that in India today violence is unleashed in most cases by Hindus fanatics. Their obsessive chauvinistic and xenophobic propaganda, disseminated through very sophisticated channels of communication, has contributed to widening the rift between the two communities. The rift has become a chasm, and saffron ideology has spread its tentacles into large sections of the population that did not earlier subscribe to the Hindutva doctrine. The bio-evolutionary vernacular of culture finds a fertile soil not only among the unemployed but also the urban and rural middle classes, which, having succumbed to consumerism, have now become victims of the crisis engendered by the so-called 'liberal' economic reforms. Its propaganda leaflets tend to racialize the boundaries between groups, which were often more diffuse and fluid, for the benefit of the Hindu 'community', whose origin goes back to the vague and arbitrarily defined *Bharatvarsha.* Only the members of this community can be considered as the genuine sons of the 'Indian Motherland', the exclusive descendants of the Aryans now incarnated by the god Rama, who has become a historical figure. This means that the hundred million Muslims find themselves reduced to the status of foreigners in this 'Fatherland'.

In fact, with the inauguration of the 'Hindu Kingdom' (*Hindu Raj*), which is basically an ethnic and biological notion signifying nation (*rashtra*) rather than a political idea, the only choice available to the Muslims would be assimilation, expulsion or annihilation.

There is no doubt that Rama is not a very popular god in the south, where there are few temples dedicated to him. It is interesting to note that the champions of Dravidian culture, who hate the Brahmins because they equate them with their Aryan conquerors, have proposed a reinterpretation of Valmiki's *Ramayana.* In this version of the epic, the indigenous demon Ravana is the hero and not the vanquished villain, while Rama is depicted as an epitome of immorality and wickedness.[3] However, in view of the pragmatism that has defined political trends until now, radical Hinduism may well replace mythology, considered outdated by some by a more nationalistic and patriotic ideology. In fact, the riots planned by its leaders in Hubli and Bangalore[4] in August and October 1994 gave Karnataka the distinction of being the Indian state with the largest number of communal clashes during that year (Engineer 1995: 250) (Maps 11 and 12). However, the electoral gains expected from this communal strife proved to be less prolific than hoped, with the BJP winning 48 out of 124 seats in the state Legislative Assembly.[5] But since they had only 4 seats in 1989, the jump is significant. Also, under the guidance of their leaders, the cadres of these radical parties have now decided to launch all kinds of militant campaigns not necessarily centred around Lord Rama. For example, they are now engaged in social work among the poor, and they have started organizing training camps for Harijans so that they can become temple priests (McKean 1992: 97), and conducting mass reconversions of Muslims to Hinduism (ibid. 98). Their proclaimed ambition is to win over the south. With this aim, the saffron party has visited no less than one hundred and ten villages in Tamil Nadu in a 'Chariot of Wisdom' (*Jnana Ratham*), which is actually a van provided with sophisticated audio-visual equipment to propagate a religious and nationalistic conception of Hinduism.

Considering the decline in the Congress party's traditional supporters (especially Muslims) and the fact that it has lost power in eight states since 1990, the election result was not totally unexpected. The BJP is now at the helm in the capital and also in Gujarat. In Maharashtra, it came to power in 1995 by forming an alliance with the Shiv Sena and remained so for three years. These two states, which are the most industrialized in India, present the modern face of the religious phenomenon that is to all appearances the most archaic. The BJP is also an important party in Karnataka, Andhra Pradesh, Bihar, Madhya Pradesh, Rajasthan, Orissa, Manipur and Himachal Pradesh. Let us remember that it gained a majority of seats in Uttar Pradesh in the 1993 elections. Strengthened by the electoral performance of the BJP, its sister organization, the VHP, announced, in preparation for the 1996 elections to the Lok Sabha, its intention to launch a campaign for the liberation of Varanasi (Benares), similar to the one carried out in Ayodhya in 1992.

It is feared that this political success and religious activism may have two tragic consequences. Firstly, the members of India's two major communities are likely to be torn apart by the contradictory appeals of territorial and religious nationalism, Hindus and Muslims alike. And secondly, the whole country will be stalked by violence and fear; and the rift between Hindus and Muslims may become so wide that only hatred is able to cross it.

NOTES

1. See Appendix III.
2. See Appendix II.
3. Irschick (1969: 295) with regard to the nineteenth century and to Richman (1992) for the twentieth century. Similar versions are also available in Maharashtra among militants of the Mahar caste who call themselves Dalits, and also among other Scheduled Castes desirous of establishing a positive identity.
4. Chapter 6.
5. RESULTS OF ASSEMBLY ELECTIONS IN KARNATAKA

Year	1983	1985	1989	1994
Congress (I)	82	66	178	35
Janata Dal	95	139	24	116
Janata Party	0	0	2	0
BJP	18	3	4	40

Source: India Today (15 March 1995).

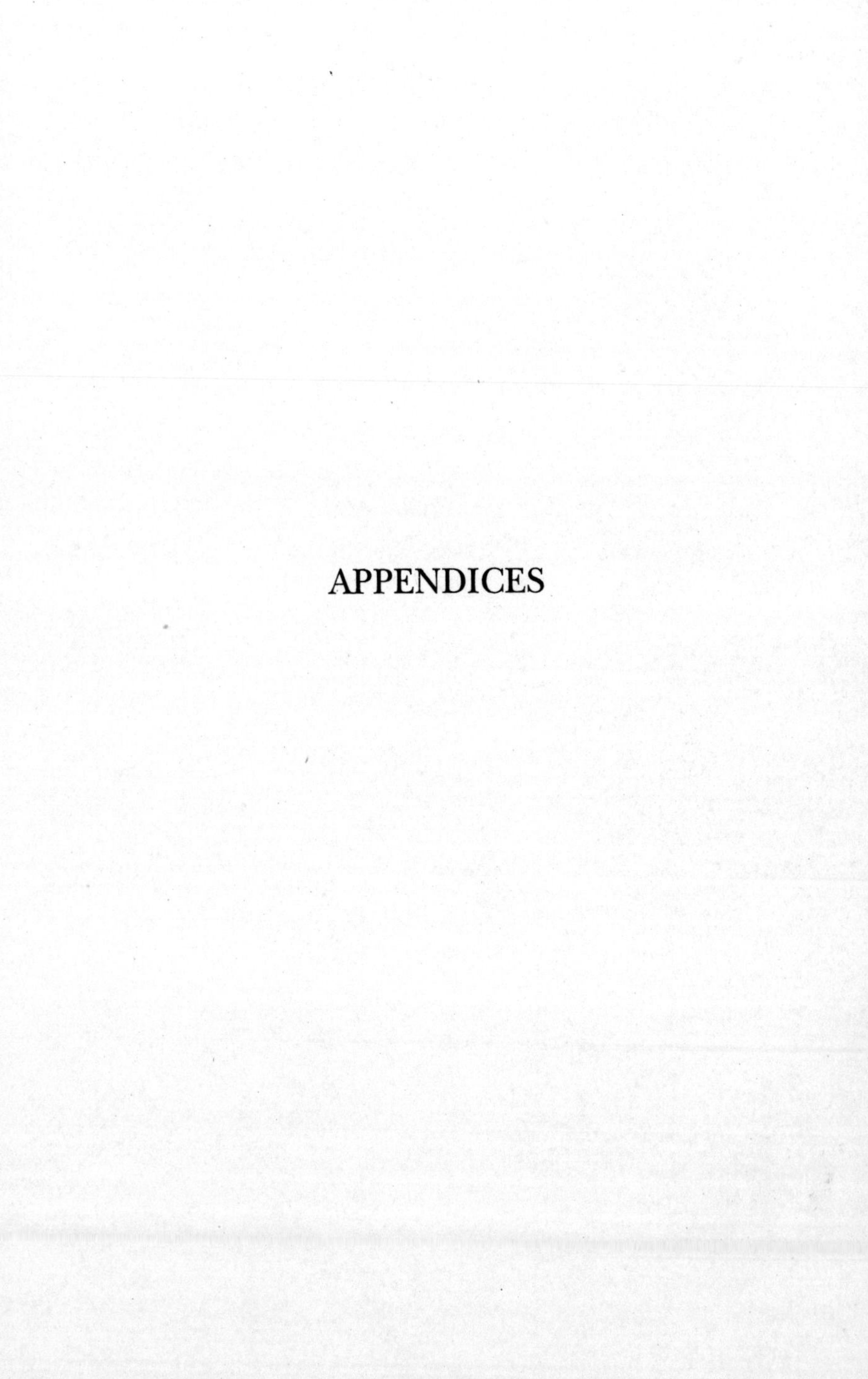

APPENDICES

APPENDIX I

Socio-economic Differences between various Religious Communities in India (1987-1988)

A survey conducted by the National Sample Survey Organization (NSSO) in 1987-8 gives us an idea of the socio-economic conditions of various religious communities in India on the basis of indicators such as occupation, ownership of landed property and levels of income and education. It is based on a sample of about 1,30,000 households spread over 8,400 villages and 4,000 cities all over the country (*Source*: *Muslim India*, No. 140, 15 July 1994).

TABLE 14: CLASSIFICATION OF OCCUPATION OF PERSONS PER HOUSEHOLD ACCORDING TO RELIGION—RURAL INDIA

(*in per cent*)

Occupation	Hindus	Muslims	Christians	Others
Agriculture	43.9	36.3	37.9	38.6
Non-agricultural	11.7	21.2	10.9	22.9
Agricultural Labour	28.3	24.4	28.4	21.7
Other Types of Labour	8.3	9.9	10.9	4.6
Other Occupations	7.9	8.1	11.9	12.3

TABLE 15: CLASSIFICATION OF OCCUPATIONS OF PERSONS PER HOUSEHOLD ACCORDING TO RELIGION—URBAN INDIA

(*in per cent*)

Occupation	Hindus	Muslims	Christians	Others
Self-Employed	35.9	53.4	21.4	44.6
Salaried Job	46.7	28.9	56.1	38.3
Casual Employment	12.1	13.4	12.3	10.5
Others	5.4	4.3	10.2	6.6

TABLE 16: EMPLOYMENT MODEL ACCORDING TO RELIGION

(*in per cent*)

Sex/Residence and Religion	Self-employed	Salaried Job	Casual Employment	Total	Rate of Employment
Men (*Urban*)					
Hindus	39.1	46.4	14.5	100.00	52.0
Muslims	53.3	29.9	16.7	100.00	49.1
Christians	29.7	53.4	17.0	100.00	48.9
Women (*Urban*)					
Hindus	4.0	27.7	26.4	100.00	15.9
Muslims	60.0	15.7	24.3	100.00	11.4
Christians	34.3	51.5	14.2	100.00	23.6
Men (*Rural*)					
Hindus	58.5	10.1	31.4	100.00	54.2
Muslims	59.0	7.5	33.5	100.00	50.5
Christians	52.1	12.0	35.9	100.00	-
Women (*Rural*)					
Hindus	59.9	3.6	36.5	100.00	33.7
Muslims	67.9	3.0	29.1	100.00	19.6
Christians	57.6	9.9	32.4	100.00	37.3

TABLE 17: DIVISION OF PERSONS ACCORDING TO RELIGION AND AREA OF CULTIVATED LAND—RURAL INDIA

(*in per cent*)

Area in Acres	Hindus	Muslims	Christians	Others
0.0	28.0	34.7	30.4	40.7
<1	17.3	24.4	27.5	12.1
1-1.25	18.3	17.5	18.9	8.5
2.5-5	16.3	12.9	14.3	12.0
+5	20.1	10.5	8.9	26.7
Total	100	100	100	100

TABLE 18: LEVEL OF MONTHLY EXPENDITURE (RE. 1.00 = 0.20 FF) PER PERSON PER HOUSEHOLD ACCORDING TO RELIGION—RURAL INDIA

(*in per cent*)

Rupees	Hindus	Muslims	Christians	Others
<80	13.7	12.0	12.5	9.6
90-110	22.8	23.1	15.7	12.7
110-160	31.3	33.6	27.1	26.4
+160	31.6	30.5	43.2	46.7
Total	99.4	99.2	98.5	95.4

TABLE 19: LEVEL OF MONTHLY EXPENDITURE (IN RS.) PER PERSON PER HOUSEHOLD ACCORDING TO RELIGION—URBAN INDIA

(*in per cent*)

Rupees	Hindus	Muslims	Christians	Others
<110	13.1	22.0	11.0	11.7
110-160	22.5	31.5	17.2	15.2
160-310	41.2	35.6	33.4	38.1
+310	22.5	10.7	35.5	34.0

TABLE 20: LEVEL OF EDUCATION ACCORDING TO RELIGION (AND SEX)—RURAL INDIA

(*in per cent*)

Level of	Hindus		Muslims		Christians		Others	
Education	Male	Female	Male	Female	Male	Female	Male	Female
Illiterate	51.3	75.0	58.2	76.1	33.7	43.1	45.3	61.4
<Primary	19.0	11.8	18.6	13.1	20.5	17.8	17.9	15.7
Middle School	22.7	11.2	19.1	9.9	35.4	29.2	25.5	19.4
High School	5.7	1.7	3.4	0.8	9.3	8.1	9.0	3.1
University	1.2	0.2	0.6	–	1.8	1.5	2.3	0.3

TABLE 21: LEVEL OF EDUCATION ACCORDING TO RELIGION (AND SEX)—URBAN INDIA

(*in per cent*)

Level of	Hindus		Muslims		Christians		Others	
Education	Male	Female	Male	Female	Male	Female	Male	Female
Illiterate	25.3	42.2	42.4	59.5	18.8	22.7	18.0	31.2
<Primary	18.8	17.2	20.9	18.5	16.0	17.5	15.6	14.47
Middle School	30.5	25.3	26.3	16.8	36.7	33.4	30.0	8.5
High School	17.2	10.7	8.0	4.3	20.1	20.8	23.6	17.5
University	7.9	4.2	2.3	0.8	8.1	5.5	11.7	7.9

APPENDIX II

The Underrepresentation of Muslims in some Socio-economic Sectors in Karnataka

TABLE 22: PERCENTAGE OF MUSLIMS IN GOVERNMENT SERVICE IN KARNATAKA (1981)

Employees	Class I Officers	Class II Technical Staff	Class III Non-technical Staff	Class IV Workers
Central Government	1.61	3.00	4.41	5.12
State Government	3.30	4.48	4.62	6.35
Public Sector	3.19	4.30	12.14	10.46

TABLE 23: PERCENTAGE OF MUSLIMS IN THE JUDICIAL SERVICE (1981)

State	Total	Muslims	%
Karnataka	223	16	7.17
Maharashtra	614	19	3.09
India	4898	303	6.19

TABLE 24: ECONOMIC PARTICIPATION IN KARNATAKA (1981)

Community	% of Population	% of Elites
Hindus	82.7	85.3
Muslims	11.2	4.5

Sources: Muslim India, Nos. 10 and 12, 1983.

TABLE 25: POLITICAL REPRESENTATION OF CASTES AND COMMUNITIES IN KARNATAKA (1988)

(*in per cent*)

Dev. Caste/ Community	Population	MLAs	MLCs	MPs	ZPMs	ZPPs
Lingayats	15.3	26.0	35.3	28.6	29.6	31.6
Vokkaligas	10.8	19.6	19.1	17.9	21.8	31.6
Brahmins	3.5	4.1	10.3	7.1	3.2	0
Marathas	2.9	3.7	0	0	2.3	5.3
Urs	0.3	0.5	0	3.6	0.1	0
Total	39.5	61.6	77.9	57.1	61.7	89.5
Others Total	24.8	16.0	13.2	21.4	23.8	0

Notes: MLA = Member of Legislative Assembly,
MLC = Member of Legislative Council,
MP = Member of Parliament,
ZPM = Member of *Zilla Parishad,*
ZPP = President of *Zilla Parishad.*

Source: Compilation of data from *Karnataka Third Backward Classes Commission Report,* vol. 1, 1990.

TABLE 26: ACCESS TO EMPLOYMENT AND EDUCATION IN KARNATAKA (1988)

Caste/ Community	Population %	Employment			University	Middle School
		AB	C	D		
I. Very Little Access						
Marathas	2.9	0.9	2.2	2.3	1.0	0.4
Total	15.9	5.9	9.6	12.9	5.8	0.3
II. Little Access						
Muslims	11.7	5.8	8.0	11.3	5.7	0.3
Total	20.7	10.7	15.1	18.8	12.6	0.3
III. Lot of Access						
Lingayats	15.3	20.6	18.0	12.1	15.7	0.5
Vokkaligas	10.8	14.4	11.8	13.8	11.6	0.4
Brahmins	3.5	19.5	13.8	5.1	21.5	1.0
Christians	2.1	1.8	3.0	3.1	2.3	0.6
Urs	0.1	0.2	0.1	0.1	0.1	0.3
Total	38.5	67.9	57.1	43.0	61.2	0.7
IV. Others Total	24.9	15.5	18.2	25.3	20.4	0.3

Note: *AB = Officers, C = Clerical Staff, D = Class IV Employees

Source: Compilation of data from *Karnataka Third Backward Classes Commission Report,* vols. 1 and 2, 1990.

TABLE 27: CORRELATION BETWEEN THE INDEX OF ECONOMIC DEVELOPMENT AND THE PERCENTAGE OF MUSLIMS IN VARIOUS DISTRICTS (1991)

District	Relative Development Index (India =100)	% of Muslims
Bangalore	178	11.61
Belgaum	107	9.62
Bellary	104	12.41
Bidar	64	18.99
Bijapur	80	12.88
Chikmagalur	145	7.96
Chitradurga	97	9.17
Dakshin Kannad	186	13.19
Dharwad	99	15.84
Gulbarga	74	17.30
Hassan	111	5.62
Kodagu	211	13.35
Kolar	71	11.41
Mandya	78	4.12
Mysore	93	6.88
Raichur	91	12.88
Shimoga	112	10.50
Tumkur	80	7.24
Uttar Kannad	81	9.71

Sources: Profiles of Districts (1993) and *Census of India* (1981).

The last table gives an idea of regional disparities.

This economic development index reflects the importance of the principal sectors of the Indian economy (cf. *Profiles of Districts*, November 1993, Centre for Monitoring Indian Economy Pvt. Ltd., Bombay).

APPENDIX III

Hindu Muslim Riots

TABLE 28: DECENNIÁL CHANGES IN THE 'VIOLENCE INDEX' FROM 1955 TO 1990

Year	No. of Killed	No. of Injured
1965	1.31396714	4.17077465
1975	0.59115282	4.22754692
1985	0.87951135	7.39311494

Sources: Muslim India, Nos. 81, 103 and 108.

Figure 11 shows the rising number of Hindu-Muslim riots, in addition to the highest points reached in certain years. Figure 12 shows the variations in what can be called the ' violence index', i.e. the proportion between the number of incidents and the number of killed and also the proportion between the number of incidents and the number of injured, the exact figures for which are indicated in Table 28.

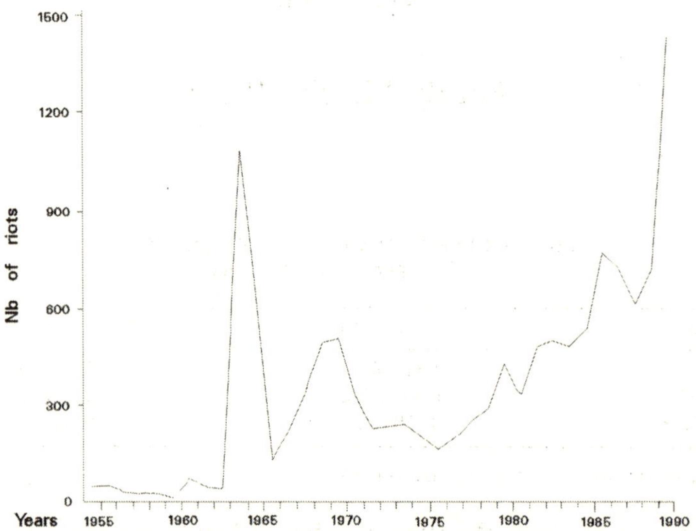

Figure 11: Increse in the number of Hindu-Muslim riots in India from 1954 to 1990

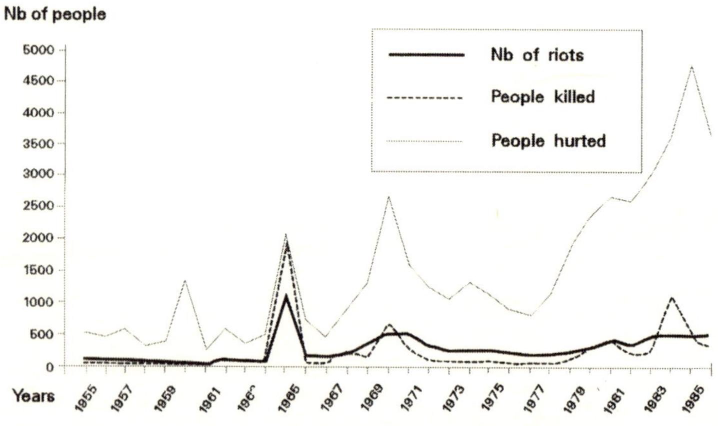

Figure 12: Correlation between the number of riots, the number of persons killed, and the number of injured in India from 1954 to 1985

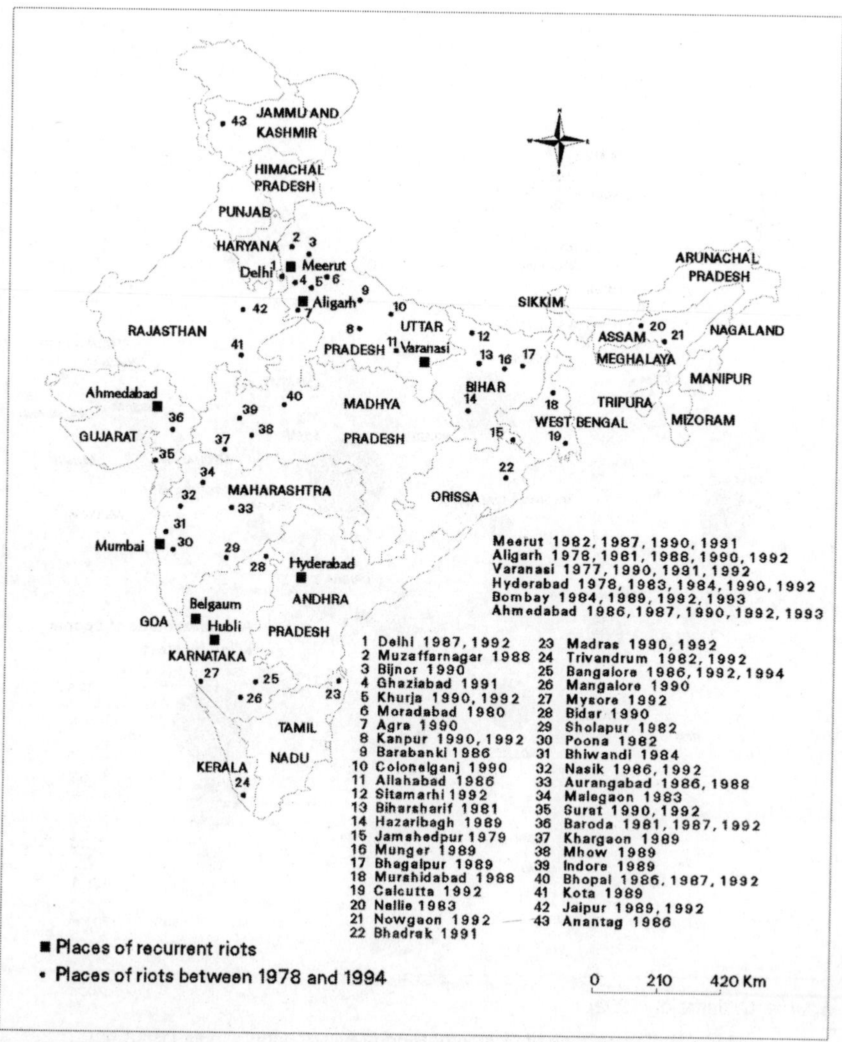

Source: Graff (1993).

Map 11: Location of Hindu-Muslim riots in India between 1978 and 1993

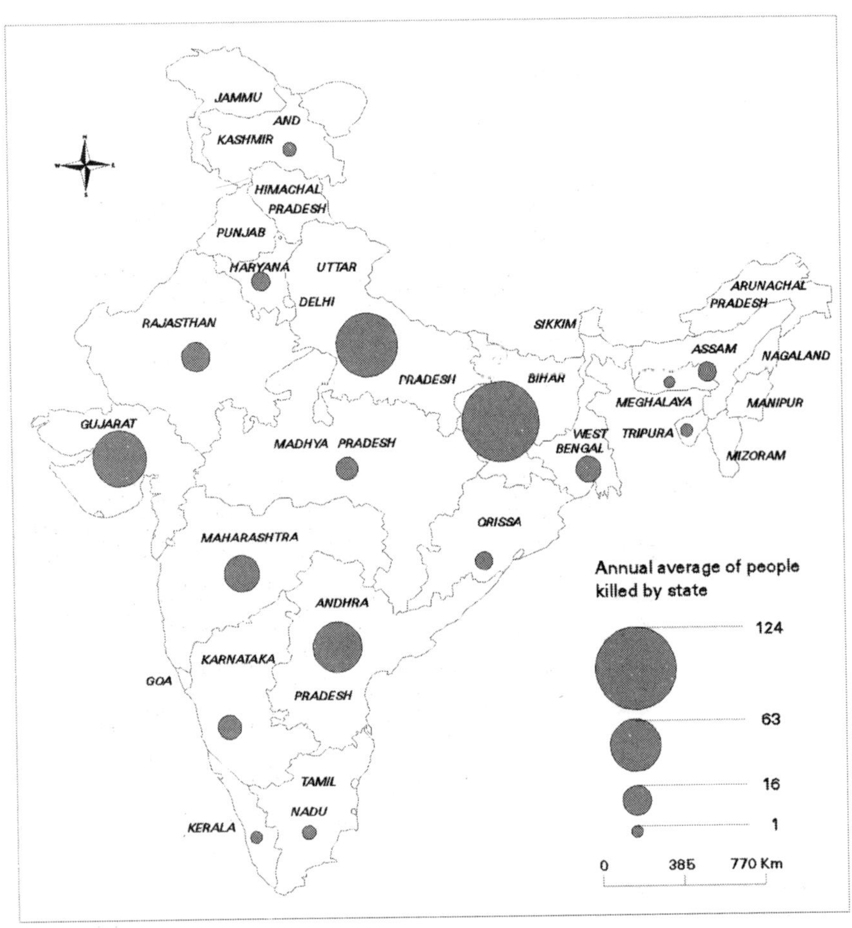

Source: C. Jaffrelot (1992).

Map 12: Distribution of victims of Hindu-Muslim riots in India (1986-90)

APPENDIX IV

Differences in Socio-economic Development between the various taluks of Karnataka (1981)

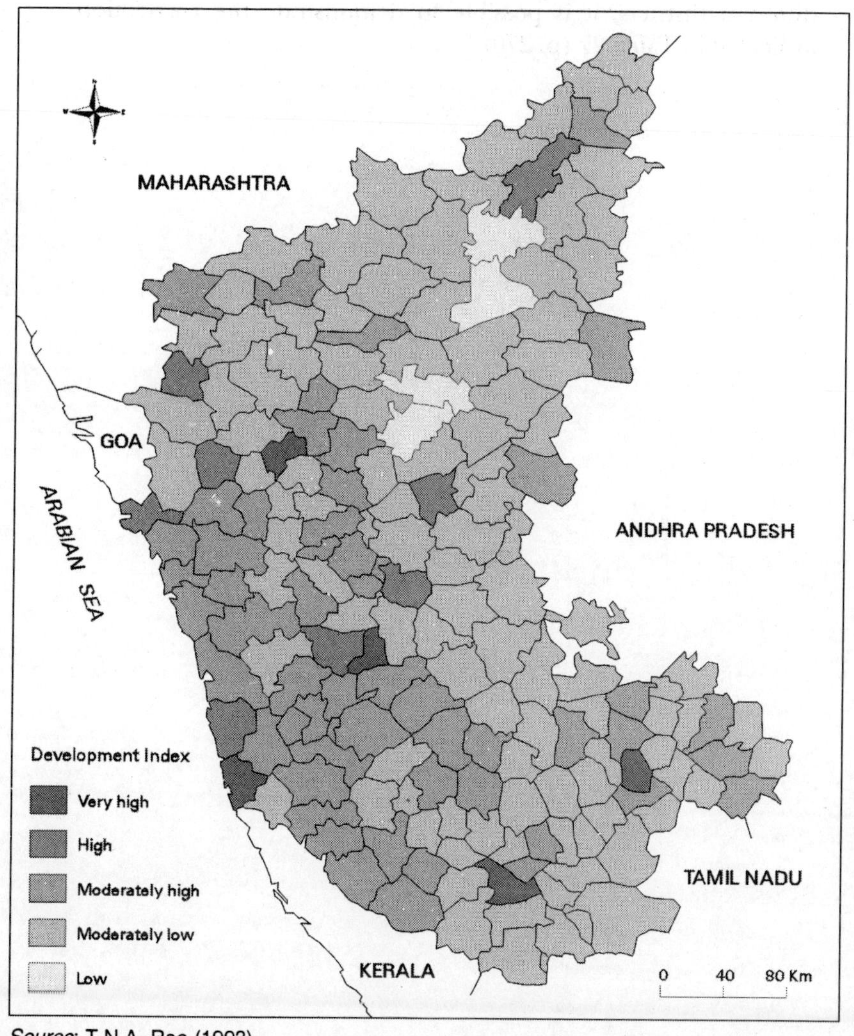

Source: T.N.A. Rao (1993).

Map 13: Disparities in economic development in Karnataka

Map 13 gives an overall view of the development level of various taluks in Karṇataka state on the basis of an index obtained by putting together statistical data regarding economic production (agricultural and industrial), hubs of employment, types of settlements, infrastructure and environment (T.N.A. Rao [1993]).

Though there is no strict correlation, we notice that by comparing this map with Map 3 (p. 32) showing the percentage of Muslims in different districts, it is possible to demonstrate the correlation indicated in Table 27 (p. 270)

Glossary

Kannada, the language of Karnataka, especially its colloquial form, can be transliterated in many different ways. We have however adhered mostly to the transliteration principles proposed by Kittel in his *A Kannada-English Dictionary* (1983), which is still used as a reference book though it was compiled more than a hundred years ago. We have not found it necessary to indicate the Sanskrit terms separately because the religious vocabulary is full of them and Kannadigas do not distinguish them from Kannada words in their speech. For Arabic and Persian terms, marked with an asterisk, we have followed Feronzsons (no date mentioned) and Platts (1970). Names of places and cities have not been transliterated nor the names of political parties, with the exception of some associations.

*ᶜalam**, standard, centre of festivities in sacred places
*alawa**, fire-pit used during *Muharram* celebrations
*ᶜalim**, (pl. *ulama*), scholar, expert in religious sciences
*ᶜaqiqa**, sacrifice performed on the seventh day after the birth of a child, tonsure ceremony
*ashraf**, nobility, an Indian Muslim of foreign descent
*asthna**, cenotaph of a Muslim saint
asura, divine, anti-god, demon
*awliya** (pl. of *wali*), God's friends or protégés, Muslim saints (cf. *pir*)

*baba**, 'old man', saint (cf. *pir*)
Badigar, carpenters caste
Bajantri, musicians caste
bali, sacrifice by killing
Banajiga, merchant caste (Lingayat)
*baraka**, charisma of a Sufi or a saint
*barah wafat**, twelfth day of the third lunar month, Prophet's death (and birth) anniversary
Bedar, hunter caste (Scheduled Caste)
*be shar**, 'outlaw', a mystic who does not follow the Islamic law
*buraq**, hippogryph on which Muhammad rode to Mecca, the

Prophet's celestial mount which carried him to Paradise

Chambhar, caste of cobblers (and farmers) of Maharashtra
*chilla**, forty days' seclusion—*ma'kusa,* mortification of the flesh

dakshina, 'ritual honorarium', salary
*dargah**, 'royal court', tomb of a Muslim saint
darshana, view (of a holy person or a god)
*dar ul-harb**, 'abode of war', enemy territory
*dar ul-Islam**, 'Abode of Islam', land governed by a Muslim prince
*darwish**, member of a Muslim mendicant order, dervish (cf. fakir)
desai, title of the head of Hindu district
devaru, god or deity
devasthanam, temple
*dhikr**, 'memory', mystical concentration while repeating the many names of God (cf. *zikr*)
*dhimmi**, non-Muslim resident enjoying certain rights in an Islamic state
*din**, religion
dodda, big, older
dosa, fault, disorder; by extension sickness
*duldul**, the name of the mule given to Ali by the Prophet; small votive horses

*fana**, a mystic's 'annihilation' in God
fakir*, 'poor', mystic, religious mendicant
*fatiha**, the first *Surah* of the Koran; prayer
*fiqh**, science of Muslim law
*faqih**, expert in Muslim law

*gali**, ghost, evil spirit
*galif**, brocade sheet covering the tomb of a Muslim saint
*ghali**, exorcist
*ghusl**, ritual bath
*golakh**, box for receiving offerings in a *dargah*
gudi, temple
Gujjar, farmers caste (originally from Gujarat)

*hadith**, Traditions; words attributed to the Prophet by sources other than the Koran

*hafiz**, one who knows the Koran by heart
Hanabar (or Krishna Goli), low caste of farmers
*hanafi**, follower of the Sunni school of law founded by Abu Hanifa (eighth century)
*haqiqa(t)**, '(divine) Reality', term belonging to the mystic vocabulary
Helava, caste of genealogists
Hindustan, the Indo-Gangetic plain, and by extension the whole of India
Hugar, florists caste

*ᶜId ul-adha**, time of pilgrimage when it is necessary to sacrifice an animal
*ᶜId ul-Fitr**, celebration at the end of the *Ramadan* fast
*ᶜidgah**, prayer ground (usually bounded by a white wall with a niche on one side)
*illa**, second part of the profession of faith
*ᶜilm**, scholar of religious sciences, knowledge of religious duties
*imam**, guide, community head

*jalal**, Divine Majesty, splendour, anger, a Sufi's evil attributes
*jama'at**, group, community, guild
*jama'at-i Islam**, politico-religious movement founded by Maulana Maududi in 1941
Jangama, highest caste among Lingayats, household priests or ascetics said to be 'without passion' (*virakta*)
*jhanda**, banner, centre of a sacred square
*jinn** (pl. *jann*), 'spirit', demon, ghost

*karamat**, miracle performed by a Muslim saint
Kasai, butchers caste (Muslim)
*khadim**, servant (in a *dargah*)
*khalifa**, Prophet's 'successor' or a Sufi shaikh, community's (supreme) head
*khanqah**, Sufi pilgrim shelter
*khilafat**, Caliph's functions
*khwaja**, 'Master', title of respect given to a Sufi shaikh
Kuruba, caste of shepherds or cowherds who are now farmers

*langar**, community kitchen attached to a Sufi pilgrim shelter or a *dargah*

Lingayat, 'he who wears the *linga*', a Virashaiva caste
*lodi**, protective thread or metal bracelet

Madar, caste of sweepers, garbage collectors (Scheduled Caste)
Madiga, tanners and peasants caste (Scheduled Caste)
*madrasa**, Muslim religious teaching institution
*maduli**, amulet
*majdhub**, ecstatic, enlightened, simple-minded
Mahar, Scheduled caste of Maharashtra
*mahbub**, 'beloved', title of high-ranking mystic
*malamati**, 'blamed', one who performs blameworthy actions to hide his high spiritual rank
*malang**, *be shar* dervish, wandering mendicant
*malfuzat**, collection of a Sufi shaikh*'s* words and anecdotes about him
Mang, Scheduled Caste of Maharashtra
*mannat**, 'wish'
Markandar, farmers caste
*matam**, mourning, mortification of the flesh by Shias during *Muharram*
*maulwi** (cf. *'alim mullah*), person giving religious instruction
*mazar**, 'place for a visit', tomb of a Muslim saint or nobleman
*mazhar**, manifestation, epiphany
*mi'raj**, Muhammad's journey to Paradise
*mirza**, Muslim from Persia or Turkey, nobleman
mlechha, 'barbarian', 'impure', Muslims in the eyes of Hindus
*morchal**, ritual fly-whisk made of peacock feathers
*Muharram**, first lunar month of the Islamic calendar, commemoration of Husain ibn 'Alim's death in 680 in the battle of Karbala
*mujahid**, one who wages a holy war (cf. *jihad*)
*mujawar**, servant of a shrine, officiant
*mullah** (cf. *'alim, maulwi*), 'master', 'lord', title given to doctors of theology; one who supervises rituals
*murid**, disciple of a Sufi master
*murshid** (cf. *pir*, shaikh), guide, spiritual leader
murti, image, representation, idol of a deity
*musulmani**, popular Indian term for circumcision, generic term designating Muslims

*nabi**, Prophet
*nadhr**, 'wish', votive offering
*nafs**, 'soul', base instincts
Navalgar, barbers caste

panjah, 'hand', relic or emblem of Muslim saints
Pattegar, farmers caste (originally from Rajasthan)
Pinjari (or Pindari), cotton-carders caste (Muslim)
*pir**, 'old man', head of a mystic order (cf. shaikh), spiritual master who guides disciples (cf. *murshid*), Muslim saint (cf. *baba, wali*)
*pirzada** (pl. *pirzade*), 'sons of the *pir*', officiant in a *dargah*
pishaci, particularly evil formless demon
pradakshina, ritual circumambulation

*qadi**, 'judge' who applies Islamic law
*qalandar**, wandering dervish
*qawwali**, musician specializing in singing Muslim religious songs
*qibla**, direction of Mecca
qutb, 'pole', 'axis', highest rank in the hierarchy of saints

*Ramazan**, (=*Ramadan*), ninth lunar month of the Islamic calendar during which the Koran was revealed; by extension, fast observed during this month
*raqs**, ecstatic dance performed by Sufis
*rasul**, God's messenger
*roza**, fast

*sajjada-nashin**, 'he who sits on a prayer-rug'; successor of a *pir*
shakti, 'power', 'energy' or the power wielded by a deity
*sama**, concert of mystical music meant to induce a trance
samadhi, tomb of a Hindu ascetic
*sayyid**, a descendant of the Prophet, a higher class among the *ashraf*
*shabe barat**, 'night of pardon', on the full-moon of the eighth lunar month of *Sha'ban*
*shafi'i**, follower of the Sunni school of law founded by al-Shafi'i (ninth century)
*shahid**, martyr, person who gives his life for the cause of Islam
shaikh* (cf. *pir, murshid*), 'old man', Sufi teacher; a person of Arab descent, second highest class among the *ashraf*
*shari'a(t)**, Muslim canonic law

*sharif** (pl. *ashraf*), 'nobleman', Muslims descended from Arab, Persian, Turkish or Afghan immigrants; the upper strata of Muslim society placed above local converts
*shirk**, 'associationism'; by extension polytheism or idolatry
*silsila**, 'chain' of initiation that links a Sufi saint through his spiritual teachers to the founder of his order and thence to Ali or the Prophet; mystical order
*sufi**, 'wool(ly)', follower of Islamic mysticism
*sunna**, a good custom that serves as a norm (cf. *hadith*)
*sunni**, 'one who follows the *sunna*', Muslims who accept the complete authority of the first four Caliphs

*tabarruk**, blessings, relics, food blessed by the *pir*
*tabligh**, missionary work, preaching
*tabut**, 'casket', ritual structure made during *Muharram*
*tadhkira**, 'notes', biography or biographical dictionary of Muslim mystics
*ta'ifa**, (cf. *silsila, tariqa*), group, mystical order
Talawar, farmers caste (said to be an old martial tribe)
tapas, 'burning'; ascetic excitement, penance
*Tariqa**, 'way', esoteric mystical journey, mystical brotherhood
*tawaf**, circumambulation (of the Ka'aba at Mecca)
*ta'widh**, amulet bearing Koranic formulas prepared by a Sufi or a *pir*
*ta'ziya**, mourning, ceremonies commemorating Husain's death during the first ten days of the lunar month of *Muharram*
tirtha, 'ford'; sanctified water; place of pilgrimage

*ulama** (sing. *'alim*), 'scholars', authorities on religious matters in Islam as opposed to mystics
*umma**, (universal) community of believers
*'urs**, 'marriage', ceremony commemorating a Muslim saint's death anniversary, i.e. his mystical union with Allah
utsavmurti, 'moveable form'; divine idol that can be taken in a procession

vibhuti, holy ashes
vira, hero
Virashaiva, 'heroic Shaivites'; sect comprising Lingayat castes

*wahhabi**, follower of a reform movement launched in Arabia in the eighteenth century by Abd al-Wahhab; by extension supporter of reforms

*walaya**, 'friendship', protection extended by God

*wali**, (pl. *awliya*), friend, God's protégé, Muslim saint (cf. *pir*)

*waqf**, donation for religious purposes; mortmain properties

*wilayat**, territory; a saint's spiritual jurisdiction over a province, sainthood

*zakat**, duty to give alms (one of the five pillars of Islamic faith)

*zamindar**, notable or hereditary chief controlling land (under the Mughal Empire)

*zat**, 'caste' (in the case of Muslims)

*zebah**, sacrifice

*zikr**, mystical repetition (cf. *dhikr*)

*ziyarat**, visit to a Muslim saint's tomb

Bibliography

Abbot, J.E., N.R. Godbole and J.F. Edward, 1935, *Nectar from Indian Saints. An English Translation of Mahipati's Marathi Bhaktalilamrit* (Chapters 1-12, 41-51). Poona: Arabhusban Press.

Ahmad, A., 1964, *Studies in Islamic Culture in the Indian Environment.* Oxford: Clarendon Press.

Ahmad, A., 1993, *Indian Muslims. Issues in Social and Economic Development.* Delhi: Khama Publishers.

Ahmad, I. (ed.), 1973, *Caste and Social Stratification among the Muslims in India.* Delhi: Manohar.

——— 1981, 'The Islamic Tradition in India', *Islam and the Modern Age* 12, 1, 44-62.

Ahmad, M., 1988, 'Islamic Revivalism in Pakistan', in J.W. Björkman (ed.): *Fundamentalism, Revivalists and Violence in South Asia.* Delhi: Manohar, 88-106.

1991, 'Islamic Fundamentalism in South Asia: The Jamaat-i-Islami and the Tablighi Jamaat of South Asia', in E.M. Marty and R.S. Appleby (eds): *Fundamentalism Observed,* vol. 1. Chicago: Chicago University Press, 457-530.

Ahmad, R. and M. Sarwar (eds), 1981, *Documentation on South Asia.* Lahore: Centre for South Asian Studies.

Ahmad, I., 1984, 'Political Economy of Communalism in Contemporary India', *Economic and Political Weekly,* XIX, 22/23, 2-9 June, 903-6.

Alam, M., 1989, 'Indo-Islamic Interaction in Medieval India', *Itinerario,* 1, 37-59.

Anawati, G.C. and L. Gardet, 1986, *Mystique musulmane. Aspects et tendances. Expériences et techniques.* Paris: Vrin (1st edn. 1961).

Andersen, W.K. and S.D. Damle, 1987, *The Brotherhood in Saffron: The Rastriya Swayamsevak Sangh and Hindu Revivalism.* Aldershot: Westview Press.

Anderson, B.R., 1991, Imagined Communities, New York & London: Verso (rev. ed.; orig. 1983).

Ansari, S., 1982, 'Interrelationship between Hindus and Muslims in India (A Sociological Analysis)', *Indian Journal of Social Research,* 23, 3, 186-9.

Arberry, A., 1950, *Sufism: An Account of the Mystics of Islam.* London.

Assayag, J., 1983, Religion et société chez les Liṅgāyat-Viraśaiva—Inde du Sud, Karnataka. Thése de 3e cycle inédite, Université de Paris X-Nanterre.

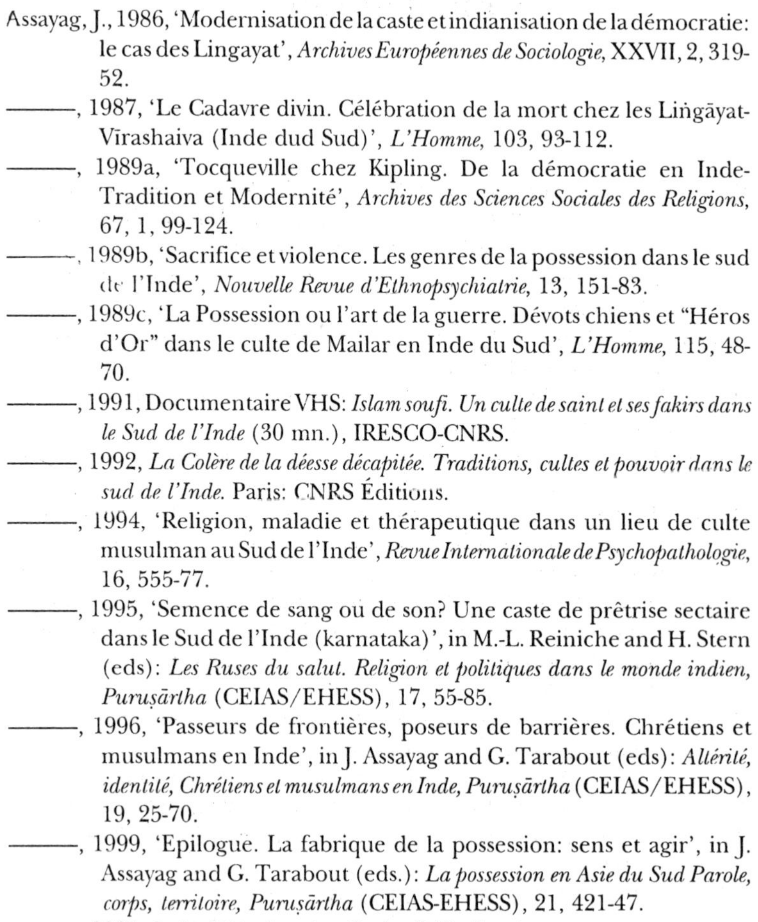

Assayag, J., 1986, 'Modernisation de la caste et indianisation de la démocratie: le cas des Lingayat', *Archives Européennes de Sociologie*, XXVII, 2, 319-52.

———, 1987, 'Le Cadavre divin. Célébration de la mort chez les Liṅgāyat-Vīrashaiva (Inde dud Sud)', *L'Homme*, 103, 93-112.

———, 1989a, 'Tocqueville chez Kipling. De la démocratie en Inde-Tradition et Modernité', *Archives des Sciences Sociales des Religions*, 67, 1, 99-124.

———, 1989b, 'Sacrifice et violence. Les genres de la possession dans le sud de l'Inde', *Nouvelle Revue d'Ethnopsychiatrie*, 13, 151-83.

———, 1989c, 'La Possession ou l'art de la guerre. Dévots chiens et "Héros d'Or" dans le culte de Mailar en Inde du Sud', *L'Homme*, 115, 48-70.

———, 1991, Documentaire VHS: *Islam soufi. Un culte de saint et ses fakirs dans le Sud de l'Inde* (30 mn.), IRESCO-CNRS.

———, 1992, *La Colère de la déesse décapitée. Traditions, cultes et pouvoir dans le sud de l'Inde.* Paris: CNRS Éditions.

———, 1994, 'Religion, maladie et thérapeutique dans un lieu de culte musulman au Sud de l'Inde', *Revue Internationale de Psychopathologie*, 16, 555-77.

———, 1995, 'Semence de sang ou de son? Une caste de prêtrise sectaire dans le Sud de l'Inde (karnataka)', in M.-L. Reiniche and H. Stern (eds): *Les Ruses du salut. Religion et politiques dans le monde indien, Puruṣārtha* (CEIAS/EHESS), 17, 55-85.

———, 1996, 'Passeurs de frontières, poseurs de barrières. Chrétiens et musulmans en Inde', in J. Assayag and G. Tarabout (eds): *Altérité, identité, Chrétiens et musulmans en Inde, Puruṣārtha* (CEIAS/EHESS), 19, 25-70.

———, 1999, 'Epilogue. La fabrique de la possession: sens et agir', in J. Assayag and G. Tarabout (eds.): *La possession en Asie du Sud Parole, corps, territoire, Puruṣārtha* (CEIAS-EHESS), 21, 421-47.

———, 2001, *Inde. Désir denation.* Paris: Odile Jacob.

Ayoub, M., 1978, *Redemptive Suffering in Islam: A Study of the Devotional Aspects of Ashura in Twelver Shi'ism.* The Hague/Paris/New York: Mouton.

Babb, L., 1975, *The Divine Hierarchy: Popular Hinduism in Central India.* New York: Columbia University Press.

Bahjant, B.P., 1932, *The Philosophy of Jnanadeva.* Poona: Pandharpur Research.

Baljon, M.S., 1989, 'Shah Waliullah and the Dargah', in C.W. Troll (ed.): *Muslim Shrines in India. Their Character, History and Significance.* Delhi: Oxford University Press, 189-97.

Basu, T. et al., 1993, *Khaki Shorts and Saffron flags. A Critique of the Hindu Right.* Hyderabad: Orient Longman Limited.

Bayly, C.A., 1983, *Rulers, Townsmen and Bazaars. North Indian Society in the Age of British Expansion, 1770-1870.* Cambridge: Cambridge University Press.

Bayly, C.A., 1985, 'The Pre-history of "communalism"? Religious Conflicts in India, 1700-1860', *Modern Asian Studies,* 19, 2, 177-203.

———, 1988, *Indian Society and the Making of the British Empire,* Cambridge: Cambridge University Press.

Bayly, S., 1986, 'Islam in Southern India: "purist" or "syncretic"?' in C.A. Bayly and D.H.A. Kolff (eds): *Two Colonial Empires: Comparative Essays on the History of India and Indonesia in Nineteenth Century.* Dordrecht, 35-73.

———, 1989, *Saints, Goddesses and Kings. Muslims and Christians in South Indian Society 1700-1900.* Cambridge: Cambridge University Press.

———, 1993, 'The Limits of Islamic Expansion in South India', in A.L. Dallapiccola and Zingel-Avé Lallemand (eds): *Islam and Indian Religions.* Stuttgart: Franz Steiner Verlag, 453-90.

Beck, B.E.F., 1981, 'The Goddess and the Demon. A local South Indian Festival and its wider Context', in M. Biardeau (ed.): *Autour de la Déesse hindoue, Puruṣārtha* (CEIAS/EHESS), 5, 83-136.

Bharati, A., 1981, *Hindu Views and Ways and Hindu-Muslim Interface. An Anthropological Assessment.* Delhi: Munshiram Manoharlal.

Biardeau, M., 1981a, 'Introduction', in M. Biardeau (ed.): *Autour de la Déesse hindoue, Puruṣārtha* (CEIAS/EHESS), 5, 9-16.

———, 1981b, 'Deva/asura. Dieux célestes et "démons" de l'hindouisme', in Y. Bonnefoy (ed.): *Dictionnaire des mythologies,* vol. I. Paris: Flammarion, 294-5.

———, 1981c, 'Devi. La Déesse en Inde', in Y. Bonneyfoy (ed.): *Dictionnaire des mythologies,* vol. I. Paris: Flammarion, 295-8.

Bombay State Gazetteer, 1893, Bombay: Government Central Book Society.

Bouchon, G., 1986, 'Quelques aspects de l'islamisation des régions maritimes de l'Inde à l'époque médiévale (XII-XVIe siècle)', in M. Gaborieau (ed.): *Islam et société en Asie du Sud, Puruṣārtha* (CEIAS/EHESS), 9, 29-36.

Bourdieu, P., 1982, *Ce que parler veut dire.* Paris: Les Éditions de Minuit.

Brass, P.R., 1990, *The Politics of India since Independence.* Cambridge: Cambridge University Press.

———, 1991, *Ethnicity and Nationalism. Theory and Comparison.* Delhi: Sage Publications.

Brittelbank, K., 1993, 'Curiosities, Conspicious Piety and the Maker of Time. Some Aspects of Kinship in Eighteenth-Century South India', *South Asia,* XVI, 2, 41-56.

Brown, J.M., 1990, *Gandhi, Prisoner of Hope.* New Haven & London: Yale University Press.

Bruinessen, M. van, 1991, 'Haji Bektash, Sultan Sahak, Sha Mina Sahib and Various Avatars of a Running Walls', *Turcica* (*Revue d'études turques*), XXI-XXIII, 55-73.

Census of India, 1931, Bengal & Sikkim (1933), 5, part 1: Calcutta.

———, 1981, Population Series-I, India, Paper 3 of 1984.

———, 1981, Portrait of Population of Karnataka. Directorate of Census Operations, Karnataka: Delhi.

———, 1991, Religion Series-I, India, Paper 1 of 1995.

Certeau, M. de, 1975a, 'Le langage altéré. La parole de la possédée', in M. de Certeau: *L'écriture de l'histoire*. Paris: Gallimard, 249-73.

———, 1975b, *Histoire et psychanalyse entre science et fiction*. Paris: Gallimard.

Chand, T., 1936, *Influence of Islam on Indian Culture*. Allahabad: Indian Law Press.

Chandra, B., 1987, *Communalism in Modern India*. Delhi: Vikas Publishing House.

Chelhod, J., 1955, *Le Sacrifice chez les Arabes. Recherches sur l'évolution, la nature et la fonction des rites sacrificiels en Arabie Occidentale*. Paris: PUF.

Clauss, P.J., 1975, 'The Siri Myth and Ritual: a Mass Possession Cult of South India', *Ethnology*, 14, 1, 47-58.

Coccari, D.M., 1989, 'Protection and Identity: Banaras' Bïr Babas as Neighborhood Guardian Deities', in S.B. Freitag (ed.): *Culture and Power in Banaras. Community, Performance, and Environment, 1800-1980*. Delhi: Oxford University Press, 130-46.

Cole, J.R.I., 1988, *Roots of North Indian Shi'ism in Iran and Irak*. Berkeley/Los Angeles/London: University of California Press.

Conklin, G.H., 1976, 'Muslim Family Life and Secularisation in Dharwar, Karnataka', in I. Ahmad (ed.): *Family, Kinship and Marriage among Muslims in India*. Delhi: Manohar, 127-40.

Coslovi, F., 1993, 'About Peculiarities of Sufism in India, Muhammad Gisudiraz and the Ni'matullahi in the Dekkan', in A.L. Dallapiccola and S. Zingel-Avé Lallemand (eds): *Islam and Indian Religions*. Stuttgart: Franz Steiner Verlag, 155-67.

Crapanzano, V., 1973, *The Hamadsha. A Study in Moroccan Ethnopsychiatry*. Berkeley: University of California Press.

Currie, P.M., 1989, *The Shrine and Cult of Mu'în al-din Chistî of Ajmer*. Delhi: Oxford University Press.

Dakhlia, J., 1990, *L'oubli de la cité. La mémoire collective à l'épreuve du lignage dans le Jerid tunisien*. Paris: Éditions de la Découverte.

Dallapiccola, A.L. and S. Zingel-Avé Lallemant (eds), 1993, *Islam and Indian Religions*. Stuttgart: Franz Steiner Verlag.

Dale, S.F., 1980, *Islamic Society on the South Asian Frontier: The Mappila of Malabar, 1498-1922*. Oxford: Oxford University Press.

Dale, S.F. and M. Gangadhara Menon, 1978, 'Nerccas: Saint-martyr Worship among the Muslims of Kerala', *Bulletin of the School of Oriental and African Studies*, 41, 3, 523-38.

Das, V., 1984, 'For a Folk-theology and a Theological Anthropology of Islam', *Contributions to Indian Sociology*, 18, 2, 293-300.

Das, V. (ed.), 1992, *Mirrors of Violence. Communities, Riots and Survivors in South Asia.* Delhi: Oxford University Press.

Das Gupta, S.B., 1976, *Obscure Religious Cult.* Calcutta, K.L. Mukopadhyay (rpt. 1946).

Deleury, G.A., 1960, *The Cult of Vithoba.* Poona: Deccan College.

Desai, P.B. (ed.), 1970, *A History of Karnataka (From Pre-history to Unification).* Dharwad: Karnatak University.

Desai, P.B., 1957, *Jainism in South India.* Sholapur.

Devereux, G., 1975, 'Acculturation antagoniste (1943)', in G. Devereux: *Ethnopsychanalyse complémentariste.* Paris: Flammarion.

Digby, S., 1970, 'Encounters with Jogis in Indian Sûfî hagiography' (Communication à la School of Oriental and African Studies, University of London), unpublished.

———, 1984, 'Qalandars and Related Groups. Element of Social Deviance in the Religious Life of the Delhi Sultanate of the Thirteenth and Fourteenth Century', in Y. Friedmann (ed.): *Islam in Asia,* vol. I, *South Asia.* Jerusalem: The Magnes Press, 60-108.

———, 1986, 'The Sufi Shaikh as a Source of Authority in Mediaeval India', in M. Gaborieau (ed.): *Islam et société en Asie du Sud, Puruṣārtha* (CEIAS/EHESS), 9, 57-78.

———, 1990, 'The Naqshbandi in the Deccan in the Late Seventeenth Century and Early Eighteenth Century: Bâbâ Palangposh, Bâbâ Musafîr and their Adherents', in M. Gaborieau, A. Popovic and T. Zarcone (eds): *Naqshbandi. Cheminement et situation actuelle d'un ordre mystique musulman.* Istanbul/Paris: Éditions Isis, 167-207.

———, 1994, 'To Ride a Tiger or a Wall? Strategies of Prestige in Indian Sufi Legend', in W.M. Callewaret and R. Snell (eds): *According to Tradition. Hagiographical Writing in India.* Wiesbaden: Harrassowitz Verlag, 99-129.

Dixit, V.G., 1977, *Raja-bag Sawar-Yogi chakravarti Changadev* (in Kannaḍa). Dharwar: Changadev Devasthan Samiti (Yamanur).

Douglas, M., 1989, *Ainsi pensent les institutions.* Paris: Édition Usher (1st edn. 1986).

D'Souza, V., 1955, *The Navayat of Kanara, a Study in Culture Contact.* Dharwar: Karnatak University.

Dumont, L., 1957, *Une Sous-caste de l'Inde du Sud. Organisation sociale et religion des Pramalai Kallar.* Paris: Mouton & Co. La Haye.

———, 1970, *Religion, Politics and History.* Paris/La Haye: Mouton Éditeur.

———, 1975, 'Définition structurale d'un dieu populaire tamoul: Aiyanar, le maître', in L. Dumont: *La Civilisation indienne et nous.* Paris: Colin, 92-110.

During, J., 1988, *Musique et extase. L'audition mystique dans la tradition soufie.* Paris: Albin Michel.

Eaton, R.M., 1974, 'Sufi Folk Literature and the Expansion of Indian Islam', *History of Religions*, XIV, 2, 117-27.

———, 1978, *Sufi of Bijapur, 1300-1700. Social Roles of Sufis in Medieval India.* Princeton: Princeton University Press.

———, 1994, *The Rise of Islam and the Bengal Frontier, 1204-1760 A.D.* Delhi: Oxford University Press.

Edward, J.F., 1941, *Dnyaneshwar. The Out-cast Brahmin.* Poona: Aryabhusan Press.

Eliade, M., 1948, *Les Techniques du yoga.* Paris: Gallimard.

Engineer, A.A., 1991, 'Remaking Indian Muslim Identity', *Economic and Political Weekly*, XXVI, 20, 1036-8.

———, 1995, 'Communalism and Communal Violence 1994', *Economic and Political Weekly*, XXX, 5, 249-50.

Engineer, A.A. (ed.), 1984, *Communal Riots in Post-Independence India.* Hyderabad: Sangam Book.

———, 1990, *Babri-Masjid-Ramjanambhoomi Controversy.* Delhi: Ajanta.

Ernst, C.W., 1985, 'From Hagiography to Martyrology: Conflicting Testimonies to a Sufi Martyr of the Delhi Sultanate', *History of Religion*, 24, 4, 308-27.

———, 1992, *Eternal Garden. Mysticism, History, and Politics at a South Asian Sufi Center.* Albany: State University of New York Press.

———, 1993, 'The Khuldabad-Burhampur Axis, and Local Sufism in the Deccan', in A.L. Dallapiccola and S. Zingel-Avé Lallemand (eds), *Islam and Indian Religions.* Stuttgart: Franz Steiner Verlag, 169-83.

Ewing, K., 1984a, 'The Sufi as Saint, Curer and Exorcist in Modern Pakistan', *Contributions to Asian Studies*, 18, 108-14.

———, 1984b, 'Malangs of the Punjab: Intoxication or Adab as the Path to God?', in B.D. Metcalft (ed.): *Moral Conduct and Authority. The Place of adab in South Asian Islam.* Berkeley: University of California Press, 357-71.

———, 1988, 'Ambiguity and Shari'at: A Perspective on the Problem of Moral Principles in Tension', in K.P. Ewing (ed.): *Shari'at and Ambiguity in South Asian Islam.* Berkeley and Los Angeles: University of California Press, 1-22.

Fahdh, T., 1971, 'Anges, démons et djinns en Islam', in *Génies, anges et démons* (Coll. 'Sources Orientales', VIII). Paris: Éditions du Seuil, 155-214.

Feronzsons Urdu-English Dictionary. Lahore: Feronzsons Ltd. (date unknown).

Filliozat, J., 1963, 'La nature du yoga dans sa tradition', in T. Brosse, *Études instrumentales des techniques du yoga.* Paris, Publications de l'École francaise d'Extrême-Orient, vol. LXII, I-XXVIII.

———, 1980, 'Sur les contreparties indiennes du soufisme', *Journal Asiatique*, CCLXVIII, 3/4, 250-73.

Foucault, M., 1963, *Naissance de la clinique. Une archéologie du regard médical.* Paris: PUF.

———, 1972, *Histoire de la folie à l'âge classique.* Paris: Gallimard.

Freitag, S., 1990, *Collective Action and Community. Public Arena and the Emergence of Communalism in North India.* Berkeley: University of California Press.

Freud, S., 1975, *Moïse et le monothéisme.* Paris: Gallimard (1st edn. 1939).

Friedmann, Y., 1986, 'Islamic Thought in Relation to the Indian Context', in M. Gaborieau (ed.): *Islam et société en Asie du Sud.* Paris: *Puruṣārtha* (CEIAS/EHESS), 9, 79-91.

Fruzetti, L.M., 1981, 'Muslim Rituals: The Household Rites *vs.* The Public Festivals in Rural India', in I. Ahmad (ed.): *Ritual and Religion among Muslims in India.* Delhi: Manohar, 91-112.

Frykenberg, R.E., 1981, 'On the Study of Conversion Movements: A Review Article and a Theoretical Note', *Indian Economic and Social History Review,* 17, 121-38.

———, 1991, 'The Emergence of Modern "Hinduism" as a Concept and as an Institution: A Reappraisal with Special Reference to South India', in G.D. Sontheimer & H. Kulke (eds): *Hinduism Reconsidered.* Delhi: Manohar, 29-49.

Fuller, C.J., 1988, 'The Hindu Pantheon and the Legitimation of Hierarchy', *Man,* 23, 19-39.

Fusfeld, W., 1988, 'The Boundaries of Islam and Infidelity', in K.P. Ewing (ed.): *Sharia't and Ambiguity in South Asian Islam.* Berkeley and Los Angeles: University of California Press, 205-19.

Gaborieau, M., 1975, 'Légende et culte du saint musulman Ghāzī Miyān au Népal occidental et en Inde du Nord', *Objets et Mondes,* XV, 3, 289-318.

———, 1985, 'From Al-Beruni to Jinnah: idiom, ritual and ideology of the Hindu-Muslim confrontation in South Asia', *Anthropology Today,* 1, 3, 7-14.

———, 1986, 'Les Ordres mystiques dans le sous-continent indien. Un point de vue ethnologique', in A. Popovic & G. Veinstein (eds): *Les Ordres mystiques dans l'Islam. Cheminements et situation actuelle.* Paris: Éditions de l'EHESS, 105-34.

———, 1989, 'A Nineteenth-Century Indian "Wahhabi" Tract Against the Cult of Muslim Saints: Al-Balagh al-Mubin', in C.W. Troll (ed.): *Muslim Shrines in India. Their Character, History and Significance.* Delhi: Oxford University Press, 198-239.

Gaborieau, M. (ed.), 1986, *Islam et société en Asie du Sud.* Paris: *Puruṣārtha* (CEIAS/EHESS), 9.

Gardet, L., 1952, 'Un problème de mystique comparée: la mention du nom divin (*dhikr*) dans la mystique musulmane', *Revue thomiste,* LII, 1, 642-79.

Gazetteer of India, 1982, Karnataka State Gazetteer. Bangalore: Government of Karnataka Publication.

Gazetteer of the Bombay Presidency, 1884, vol. XXI, Belgaum. Bombay: Government Central Press.

———, 1884, vol. XXII, Dharwar. Bombay: Government Central Press.

———, 1884, vol. XXIII, Bijapur. Bombay: Government Central Press.

———, 1893, Dharwar. Bombay: Government Central Book Society.

Geertz, C., 1968, *Islam Observed. Religious Development in Morocco and Indonesia.* Chicago & London: The University of Chicago Press.

———, 1973, *The Interpretation of Cultures.* New York: Basic Books.

Gellner, E., 1969, *Saints of the High Atlas.* London: Weindenfeld & Nicholson.

———, 1981, *Muslim Society.* Cambridge: Cambridge University Press.

———, 1989, *Nations et nationalisme.* Paris: Payot (1st edn. 1983).

Ghauri, I.A., 1975, 'Muslims in the Deccan in the Middle Ages: An Historical Survey', in *Islamic Culture,* XLIX, 3, 151-64.

Gilsenan, M., 1973, *Saint and Sufi in Modern Egypt. An Essay in the Sociology of Religion.* Oxford: Clarendon Press.

Gold, D., 1987, *The Lord as Guru. Hindi Sants in North Indian Tradition.* New York/Oxford: Oxford University Press.

———, 1991, 'Organized Hinduisms: From Vedic Truth to Hindu Nation', in E.M. Marty and R.S. Appleby (eds): *Fundamentalism Observed,* vol. 1. Chicago: Chicago University Press, 531-93.

Goldziher, I., 1967, 'On the Veneration of the Dead in Paganism and Islam', in S.M. Stern (ed.): *Muslim Studies,* I. London: George Allen and Unwin Ltd (1st edn. 1884), 209-35.

Gonda, J., 1965, *Les Religions de l'Inde, II, L'hindouisme récent.* Paris: Payot (1st edn. 1963).

Goody, J., 1994, *La Culture des fleurs.* Paris: Éditions du Seuil (1st edn. 1993).

Gopal, S. (ed.), 1991, *Anatomy of a Confrontation. The Babri-Masjid-Ramjanmabhumi Issue.* New Delhi: Vikas Publishing House.

Gordon, S., 1993, *The Maratha, 1600-1818. The New Cambridge History of India,* II, 4. Cambridge: Cambridge University Press.

———, 1994, 'Scarf and Sword: Thugs, Marauders, and State-formation in Eighteenth-Century Malwa', in S. Gordon, *Maratha, Marauders, and State Formation in Eighteenth Century India.* Delhi: Oxford University Press, 1-22.

Graff, V., 1993, 'Le désarroi des musulmans indiens. Chronique d'une crise annoncée', in J. Racine (ed.): *L'Inde et la question nationale, Hérodote,* 71, 116-39.

Gupta, D., 1982, *Nativism in a Metropolis. The Shiv Sena in Bombay.* Delhi: Manohar.

———, 1991, 'Communalism and Fundamentalism, Some notes on the Nature of Ethnic Politics in India', *Economic and Political Weekly,* Annual Number, XXVI, 11/12, 573-82.

Gupta, R., 1976, *Hindu-Muslim Relations.* Lucknow: Ethnographic and Fold Culture Society, U.P.

Halbfass, W., 1988, *India and Europe: An Essay in Understanding.* Albany: State University of New York Press.

Halbwachs, M., 1975, *Les Cadres sociaux de la mémoire.* Paris/La Haye: Mouton Éditeur (1st edn. 1925).

Hardgrave, R.L., 1977, 'The Mappila Rebellion, 1921: Peasant Revolt in Malabar', *Modern Asian Studies,* 11, 1, 57-99.

Hardy, P., 1972, *The Muslims of British India.* Cambridge: Cambridge University Press.

———, 1979, 'Modern European and Muslim Explanations of Conversion to Islam in South Asia: A Preliminary Survey of Literature', in N. Levtzion (ed.): *Conversion to Islam.* New York: Holmes & Meier, 177-206.

Haroon, M., 1991, *Muslims of India. Their Literature on Education, History, Politics, Religion, Socio-Economic and Communal Problem.* Delhi: Indian Bibliography Bureau.

Hasan, M., 1988, 'Indian Muslims since Independence: in Search of Integration and Identity', *Third World Quaterly,* 10, 2, 818-42.

———, 1990, 'Sectarianism in Indian Islam: The Shia/Sunni Divide in the United Provinces', *The Indian Economic and Social History Review,* 27, 2, 209-28.

———, 1991, 'Competitings Symbols and Shared Codes: Inter-Community Relations in Modern India', in S. Gopal (ed.): *Anatomy of a Confrontation. The Babri-Masjid-Ramjanmabhumi Issue.* Delhi: Vikas Publishing House, 105-20.

Heesterman, J.C., 1985, *The Inner Conflict of Tradition.* Chicago & London: University of Chicago.

Herklots, M.D. (& Ja'far Sharif), 1972, *Islam in India or the Qânûn-i-Islâm. The Customs of the Musalmâns of India.* London: Curzon Press (1st edn. 1921).

Hollister, J.N., 1953, *The Shi'a of India.* London: Luzac and Co. (nouvelle édition 1979, Delhi: Oriental Book Reprint Corporation).

Hughes, T.P., 1964, *A Dictionary of Islam.* Lahore: Premier Book House (1st edn. 1885).

Hussain Khan, C.G., 1994, *Marriage and Kinship among Muslims in South India.* Jaipur and Delhi: Rawat Publications.

Hussaini, S.S.K., 1970, 'Bund Sama', *Islamic Culture,* XLIV, 3, 177-85.

———, 1983, *Sayyid Muhammad Al-Husaynî-i-Gîsûdirâz (721/1321-825/1422) on Sufism.* Delhi: Idarah-i Adabiyat-i Delhi.

Inden, R., 1986, 'Orientalist Constructions of India', *Modern Asian Studies,* 20, 301-46.

Irschick, E.F., 1969, *Politics and Social Conflicts in South India. The Non-Brahman Movement and Tamil Separatism, 1916-1929.* Bombay: Oxford University Press.

Jackson, P. (ed.), 1988, *The Muslims of India. Beliefs and Practices.* Bangalore: Theological Publication in India.

Jaffrelot, C., 1991, 'Les émeutes entre hindous et musulmans. Essai de hiérarchisation des facteurs culturels, économiques et politiques', *Culture et Conflits*, 5, 25-54.

———, 1993a, *Les Nationalistes hindous. Idéologie, implantation et mobilisation des années 1920 aux années 1990.* Paris: Presses de la Fondation Nationale des Sciences Politiques.

———, 1993b, 'Le nationalisme hindou: de la construction idéologique à la mobilisation politique', in G. Kepel (ed.): *Les Politiques de dieu.* Paris: Éditions du Seuil, 223-64.

Jamous, R., 1991, *La Relation frère-soeur. Parenté et rites chez les Meo de l'Inde du Nord.* Paris: Éditions de l'EHESS.

Jones, K.W., 1976, *Arya Dharm: Hindu Consciousness in 19th Century Punjab.* Berkeley: University of California Press.

Kadan, K.N., 1988, 'The Birth of a Rationalist', in E. Zelliot and M. Bernsten (eds): *The Experience of Hinduism. Essays on Religion in Maharashtra.* Toronto: University of Toronto, 280-90.

Kakar, S., 1982, *Shamans, Mystics and Doctors. A Psychological Inquiry into India and Its Healing Traditions.* Delhi: Oxford University Press.

Kapferer, B., 1983, *A Celebration of Demons. Exorcism and the Aesthetics of Healing in Sri Lanka.* Bloomington: Indiana University Press.

Karve, I., 1962, 'On the Road: A Maharashtrian Pilgrimage', *Journal of Asian Studies*, 22, 1, 13-29.

Katzenstein, M.F., 1979, *Ethnicity and Equality. The Shiv Sena Party and Preferential Policies in Bombay.* Ithaca and London: Cornell University Press.

Kaul, R., 1993, *Caste, Class and Education. Politics of the Capitation Fee Phenomenon in Karnataka.* Delhi. Sage Publications.

Khan, M.I., 1994, *Kashmir's Transition to Islam. The Role of Muslim Rishis (Fifteenth to Eighteenth Century)*. Delhi, Manohar.

Kittel, Rev. F., 1983, *A Kannada-English Dictionary.* New Delhi, Asian Educational Services (1st edn. 1884, Mangalore Basel Mission Book).

Kohli, A., 1991, *Democracy and Discontent. India's Growing Crisis of Governablity.* Cambridge: Cambridge University Press.

Kuiper, F.B.J., 1983, *Ancient Indian Cosmogony.* Delhi: Vikas Publishing House.

Kumar, N., 1989, 'Work and Leisure in the Formation of Identity: Muslim Weavers in a Hindu City', in S. Freitag (ed.): *Culture and Power in Banaras. Community, Performance, and Environment, 1800-1980.* Delhi: Oxford University Press, 147-70.

Kumar, P. (ed.), 1992, *Towards Understanding Communalism.* Chandigarh:

Centre for Research in Rural and Industrial Development.

Kurin, R., 1984, 'Morality, Personhood and the Exemplary Life: Popular Conceptions of Muslims in Paradise', in B.D. Metcalf (ed.): *Moral Conduct and Authority. The Place of adab in South Asian Islam.* Berkeley: University of California Press, 196-220.

Lawrence, B.B., 1982, 'Islam in India: The Function of Institutional Sufism in the Islamization of Rajasthan, Gujarat and Kashmir', *Contributions to Asian Studies,* 17, 27-43.

———, 1983, 'The early Chisthi Approach to Samā', in M. Israel and N.K. Wagle (eds.): *Essays in honour of Professor Aziz Ahmad.* Delhi: Manohar, 69-93.

———, 1984, ' Early Indo-Muslim Saints and Conversions', in Y. Friedmann (ed.): *Islam in Asia,* vol. 1, *South Asia.* Jerusalem: The Magnes Press, 109-45.

———, 1987, 'The Sant Movement and North Indian Sufis', in K. Schomer and W.H. Mc Leod (eds): *The Sants. Studies in a Devotional Tradition of India.* Delhi: Motilal Banarsidass, 359-73.

———, 1993, 'Biography and the 17th century Qadiriya of North India', in A.L. Dallapiccola and S. Zingel-Avé Lallemant (eds): *Islam and Indian Religions.* Stuttgart: Franz Steiner Verlag, 399-416.

Le Goff, J., 1977, 'L'Occident médiéval et l'Océan indien: un horizon onirique', in J. Le Goff: *Pour un autre Moyen Age. Temps, travail et culture en Occident, 18 essais.* Paris: Gallimard, 280-98.

Leiris, M., 1980, *La Possession et ses aspects théâtraux chez les Éthiopiens de Gondar.* Paris: Le Sycomore (1st edn. 1958).

Lévi-Strauss, C., 1964, *Mythologiques* I: *le cru et le cuit.* Paris: Plon.

Lombard, D., 1986, 'Les *tareka* en Insulinde', in A. Popovic & G. Veinstein (eds): *Les Ordres mystiques dans l'Islam. Cheminements et situation actuelle.* Paris: Éditions de l'EHESS, 139-64.

Madan, T.N., 1987, 'Secularism in its Place', *The Journal of Asian Studies,* 46, 2, 747-59.

Malinowski, B., 1974, *Les Jardins de corail.* Paris: Maspéro (1st edn. 1935).

Malkhani, K.R., 1981, *The RSS Story.* New Delhi: Impex India.

Manor, J., 1978, *Political Change in an Indian State, Mysore 1917-1955.* New Delhi: South Asia Books.

———, 1979, 'Language, Religion and Political Identity in Karnataka', in D. Taylor and M. Yapp (eds): *Political Identity in South Asia.* London: Curzon Press, 170-90.

———, 1989, 'Karnataka: Caste, Class, Dominance and Politics in a Cohesive Society', in F.R. Franckel and M.S.A. Rao (eds): *Dominance and State Power. Decline of a Social Order,* vol. 1. Delhi: Oxford University Press, 322-51.

Marriott, McKim, 1955, 'Western Medecine in a Village of Northern India', in B.D. Paul (ed.): *Health, Culture and Community*. New York: Russell Sage Foundation, 239-68.

Massignon, L., 1954, *Essai sur les origines du lexique technique de la mystique musulmane*, Paris: Vrin.

Masselos, J., 1982, 'Change and Custom in the Format of the Bombay Mohurrum during the Nineteenth and Twentieth Centuries', *South Asia*, V, 2, 47-67.

Mathew, G., 1982, 'Politicisation of Religion. Conversion to Islam in Tamil Nadu', *Economic and Political Weekly*, XVII, 25, 1027-34 and 26, 1068-72.

Mathur, Y.B., 1969, 'The Mujahidin Movement in Modern India', *Studies in Islam*, V, 2/4, 193-217.

Mauss, M., 1960, 'Les techniques du corps (1936)', in M. Mauss: *Sociologie et anthropologie*. Paris: PUF.

McDonald, D.S. and H. Masse, 1961, 'Djinn', in B. Lewis, Ch. Pellat and J. Schascht (eds): *Encyclopaedia of Islam*, vol. II. Leiden, E.J. Brill/ London: Luzac & Co. 546-60.

Mc Guire, J. and P. Reeves (eds), 1994, *After Ayodhya, South Asia*, XVIII, Special Issue.

Mc Kean, L.D., 1992, Towards a Politics of Spirituality: Hindu Religious Organisations and Indian Nationalism. PhD thesis, Department of Anthropology, Sydney University (Chicago University Press, 1996).

Metcalf, B.D., 1982, *Islamic Revival in British India: Deoband, 1860-1900*. Princeton: Princeton University Press.

Métraux, A., 1959, *Le Vaudou haïtien*. Paris: Gallimard.

Michell, G. (ed.), 1986, *Islamic Heritage of the Deccan*. Bombay: Marg Publications.

Miller, R.E., 1976, *Mappila Muslims of Kerala. A Study in Islamic Trends*. Madras: Orient Longman.

Minault, G., 1982, *The Khilafat Movement: Religious Symbolism and Political Mobilization in India*. New York: Columbia University Press.

Mokashi, D.B., 1990, *Phalki. A Pilgrimage to Pandharpur*. Hyderabad: Orient Longman Limited.

Molé, M., 1963, 'La danse extatique en Islam', in *Les Danses sacrées* (coll. 'Sources orientales', VI). Paris: Éditions du Seuil, 145-280.

———, 1965, *Les Mystiques musulmans*. Paris: PUF.

Mujeeb, M., 1967, *The Indian Muslims*. London: George Allen and Unwin.

Mysore State Gazetteer, 1930, *Gazetteer*, vol. V, ed. by C. Hayaravadana Rao. Bangalore: Government Press.

Nichter, M., 1989, *Anthropology and International Health*. South Asians Studies. Dordrecht/Boston/London: Kluwer Academic Publishers.

Nizami, K.A., 1974, *Some Aspects of Religion and Politics in India during the Thirteenth Century*. Delhi: Idara-i Adabiyat-i Delhi.

Obeyesekere, G., 1984, *The Cult of the Goddess Pattini.* Chicago: University of Chicago Press.

O'Flaherty, W.D., 1976, *The Origins of Evil in Hindu Mythology.* Delhi: Motilal Banarsidass.

Padmanabha, P., 1971, *Special Study Report on Bhuta Cult in South Kanara District.* Mysore: Census of India, Series 14.

Pandey, G., 1990, *The Construction of Communalism in Colonial North India.* Delhi: Oxford University Press.

———, 1994, 'The New Hindu History', *South Asia,* XVII, 97-112.

Parabrahma Sastri, P.V., 1982, *The Kakativas of Warangal.* Hyderabad: Orient Longman Limited.

Pathan, S.K., 1979, Religion in its Socio-cultural Setting among the Muslims in a South Indian Village. Dharwad: Dharwad University (unpublished, PhD).

Pfeiderer, B., 1981, 'Mira Datar Dargah: the Psychiatry of a Muslim Shrine', in I. Ahmad (ed.): *Ritual and Religion among Muslims in India.* Delhi: Manohar, 195-233.

Platts, J.T., 1970, *A Dictionary of Urdû, classical Hindi and English.* Oxford: Oxford University Press.

Popovic, A. and G. Veinstein, (eds), 1986, *Les Ordres mystiques dans l'Islam. Cheminements et situation actuelle.* Paris: Éditions de l'EHESS.

Pouchepadass, J., 1979, 'Délinquance de fonction et nomalisation coloniale: les "tribus criminelles" dans l'Inde britannique', in *Les Marginaux et les exclus de l'histoire.* Paris: Union Générale d'édition, 122-54.

Racine, J.L., 1994, *Les Attaches de l'homme. Enracinement paysan et logiques migratoires en Inde du Sud.* Paris/Pondichéry: Institut français de Pondichéry et Éditions de la Maison des Sciences de l'homme.

Rajgopal, P.R., 1987, *Communal Violence in India.* Delhi: Uppal Publishing House.

Ranade, R.D., 1961, *Pathway to God in Marathi Literature.* Bombay: Bharatiya Vidya Bhavan.

Rao, B.V., 1989, *Socio-economic Change in Belgaum District (A Historical Probing).* Bombay: Himalaya Publishing House.

Rao, T.N.A., 1993, *Balanced Regional Development. Levels of Development of Karnataka.* Belgaum: Academy of Regional Science and Humanities (ACARSH).

Rao, V.D., 1969, 'The Maratha Bardic Poetry', *The Modern Review,* 124, 749-52.

Ray, A. and J. Kumpatla, 1987, 'Zilla Parishad Presidents in Karnataka: Their Social Background and Implications for Development', *Economic and Political Weekly,* XXII, 17-24, 1828-32.

Reiniche, M.-L., 1975, 'Les "démons" et leur culte dans la structure du panthéon d'un village du Tirunelveli', *Puruṣārtha* (CEIAS), 2, 173-203.

Reiniche, M.-L., 1979, *Les Dieux et les hommes. Étude de cultes d'un village du Tirunelveli, Inde du Sud.* Paris/La Haye: Mouton Éditeur.

———, 1981, 'Hindouisme populaire', in Y. Bonnefoy (ed.): *Dictionnaire des mythologies*, vol. I. Paris: Flammarion, 519-26.

Richards, J.F., 1974, 'The Islamic Frontier in the East: Expansion into South Asia', *South Asia*, 4, 91-109.

———, 1993, *The Mughal Empire*, The New Cambridge History of India, I, 5. Cambridge: Cambridge University Press.

Richman, P., 1992, 'E.V. Ramasami's Reading of the Ramayana', in P. Richman (ed.): *Many Ramayanas. The Diversity of a Narrative Tradition in South Asia.* Delhi: Oxford University Press.

Ricœur, P., 1991, *Temps et récit. L'intrigue et le récit historique*, vol. 1. Paris: Éditions du Seuil.

Rizvi, S.A.A., 1978-82, *A History of Sufism in India*, 2 vols. Delhi: Munshiram Manoharlal.

Robinson, F., 1974, *Separatism Among Indian Muslims. The Politics of the United Provinces Muslims, 1860-1923.* Cambridge: Cambridge University Press.

———, 1983, 'Islam and Muslim Society in South Asia', *Contributions to Indian Sociology*, 17, 2, 185-203.

Rollier, F., 1983, Murugmalla. Possession et rituels thérapeutiques dans un tombeau musulman d'Inde du Sud. Étude ethnopsychiatrique. Mémoire pour le CES de psychiatrie, Université de Paris IV.

Rouget, G., 1990, *La Musique et la transe. Esquisse d'une théorie générale des relations de la musique et de la possession.* Paris: Gallimard *TEL* (1st edn.).

Roy, A., 1983, *The Islamic Syncretistic Tradition in Bengal.* Princeton: Princeton University Press.

———, no date, 'Islamization in South Asia with Special Reference to the Bengali-speaking Region: A Conceptual and Historical Revaluation', *Indo-British Review*, XIX, 1, 21-41.

Rushdie, S., 1989, *Les Versets sataniques.* Christian Bourgois Éditeur (1st edn. 1988).

———, 1993, *Patries imaginaires. Essais et critiques, 1981/1991.* Christian Bourgois Éditeur (1st edn. 1992).

Saiyid, A.R., 1981, 'Ideal and Reality in the Observance of Moharram', in I. Ahmad (ed.): *Ritual and Religion among Muslims in India.* Delhi: Manohar, 113-42.

Saksena, N.S. (ed.), 1990, *Communal Riots in India.* Delhi: Noira.

Sarkar, J., 1992, *Shivaji and his Time.* Bombay: Orient Longman (1st edn. 1952).

Satyaprakash, 1985, *Muslims in India. Bibliography of their Religious, Socio-Economic and Political Literature* (Compiled and edited by). Indian Documentation Service. Gurgaon: Haryana.

Schimmel, A.D., 1975, *Mystical Dimensions of Islam.* Chapel Hill: The University of North Carolina Press.

———, 1980, *Islam in the Indian Subcontinent.* Leiden-Köln: E.J. Brill.

———, 1993, 'Introduction', in A.L. Dallapiccola and S. Zingel-Avé Lallemand (eds): *Islam and Indian Religions.* Stuttgart: Franz Steiner Verlag, 1-9.

Schomer, K. and W.H. McLeod (eds), 1987, *The Sants. Studies in a Devotional Tradition of India.* Delhi: Motilal Banarsidass.

Schwerin, K.G., 1984, 'Saint Worship in Indian Islam: The Legend of the Martyr Salar Masud Ghazi', in I. Ahmad (ed.): *Ritual and Religion among Muslims in India.* Delhi: Manohar, 143-61.

Select Bibliography on Indian Muslims, 1984, Indian Council of Social Sciences Research. Southern Regional Center. Hyderabad: Osmania University Library.

Seminar, Secularism in Crisis, 125, Jan. 1970.

———, Indian Muslims, 174, Feb. 1974.

———, The Muslims Condition, 240, Aug. 1979.

———, Urdu, 332, Oct. 1983.

———, Communal Divides, 374, Oct. 1990.

———, Islam, 416, Apr. 1994.

Sherwani, H.K., 1973-4, *History of Medieval Deccan (1295-1724),* vols. I & II. Hyderabad: The Government of Andhra Pradesh.

Shulman, D.D., 1984, 'The Enemy within: Idealism and Dissent in South India Hinduism', in S.N. Einsenstadt, R. Kahane and D.D. Shulman (eds): *Orthodoxy, Heterodoxy and Dissent in India.* Berkeley/Los Angeles/London: University of California Press, 11-56.

———, 1986, 'Battle as Metaphor in Tamil Folk and Classical Traditions', in Stuart H. Blackburn and A.K. Ramanujan (eds): *Another Harmony. New Essays on the Folklore of India.* Berkeley: University of California Press, 105-30.

Siddiqui, I.H., 1985, 'A New Look at Deccani Sufism', in C.W. Troll (ed.): *Islam in India.* Delhi: Vikas Publishing House, 237-49.

Singh, G., 1993, 'Hindutva's Low Intensity War against Bombay's Riot Victims', *Economic and Political Weekly,* 8 May, XXVIII, 908-10.

Skyhawk, H. van, 1990, *Bhakti und Bhakta. Religionsgeschichtliche Untersuchungen zum Heilsbegriff zur religiösen Umwelt des Sri Sant Ekanath.* Stuttgart: Steiner Verlag Wiesbaden GMBH.

———, 1993, 'Vaisnava Perception of Muslims in 18th Century Maharashtra', in A.L. Dallapiccola and S. Zingel-Avé Lallemand (eds): *Islam and Indian Religions.* Stuttgart: Franz Steiner Verlag, 203-16.

Sontheimer, G.-D. and H. Kulke (eds), 1991, *Hinduism Reconsidered.* Delhi: Manohar.

Stein, B., 1980, *Peasant State and Society in Medieval South India.* Delhi: Oxford University Press.

Stein, B., 1985, 'Note on "Peasant Insurgency" in Colonial Mysore: Event and Process', *South Asia Research*, 5, 1, 11-29.

Subhan, J.A., 1970, *Sufism. Its Saints and Shrines. An Introduction to the Study of Sufism with Special Reference to India.* New York: Samuel Weiser Inc. (1st edn. Lahore 1938).

Subrahmanyam, S., 1994, 'Introduction', in S. Subrahmanyam (ed.): *Money and the Market in India, 1100-1700.* Delhi: Oxford University Press.

Tarabout, G., 1986, *Sacrifier et donner à voir en pays Malabar. Les fêtes de temple au Kérala (Inde du Sud): étude anthropologique.* Paris: École francaise d'Extrême-Orient, vol. CXLVII.

———, 1990, 'Sacrifice et renoncement dans les mythes de fondation de temples au Kérala', in M. Detienne (ed.): *Tracés de fondation.* Peeters Louvain/Paris: Bibliothèque de l'École Pratique des Hautes Études, vol. CXIII, 211-32.

Thapar, R., 1985, 'Syndicate Moksha', *Seminar* 313, Sept., 14-22.

Thapar, R., H. Mukhia and B. Chandra, 1977, *Communalism and the Writing of Indian History.* Delhi: People's Publication House.

Thursby, G.R., 1975, *Hindu-Muslim Relations in British India. A Study of Controversy, Conflict, and Communal Movements in Northern India, 1923-1928.* Leiden: E.J. Brill.

Thimmaiah, G., 1993, *Power Politics and Social Justice. Backward Castes in Karnataka.* Delhi: Sage Publications.

Thimmaiah, G. and A. Aziz, 1983, 'The Political Economy of Land Reform in Karnataka, A South Indian State', *Asian Survey*, XXIII, 7, 819-27.

Toffin, G., 1992, 'The logic and Conflicts of a Nepalese Pantheon', in B. van den Hoek, D. Kolff and M. Ort (eds): *Ritual, State and History in South Asia: Studies in Honour of J.C. Heesterman.* Leiden: E.J. Brill, 677-94.

Trimingham, J.S., 1971, *The Sufi Orders in Islam.* London: Oxford University Press.

Troll, C.W., 1989, *Muslim Shrines in India. Their Character, History and Significance.* Delhi: Oxford University Press.

Tyan, E., 1961, '*Djihâd*', in B. Lewis, Ch. Pellat and J. Schascht (eds): *Encyclopaedia of Islam*, vol. II. Leiden, E.J. Brill/London: Luzac & Co., 538-40.

Upadhyaya, U.P., 1984, *Bhuta Worship. Aspect of a Ritualistic Theatre.* Udipi: Regional Resources Centre for Folk Performing Arts.

Vitray-Meyerovitch, Eva de, 1977, *Rûmî et le soufisme.* Paris: Éditions du Seuil.

Vaudeville, C., 1974a, 'Pandharpur. The City of Saints', in H.M. Buck and G.E. Yocum (eds): *Structural Approaches to South India Studies.* Chambersburg: Pennsylvania, Wilson Books, 137-61.

———, 1974b, *Kabir*, 2 vols. Oxford: Oxford University Press.

———, 1987a, 'Sant Mat: Santism as the Universal Path to Sanctity', in K. Schomer and W.H. McLeod (eds): *The Sants. Studies in a*

Devotional Tradition of India. Delhi: Motilal Banarsidass, 21-40.

Vaudeville, C., 1987b, 'The Shaiva-Vaishnava Synthesis in Maharashtrian Santism', in K. Schomer and W.H. Mc Leod (eds): *The Sants. Studies in a Devotional Tradition of India.* Delhi: Motilal Banarsidass, 215-28.

———, 1987c, 'The Shaivaite Background of Santism in Maharashtra', in M. Israel and N.K. Wagle (eds): *Religion and Society in Maharashtra.* Toronto: University of Toronto, 32-45.

Varenne, J., 1971, 'Anges, démons et génies dans l'Inde', in *Génies, anges et démons* (Coll. 'Sources Orientales', VIII), Paris: Éditions du Seuil, 257-93.

Veer, P. van der, 1987, 'God Must be Liberated! A Hindu Liberation Movement in Ayodhya', *Modern Asian Studies,* 21, 2, 283-301.

———, 1988, *Gods on Earth. The Management of Religious Experience and Identity in a North Indian Pilgrimage Centre.* London-Atlantic Highlands, NJ: Athlone Press.

———, 1992, 'Playing or Praying: A Sufi Saint's Day in Surat', *The Journal of Asian Studies,* 51, 3, 545-64.

Wadley, S.S., 1975, *Shakti Power in the Conceptual Structure of Karimpur Religion.* Chicago: Chicago Press.

Wagle, N.K., 1983, 'The Ordeal on the Mosque of Rânjangâv: An Aspect of Dispute Resolution in 18th Century Maharashtra', in M. Israel and N.K. Wagle (eds): *Islamic Society and Culture. Essays in Honour of Professor Aziz Ahmad.* Delhi: Manohar, 315-34.

———, 1991, 'Hindu-Muslim Interaction in Medieval Maharashtra', in G.D. Sontheimer & H. Kulke (eds): *Hinduism Reconsidered.* Delhi: Manohar, 51-66.

Weinberger-Thomas, C., 1989, 'Cendres d'immortalité. La crémation des veuves en Inde', *Archives de Sciences Sociales des Religions,* 67, 1, 9-52.

Weiner, M., 1967, *Party Building in a New Nation. The Indian National Congress.* Chicago: The University of Chicago Press.

Weiner, M. and M.F. Katzenstein, 1981, *India's Preferential Policies. Migrants, The Middle Classes, and Ethic Equality.* Chicago and London: The University of Chicago Press.

Wink, A., 1986, *Land and Sovereignty in India. Agrarian Society and Politics under 18th Century Maratha Swaraja.* Cambridge: Cambridge University Press.

———, 1990, *Al-Hind. The Making of the Indo-Islamic World,* vol. 1, *Early Medieval India and the Expansion of Islam (7-11th centuries).* Leiden/ New York: E.J. Brill.

———, 1993, 'Islamic Society and Culture in the Deccan', in A.L. Dallapiccola, and S. Zingel-Avé Lallemand (eds): *Islam and Indian Religions.* Stuttgart: Franz Steiner Verlag, 217-27.

Zelliot, E., 1982, 'A Medieval Encounter between Hindu and Muslim: Eknath's Drama-Poem Hindu-Turk samvad', in F.W. Clothey (ed.): *Images of Man: Religion and Historical Process in South Asia.* Madras, 254-69.

———, 1987, 'Four Radical Saints in Maharashtra', in M. Israel and N.K. Wagle (eds): *Religion and Society in Maharashtra.* Toronto: University of Toronto, 131-44.

Zelliot, E. and M. Bertsen (eds.), 1988, *The Experience of Hinduism Essays on Religion in Maharashtra.* Albany: State University of New York Press.

Zimmermann, F., 1989, *Le Discours des remèdes au pays des épices.* Paris: Payot.

Index